LCAA

BI 3023413 1

D1426450

INDIGENOUS PSYCHOLOGIES

CROSS-CULTURAL RESEARCH AND METHODOLOGY SERIES

Series Editors

Walter J. Lonner, *Department of Psychology, Western Washington University (United States)*
John W. Berry, *Department of Psychology, Queen's University, Kingston, Ontario (Canada)*

Volumes in this series:

INDIGENOUS PSYCHOLOGIES

Research and Experience in Cultural Context

edited by
Uichol Kim
John W. Berry

Volume 17, Cross-Cultural Research and Methodology Series

SAGE Publications
International Educational and Professional Publisher
Newbury Park   London   New Delhi

For information address:

SAGE Publications, Inc.
2455 Teller Road
Newbury Park, California 91320
E-mail: order@sagepub.com

SAGE Publications Ltd.
6 Bonhill Street
London EC2A 4PU
United Kingdom

SAGE Publications India Pvt. Ltd.
M-32 Market
Greater Kailash I
New Delhi 110 048 India

Printed in the United States of America

Library of Congress Cataloging-in-Publication Data

Indigenous psychologies : research and experience in cultural context
    / edited by Uichol Kim, John W. Berry.
        p.   cm. — (Cross-cultural research and methodology series ;
    v. 17)
    Includes bibliographical references and index.
    ISBN 0-8039-5141-8 (cloth)
    1. Ethnopsychology.   I. Kim, Uichol.   II. Berry, John W.
III. Series.
GN502.I53   1993   93-5196
155.8—dc20   CIP

96 97 98 99 00 01 10 9 8 7 6 5 4 3 2

Sage Production Editor: Rebecca Holland

CONTENTS

SERIES EDITOR'S INTRODUCTION

The Sage Series on Cross-Cultural Research and Methodology was created to present comparative studies on cross-cultural topics and interdisciplinary research. Inaugurated in 1975, the series is designed to satisfy a growing and continuing need to integrate research method and theory and to dissect issues from a comparative perspective; a truly international approach to the study of behavioral, social, and cultural variables can be done only within such a methodological framework.

Each volume in the series presents substantive cross-cultural studies and considerations of the strengths, interrelationships, and weaknesses of the various methodologies, drawing upon work done in anthropology, political science, psychology, and sociology. Both individual researchers knowledgeable in more than one discipline and teams of specialists with differing disciplinary backgrounds have contributed to the series. Although each individual volume may represent the integration of only a few disciplines, *the cumulative totality of the series reflects an effort to bridge gaps of methodology and conceptualization across the various disciplines and many cultures.*

A persistent—some would say intractable—methodological problem in cross-cultural research in any of the behavioral sciences concerns *generalizability.* Because the term *cross-cultural* implies comparisons between two or more cultures on some dimension of interest, it is critical to establish equivalence between the cultures on that dimension. Failure to do so results in flawed research, and this typically means that one cannot make generalizations. Because of this problem of comparability, many scholars prefer to study concepts that are valid and meaningful *within* a specific culture only— a viewpoint that can be described as *cultural* psychology or, more typically, "mainstream" psychology, which tends to ignore the issue of comparability. On the other hand, cross-culturalists may prefer to study intensely and carefully concepts or "worldviews" within particular cultures of interest to get a better idea about what can or cannot serve as common bases of comparison across various cultures. Whichever of these two views prevails, both are interested in *indigenous* concepts that are relevant for psychological inquiry.

Thus the researcher will want to know what is native to, or rooted in, specific societies or cultures. And that is what this volume in the series is all about—indigenous psychologies. To the extent that there is, as some believe, a current movement to "indigenize" psychology, this volume takes on added importance.

One of the two editors of the volume, John W. Berry, is also series coeditor. Thus, although I have written this brief summary without him, he obviously endorses the volume's contribution to the series. The first editor, Uichol Kim, is a native of Korea and studied with Berry at Queen's University, in Canada. I am pleased that their student-teacher relationship has thrived and has resulted in this interesting and important book of readings, which contains chapters from many psychologists who are intimately familiar with their own countries and how psychology fits in them.

—Walter J. Lonner
Western Washington University

1

INTRODUCTION

UICHOL KIM
JOHN W. BERRY

Wilhelm Wundt, considered the father of modern psychology, established psychology as an independent branch of science in 1879 (Boring, 1921). Wundt recognized two traditions in psychology: *Naturwissenschaften* (the natural sciences tradition) and *Geisteswissenschaften* (the cultural sciences tradition) (van Hoorn & Verhave, 1980). Wundt was influential in establishing psychological experiments in general psychology (reflecting the *Naturwissenschaften* tradition). The experimental approach became the sine qua non of psychological research and has become the defining feature of general psychology (Koch & Leary, 1985; Lachenmeyer, 1970; LeVine, 1974). Wundt, however, articulated the limitations of the experimental method (Danziger, 1983) and pointed out that thinking is heavily conditioned by language, customs, and myths, which are the primary areas for *Völkerpsychologie* (cultural psychology or ethnopsychology; Danziger, 1979). He regarded *Völkerpsychologie* as a "more important branch of psychological science which was destined to eclipse experimental psychology" (Danziger, 1983, p. 307). In the latter part of his life, Wundt devoted himself to examining sociocultural influences in psychological processes by writing a 10-volume work on *Völkerpsychologie* (1910-1920). The indigenous psychologies approach represented in this volume is a direct descendant of Wundt's *Geisteswissenschaften* tradition.

Wundt recognized that although the experimental method is appropriate for investigating some basic psychological processes, it is inappropriate for

AUTHOR'S NOTE: Uichol Kim would like to express his gratitude for the financial support provided by the Department of Psychology and the College of Social Sciences, University of Hawaii. He would also like to thank Ann-Marie Horvath and Genie Lester for their editorial assistance.

studying psychological phenomena that are shaped by language and culture (Allport, 1968; Berry, 1983; Danziger, 1979). As early as 1866, he stated that "attempts to subsume mental processes under the types of laws found in the physical sciences will never be successful" (quoted in Blumenthal, 1983, p. 117). General psychology, however, rejected the cultural sciences tradition advocated by Wundt and established the natural sciences paradigm as the dominant framework (Danziger, 1983; Koch & Leary, 1985).

The cultural sciences tradition recognizes the need to develop theories and methods that are appropriate for human beings. In this tradition, human qualities and their cultural contexts are incorporated into the research design. It is a version of science that encompasses the physical, biological, social, and applied sciences. Cultural anthropology, ethnoscience, and cross-cultural psychology are other examples of this tradition.

The first part of this introduction provides a brief description of the indigenous psychologies approach. Within this section the *cross-indigenous approach* is delineated. The second section provides a brief overview of the history of the cultural sciences tradition and summarizes critical features of this tradition by examining the works of five prominent scholars: Giovanni Battista Vico, Johannes Gottfried Herder, Hayim Steinthal, Moritz Lazarus, and Wilhelm Wundt. The section also provides comparisons between the indigenous psychologies approach and sister disciplines in the cultural sciences tradition, such as cultural anthropology, ethnoscience, and cross-cultural psychology. Finally, we offer a brief overview of the chapters in this volume.

THE INDIGENOUS PSYCHOLOGIES APPROACH

Webster's Third New International Dictionary defines the word *indigenous* as follows: "native: (1) not introduced directly or indirectly according to historical record or scientific analysis into a particular land or region or environment from the outside, (2) originating or developing or produced naturally in a particular land or region or environment, (3) of, relating to, or designed for natives" (Merriam-Webster, 1976). This definition contains three key features: (a) what something indigenous is (i.e., native), (b) what it is not (i.e., transported or transplanted from another region), and (c) what it is for (i.e., designed for natives). *Psychology* has been defined as the scientific study of human behavior (or the mind). Combining these two definitions, *indigenous psychologies* can be defined as the scientific study of human behavior (or the mind) that is native, that is not transported from other regions, and that is designed for its people.

Although scientific investigation of indigenous knowledge is still in its infancy, this chapter outlines a framework for the development of indigenous psychologies by reviewing their current status. The following paragraphs delineate six fundamental assumptions and research strategies that are shared in the indigenous psychologies approach.

First, the indigenous psychologies approach emphasizes understanding rooted in the ecological context (Berry, Chapter 16; Georgas, Chapter 4), philosophical context (Boski, Chapter 5; de Silva, Chapter 14), cultural context (Choi, Kim, & Choi, Chapter 12; Enriquez, Chapter 9; Ho, Chapter 15; Jodelet, Chapter 11), political context (Ardila, Chapter 10; Moghaddam, Chapter 7; Trimble & Medicine, Chapter 8), and historical context (Diaz-Guerrero, Chapter 3; Lomov, Budilova, Koltsova, & Medvedev, Chapter 6; Sinha, Chapter 2). The indigenous psychologies approach attempts to document, organize, and interpret the understanding people have about themselves and their world. It emphasizes the use of natural taxonomies as units of analysis. It examines how individuals and groups interact within their context. This information is then used as a tool for discovering psychological invariants. The second step involves explaining causes behind the observed invariants. The third step consists of comparing results across different contexts for further refinement and extension.

Second, indigenous psychologies are not studies of *exotic* people in faraway places. Although indigenous studies with native peoples are necessary (Trimble & Medicine, Chapter 8), indigenous understanding is needed for "developed" countries (Berry, Chapter 16; Jodelet, Chapter 11) as well as for "developing" countries (Choi et al., Chapter 12; Ho, Chapter 15), "underdeveloped" countries (Ardila, Chapter 10; Diaz-Guerrero, Chapter 3; Enriquez, Chapter 9; Moghaddam, Chapter 7; Sinha, Chapter 2), and countries that espouse sets of sociopolitical ideologies different from those found elsewhere (Boski, Chapter 5; Lomov et al., Chapter 6). The indigenous psychologies approach affirms the need for each culture to develop its own indigenous understanding.

Third, within a particular society there can be a multitude of perspectives not shared by all groups (Georgas, Chapter 4; Lomov et al., Chapter 6; Trimble & Medicine, Chapter 8). Moghaddam (Chapter 7) points out the existence of *dualism* and *parallelism* in developing countries such as Iran. Dualism describes a situation where one sector of a society is developed and "Westernized" and the other sector remains "traditional." Even within a particular culture, these two sectors have limited interaction and operate *parallel* to each other. In addition, the existence of cultural diversity within a particular society could produce the need for different types of explanations and interpretations (Georgas, Chapter 4; Lomov et al., Chapter 6; Trimble & Medicine, Chapter 8).

Fourth, acceptance of the indigenous psychologies approach does not affirm or preclude the use of a particular method. The indigenous psychologies approach is part of the scientific tradition, and an important aspect of the scientific endeavor is the discovery of appropriate methods for investigating the phenomenon of interest. Scientists should not and cannot be bound to a particular method (Boulding, 1980; Enriquez, Chapter 9; Trimble & Medicine, Chapter 8). The use of multiple methods (Campbell & Fiske, 1959) is recommended to increase the researcher's confidence that a particular finding is valid and not an artifact of research methods (Berry, Chapter 16; Enriquez, Chapter 9). Results from multiple methods could be integrated to provide a more comprehensive and robust understanding of psychological phenomena.

Fifth, one cannot assume a priori that a particular perspective is inherently superior to another. The assumption that a person must be born and raised in a particular culture to understand it is not always valid. It can be true that such persons may have insights about and understanding of their own culture that an outsider may not possess. Insiders, however, may be bound by, and blind to, their own cultural influences (Berry, Chapter 16; Enriquez, Chapter 9; Sinha, Chapter 2). Within a particular culture people share common viewpoints (i.e., tacit knowledge) and consider such ideas *natural,* not *cultural.* As Wirth (1946) observes, "The most important thing . . . that we can know about a person is what he (or she) takes for granted, and the most elemental and important facts about a society are those things that are seldom debated and generally regarded as settled" (p. xxiv). Someone with an external point of view can call attention to those things that are assumed to be natural but are actually cultural. Kleinman (1980) suggests that cross-indigenous comparisons may serve as mirrors for understanding one's own culture.

Sixth, as with other scientific traditions, one of the goals of the indigenous psychologies approach is the discovery of universal facts, principles, and laws. It does not, however, assume a priori the existence of psychological universals. If they exist, they need to be theoretically and empirically verified. The discovery process, however, differs qualitatively from that of general psychology. In the indigenous psychologies approach, individual, social, cultural, and temporal variations are incorporated into the research design, rather than eliminated or controlled. This approach advocates the use of cross-cultural (Berry, Chapter 16) and cross-indigenous investigations (Enriquez, Chapter 9).

Cross-Indigenous Approach

There are two stages of discovery in the indigenous psychologies approach. First is the description and explanation of psychological phenomena rooted

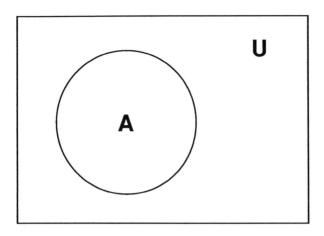

U   = universe (total range of the phenomenon)
U'   = measured universe of the phenomenon
A   = existence of the phenomenon in culture A
U' = A

Figure 1.1. The Cross-Indigenous Approach: Existing Western Scientific and Academic Psychology

in a particular culture. The second aspect involves comparing results from one indigenous psychology with others in search of universal generalizations. This second phase has been called the *cross-indigenous approach* (Enriquez, Chapter 9).

Figure 1.1 illustrates, through use of a Venn diagram, an indigenous psychology of one particular culture. The figure has three components: the universe (U, the total range of phenomenon), the measurement of a phenomenon (U'), and the existence of a phenomenon in a particular culture (A). In science, U' does not equal U (i.e., it is rare to investigate the full range of a phenomenon); only some aspects of the phenomenon can be sampled and investigated.

In Figure 1.1, the measured universe, U', equals the existence of a phenomenon in a particular culture, A. Discoveries made in culture A are often assumed to be the measured universe, or a representation of the universe. This position reflects the current status of general psychology, which assumes that psychological results are universal. Existing psychological knowledge, however, can best be characterized as American psychology (i.e., of, by, and for the United States) and not as a universal psychology (Moscovici, 1972; Murphy & Kovach, 1972; Sampson, 1977; see also Ardila, Chapter 10; Berry, Chapter 16; Diaz-Guerrero, Chapter 3; Enriquez, Chapter 9; Ho, Chapter 15; Sinha, Chapter 2).

Criticism of general psychology can be divided into two camps: those who attack its external validity and those who question its internal validity. Several contributors to this volume (e.g., Ardila, Chapter 10; Berry, Chapter 16; Boski, Chapter 5; Diaz-Guerrero, Chapter 3; Ho, Chapter 15; Trimble & Medicine, Chapter 8; Sinha, Chapter 2) question the external validity of existing psychological knowledge. They contend that general psychology has focused on assumptions, issues, and problems of the United States and that the results are limited to U.S. society and are not generalizable to other cultures. As a consequence, psychological knowledge is an example of *imposed etic* and not true *etic* knowledge (see Berry & Kim, Chapter 17, for further discussion; see Berry, 1989, for a detailed discussion).

In addition to errors of commission, Azuma (1984) points out that general psychology has committed errors of omission. He points out that American psychologists cannot appreciate phenomena found outside of the United States: "When a psychologist looks at a non-Western culture through Western glasses, he may fail to notice important aspects of the non-Western culture since the schemata for recognizing them are not provided by his science" (p. 49). In general psychology the full range of psychological phenomena is not typically investigated, and thus psychological results have limited external validity.

One consequence of focusing on issues and problems of the United States is neglect of scientific contributions made by researchers in other countries (Berry, Chapter 16; Enriquez, Chapter 9; de Silva, Chapter 14; Ho, Chapter 15; Lomov et al., Chapter 6). For example, de Silva (Chapter 14) notes that Buddhism contains a "highly systematic psychological account of human behavior and mind." This knowledge can be used to test, supplement, complement, or refute existing psychological theories and can be applied for therapeutic purposes. Durojaiye (Chapter 13) points out that most definitions of intelligence focus on cognitive aspects and neglect the all-important social dimensions.

The second line of criticism deals with the limited internal validity of psychological knowledge. Psychological theories and methods developed in the United States adopted the individual as the basic unit of analysis, affirming the individualistic bias (Koch & Leary, 1985; Sampson, 1977; Spence, 1985). Several contributors to this volume (Choi et al., Chapter 12; Enriquez, Chapter 9; Ho, Chapter 15) suggest that an alternative unit of analysis (i.e., human relationships) be used in understanding cultures of Asia (i.e., China, Japan, Korea, and the Philippines).

A more fundamental challenge is the question of the scientific validity of general psychology. The basic assumption of psychology as a branch of the natural sciences and the use of experimental methods have been seriously challenged, by Cronbach (1975), Gibson (1985), Kantor (1979), and Toulmin and Leary (1985), among others. These prominent psychologists point out that general psychology has largely failed to discover or amass empirical facts and laws because of its inappropriate emulation of the natural sciences.

There is now worldwide recognition of the limited scientific validity and utility of existing psychological knowledge, and calls for indigenization are being heard. In recent years the need for indigenous psychologies has been recognized in Canada (Berry, 1974), China (Ching, 1984), Fiji (Samy, 1978), France (Moscovici, 1972), Germany (Graumann, 1972), Hong Kong (Ho, 1982), India (Sinha, 1984), Japan (Azuma, 1984), Korea (Kwon, 1979), Mexico (Diaz-Guerrero, 1977), the Philippines (Enriquez, 1977), Scandinavia (Smedslund, 1984), Taiwan (Yang, 1986), Turkey (Kagitcibasi, 1984), Venezuela (Salazar, 1984), and Zambia (Serpell, 1984).

In Figure 1.2, a phenomenon is compared between two cultures: Culture A and Culture B. This type of a comparison yields two kinds of knowledge: culture specific and culturally shared. In the United States, for example, most definitions of intelligence focus on cognitive ability (Berry, 1984; Durojaiye, Chapter 13). Dasen (1984) found that the Baoulé culture, like American culture, views intelligence in terms of literacy, memory, and the ability to process information quickly. This form of intelligence is, however, regarded as meaningful only when applied for the well-being of the community. Dasen found that in addition to cognitive abilities, the Baoulé emphasize social intelligence (defined as the ability to get along with one another and to serve the group). Similar conceptions have been discovered in numerous other cultures (Berry, 1984; Berry & Bennett, 1992; Stevenson, Azuma, & Hakuta, 1986; see also Durojaiye, Chapter 13).

Dasen (1984) also found a unique feature of intelligence among the Baoulé that is not found in North America or Europe: "to be lucky and to bring good luck." This may reflect a spiritual aspect that is often neglected in North America and Europe. It may be found in cultures where spiritual influences are considered real and part of everyday life. By comparing intelligence in two cultures, one not only discovers culturally unique and culturally shared characteristics, but increases the total range of the measured phenomenon, U'.

Comparisons between two cultures may yield results that do not reflect true differences but represent research artifacts. Leff (1981) reports that in an epidemiological study of schizophrenia the rate of schizophrenic patients in psychiatric hospitals in New York and London differed significantly (62% versus 34%). Leff attributes this difference to problems of diagnosis rather

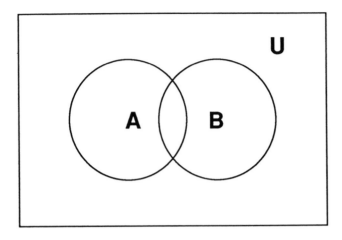

U	= universe (total range of the phenomenon)
A - (A∩B)	= existence of the phenomenon only in culture A
B - (A∩B)	= existence of the phenomenon only in culture B
A∩B	= culturally shared (<u>derived etic</u> of cultures A and B)
A∪B = U'	= measured universe of the phenomenon

Figure 1.2. Comparing a Phenomenon Between Two Cultures

than to cultural differences. When he used trained clinicians who adopted the same standard of diagnosis, the difference became insignificant (29% versus 35%). Similarly, Yap (1974) analyzed what are purported to be culture-specific mental disorders (such as *latah, amok, witiko, koro, brain fag, pibloqtog, susto*). Although symptoms are manifested in culture-specific forms, Yap contends that the underlying nature of these syndromes could be classified and integrated into the existing body of knowledge. The above two reanalyses suggest that observed "differences" between two or more cultures may actually be nothing more than artifacts of research.

Figure 1.3 illustrates a situation in which a phenomenon is compared in three different cultures. In this diagram there are three types of information: culture-specific characteristics, shared characteristics between two cultures, and shared characteristics in all three cultures. The representativeness of the measured phenomenon, U', has been increased significantly.

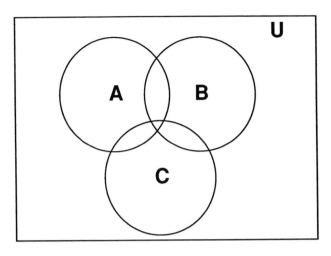

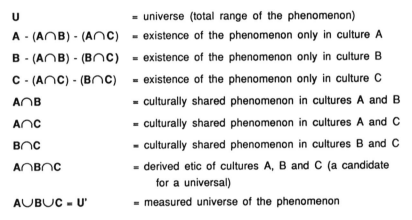

U	= universe (total range of the phenomenon)
A - (A∩B) - (A∩C)	= existence of the phenomenon only in culture A
B - (A∩B) - (B∩C)	= existence of the phenomenon only in culture B
C - (A∩C) - (B∩C)	= existence of the phenomenon only in culture C
A∩B	= culturally shared phenomenon in cultures A and B
A∩C	= culturally shared phenomenon in cultures A and C
B∩C	= culturally shared phenomenon in cultures B and C
A∩B∩C	= derived etic of cultures A, B and C (a candidate for a universal)
A∪B∪C = U'	= measured universe of the phenomenon

Figure 1.3. Comparing a Phenomenon Across Three Cultures

Forms of address can be used as an example to illustrate the above diagram. In several European languages, two pronouns are used to mark social relationships. In French, for example, *tu* represents the informal form and *vous* represents the formal form. A similar distinction is also found in other European languages, such as German, Spanish, and Italian (Brown, 1965). In a typical dyadic relationship, a person of higher social standing could use the *tu* form to address someone of lower standing. The person of lower standing does not usually reciprocate with the *tu* form, but uses the *vous* form. Brown (1965) postulates that this dyadic usage reflects unequal status. Second, the *tu* form is used between dyads of intimate equals and the *vous* form is used between strangers. These usages reflect social distance.

Brown (1965) postulates the *invariant norm of address* that regulates the pronominal usage. This norm states that two underlying dimensions that regulate the actual types of pronouns used are status and solidarity. Results from a series of studies of European languages confirm the invariant norm of address. Although comparable "formal" and "intimate" pronouns once existed in the English language (*thou/thee*), their usage is no longer maintained. In a study of the nominal forms of address for English,[1] Brown found support for the two underlying rules of address. This norm would constitute a culturally shared characteristic among these European languages.

In Korean and Japanese languages, there are no pronominal equivalents to the *tu/vous* forms. Rather, the levels of formality are directly coded in the verb endings. There are three levels of formality in Japanese, and six levels of formality in Korean (Martin, 1964). The coding of formality in verb endings represents a shared characteristic between Korean and Japanese that is not shared with European languages. Although there are differences among these languages in the form of expression, there is a suggestion of tentative universal rules of address (Kroger, Wood, & Kim, 1984). In a further empirical analysis of Chinese, Greek, and Korean nominal forms of address, Brown's (1965) invariant norm of address has been confirmed. Thus this norm could be considered a candidate for a true etic.

Similar to the norms of address, Ho (Chapter 15) suggests that the norm of reciprocity could be considered universal. It is, however, manifested in various ways in different cultures. In his analysis of key concepts in China, Japan, and the Philippines, he found that these cultures emphasize collective reciprocity. It is reflected in the Chinese concepts of *renqing* (meaning "favor") and *renqingzhai* ("indebtedness to a favor"), the Japanese concept of *on* ("obligation"), and the Filipino concept of *utang la loob* ("debt of gratitude"). In contrast to Western notions of reciprocity, where the individual is the unit of analysis, in Asian cultures interpersonal relatedness is emphasized (Choi et al., Chapter 12; Enriquez, Chapter 9; Ho, Chapter 15). Empirical studies in Korea and Canada, for example, confirm the above observations (Choi et al., Chapter 12; Kim & Choi, in press).

There are, however, cases where an overlap among various cultures is not found. Figure 1.4 represents this possibility. In discussing this figure, the example of incest taboo can be used. The incest taboo (i.e., a sanction against inbreeding or sexual intimacy among family members and close relatives) has been found in almost all cultures (van den Berghe, 1983). One possible reason for enforcement of incest taboo is that infants born from incestuous relations are more likely to possess genetic deformities. There have been some cultures, however, about 40 in all, in which the incest taboo has not been strictly enforced (van den Berghe, 1983). For instance, the incest taboo was not practiced in some royal families and in some secluded communities,

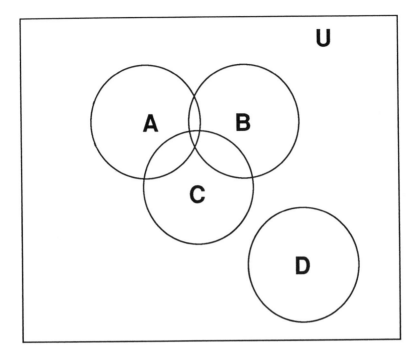

$$A \cap B \cap C \cap D \qquad = 0, \text{ There is no overlap}$$

$$A \cup B \cup C \cup D = U' \qquad = \text{measured universe of the phenomenon}$$

Figure 1.4. Comparing a Phenomenon Across Four Cultures

such as the Hawaiian Islands (Daws, 1968). Early settlers in Hawaii, for example, emigrated in small bands, traveling great distances, and thus outbreeding was not a realistic possibility. However, because of a relatively high number of offspring with genetic deformities, there are some suggestions that infanticide was practiced (Daws, 1968). In such a case, infanticide could be interpreted as an alternative way of reducing genetic deformities.

From systematic studies of indigenous psychologies across different cultures, it is possible to look for general principles and universals. Cross-indigenous psychologies, complemented with cross-cultural psychology, can lead to the discovery of *true etics* rather than *imposed etics*. With the cross-indigenous approach, not only can universal regularities be discovered, but the total range of a phenomenon investigated is increased.

In summary, the indigenous psychologies approach upholds the view that each culture needs to be understood from within its own reference frame. This approach advocates systematic and in-depth description of the behaviors, values, customs, and beliefs of a particular culture. It shares a family resemblance to other disciplines in the cultural sciences tradition: ethnoscience, cultural anthropology, and cross-cultural psychology. Its lineage can be traced back to the cultural sciences tradition.

THE CULTURAL SCIENCES TRADITION

Historical Overview

There are five prominent scholars in the cultural sciences tradition who have pointed out that the human world is complex and ever changing. These scholars suggest that the nature of knowledge for human subjects differs from the nature of knowledge for physical objects. Theories and methods developed in natural sciences are thus of limited use in our attempts to understand human beings. As a result, researchers need to adopt different levels, units, and methods of analysis for human subjects. The first leading figure representing the cultural sciences tradition is an Italian philosopher, Giovanni Battista Vico (1688-1744). The following description of Vico's work is summarized from the work of Berlin (1976).

Vico separated the natural world from the human world. He noted that nature exists prior to, and independent of, human creation. Human beings are mere observers of nature and thus their understanding about nature can be only indirect and inferential (i.e., we can classify the contents of the natural world into regularities, dissect them, combine and recombine them, simulate them, and superimpose mathematical techniques on them, but our results yield only correlations between two or more observed events, and we infer causality between the events). In the human world, direct, firsthand knowledge is possible because each individual is not just an observer but an actor participating in, reacting to, and contributing to its development. Art, history, society, culture, language, mathematics, and even science are *products* of collective human effort. As creators of these products, human beings can have direct, firsthand knowledge of their world. In the human world, "we judge human activity in terms of purposes, motives, acts of will, decisions, doubts, hesitations, thoughts, hopes, fears, and desires; these are among the ways in which we distinguish human beings from the rest of nature" (Berlin, 1976, p. 22).

Vico used the following analogy to articulate the limits of the physical and mathematical models in explaining the human world: to conceive of animate objects in human terms is considered irrational (i.e., a misapplication of categories, called *anthropomorphism* or *animism*), and the reverse tendency to explain humans in terms of mechanical laws is equally erroneous. Vico stated that humans possess an imaginative faculty that allows individuals to examine their own feelings, thoughts, and acts, as well as those of others and of other cultures. Humans embody their feelings, attitudes, and thoughts in symbols. These symbols are natural means of self-expression and are dependable reflections of the mind and outlook of the creator. Vico suggested using *fantasia* (translated as "reconstructive imagination"; Berlin, 1976) as a tool for understanding the human world. Those who possess *fantasia* can trace a symbol to its origins, reconstruct it, understand its effects, and assess its value. Within the diverse expressions, there can be a unified understanding of humans. Through the use of *fantasia,* social scientists can penetrate to the core of these symbolic representations to understand their underlying dynamics. Vico advocated historical and comparative analyses of culture to ascertain the unified understanding of humans (a thesis later adopted by Wundt, 1916).

Another key figure representing the cultural sciences tradition is Johannes Gottfried Herder (1744-1803). Like Vico, he saw limitations in the rationalist and empiricist approaches to understanding the human world and rejected the strict application of natural laws in the human sphere (Berlin, 1976). He argued instead for what Berlin (1976) labels *populism, expressionism,* and *pluralism.* The following description of Herder's work is also summarized from the work of Berlin (1976).

Populism is the "belief in the value of belonging to a group or a culture" (Berlin, 1976, p. 153). *Volkgeist* is an example of a natural way to group human beings. It is defined by Lazarus and Steinthal (1860) as "a similar consciousness of many individuals, plus an awareness of this similarity, arising through similar descent and spatial proximity" (cited in Allport, 1968, p. 49). Herder pointed out that each culture develops its own *Volkgeist,* and its development is influenced by factors such as ecology, education, physical and biological needs, and relations with neighbors. *Volkgeist* is expressed in speech, mythology, religions, folklore, art, literature, morality, custom, and law. *Volkgeist* shapes how people live, contemplate goals, imagine, think, feel, and behave and is communicated and shared through language. Individuals within a particular cultural community are united by common *Volkgeist* experiences.

Expressionism is the "doctrine that human activity in general, and art in particular, express the entire personality of the individual or the group, and are intelligible only to the degree to which they do so" (Berlin, 1976, p. 153). Herder believed that self-expression represents the very essence of a creative human being. He believed that human products such as works of art are forms of communication, expressions of a person's creativity. Other people could appreciate and understand these individual and cultural products through the process of *einfühlen* ("empathy").

Pluralism is "the belief not merely in multiplicity, but in the incommensurability of the values of different cultures and societies" (Berlin, 1976, p. 153). Herder claimed that every culture possesses its own unique character: "All explanation, all understanding, indeed, all living, depends on a relationship to a given social whole and its unique past, and that is incapable of being fitted into some repetitive, generalized pattern" (Berlin, 1976, p. xxiv). Herder noted that the tendency to judge ancient societies or other cultures by using one's own standard reflects cultural arrogance that could lead to distorted views. Herder believed that cultural diversity and social change are not only inescapable, but desirable. They are intrinsic parts of the creative aspect of human nature.

Hayim Steinthal (1823-1899) and Moritz Lazarus (1824-1903) provided a unique contribution to the cultural sciences tradition by empirically documenting the existence of diverse cultural patterns. They published the first journal in psychology, titled *Zeitschrift für Völkerpsychologie und Sprachwissenschaft* (Journal of Ethnopsychology and Linguistics; Danziger, 1983). The journal covered topics such as religion, mysticism, geological and geographic knowledge, biological and medical knowledge, and the development and use of language, customs, beliefs, tales, and myths (Danziger, 1983). This knowledge was analyzed as to its cultural implications (Danziger, 1983). The goal was to verify empirically the existence of *Völkgeist.*

Steinthal and Lazarus emphasized the use of systematic observation and documentation, rather than speculation on the existence of cultural differences. They relied on accounts of ethnographies compiled by writers, travelers, explorers, missionaries, and administrative officials (Danziger, 1983). They believed that the dialectical relationship between individuals and a community should be a topic for psychology rather than for philosophy, legal theory, or politics (Danziger, 1983). They contended that culture and history involve psychological processes that are amenable to systematic empirical analysis (Danziger, 1983).

The most important figure for psychology is Wilhelm Wundt. As a key figure representing both the natural sciences tradition and the cultural sciences tradition, Wundt believed these two approaches to be complementary rather than mutually exclusive (Danziger, 1983). Wundt credited Steinthal and Lazarus with introducing the concept of *Völkerpsychologie* and with compiling the *Zeitschrift für Völkerpsychologie und Sprachwissenschaft.*

Wundt cited the work of Vico and Herder and affirmed their viewpoints in the need for a historical and cultural analysis. Wundt's unique contribution is the amalgamation of the psychological level of analysis with the cultural level of analysis. He provided further extensions and refinement of ideas laid down by Vico, Herder, and Steinthal and Lazarus.

Wundt (1916) considered *Völkerpsychologie* to be a new field of knowledge in which human actors occupy center stage, affirming the position of Vico and Herder. He pointed out that language, mythology, art, customs, and religions are products of collective human effort and "all phenomena with which mental sciences deal are, indeed, creations of the social community" (p. 2). He defined *Völkerpsychologie* as "investigations concerning the relations which the intellectual, moral, and other mental characteristics of people sustain to one another, as well as to studies concerning the influence of these characteristics upon the spirit of politics, art, and literature" (p. 2).

Wundt noted that individual psychological processes (i.e., individual consciousness) can be systematically investigated in a laboratory setting through controlled experimentation. Cultural patterns and dynamics, however, cannot be brought into a laboratory setting. Moreover, *Völkerpsychologie* represents a cultural level of analysis that encompasses the individual consciousness:

> In the analysis of higher mental processes, folk psychology [*Völkerpsychologie*] is an indispensable supplement to the psychology of individual consciousness. Indeed, in the case of some questions the latter already finds itself obliged to fall back on the principles of folk psychology. Nevertheless, it must not be forgotten that just as there can be no folk community apart from individuals who enter into reciprocal relations within it, so also does folk psychology, in turn, presuppose individual psychology, or, as it is usually called, general psychology. The former, however, is an important supplement to the latter, providing principles for interpretation of the more complicated processes of individual consciousness. (Wundt, 1916, p. 3)

Wundt asserted that *Völkerpsychologie* is necessary to provide a complete account of psychogenesis and that psychological investigations at the individual level cannot adequately do so. Developmental analysis of individuals, for example, cannot fully account for psychogenesis, because a child is born into a preexisting cultural community and is shaped by it. The cultural community and intermediate social groups (such as family, tribe, and local community) into which a child is born must be examined historically, as they are not fixed entities, but have evolved through time and space. Wundt reaffirmed the positions of Vico and Herder, who asserted that each culture needs to be understood from its own frame of reference and that the analysis of the

historical evolution of a particular culture is fundamental to an understanding of people of that culture.

Wundt stressed that *Völkerpsychologie* is expressed in observable products such as language, myths, customs, and folkways. These products can be
understood through ethnographic, comparative, and historical analyses.
From these analyses, inferences can be made about their underlying nature and processes. Wundt believed that the basic psychological processes
underlying individual consciousness and cultural products are universal
(Danziger, 1983).

Wundt's grand design was first to separate different levels of analysis
(physiological, individual, and cultural) and to discover for each level an
appropriate unit and method of analysis (e.g., consciousness and introspection at the individual level and *Völkerpsychologie* at the cultural level). Once
basic processes are discovered at each level, Wundt proposed that this
knowledge could be integrated to provide coherent and universal understanding of human beings.

The five scholars discussed above provided a rich framework for understanding the human world. First, they argued that the human world is much
more complex than the physical world, and that methods used by the natural
sciences have limited applicability. Additional tools, such *fantasia, ein-
fuhlen,* and introspection need to be utilized in the human world. This point
has been echoed by authors in the present volume (Boski, Chapter 5; Choi
et al., Chapter 12; Enriquez, Chapter 9; Jodelet, Chapter 11).

The second major contribution of these scholars is their emphasis on systematic observation and documentation. They articulated the importance of
descriptive research and historical analysis as the first step in discovering
invariants within a particular culture. This point is elaborated by numerous
authors in the present volume (Berry, Chapter 16; Choi et al., Chapter 12;
de Silva, Chapter 14; Diaz-Guerrero, Chapter 3; Enriquez, Chapter 9; Ho,
Chapter 15; Jodelet, Chapter 11; Sinha, Chapter 2; Trimble & Medicine,
Chapter 8).

The five scholars' third major point is the acceptance of the diversity of
viewpoints, life-styles, and cultures as being natural. Diversity appears in
response to a culture's unique history, ecological pressures, and collective
needs. This point is affirmed by several authors in the present volume (Berry,
Chapter 16; Boski, Chapter 5; Diaz-Guerrero, Chapter 3; Durojaiye, Chap-
ter 13; Enriquez, Chapter 9; Georgas, Chapter 4; Lomov et al., Chapter 6;
Sinha, Chapter 2; Trimble & Medicine, Chapter 8). The use of one standard
to judge other individuals or cultures reflects an inability to go beyond one's
personal and cultural boundaries. This limitation is known as *egocentrism* at
the individual level and *ethnocentrism* at the cultural level. Scientists are
susceptible to both.

Fourth, these five scholars separated the content of representation from the style of representation. Although there are variations in human experiences across cultures in terms of their content, greatest variations occur in how the content is manifested. For example, all human beings have basic needs, such as for food, water, air, rest, and sexual expression. The greatest diversity appears in how these needs are satisfied. This point is elaborated by Boski (Chapter 5) and Ho (Chapter 15).

Scientific Approach

The cultural sciences tradition affirms the need to develop a descriptive understanding of a phenomenon in order to discover psychological and cultural invariants. A part of the discovery process involves uncovering an appropriate unit of analysis that can be used in analyzing, testing, and verifying observed patterns. The next step in the discovery process involves explaining these patterns. In this stage, the researcher systematically manipulates the unit of analysis to explore and experiment with the phenomenon.

The rationale for the cultural sciences approach and its relationship to the physical and biological sciences approach is depicted in Figure 1.5. In the physical sciences, the objects of investigation (i.e., inanimate objects) do not possess life. In Newtonian mechanics, for example, objects of investigation are relatively stable, homogeneous, and isolable (compared with animate objects) (Boulding, 1980). Physical objects (e.g., mass such as NaCl) are reactive to external stimuli (e.g., force, such as electrical attraction), and experimental replications can be performed by using new, identical raw material (e.g., the formation of NaCl). In order to explain the cause of the chemical reaction (the question of *why*), researchers need to understand the nature of the objects (*what*) and the process of chemical reaction (*how*).

Organisms, on the other hand, do not simply react to external stimuli. They interact with and adapt to their ecology. They possess central nervous systems that record their experiences. This learning may affect the behavior of the organism for the rest of its life (e.g., food poisoning and subsequent aversion to particular foods) and may be transmitted to its offspring to increase their chances of survival (e.g., taste aversion found in rats and color aversion found in pigeons). For this reason, ethologists such as Konrad Lorenz and Niko Tinbergen emphasize the need to investigate animals in their natural habitats. Tinbergen (1965) contends that animals adapt to, and their behaviors are meaningful in, particular ecological niches. Roeder (1965) points out that "a tiger's teeth and a fish's fins have evolutionary significance not only in their shape, but also in *how* and *where* they are used" (p. 7; emphasis added).

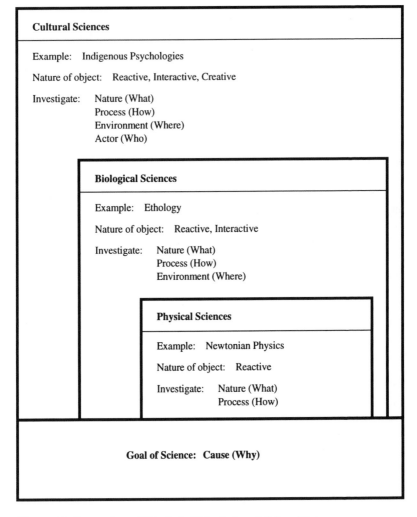

Figure 1.5. Comparison of Physical, Biological, and Cultural Sciences

During the descriptive phase, the goal of ethologists is to uncover stable parameters (i.e., units of analysis) and isolable subsystems (i.e., ecological niches). Ethologists have successfully discovered units of analysis such as fixed action patterns, species-specific defense mechanisms, and innate releasing mechanisms that are used to investigate complex patterns of animal behavior. As a result, in the biological sciences, in addition to knowing *what* and *how,* researchers need to know *where.*

At the physiological and biochemical levels, humans respond much like other animate objects (e.g., the knee-jerk reflex). At the individual and cultural levels, humans are interactive; they have successfully adapted to their ecology (Berry, Chapter 16; Georgas, Chapter 4). As in ethology, research must be conducted in naturalistic settings first to discover appropriate units of analysis. These must then be used systematically to unravel the complex and interactive nature of human thought and behavior (Choi et al., Chapter 12; Ho, Chapter 15; Jodelet, Chapter 11; Trimble & Medicine, Chapter 8).

There is, however, a central difference between humans and other organisms. Humans have the potential to be self-aware and creative. As pointed out above, humans possess the ability to understand, explain, predict, and control their environments. This creative feature allows the human being not only to adapt to the ecology, but to understand it and control it. As a result, in the human sciences, in addition to knowing *what, how,* and *where,* we need to know *who* (as individuals and as members of a culture).

As depicted in Figure 1.5, the cultural sciences approach represents a broader and more inclusive approach to science, encompassing both the physical and the biological sciences. Indigenous psychologies represent one version of the cultural sciences tradition. There are other approaches that share family resemblance to the indigenous psychologies approach: cultural anthropology, ethnoscience, and cross-cultural psychology. The indigenous psychologies approach differs from the above approaches in several areas.

Cultural Anthropology

The closest cousin to the indigenous psychologies approach is cultural anthropology. The two differ, however, in several aspects. First, cultural anthropology has traditionally used a particular method, ethnography, in the discovery process. Although ethnography is a useful descriptive tool, its results can be method bound. The reliability, validity, and interpretation of the data are not strictly verifiable. In science, results need to be verifiable by other researchers and through the use of different research methods. In cultural anthropology, an anthropologist rarely reexamines a finding of another anthropologist by replicating the study at the same field site, with the same instrument, and with the same population. One notable exception is Freeman's (1983) controversial fieldwork in Samoa challenging Margaret Mead's (1928) interpretations. Freeman, however, used a very different framework, research design, and population, and his study cannot be viewed as a robust replication. Although his reanalysis is not ideal, a better-designed replication is considered necessary in the indigenous psychologies approach.

Second, cultural anthropologists rely heavily on informants to serve as translators and interpreters of events in a community if the anthropologists themselves do not have the necessary language or cultural understanding. The perspective provided by an informant can be limited and may not accurately represent the people being investigated. The data provided by an informant need to be verified systematically by other members of the community. This type of verification has become more frequent in recent years.

Third, although the indigenous psychologies approach emphasizes the need to understand a culture from its own perspective, it does not uphold the strict cultural relativity position, which argues that each culture is unique and needs to be understood within its own context and that comparisons among cultures are unwarranted. According to Rossi (1980), most cultural anthropologists "reject ethnocentrism and uphold the principle of *cultural relativism*" (p. 2). The indigenous psychologies approach does not preclude the existence of, or the discovery of, psychological universals. The question of universality, or of possible generalizability, needs to be entertained. Just as general psychology cannot assume that its results are universal a priori, one cannot assume that one's findings are unique to a particular culture. The existence of psychological universals is a theoretical and empirical issue that cannot be decided a priori.

Fourth, the indigenous psychologies approach recognizes the need to examine the dialectical influences of the individual and the culture. It acknowledges the existence of diversity at both individual and cultural levels. Cultural anthropology places greater emphasis on the collective level and the indigenous psychologies approach places greater emphasis on the individual level. For example, Heelas and Lock's edited volume *Indigenous Psychologies: The Anthropology of the Self* (1981) reflects an anthropological emphasis. The editors define indigenous psychologies as "the cultural views, theories, conjectures, classifications, assumptions, and metaphors—together with notions embedded in social institutions—which bear on psychological topics" (p. 3). The book focuses on the collective representation of psychological issues, and the psychological perspective is secondary. The indigenous psychologies approach, advocated in the present volume, puts a greater emphasis on the psychological and dialectical processes.

Ethnoscience

Like the ethnoscience tradition, the indigenous psychologies approach examines the systems of folk classification and categorization. Researchers in the ethnoscience tradition (e.g., Naomi Quinn, Paul Kay, Roy D'Andrade,

Geoffrey White, Eleanor Rosch, Barbara Lloyd, George Lakoff, Catherine Lutz, and Roger Kessing) investigate topics such as biological classification, color categorization, kinship terminologies, cognition, memory, and emotion (for examples of their work, see Holland & Quinn, 1987; Rosch & Lloyd, 1978; Stigler, Shweder, & Herdt, 1990). Both the ethnoscience tradition and the indigenous psychologies approach emphasize the need for systematic and in-depth description of a phenomenon in its natural environment.

Cognition and Categorization, edited by Rosch and Lloyd (1978), and *Cultural Models in Language and Thought,* edited by Holland and Quinn (1987), represent this tradition. Ethnoscience recognizes the limitations of the arbitrary classification systems that are often imposed upon their subject matter. Ethnoscientists suggest that the system of classification be examined from categories developed by people in their natural settings. Classifications arise out of people's interaction with their environments. Rosch and Lloyd (1978) emphasize the importance of documenting "real world categories, the cognitive processes underlying categorization, and the nature of representation" (p. 3). Four contributions in this volume (Choi et al., Chapter 12; Enriquez, Chapter 9; Jodelet, Chapter 11; Trimble & Medicine, Chapter 8) employ a similar ethnoscientific approach.

In psychology, Heider (1958) advocates the development of *naive psychology.* He suggests that common sense be used as a starting point of research in interpersonal relations. Although intuitive knowledge has limited applicability in the physical sciences, it can be useful in understanding human behavior: "The ordinary person has a great and profound understanding of himself and of other people which, though unformulated or only vaguely conceived, enables him to interact in more or less adaptive ways" (p. 2). Heider comments that commonsense psychology can contribute to scientific understanding of human relations in two ways. First, people's conceptions about other people and social situations shape their behavior. This descriptive knowledge can aid in the prediction of their actual behavior. Second, he suggests that there are elements of truth contained in these commonsense viewpoints (for further discussion, see Bruner, 1990; Choi et al., Chapter 12).

Cross-Cultural Psychology

The closest sibling to the indigenous psychologies approach is cross-cultural psychology. Cross-cultural psychology is broadly defined as the "scientific study of the ways in which social and cultural forces shape human behavior" (Segall, Dasen, Berry, & Poortinga, 1990, p. 3). The goals of cross-cultural psychology are threefold: to transport and test existing psychological theories in different cultural settings to verify their generalizability and applicability, to explore and develop psychological understanding rooted in a particular cultural context, and to compare knowledge obtained from the first two goals and integrate them to arrive at a more universal description and explanation (Berry, 1980).

Cross-cultural psychology recognizes the two possible starting points in research. Berry (1989) summarizes the two contrasting perspectives through the use of the emic/etic distinction. He notes that the etic approach attempts to derive a universal understanding of a phenomenon. In this approach, theories and methods are abstracted and created by researchers in advance, based on standardized or absolute criteria. They are then tested on existing cultures to study variations on the standardized criteria. This is the position of general psychology. The emic approach, on the other hand, represents an approach similar to that of ethnoscience and cultural anthropology. It examines one cultural system from its own internal viewpoint. The goals of this approach are to discover indigenous units of analyses in an attempt to provide a systematic understanding of its structure.

Cross-cultural psychology attempts to incorporate both emic and etic approaches (Berry, 1989). Theories and methods are typically developed in one culture. They are then transported to and imposed upon another. They are, however, adapted in the other culture to incorporate the indigenous knowledge system. The final results are then compared between two or more cultures to discover commonality and/or differences. Theories are then verified, modified, reanalyzed, revised, or rejected.

In the area of cognition, *Indigenous Cognition: Functioning in Cultural Context*, edited by Berry, Irvine, and Hunt (1988), represents the cross-cultural tradition. This book emphasizes the need to adopt an approach through which people are investigated in their respective cultural contexts, which are "informed by *their* views and *their* understanding of what *their* cognitive life is about" (p. 2). Theories and instruments, nevertheless, have been largely developed within one cultural tradition and then tested in other cultures.

The main difference between indigenous psychology and cross-cultural psychology lies in the starting point of research (Enriquez, Chapter 9). To use the terminology employed by Enriquez (Chapter 9), the indigenous psychologies approach represents *indigenization from within,* whereas cross-cultural psychology represents *indigenization from without.* Indigenization from without examines particular issues, concepts, and methods that are developed and are of interest to a particular scientific community (most often the United States) and are studied in other cultures (e.g., Third World countries). There can be various attempts to modify the instruments to incorporate local indigenous perspectives, but these attempts, nevertheless, are external impositions (Enriquez, Chapter 9). Although these approaches attempt to incorporate and synthesize another culture's perspective, the issues, concepts, and methods have been preselected and reflect the interests of the investigator. Enriquez notes that strict adherence to this type of research could end up as a form of psychological and cultural "colonization."

Indigenization from within involves the study of issues and concepts that reflect the needs and realities of a particular culture. For example, issues such as illiteracy, poverty, national development, and rural psychology are salient topics for India, but not necessarily for industrialized nations (Sinha, Chapter 2). Boski (Chapter 5) notes that in addition to indigenous issues, intellectual styles (i.e., preferred epistemology or methodology) need to be examined. Intellectual style often reflects how one defines the situation, the method one adopts, and the interpretation one chooses. Strict adherence to indigenization from within, however, could result in cultural parochialism and ethnocentrism (Sinha, Chapter 2).

The cross-cultural psychology and indigenous psychologies approaches are not mutually exclusive; rather, they are complementary approaches. The main difference lies in the starting point of research. Integration of these two approaches is necessary if we are to discover true psychological universals (Berry & Kim, Chapter 17). Examples of integration of the cross-cultural and cross-indigenous approaches can be found in the three studies of individualism and collectivism discussed below.

First, Hofstede (1980, 1983), in a study of more than 117,000 IBM employees in 66 countries, found a dimension of cultural variations he calls *individualism*. It is considered to be a bipolar dimension, with individualism on one end and collectivism on the other. Hofstede (1980) used an instrument that was developed in one culture and tested in various countries.

Second, Michael Bond and his colleagues extracted 40 indigenous Chinese values from the philosophical literature and created an instrument, called the Chinese Values Survey, that was then translated and administered to a group of university students in 20 different countries (Chinese Cultural Connection, 1987). These researchers found a dimension that correlated highly with Hofstede's (1980) individualism. These two studies can be considered examples of the cross-cultural approach.

Finally, Triandis and his colleagues (1986) developed an attitude instrument to which collaborators from numerous cultures contributed items. These researchers found two dimensions that correlated highly with Hofstede's (1980) individualism. This study can be considered a version of the cross-indigenous approach. Both the cross-cultural approach and the cross-indigenous approach yielded a consistent pattern of results and suggest that the results are robust (for a review, see Kim, Triandis, Choi, Kagitcibasi, & Yoon, 1993).

OVERVIEW OF THE CHAPTERS

This book contains 17 contributions representing various parts of the world. Chapter 2, by Durganand Sinha, reviews the indigenization process in India by addressing four key questions: why it is needed, when it started, what it is, and how to achieve it. The chapter articulates the need to integrate indigenous systems of knowledge passed down through Indian heritage with the scientific tradition and the challenges of national development.

In Chapter 3, Rogelio Diaz-Guerrero articulates a framework for developing a Mexican ethnopsychology and reviews the *historic-sociocultural premises* (culturally significant values held by a majority of people) studied over the past 20 years in different parts of Mexico. He has found several dimensions of historic-sociocultural premises to be relatively robust: affiliative obedience, machismo, respect over love, and virginity.

In Chapter 4, James Georgas examines the functional relationship between ecological and social variables across different ethnic groups and time. He uses the ecological-social model to investigate changing interpersonal relationships, family values, and community cohesiveness in Greece.

In Chapter 5, Pawel Boski examines the development of Polish psychology in three areas: indigenous problems, cultural values, and intellectual styles. He notes that in addition to indigenous issues, Polish cultural values affirm humanism. Humanistic values are reflected in intellectual style, which affects how one defines the situation, the method one adopts, and the interpretation one chooses. Boski examines how these three facets shaped the development of Polish psychology.

Lomov, Budilova, Koltsova, and Medvedev, in Chapter 6, examine the close relationship among religion, science, and social life in Russia. The authors outline ideas put forth by prominent Russian scholars such as Nadezhdin, Lomonsov, Sechenov, and Bekhterev. They point out that in Russia, psychological knowledge is widely disseminated (e.g., Sechenov's *Reflexes of the Brain* has been widely read and discussed), and they note that religion and science are integral parts of social life in the Russian culture.

In Chapter 7, Fathali Moghaddam suggests that in most developing countries, two competing systems (i.e., traditional and indigenous versus modern and imported) operate parallel to one another. He points out that the developed, "Westernized" sector does not interact with the "traditional" sector. This creates a competing subculture within one society, resulting in two psychologies that reflect two different realities.

Chapter 8, authored by Joseph Trimble and Beatrice Medicine, refutes the melting pot theory of the United States and articulates the need to acknowledge diverse Native Indian communities. The authors suggest that each community needs to be examined from its own historical, cultural, spiritual, ecological, and acculturative context. Any integrative understanding of these communities must first come from an internal analysis.

In Chapter 9, Virgilio Enriquez traces the acceptance of general psychology as a part of the colonial background of the Philippines. In the early 1970s a new movement developed, urging a new brand of psychology called *liberation psychology*. The movement instilled a new consciousness in Filipino psychology by forcing the discipline to examine the colonial imposition and to revalidate its cultural and theoretical orientation. Enriquez provides a description of *Sikolohiyang Pilipino* that explores the nature and dynamics of the Filipino psyche.

Chapter 10, by Ruben Ardila, articulates the limitations of general psychology and provides guidelines for the development of a more appropriate psychology for developing countries. Ardila notes that in Third World countries the emphasis is on application and problem solving rather than on basic research. He points out several areas that are of concern to Third World nations: use of human resources, achievement motivation, education, poverty, health and disease, and life expectancy.

In Chapter 11, Denise Jodelet utilizes the social representation perspective to examine how ideas developed in the scientific community filtered down to a rural community in France. Jodelet focuses specifically on those concepts that deal with disturbances of the mind and body.

Chapter 12, by Sang-Chin Choi, Uichol Kim, and Soo-Hyang Choi, examines key concepts that are indigenous to Korean culture and that illuminate facets of interpersonal relatedness. The results confirm the collectivist orientation of Korean culture. The authors suggest that emotional concepts such as *cheong* ("affection") occupy center stage in Korean culture. This emphasis contrasts sharply with the Western emphasis on rationality.

In Chapter 13, Michael Durojaiye investigates the meaning of intelligence in Nigeria. He has found a strong social dimension of intelligence. In Nigeria, intelligence is not interpreted as a genetic or rational construct, but as a social construct. Intelligence is meaningful not as an individual entity, but as a construct that is socially defined, propagated, and reified.

In Chapter 14, Padmal de Silva examines concepts and perspectives developed in Buddhism and their relevance to therapeutic practices. He notes that Buddhism contains a "highly systematic psychological account of human behavior and mind," and this knowledge can be used to test, supplement, complement, or refute existing psychological theories and can be applied for therapeutic purposes.

In Chapter 15, David Ho proposes a conceptual framework for Asian social psychology and examines key concepts in the Chinese, Japanese, and Filipino cultures. In his analysis, he notes that these concepts reflect cultural collectivism and relatedness. The reciprocity rules follow collective norms rather than the individualistic norms found in the United States.

In Chapter 16, John Berry articulates the need to develop an indigenous psychology of Canada. He outlines special features of Canadian society: vast land mass and low population density; cultural, social, and linguistic dualism; and cultural pluralism. He provides an integrated framework to address how these areas could be addressed by different branches of psychology (e.g., social, clinical, educational, and work).

The final chapter outlines a comparative framework for integrating the cross-indigenous approach with the cross-cultural approach. This integrated approach avoids the main problems of general psychology (i.e., it is culture blind and culture bound) and provides a comprehensive body of knowledge that could yield a veritable universal psychology.

NOTE

1. Nominal forms of address such as *Dr., Mr.,* and *Mrs.* are considered formal in the English language. First names and nicknames are considered informal. See Kroger, Wood, and Kim (1984) for a full description.

REFERENCES

Allport, G. (1968). Historical background of modern social psychology. In G. Lindzey & E. Aronson (Eds.), *Handbook of social psychology* (Vol. 1). Reading, MA: Addison-Wesley.

Azuma, H. (1984). Psychology in a non-Western country. *International Journal of Psychology, 19,* 145-155.

Berlin, I. (1976). *Vico and Herder: Two Studies in the History of Ideas.* New York: Viking.

Berry, J. W. (1974). Canadian psychology: Some social and applied emphases. *Canadian Psychologist, 15,* 132-139.

Berry, J. W. (1980). Introduction to methodology. In H. C. Triandis & J. W. Berry (Eds.), *Handbook of cross-cultural psychology* (Vol. 2). Boston: Allyn & Bacon.

Berry, J. W. (1983). Wundt's *Völkerpsychologie* and the comparative study of human behavior. In G. Eckardt & L. Sprung (Eds.), *Advances in historiography of psychology.* Berlin: VEB Deutscher Verlag der Wissenschaften.

Berry, J. W. (1984). Toward a universal psychology of cognitive competence. *International Journal of Psychology, 19,* 335-361.

Berry, J. W. (1989). Imposed etics, emics and derived etics: The operationalization of a compelling idea. *International Journal of Psychology, 24,* 721-735.

Berry, J. W., & Bennett, J. A. (1992). Cree conceptions of cognitive competence. *International Journal of Psychology, 27,* 73-88.

Berry, J. W., Irvine, S. H., & Hunt, E. B. (Eds.). (1988). *Indigenous cognition: Functioning in cultural context.* Dordrecht, Netherlands: Martinus Nijhoff.

Blumenthal, A. R. (1983). Wilhelm Wundt and early American psychology: A clash of cultures. In R. W. Rieber (Ed.), *Wilhelm Wundt and the making of a scientific psychology*. New York: Plenum.

Boring, E. G. (1921). *A history of experimental psychology*. Englewood Cliffs, NJ: Prentice-Hall.

Boulding, K. (1980). Science: Our common heritage. *Science, 207,* 821-826.

Brown, R. (1965). *Social psychology*. New York: Free Press.

Bruner, J. (1990). *Acts of meaning*. Cambridge, MA: Harvard University Press.

Campbell, D. T., & Fiske, D. W. (1959). Convergent and discriminant validation by the multitrait-multimethod matrix. *Psychological Bulletin, 56,* 81-105.

Chinese Cultural Connection. (1987). Chinese values and the search for a culture-free dimension of culture. *Journal of Cross-Cultural Psychology, 18,* 143-164.

Ching, C. C. (1984). Psychology and the four modernizations in China. *International Journal of Psychology, 19,* 57-63.

Cronbach, L. J. (1975). The two disciplines of scientific psychology. *American Psychologist, 30,* 671-684.

Danziger, K. (1979). Social origins of modern psychology. In A. R. Buss (Ed.), *Psychology in social context*. New York: Irvington.

Danziger, K. (1983). Origins and basic principles of Wundt's *Völkerpsychologie*. *British Journal of Social Psychology, 22,* 303-313.

Dasen, P. (1984). The cross-cultural study of intelligence: Piaget and the Baoulé. *International Journal of Psychology, 19,* 407-434.

Daws, G. (1968). *Shoal of time: A history of the Hawaiian Islands*. Honolulu: University of Hawaii Press.

Diaz-Guerrero, R. (1977). A Mexican psychology. *American Psychologist, 32,* 934-944.

Enriquez, V. G. (1977). Toward cross-cultural knowledge through cross-indigenous methods and perspectives. *Philippine Journal of Psychology, 12,* 9-16.

Freeman, D. (1983). *Margaret Mead and Samoa: The making and unmaking of an anthropological myth*. Cambridge, MA: Harvard University Press.

Gibson, J. J. (1985). Conclusions from a century of research on sense perception. In S. Koch & D. E. Leary (Eds.), *A century of psychology as science*. New York: McGraw-Hill.

Graumann, C. F. (1972). The state of psychology, I. *International Journal of Psychology, 7,* 123-134.

Heelas, P., & Lock, A. (Eds.). (1981). *Indigenous psychologies: The anthropology of the self*. London: Academic.

Heider, F. (1958). *The psychology of interpersonal relations*. New York: John Wiley.

Ho, D. Y. F. (1982). Asian concepts in behavioral science. *Psychologia, 25,* 228-235.

Hofstede, G. (1980). *Culture's consequences: International differences in work-related values*. Beverly Hills, CA: Sage.

Hofstede, G. (1983). National cultures revisited. *Behavior Science Research, 18,* 285-305.

Holland, D., & Quinn, N. (Eds.). (1987). *Cultural models in language and thought*. Cambridge: Cambridge University Press.

Kagitcibasi, C. (1984). Socialization in traditional society: A challenge to psychology. *International Journal of Psychology, 19,* 145-157.

Kantor, J. R. (1979). Psychology: Science or nonscience? *Psychological Bulletin, 29,* 155-163.

Kim, U., & Choi, S. C. (in press). Individualism, collectivism, and child development: A Korean perspective. In P. M. Greenfield & R. Cocking (Eds.), *Cognitive socialization of minority children: Continuities and discontinuities*. Hillsdale, NJ: Lawrence Erlbaum.

Kim, U., Triandis, H. C., Choi, S. C., Kagitcibasi, C., & Yoon, G. (Eds.). (1993). *Individualism and collectivism: Theory, method, and application*. Manuscript submitted for publication.

Kleinman, A. (1980). *Patients and healers in context of culture*. Berkeley: University of California Press.

Koch, S., & Leary, D. E. (1985). Introduction. In S. Koch & D. E. Leary (Eds.), *A century of psychology as science*. New York: McGraw-Hill.

Kroger, R. O., Wood, L. A., & Kim, U. (1984). Are the rules of address universal? III: Comparison of Chinese, Greek, and Korean usage. *Journal of Cross-Cultural Psychology, 15,* 273-284.

Kwon, T. H. (1979). Seminar on Koreanizing Western approaches to social science. *Korea Journal, 19,* 20-25.

Lachenmeyer, C. W. (1970). Experimentation: A misunderstood methodology in psychological and social-psychological research. *American Psychologist, 25,* 617-624.

Leff, J. (1981). *Psychiatry around the globe: A transcultural view*. New York: Marcel Dekker.

LeVine, M. (1974). Scientific method and the adversary model: Some preliminary thoughts. *American Psychologist, 29,* 661-667.

Martin, S. (1964). Speech levels in Japan and Korea. D. Hymes (Ed.), *Language in culture and society*. New York: Harper & Row.

Mead, M. (1928). *Coming of age in Samoa*. New York: Morrow.

Merriam-Webster, G. C. (1976). *Webster's third new international dictionary*. Chicago: Encyclopedia Britannica.

Moscovici, S. (1972). Society and theory in social psychology. In J. Israel & H. Tajfel (Eds.), *The context of social psychology*. London: Academic.

Murphy, G., & Kovach, J. K. (1972). *Historical introduction to modern psychology* (3rd ed.). New York: Harcourt Brace Jovanovich.

Roeder, K. D. (1965). Introduction. In N. Tinbergen, *Animal behavior*. New York: Time-Life.

Rosch, E., & Lloyd, B. B. (Eds.). (1978). *Cognition and categorization*. Hillsdale, NJ: Lawrence Erlbaum.

Rossi, I. (1980). Introduction. In I. Rossi (Ed.), *People in culture: A survey of cultural anthropology*. New York: Praeger.

Salazar, J. M. (1984). The use and impact of psychology in Venezuela. *International Journal of Psychology, 19,* 113-122.

Sampson, E. E. (1977). Psychology and the American ideal. *Journal of Personality and Social Psychology, 35,* 767-782.

Samy, J. (1978). Development and research for the Pacific, and session on theory and methods. In A. Marmak & G. McCall (Eds.), *Paradise postponed: Essays on research and development in the South Pacific*. Rushcutters Bay, NSW: Pergamon.

Segall, M. H., Dasen, P. R., Berry, J. W., & Poortinga, Y. H. (1990). *Human behavior in global perspective: An introduction to cross-cultural psychology*. New York: Pergamon.

Serpell, R. C. (1984). Commentary on the impact of psychology on Third World development. *International Journal of Psychology, 19,* 179-192.

Sinha, D. (1984). Psychology in the context of Third World development. *International Journal of Psychology, 19*(1-2), 17-29.

Smedslund, J. (1984). The invisible obvious: Culture in psychology. In K. M. J. Lagerspetz & P. Niemi (Eds.), *Psychology in the 1990's*. Amsterdam: North-Holland.

Spence, J. (1985). Achievement American style: The rewards and costs of individualism. *American Psychologist, 40,* 1285-1295.

Stevenson, H., Azuma, H., & Hakuta, K. (Eds.). (1986). *Child development and education in Japan*. New York: W. H. Freeman.

Stigler, J. A., Shweder, R. A., & Herdt, G. (Eds.). (1990). *Cultural psychology: Essays on comparative human development*. New York: Cambridge University Press.

Tinbergen, N. (1965). *Animal behavior*. New York: Time-Life.

Toulmin, S., & Leary, D. E. (1985). The cult of empiricism in psychology and beyond. In S. Koch & D. E. Leary (Eds.), *A century of psychology as science.* New York: McGraw-Hill.

Triandis, H. C., Bontempo, R., Betancourt, H., Bond, M., Leung, K., Brenes, A., Georgas, J., Hui, C. H., Marin, G., Setiadi, B., Sinha, J. P. B., Verma, J., Spangenberg, J., Tousard, H., & de Montmollin, G. (1986). The measurement of the etic aspects of individualism and collectivism across cultures. *Australian Journal of Psychology, 38,* 257-267.

van den Berghe, P. L. (1983). Human inbreeding avoidance: Culture in nature. *Behavioral and Brain Sciences, 6,* 91-123.

van Hoorn, W., & Verhave, T. (1980). Wundt's changing conceptions of a general and theoretical psychology. In W. G. Bringmann & R. D. Tweeney (Eds.), *Wundt studies: A centennial collection.* Toronto: Hogrefe.

Wirth, L. (1946). Preface. In K. Mannheim, *Ideology and utopia: An introduction to sociology of knowledge.* New York: Harcourt, Brace.

Wundt, W. (1916). *Elements of folk psychology: Outlines of a psychological history of the development of mankind* (E. L. Schaub, Trans.). London: George Allen & Unwin.

Yang, K. S. (1986). Chinese personality and its change. In M. H. Bond (Ed.), *The psychology of the Chinese people.* Hong Kong: Oxford University Press.

Yap, P. W. (1974). *Comparative psychiatry: A theoretical framework.* Toronto: University of Toronto.

2

INDIGENIZATION OF PSYCHOLOGY IN INDIA AND ITS RELEVANCE

DURGANAND SINHA

Rudyard Kipling, in "The Elephant's Child," wrote:

> I keep six honest serving men
> (They taught me all I knew);
> Their names are What and Why and When
> And How and Where and Who.

This chapter deals with the first four of the "honest serving men." In other words, it is concerned with the following issues related to indigenization of psychology in India: why we need it, when it started, what it is, and how to achieve it.

WHY INDIGENIZATION OF PSYCHOLOGY IS NEEDED IN INDIA

In India the roots of psychology can be traced to the vast storehouse of knowledge contained in ancient philosophical and religious texts, in epics, and in the rich folklore. These sources contain valuable material concerning the nature of human beings, their personalities and their social and interpersonal interactions. But the knowledge contained therein is based on the intuitions of seers and speculations and can hardly be regarded as scientific in

---

AUTHOR'S NOTE: An earlier version of this chapter was presented at the Symposium on Indigenous Psychologies during the Eighth International Conference of Cross-Cultural Psychology, Istanbul, Turkey, 1986.

the modern sense of the term. Thus when modern scientific psychology, based on the empirical, mechanistic, and materialistic orientations of the West, was imported to India as part of the general transfer of knowledge, it came in as a "ready-made intellectual package in the first decade of this century" (Nandy, 1974, p. 7). It tended to sweep away the traditional psychology, at least among those who had been involved in modern Western education. In fact, this transfer in a way constituted an element of the political domination of the West over the Third World countries and the general process of modernization and Westernization. The domination was so great that for almost three decades, until about the time India achieved independence (1947), psychology remained tied to the apron strings of the West and did not show any sign of maturing. Very little originality was displayed, and Indian research added hardly anything to psychological theory or knowledge, and was seldom related to the problems of the country (D. Sinha, 1980). Research conducted was by and large repetitive and replicative in character, the object being to supplement studies done in the West by further experimentation or to examine some of their aspects from a new angle.

Thus the discipline remained at best a pale copy of Western psychology, rightly designated a "Euro-American product" with very little concern with social reality as it prevailed in India. Many Indian scholars who held positions of importance had been trained in British or American universities and looked to the West for inspiration long after their return. There was nothing as such wrong with this orientation, but it had two harmful consequences that prevented healthy growth of the discipline. First, Indian scholars became recipients rather than exchange agents of knowledge. Indian psychology became imitative and subservient, sometimes going to the ridiculous length of conceptualizing, as Nandy (1974, p. 8) points out, peculiarly Indian phenomena in American terms, such as treating caste as if it were comparable to race, communalism as if it were comparable to anti-Semitism, and the situation of untouchables as if it were comparable to that of American blacks. It is not surprising, therefore, that the members of the Review Committee of the Indian Council of Social Science Research (1973) voiced their "concern about the foreignness of social science research in India in the field of psychology in particular" (p. 43). Such replicative studies had little relevance to the problems of the country.

The second consequence was that adopting the prevailing disciplinary fashion of the West distorted the sense of priorities of Indian scholars. They accepted the salience and priorities prevailing in Western psychology at the time without bothering to reexamine them in the light of Indian needs. As I have pointed out in earlier work, "The Western models and ideas took Indian researchers away from such ideas that might have struck roots in the Indian soil" (D. Sinha, 1986, p. 111). This frequently led to a shift in local scholars' focus, away from their own country and its problems, and distracted them from core issues. As I have pointed out in the context of cross-cultural research, many studies conducted were remote and of little relevance to the problems of the country where the data had been collected (D. Sinha, 1983a). At best, they served the theoretical needs of Western psychologists who were interested in testing panhuman applications of their theories, models, and observations, but were rarely of practical relevance to the host country (D. Sinha, 1986, p. 111).

Psychology that was borrowed, being a product of a very specific environment, was characterized by features that were not obtainable in India. Scientific enterprise is rooted in the prevalent worldview of the community, and psychological knowledge in each country has certain distinctive characteristics. Being rooted in respective intellectual history and sociocultural milieu, it has its own strong and weak points (D. Sinha, 1981). As Jahoda (1980) observes, psychological data and theories are often products of a specific social milieu of advanced industrial societies whose features are literacy, impersonality, universality, and a wide range of beliefs, ideas, and attitudes. These theories have made valuable contributions toward more efficient functioning of relatively stable institutions, such as industries, the military, and educational institutions, that share many of the characteristics of similar institutions in the West. In general, such conditions of stability are almost totally absent in the developing world (Jahoda, 1973), where problems emanate from the uncertainties and instabilities that are the core characteristics of the rapid socioeconomic changes taking place. Therefore, when confronted with issues that are mainly the accompaniments of rapid changes, Western generalizations and theories appear to have very limited relevance or utility (D. Sinha, 1984b). I tend to agree with Jahoda's (1980) general conclusion that social psychology is still very weak as regards theories relevant to studies in developing countries. Thus it is not surprising that in India "there are signs of growing crisis in psychology" in the sense that unlike economics, sociology, and anthropology, it has failed to make any impact in the national life (Pareek, 1980). It seems to have been largely left out of the arena of social change and national development that is so vital to the country. This feeling of being left out has generated among psychologists a strong urge to make their research efforts relevant and an urgent need for new orientation for the discipline.

BEGINNINGS OF
INDIGENIZATION OF PSYCHOLOGY IN INDIA

Though it is difficult to date the indigenization of psychology in India to any particular year, it can be asserted that it began in somewhat imperceptible latent form with the gaining of independence in 1947. With the end of the colonial era there was a rapid growth and diversification of research in almost all the branches of the subject and a great expansion in teaching and research. Along with this trend dawned the growth of national pride and a gradual awareness of distinct identity among scholars who began to feel the need for "outgrowing the alien framework" (D. Sinha, 1980). There was an effort to link different elements of Western psychology to the Indian situation by studying variables that were operant in the Indian setting, such as job satisfaction, absenteeism, and anxiety, to mention only a few. Though there was a search for relevant Indian topics, the general framework of Western concepts and theories for understanding reality was largely employed (J. B. P. Sinha, 1976). The trend for assimilation remained weak, and the field was a long way from gaining "intellectual independence." In fact, foreign contacts and publications carried enormous prestige and mattered a lot in career advancement. As a result, not only were foreign theories and models employed, but problems were researched that were popular in the West at that time and not necessarily those that constituted vital social issues in India.

The next phase in indigenization began in the 1960s, with distinct articulation of the need to conduct problem-oriented research and relate it particularly to the psychological problems arising from the rapid socioeconomic changes and development that the country was undergoing. With meager economic resources, doing research was felt to be a privilege, and one could not only expect to remain engaged simply in "research for prestige" but also in "research for policy." Jahoda (1975), referring to cross-cultural psychology, was right in asserting that there was "a strong indication that the Third World will not indefinitely welcome or even tolerate the activities of researchers without at least some prospect for tangible returns" (p. 6). Psychologists in India began to accept the challenge of social change and national development and to address themselves increasingly to problems of modernization of agriculture, rural development, family health and welfare, population control, caste and social structure, poverty and inequality, diffusion of innovations, and the like—many of which had so far remained outside the pale of psychology in the West. This change in orientation clearly marked the beginning of the phase of indigenization of psychology in India.

It may be observed that if one takes the definition of a psychologist as provided by the International Labour Office (1969) in its *International Standard Classification of Occupations,* social change and psychological problems of national development are outside the disciplinary ethos of the subject in the West. To that extent, psychologists in India in their effort toward indigenization have extended the frontiers of the discipline.

The next phase of the indigenization of psychology in India can be characterized as one of questioning, doubt, and a search for new identity. Though the trend started to be visible in the mid-1960s, it was in the 1970s that it intensified and crystallized. Indian psychologists started to question Western theories and models and their appropriateness in the specific sociocultural context and expressed doubts about the efficacy of tools developed by Western researchers for gathering data, especially on the unsophisticated and preliterate Indian population (D. Sinha, 1983b). It was during this phase that the process of indigenization was clearly in evidence. It was reflected in the distinct urge to develop a psychology rooted in Indian soil.

WHAT IS INDIGENIZATION?

Before discussing what constitutes indigenization of psychology, it would be useful to clarify the concept of indigenization itself. According to the *Oxford English Dictionary,* the word *indigenous* has reference to flora and fauna and means "produced naturally in a region; belonging naturally to the *soil"* (emphasis added). Extending the meaning and applying it to the *process,* indigenization would imply the way in which an element is so transformed as to make it natural or suited to the region, to the soil or the special features of the environment. The problem of indigenization arises when there is a foreign transplant that has to be transformed in such a way as to make it suited or natural to the soil, or the sociocultural setting. In the context of psychology, indigenization would refer to transformations of the scientific psychology that was borrowed from the West that would allow it to take on a character suited to the sociocultural milieu of the country. As evidenced today, indigenization is visible in the shaping of a process rather than in a finished product. Strong trends toward it are in evidence all around, but it will be some time before we have a well-developed indigenized product.

Before getting into the details, it would be well to point out that indigenization is not to be confused with the revivalism that has been in evidence since independence and is often known as *Indian psychology.* There was a reaction against the behavioristic and materialistic orientation of Western psychology, its wholly mechanistic view of humankind, and the limitations inherent therein. Being limited by its methodology, which was modeled on the physical sciences, it failed to answer pertinent questions concerning complex human phenomena of personality development, emotion, integration of the individual, and societal behavior. Many psychologists in the 1950s not only rightly pointed to its superficiality and weaknesses but also talked glibly about such phenomena as transmigration of soul, rebirth, and supernatural powers. They simply culled from ancient Indian sources speculative views concerning these phenomena, whose only claim to validity was their ancient origin. This intellectual exercise to reject scientific endeavors outright was not accepted by the general run of modern psychologists, who had imbibed the empirical and scientific temper of the time and were committed to the universalism of science. It is therefore not surprising that such revivalism and uncritical worship of the past was by and large rejected, and the expression *Indian psychology* was often used in a pejorative sense. Though the scientific enterprise is influenced by historical and sociocultural factors, there is no question of distinct *kinds* of psychology (such as Indian, American, German, or Japanese) conditioned by national and continental boundaries. Science cannot be so circumscribed and pigeonholed by national boundaries. There are, of course, exceptions; for instance, Akhilananda (1948, 1952) and Paranjpe (1984) not only outline the distinctive characteristics of psychological thinking in ancient Indian texts but also emphasize their practical significance and utility for understanding problems of mental health and human interactions.

Some scholars swayed by the trend toward indigenization have resorted to a process that is superficial. In their anxiety to appear rooted in the Indian soil, they casually refer to concepts and formulations contained in different ancient Indian systems when dealing with the problem at hand. A paper titled "Stress Research in Organisations: Integration of East and West" (Singh & Sinha, 1987) presented recently in a seminar on applied social psychology in India is a case in point. All the paper's authors do is state that the words *klesh* and *dukha* approximate to the Western concept of stress and outline their origins according to the Samkhya yoga system. They express surprise that stress research in India has borrowed the perspectives and methodologies of the West and that in spite of "the tradition of such well-articulated theorizations," no attention has been paid to empirical testing. Although the authors' stated goal was to attempt to integrate the findings on Indian and Western concepts of stress, no such effort was visible. After a cursory discussion of the origins of stress according to the Samkhya yoga system, the authors switch to Western formulations, making no attempt to provide any linkage, to integrate the two traditions, or to indicate the relevance of theorizations contained in the Indian system. Such superficial efforts toward integration are much in evidence today; the paper described above provides an illustration of what may be termed *cosmetic indigenization.*

Distinct from revivalism and the type of superficial indigenization indicated above is a growing tendency toward integration of modern psychology with Indian thought (D. Sinha, 1965) and an effort to bring about a new synthesis. I mentioned above some distinctive features of psychology as enshrined in ancient Indian texts. Instead of only pointing to the similarities and parallels between ancient Indian views and modern psychological thinking on phenomena such as consciousness, dreams, and sleep, there has been an effort to locate those concepts of our ancient philosophical heritage that lend themselves to scientific investigation. Naidu, Thapa, and Das (1986) have initiated a program of investigation on the role of detachment as a moderator in the stress process. Another excellent example of such an effort toward integration is Pande and Naidu's (1986) research attempting to operational- ize the concept of *nishkama karma* (action without attachment to outcome), develop a test to measure it, and analyze the correlates. Indian texts have traditionally stressed the importance of focusing intensely on the task at hand rather than being distracted by concern about the outcome of the task. The researchers posited that individuals with an outcome orientation would show positive and greater correlation between stresses and strains than would those with high effort orientation. Statistical analysis of the test they developed yielded two distinct clusters of outcome orientation and effort orientation and indicated the expected relationship with stress.

Pande and Naidu's study represents a form of indigenization of psychol- ogy in the sense that it explored Indian cultural systems for concepts and models relevant for understanding Indian social reality and exposed them to scientific scrutiny. It represents an effort toward an integration and synthesis of the Indian system with modern scientific psychology by operationalizing concepts, measuring them, and subjecting the measurements to experimental analysis. In fact, a striking feature of contemporary psychology has been a sudden upsurge of interest almost all over the world in examining indigenous modes of health measures as prescribed in various forms of yogic practices and meditation. Not only their physiological and psychological charac- teristics but their therapeutic values have been subjected to widespread in- vestigation (Anand, Chhina, & Singh, 1969; Gellhorne & Kiely, 1972; Rao & Murthy, 1975; Vahia et al., 1973). This has produced a body of knowledge that is not only indigenous in content but has wide applicability.

Indigenization is taking place in yet another way as well. A kind of as- similation process is in operation whereby transplanted knowledge is gradu- ally being adapted to local soil. For decades, psychologists in India had been victims of "adaptology" (Agarwal, 1975) or in their zeal had resorted simply to criticizing and taking a negative view of Western ideas and theories. In the process of assimilation, effort is being made to go beyond Western theories and models to build a conceptual framework more in tune with the Indian social reality. In the process, a distinctive identity is gradually being devel- oped. Although scientific methodology has been accepted, Western theoreti- cal frameworks are being critically examined and modified to be more meaningful in the Indian sociocultural milieu. Problems that are peculiarly Indian are being taken up for investigation utilizing knowledge and tech- niques acquired from Western sources. In the process, not only is the content of psychology becoming indigenized, but a new orientation to the discipline is gradually developing.

A few details will help to make this point clear. India being a predominantly rural country, with more then 76% of the population residing in villages and nearly 63% of the net domestic product originating in rural areas, it is natural that rural development occupies a vital place in national planning. Therefore, if psychology is to be "relevant" it has to go beyond the urban middle-class collegiate bias of the West. Psychological dimensions of rural development have been studied, and efforts have been made to discover if a motivational syndrome is associated with development (N. P. Singh, 1970; S. Singh, 1976, 1978; Singh & Gupta, 1977; D. Sinha, 1969, 1974). Extending the discipline to the rural sector engendered doubts about the appropriateness of tools of data collection borrowed from the West and also about the uncritical transfer of concepts and theoretical frameworks. In fact, not only are specific rural problems being investigated by Indian psychologists and culturally appropriate tools for research being forged, but efforts are under way to develop a "rural psychology" subdiscipline (D. Sinha, 1985b), that is, psychology as applied to rural areas, whose parameters, it is contended, are distinct from those of the industrialized urban culture of Western societies. This trend is imparting a new look to psychology as it is known in the West. The basic assumptions and data base of the latter are being critically examined and questioned, and efforts have been undertaken to modify them to suit the rural Indian sociocultural setting where they will be applied.

Another excellent example of the process of assimilation is provided by the work of J. B. P. Sinha (1980) and Kakar (1971a, 1971b). After analyzing the authority patterns in Indian organizations, Kakar (1971b) pointed out how they were dominated by the parental ideology of authority relations. In the same context, cultural relativity of the participative style of management, generally considered effective in the Euro-American setting, has been emphasized, and a distinct style called the *nurturant task leader* has been postulated. It is task-oriented, having structured expectations from the subordinates, and draws upon Indian familial values (Ray, 1970), affection, dependency, and need for personalized relationship. Under the sociocultural conditions prevailing in the country, it is claimed to be more appropriate and effective.

Apart from the conceptual level, doubts have been raised about the utility of Western tests (Wig, Pershad, & Verma, 1974) and tools of data collection, which are conditioned by many sociocultural factors (D. Sinha, 1983b). Scholars are displaying caution in using these tests on unsophisticated, illiterate rural populations, and there is a systematic effort under way to develop culturally appropriate tools, as evidenced in a "grain-sorting test" for level of aspiration (D. Sinha, 1969), a test of task taking and task avoidance (Chaubey, 1974), the Story-Pictorial Embedded Figures Test for psychological differentiation (D. Sinha, 1978, 1984a), and "participative evaluation" (Bogaert, 1984) for recording the collective opinion of villagers.

These examples are illustrative of the fact that imported psychology has begun to be regarded as not "natural" to the Indian soil, and a distinct effort is being made to develop the subject in a manner that, although not sacrificing its scientific value, could take up larger issues and problems facing the country. At the same time, Western theories and models and tools of research have become assimilated to the Indian setting. This process has imparted to psychology in India a distinctive character suited to its sociocultural setting. In this effort to look for "Indianness" and to understand it in terms of its own idioms (D. Sinha, 1986, p. 761), the discipline is developing a new identity. In a sense, it is conforming to Mukherjee's (1980) dictum that "psychology has to go native if it is to be creative and relevant to society." As I have pointed out in earlier work (D. Sinha, 1986), it conforms with what has been called "endogenous development" (UNESCO, 1977); that is, "Different societies must retain their individual character, drawing their strength from their own innate modes of thought and action, adopting goals in keeping with these values, with perceived needs and with the resources at their disposal."

ACHIEVEMENT OF
INDIGENIZATION OF PSYCHOLOGY IN INDIA

Before closing, it is appropriate to point out briefly the manner in which the process of indigenization is taking place and the new orientation it is imparting to psychology in India. There is, as we have seen, a strong tendency toward indigenization of research not only in the selection of topics regarded as vital and relevant to the Indian scene, but also in using variables that are drawn from the particular sociocultural context. There is an increasing tendency to make academic pursuits more problem oriented and geared to issues generated by social and economic changes that are taking place in the country. Many topics that are directly related to the developmental needs of the country are being taken up for study. The approach is not simply academic, but there is great concern to forge intervention strategies to solve the various urgent problems of the country. Looking critically at the scene, Indian psychologists seem to be, unlike their Western counterparts, overwhelmed by the many pressing national problems and, in their anxiety for social relevance, they are tending to neglect fundamental theoretical research. In any case, the process of indigenization has caused psychology in India to be more problem oriented than it is in the West.

Faced with larger social issues, the basic orientation of the discipline as seen in the West had to undergo a transformation. Western psychology is microcosmic, placing disproportionate emphasis on narrow aspects of the problem and small segments of behavior. In spite of the correction imparted by field theory, psychology in the West is basically microsocial in orientation and concentrates almost entirely on personal characteristics of individual actors in social processes rather than on sociostructural factors (D. Sinha, 1986, p. 113). The common tendency of Western psychologists to vivisect complex human phenomena into bits and pieces, thereby missing their complexity, has been critically viewed in the Indian context. It is reflected in an observation made in the report of the Review Committee of the Indian Council of Social Science Research (1973): "Most researches done in social psychology laid disproportionate stress on narrow aspects of larger social problems and in consequence, the information gathered lacked in organization, synthesis and integration" (p. 44).

As Nandy (1974, p. 1) rightly points out, Indian psychology is at present suffering from a crisis of disciplinary culture and tends to ignore larger social issues. If psychology is concerned with problems emanating from social change and developmental processes it cannot remain confined to microcosmic individual processes but has to encompass large social, structural, and cultural influences. A need is being articulated for a "macropsychology" in which structural and systemic variables will be built into our research design so that the social reality that is brought under study does not lose its basic character and become laboratory trivialities (D. Sinha, 1986, p. 113). There is a plea for macropsychology that is distinct in orientation and approach from what the discipline has been in the West (D. Sinha, 1985a).

There is also a growing feeling that psychologists have tended to confine themselves to a narrow groove and have taken a very limited view of reality because of their unidisciplinary perspective. Such a perspective is inimical to a meaningful view of human problems, especially those concerning social change and development. As Myrdal (1968) has pointed out, all problems of living are complex and cannot be fitted into the pigeonholes of our inherited academic disciplines. In fact, the respective fields overlap so much in this area of applied research that in describing social phenomena and explaining relevant relationships, weapons from the arsenals of all disciplines can be used with profit. Benefits of mutual borrowing of concepts and techniques of analysis have been emphasized. Pareek (1980) has rightly observed:

> Psychology has, therefore, to come out of its narrow groove in which it seems to have got stuck. Although the confinement to the narrow field has given a false sense of identity to psychology in the country, it has resulted in its isolation and fragmentation regarding knowledge as well as application on the one hand, and lack of linkage with other social sciences from mutual learning and growth on the other. (p. ix)

Psychology has to assume a multidisciplinary perspective and must meaningfully interact and collaborate with other social sciences to understand and analyze the major problems of development and to work out joint strategies for solving them.

Psychology, as such, suffers from certain inherent constraints. Being modeled after mathematics and the physical sciences, its methodology tends to insulate it from the complexities of social problems. It has certainly produced a vast amount of research impressive for its neatness and precision, but often having no external referent. Methodological refinement seems to have become an end in itself, frequently leading to artificiality and triviality. Nowhere is the tyranny of methodology more apparent than when the researcher faces complex social problems for investigation. Thus, when confronted with issues emanating from social change and national development, some psychologists have questioned the appropriateness of the prevailing methodology. Rather than following a Procrustean bed policy of excluding such problems from purview because of their complexity, they are endeavoring to broaden the methodological repertoire to enable the discipline to be more problem oriented (D. Sinha, 1986, pp. 116-117).

The process of indigenization is already visible in the choice of problems for research and the variables often studied by those psychologists who are taking up issues relevant to development. Surveys of research in psychology illustrate how Indian psychologists, especially since the 1970s, have taken up larger problems of development; frequently their investigations have an interdisciplinary tinge (Mitra, 1972; Pareek, 1980, 1981). In fact, it is common, though resented by some psychologists, that many problems related to development, such as rural leadership and organizational effectiveness (which strictly belong to the domain of psychology), are being investigated by nonpsychologists, often with considerable success. In any case, the area of development is no respecter of disciplinary boundaries. Problems arising from it overlap disciplines and usefully interface with sister disciplines. This is exactly what is happening to psychology in India in its process toward indigenization. It is adopting a less insular outlook and trying to forge a kind of "grand alliance" with sister disciplines in order to meet the new challenge of analyzing, understanding, and solving problems connected with national development (D. Sinha, 1986, p. 114).

What has been the impact of this process of indigenization on the discipline itself? Many psychologists, even in India, are finding it difficult to cast off the microcosmic and individualistic orientation acquired in the West; they are bound by the prevailing disciplinary ethos, are critical about this tendency, and doubt the distinctive identity of psychology in India. Though talk of social relevance has been called a "gambit" and psychology has been characterized as an "insipid watery brew" (Nandy, 1974), the contemporary picture of psychology in India that is emerging is of a subject that is coming out of its narrow groove to enter new fields, such as social change and national development, that have remained outside the disciplinary culture prevailing in the West (International Labour Office, 1969). The conventional boundaries of the discipline are thereby being extended. In the process of casting off its age-old mold, it is acquiring a new orientation of incorporating more and more macrocosmic and structural variables in its research design, so that from a predominantly microcosmic discipline it is growing into a blend of microcosmic and macrocosmic, or a mix of *fine-grain* and *coarse-grain* analysis (D. Sinha, 1977). It is also adopting a more interdisciplinary perspective than is visible in the West. In this context, what has been termed "reverse flow" in transfer of knowledge from the East to the West has already begun (D. Sinha, 1986, p. 129), and in the course of time it is likely to have a distinct impact on the orientation, approach, and methodology of psychology.

REFERENCES

Agarwal, K. G. (1975). Psychology or adaptology. *Social Scientist,* pp. 1-5.

Akhilananda, S. (1948). *Hindu psychology.* London: George Allen & Unwin.

Akhilananda, S. (1952). *Mental health and Hindu psychology.* London: George Allen & Unwin.

Anand, B. K., Chhina, G. S., & Singh, B. (1969). Some aspects of electroencephalographic studies in yogis. In C. Tart (Ed.), *Altered states of consciousness* (pp. 503-516). New York: John Wiley.

Bogaert, M. V. (1984, March). *Adult education input for tribal development.* Paper presented at the regional workshop, Educational Components of Rural Development Projects, ANS Institute of Social Studies, Patna.

Chaubey, N. P. (1974). *Motivational dimensions of rural development: A study of risk-taking, risk-avoidance and fear of failure in villages.* Allahabad, India: Chaitanya.

Gellhorne, E., & Kiely, W. F. (1972). Mystical states of consciousness: Neurophysiological and clinical aspects. *Journal of Nervous and Mental Diseases, 154,* 399-406.

Indian Council of Social Science Research, Review Committee. (1973). *A report on social science in India* (Vol. 1). New Delhi: Author.

International Labour Office. (1969). *International standard classification of occupations.* Geneva: Author.

Jahoda, G. (1973). Psychology and the developing country: Do they need each other? *International Social Science Journal, 25,* 461-475.

Jahoda, G. (1975). Applying cross-cultural psychology in the Third World. In J. W. Berry & W. J. Lonner (Eds.), *Applied cross-cultural psychology.* Amsterdam: Swets & Zeitlinger.

Jahoda, G. (1980, September 26-29). *Has social psychology a distinct contribution to make?* Paper presented at the Conference on Social Psychology and the Developing Country, University of Lancaster.

Kakar, S. (1971a). Authority patterns and subordinate behavior in Indian organization. *Administrative Science Quarterly, 16,* 298-307.

Kakar, S. (1971b). The theme of authority in social relations in India. *Journal of Social Psychology, 84,* 93-101.

Mitra, S. K. (Ed.). (1972). *A survey of research in psychology.* Bombay: Popular Prakashan.

Mukherjee, B. N. (1980). Psychological theory and research methods. In U. Pareek (Ed.), *A survey of research in psychology.* Bombay: Popular Prakashan.

Myrdal, G. (1968). *Asian drama: An enquiry into the poverty of nations* (Vol. 1). New York: Penguin.

Naidu, R. K., Thapa, K., & Das, M. M. (1986). *On measuring detachment: An example of a scientific analog of an indigenous concept.* Unpublished manuscript, Allahabad University, Department of Psychology.

Nandy, A. (1974). The non-paradigmatic crisis in Indian psychology: Reflections on a recipient culture of science. *Indian Journal of Psychology, 49,* 1-20.

Pande, N., & Naidu, R. K. (1986). *Effort and outcome orientations as moderators of the stress-strain relationship.* Unpublished manuscript, Allahabad University, Department of Psychology.

Paranjpe, A.C. (1984). *Theoretical psychology: The meeting of East and West.* New York: Plenum.

Pareek, U. (Ed.). (1980). *A survey of research in psychology 1971-76* (Vol. 1). Bombay: Popular Prakashan.

Pareek, U. (Ed.). (1981). *A survey of research in psychology 1971-76* (Vol. 2). Bombay: Popular Prakashan.

Rao, C., & Murthy, H. N. (1975). *Comparison of different techniques of relaxation.* Paper presented at the Sixth All India Convention of Clinical Psychologists, Banaras.

Ray, A. (1970). Indian managers of the 1980s. *Economic and Political Weekly, 5*(35), 105-106.

Singh, N. P. (1970). Risk-taking and anxiety among successful and unsuccessful, traditional and progressive agricultural entrepreneurs of Delhi. *British Journal of Social and Clinical Psychology, 9,* 301-308.

Singh, S. (1976). Achievement motivation and success in farming. *British Journal of Protective Psychology and Personality Study, 21,* 17-20.

Singh, S. (1978). *Achievement motivation, decision making, orientations and work values of brothers in the contrasting farm output* (Project Report). New Delhi: University Grants Commission.

Singh, S., & Gupta, B. S. (1977). Motives and agricultural growth. *British Journal of Social and Clinical Psychology, 16,* 189-190.

Singh, S., & Sinha, A. K. (1987, February 9-12). *Stress research in organisations: Integration of East and West.* Paper presented at the seminar Applied Social Psychology in India, Bhopal University.

Sinha, D. (1965, Spring). Integration of modern psychology with Indian thought. *Journal of Humanistic Psychology,* pp. 6-21.

Sinha, D. (1969). *Indian villages in transition: A motivational analysis.* New Delhi: Associated.

Sinha, D. (1974). *Motivation and rural development.* Calcutta: Minerva.

Sinha, D. (1977). Orientation and attitude of social psychologists in a developing country. *International Review of Applied Psychology, 26,* 1-10.

Sinha, D. (1978). Story-pictorial EFT: A culturally appropriate test for perceptual disembedding. *Indian Journal of Psychology, 53,* 160-171.

Sinha, D. (1980, July 5-12). Towards outgrowing the alien framework: A review of some recent trends in psychological researches in India. In *History of psychology in various countries.* Symposium conducted at the Twenty-second International Congress of Psychology, Leipzig, GDR.

Sinha, D. (1981). Social psychology in India: A historical perspective. In J. Pandey (Ed.), *Perspectives on experimental social psychology in India* (pp. 3-17). New Delhi: Concept.

Sinha, D. (1983a). Cross-cultural psychology: A view from the Third World. In J. B. Deregowski, S. Dziurawiec, & R. C. Annis (Eds.), *Explications in cross-cultural psychology.* Lisse, Netherlands: Swets & Zeitlinger.

Sinha, D. (1983b). Human assessment in the Indian context. In S. H. Irvine & J. W. Berry (Eds.), *Human assessment and cultural factors.* New York: Plenum.

Sinha, D. (1984a). *Manual for story-pictorial EFT and Indo-Africa EFT.* Varanasi: Rupa Psychological Corporation.

Sinha, D. (1984b). Psychology in the context of Third World development. *International Journal of Psychology, 19*(1-2), 17-29.

Sinha, D. (1985a). A plea for macropsychology. In R. Diaz-Guerrero (Ed.), *Cross-cultural and national studies in social psychology* (pp. 277-283). Amsterdam: North-Holland.

Sinha, D. (1985b). Psychology in rural areas: The case of a developing country. In R. Diaz-Guerrero (Ed.). *Cross-cultural and national studies in social psychology* (pp. 431-451). Amsterdam: North-Holland.

Sinha, D. (1986). *Psychology in a Third World country: The Indian experience.* New Delhi: Sage.

Sinha, J. B. P. (1976). Outgrowing the frame. *Vikalpa, 1,* 63-67.

Sinha, J. B. P. (1980). *Nurturant task leader.* New Delhi: Concept.

Triandis, H. C. (1983). *Collectivism vs. individualism: A reconceptualization.* Unpublished manuscript.

UNESCO. (1977). *Thinking ahead: UNESCO and the challenge of today and tomorrow.* Paris: Author.

Vahia, N. S., Doonagaji, D. R., Jeste, D. V., Ravindranath, S., Kapoor, S. N., & Ardha Purkar, I. (1973). Psychophysiologic therapy based on the concepts of Patanjali. *American Journal of Psychotherapy, 27,* 557-565.

Wig, N. N., Pershad, D., & Verma, S. K. (1974). The use of psychological tests in Indian psychiatric research: A reappraisal. *Indian Journal of Clinical Psychology, 1,* 8-14.

3

MEXICAN ETHNOPSYCHOLOGY
ROGELIO DIAZ-GUERRERO

Ethnopsychology has been particularly prominent in Mexico, the cauldron where the first large-scale successful amalgamation of blood and culture took place. The resulting personalities, the psychology of the Mexican Indian and mestizo, piqued many a visitor (Ramirez, 1983). The disquieting, sulfurous, but gripping chronicles told by sixteenth-century friars and conquerors to the king of Spain about the Indians of Mexico have reverberated in recent popular literature. But more important, from the beginning of the present century Mexicans themselves have become fascinated with the psychology of the Mexican. A psychologist named E. A. Chavez (1901) initiated and analyzed the character of the mestizo, the Indian, and the criollo. In the following decades philosophers, writers, and psychoanalysts dedicated volumes to various aspects of the Mexican personality.

The first quantitative efforts to explore the psychology of the Mexican were performed by Gomez-Robleda (1948, 1962). He was a good statistician, but his psychological hypotheses and particularly his interpretations were, albeit creative, often unsophisticated. Some of my own work appears next in the quantitative arena (Diaz-Guerrero, 1952, 1961, 1982b). It is basically this work that is the focus of the present chapter.

TOWARD AN ETHNOPSYCHOLOGY

A crucial issue in cross-cultural psychology has been defining the concept of culture. In the 1980s, Rohner (1984), Jahoda (1984), and Segall (1984) participated in a heated argument as to whether or not a proper definition of culture is relevant to the conduct of cross-cultural research. I agree with Rohner and Jahoda, who consider that, sooner or later, a universal concept of culture will increase both the hermeneutic and the heuristic value of cross-cultural psychology.

Although interesting inroads have been made by Hofstede (see, e.g., Hofstede & Bond, 1984), the concern for a generalized concept of culture as it affects cross-cultural research is premature. A better route, I believe, is to approach the problem by developing specific ethnopsychologies and, concomitantly, a new systematic discipline, ethnopsychology (see Berry, 1974, 1978; Diaz-Guerrero, 1961, 1975; Jahoda, 1979; Triandis, 1977, 1978; Triandis, Vassiliou, Vassiliou, Tanaka, & Shanmugan, 1972).

The purpose of this chapter is to begin to answer the following four questions:

1. How can a discipline labeled *ethnopsychology* be conceptualized?
2. What are some of the systematic tenets of this discipline?
3. What has been discovered with Mexican populations (varying in age, sex, socioeconomic status, historical time, and geographic distribution) that can lead to a Mexican ethnopsychology?
4. What can be some of the goals of an ethnopsychology?

CONCEPTION OF ETHNOPSYCHOLOGY

An ethnopsychology should begin by accepting that human beings are subject to extremely varied stimulation. They are growing and interacting in nothing less than a very complex ecosystem. The human ecosystem, beyond all of the variables that biologists enumerate for other species, includes a powerful subjective ecosystem. It includes the ways various individuals and various groups perceive the objective ecosystem and function in it, anthropological symbols and meaning, and sociological and economic structural variables.

The most powerful of all of these factors for the psychological development of the individual are probably the subjective individual and collective perceptions of him- or herself and his or her entire ecosystem. In the development of a preliminary ethnopsychology, these perceptions can be considered the fundamental variables of concern. It is likely that they cover a large amount of the variance of personality and cognitive development.

But even in this fundamentally subjective ecosystem we must at least consider the biopsychological individual and his or her sociocultural environment. In ethnopsychology, it is fundamental to postulate that personality and cognitive development are essentially the results of a perennial dialectic between the biopsychological individual and his or her sociocultural environment. I have labeled this the *culture/counterculture dialectic* (Diaz-Guerrero, 1979).

It is my contention that the most important elements of the sociocultural environment are *historic-sociocultural premises* (HSCPs) (Diaz-Guerrero, 1967a, 1967b, 1972, 1976, 1977). An HSCP is "(a) a statement, a culturally significant statement, which is held by an operationally defined majority of the subjects in a given culture, and (b) it is also, preferably, a statement that will be held differentially across cultures" (Diaz-Guerrero, 1967a, p. 263). It has been found that some HSCPs are prescriptive, such as "The mother is the dearest being in existence" and "A woman should be a virgin until she marries." Others clearly imply a psychodynamic interplay with the environment (i.e., they embody the coping style most prevalent in a given culture). In this context the style of coping may be self-modifying or self-assertive. In the first, the individual adapts to the demands of the ecosystem; in the latter, he or she tries to modify the ecosystem (Diaz-Guerrero, 1967b).

In a major program of research drawing from large numbers of HSCPs applied to different types of populations, I extracted 13 factor scales (Diaz-Guerrero, 1972, 1973, 1982c). Given that many of these HSCPs were upheld by a majority of the individuals in several independent samples, it was simple to postulate that they represented traditional Mexican beliefs and modes of coping, and embodied a significant aspect of the Mexican culture. Once these measures were at hand, I theorized that an individual Mexican's score on these factorial scales represented his or her personal position in the culture/counterculture dialectic. In other words, how traditionally Mexican one is, or how much one has rebelled and therefore individualized oneself away from one's culture could be indicated by one's score. A number of different studies that included the prescriptive sociocultural premises of an inventory of the Mexican family (Diaz-Guerrero, 1972, 1982c) and the coping style premises that were created by a questionnaire examining *filosofía de vida* (philosophy of life) (Diaz-Guerrero, 1973, 1976) provided the material for considering the tenets fundamental to the development of an ethnopsychology.

TENETS OF AN ETHNOPSYCHOLOGY

Ten basic tenets are required in an ethnopsychology:

1. It should postulate the existence of a specific human ecosystem.
2. It should postulate that behavior, particularly personality and social behavior, is determined by a dialectical exchange of all types of information between biological and psychological dispositions of the individual and the group, and also with powerful sociocultural and other influences of the hu-

man ecosystem in which they live. Ethnopsychology must be interdisciplinary.

3. Operationally, it should agree that an important and potentially measurable aspect of the ecosystem is culture.

4. Culture includes, as cultural anthropologists and sociologists agree, verbal affirmations (traditions, norms, values, beliefs) and structural entities (material culture, organizations, institutions).

5. Culture is fundamentally an outcome of history and of the culture/counterculture dialectic.

6. For operational and theoretical advantages, it is proposed that an ethnopsychology begins its systematic explorations through the measurement and determination of individual and group differences of verbal affirmations and dimensions discovered specifically for a given culture.

7. For operational and theoretical advantages, it is proposed that these affirmations be labeled *historic-sociocultural premises,* or HSCPs.

8. HSCPs and dimensions derived from them must show significant relationships with crucial biopsychological and social science variables in a given culture.

9. HSCPs and dimensions derived from them should show significant and preferably predictable differences intraculturally and cross-culturally.

10. Other typical characteristics of individuals and groups of a given culture, discovered by probing methods other than HSCPs (e.g., through Osgood, Suci, & Tannenbaum's [1957] semantic differential or Szalay & Brent's [1967] free verbal associations) are acceptable ethnopsychological discoveries, but they must show the functional characteristics demanded by the HSCPs and, it is hoped, will eventually discover new HSCPs.

In order to give body to these tenets, corollaries of Tenets 6, 8, 9, and 10 will be illustrated with data drawn from four high school samples ($N = 839$) from three regions of Mexico (Diaz-Guerrero, 1982c). HSCPs should preferably be endorsed by a majority of the people of a given culture. In Table 3.1 it can be seen that a large majority of subjects in central, northern, and southern Mexico agree with a number of these HSCPs. Some of the dimensions that have come from these and other HSCPs are as follows: affiliative obedience, machismo, respect over love, and virginity.

Beyond consistency across geographical location of a given culture, HSCPs should show permanency as well as meaningful variation through time. In 1959 and again in 1970, to determine the impact of social change on the HSCPs a cohort study was carried out with 467 third-year junior high school students of both sexes from 17 different high schools spread over Mexico City. Junior high schools at the time in Mexico City could be divided between all-girl and mixed-sex schools, so that the effects of what we would

Table 3.1 Historic Sociocultural Premises in Several Studies

HSCPs	Range of % Endorsing
2. A person should always respect her parents.	98-83
34. To me, the mother is the dearest being in existence.	92-79
96. A good wife is always faithful to her husband.	96-79
19. One should always be loyal to one's family.	93-63
7. Small children should not interrupt the conversation of older persons.	81-56
82. Women must be protected.	83-62
100. The place for women is in the home.	88-44
27. A son should always obey his parents.	83-42
54. Men should wear the pants in the family.	79-37
76. A woman should be a virgin until marriage.	86-50
18. Every man would like to marry a virgin.	86-67
121. Most boys would like to be like their father.	84-55
52. A good wife never questions the behavior of her husband.	80-69
64. Most Mexican males feel superior to women.	71-68
21. Many daughters fear their fathers.	77-60
88. Most men prefer submissive women.	72-65
10. An adulterous woman dishonors her family.	73-49
47. Most girls would like to be like their mothers.	77-36
33. Women suffer more in their lives than men.	64-43
46. The stricter the parents, the better the child.	63-26

SOURCE: Adapted and translated from Diaz-Guerrero (1982b).

now call different habitats could be discerned. In Table 3.2 it is evident that both historical time and habitat have significant, if varied, effects upon several of the HSCPs, but no effect upon others. From the results it also appears

Table 3.2 Historic Sociocultural Premises and the Role of Women in Mexico: Time and Habitat Effects

HSCPs	Sample	1959	1970	
33. Women suffer more in their lives than men.	M	63	77	**
	F	72	61	NS
47. Most little girls would prefer to be like their mothers.	M	65	73	NS
	F	72	57	**
103. Women should be docile.	M	63	43	**
	F	57	29	**
96. A good wife should always be faithful to her husband.	M	84	91	NS
	F	94	92	NS
80. Young women should not go out at night alone with a man.	M	60	57	NS
	F	73	52	**
100. The place for women is in the home.	M	90	79	**
	F	74	60	**

SOURCE: Adapted and translated from Diaz-Guerrero (1974).
NOTE: M = mixed sample, high school; F = female sample, high school.
$**p < .01.$

to be very likely that historical time and habitat interact. Some of the changes have face validity; the meaning of others is discussed in Diaz-Guerrero (1974).

Measures developed to quantify aspects of the sociocultural ecosystem also show significant correlations with age, grade, and education of subjects in a given culture (Diaz-Guerrero, 1984a). Similarly, measures developed to quantify aspects of the sociocultural ecosystem show significant correlations with measures designed to determine cognitive development of groups of subjects in a given culture. Table 3.3 portrays interesting correlations between HSCPs of coping from the questionnaire about *filosofia de vida* and a series of dimensions from the Questionnaire of the Mexican Family with the Witkin Embedded Figures Test applied individually. Considering that almost all of the subjects had completed only primary education, and the generally lower correlations between psychological tests in Mexico compared with the developed countries, this is a clear demonstration that the HSCPs are related to cognitive style development in Mexican subjects.

Measures developed to quantify aspects of the sociocultural ecosystem also show significant correlations with measures of personality characteristics, socioeconomic status, cognitive intellectual variables, vocational dispositions, and moral development (Diaz-Guerrero & Emmite, in press).

Table 3.3 Correlations Between HSCPs and the Witkin Embedded Figures Test
              Applied Individually to 64 Mexican Mothers

Variables	Number Correct	Mean of Total Time
Active self-assertion	.37**	−.40***
Active internal control	.25*	−.27*
Machismo	−.35**	.42***
Virginity	−.31**	.35
Abnegation	−.31**	.35**
Respect over love	−.41***	.45***
Family honor	−.31**	34**
Cultural rigidity	−.38**	44***

NOTE: Mothers in the study were randomly selected by area sampling in Mexico City to represent the upper-lower and lower-middle social classes of the city.
*$p < .05$; **$p < .01$; ***$p < .001$.

GOALS OF AN ETHNOPSYCHOLOGY

There are seven goals of an ethnopsychology:

1. It will be a basic tool for exploring indigenous cultural systems, what Berry (1983) calls the "societal and social psychologies," in order to discover and understand local concepts and intracultural and individual variations. As the tables presented here indicate, the Mexican HSCPs can vary in accordance with age, historical time, education, and social class. To understand variation in indigenous beliefs, these and other variables will be useful to any program designed to determine and strengthen the positive aspects of the indigenous psychologies and to discourage the negative.
2. It will be useful for developing complete indigenous psychologies, specifically in the areas of personality, cognitive development, and social behavior.
3. It will determine the extent to which the principles of perception, learning, thinking, and so on (i.e., all of the psychological processes) apply to local populations, and if there are differences by age, sex, education, socioeconomic, rural-urban, majority-minority, and the extent of individual differences. A number of cross-cultural psychologists have been hammering at the practical importance of this knowledge for their own societies. It is expected, at the very least, that the score on the HSCP scales will be significantly correlated with motor, perceptual, learning, and thinking tasks.

4. It will test and determine the extent to which the many personality, cognitive, and sociopsychological dimensions that have been discovered in industrialized countries apply to local populations, and if there are age, sex, socioeconomic, rural-urban, and majority-minority differences, as well as the extent of the local individual differences.

5. It will utilize the data obtained through the efforts outlined above to help substantially in the interpretation of cross-cultural differences. This may be the only completely genuine way of explaining cross-cultural differences.

6. It will help cross-cultural psychology in its important goal of ascertaining universally or quasi-universally relevant and valid dimensions, laws, and theories of human behavior.

7. The development of an ethnopsychology should exemplify through its tenets the scientific approach, so badly needed for many decades, to the unfolding of a valid understanding of personality development and personality functioning in both normal and abnormal populations. Such a scientific, instead of intuitive, understanding is essential if psychotherapeutic and other personal improvement techniques are to be applied optimally to local populations.

THE PRESENT AND FUTURE
OF A MEXICAN ETHNOPSYCHOLOGY

The economic crisis and other factors have dealt a blow to the Instituto Nacional de Ciencias del Comportamiento y de la Actitud Publica, A.C. (INCCAPAC), where, with the help of dedicated colleagues and students, and the support of foundations and the Faculty of Psychology of the National University of Mexico (UNAM), most of the aforementioned studies were accomplished. INCCAPAC, barely subsisting, has continued it cross-cultural and ethnopsychological research on a lesser scale, and is now in the slow process of becoming a part of the Faculty of Psychology at UNAM.

On the other hand, a group of young graduate and postgraduate psychologists in the Graduate Department of Social Psychology at UNAM, under the leadership of Rolando Diaz-Loving, and with a somewhat different but compatible social approach (see Tenet 10) are doing research on important Mexican psychological dimensions fully concordant with a Mexican ethnopsychology. Two examples will illustrate this work.

First, Diaz-Loving and Andrade-Palos (1984) discovered, after a painstaking adaptation of Nowicki and Strickland's (1973) scale of internality-externality for children, that a clear new factor dimension was necessary for understanding the locus of control in Mexican children. Beyond the typical instrumentalism and fatalism factors found also in the United States, there was a clear affective factor found in items that indicated children obtained what they wanted by being good. This work bears upon the fourth goal of an ethnopsychology given above, but also upon Tenet 10. Something apparently typical of Mexican children has been found, and it may be one expression of the Mexican HSCP dimension of affiliative obedience. It may apply more directly to the "undiscovered Mexican," or perhaps it is a dimension of the generally traditional HSCP concerning affiliative obedience, and may imply that "it is better to use love rather than force to get results" or "in all matters of life, love is more important than power." It may also refer to what appears to be, in the Mexican culture, a confusion between power and love. But if this is the case, the importance of ascertaining the degree and real-life results of this confusion, not only in the Mexican but in all cultures, may be significant in understanding corruption and violence.

Second, La Rosa (1986) defined the self-concept conceptually and then, with brainstorming sessions in which several samples of Mexican senior high school and university students of both sexes ($N = 118$) participated, identified five dimensions of the self-concept: (a) physical (appearance and functioning), (b) occupational (role and functioning in any type of work), (c) emotional (intraindividual feelings and interpersonal interactions), (d) social (satisfaction and dissatisfaction in social interactions), and (e) ethical (congruence or incongruence with personal and cultural values). With 358 students in a more heterogeneous sample from senior high and university students of both sexes he collected survey data soliciting all the adjectives, positive and negative, that came to their minds, taking into consideration the above dimensions of the self-concept. Several thousand adjectives resulted, many with high frequency, from which 35 to 40 were selected for each dimension. Following sophisticated techniques with various samples, he determined the proper antonym for each adjective. Then, with a semantic differential format and the concept of "I am," 418 students, again from heterogeneous samples, responded to 54 selected pairs of adjectives resulting from the previous steps.

A factor analysis was performed to verify the construct validity. From 13 factors, 8 were selected that explain 59% of the total variance and are conceptually congruent. The pairs of adjectives for the physical dimension were extremely heterogeneous, and no physical factor appeared. There were 3 emotional, 2 social, and 2 ethical factors, and 1 occupational factor.

A questionnaire derived from this pilot study and 72 additional congruent adjectival scales from the Self-Concept Questionnaire was given to a heterogeneous sample of 1,083 students of both sexes, with a mean age of 21 and a standard deviation of 4.32.

From the factor analyses, 9 congruent factors explaining 49% of the variance were extracted. Factor 1 was a social affiliative factor with high loadings on courteous-noncourteous, well brought up-badly brought up, and amiable-rude. Being Factor 1, it had a mean correlation with all the other factors of

.51. There is little doubt that there several important undiscovered HSCPs for social interactions in Mexico such as those that have been found with the following underlying theme: To get places you must be courteous.

Factor 2 was one of three emotional factors with highest loadings in happy-sad, depressed-contented, bitter-jovial, frustrated-realized. This was labeled "intraindividual emotions or mood states." It had a mean correlation of .50 with the other factors. In a study with Mexican junior high students from the lower class, I found that sadness (*tristeza*) correlated highest with Spielberger's anxiety trait ($r = .48$) (Diaz-Guerrero, 1982a). I then studied the correlates of the breadth of *tristeza* with 19 clinically critical concepts in 200 junior high students of two social classes and two sexes (Diaz-Guerrero, 1982a, 1984b). Results clearly portray the psychopathological impact of sadness in Mexico as well as its differential correlates as sex and social class varies. This, and the results of a series of cross-cultural studies with the Holtzman Inkblot Test (HIT), led me to the statement (much prior to La Rosa's study) that depression is the main source of psychopathology in Mexico and anxiety the second (Diaz-Guerrero, 1985). Factor 2 of La Rosa's study uncovers another crucial dimension in the Mexican culture that should lead to the discovery of HSCPs.

Factor 3 is a social expressive factor with highest loadings in quiet-communicative, introverted-extroverted, and reserved-expressive. Factor 4 is an emotional interindividual dimension: romantic-indifferent, affectionate-cold. Factor 5 reflects an occupational dimension: responsible-irresponsible, punctual-unpunctual. Factor 6, the third emotional factor, has the following items loading on the dimension: impulsive-reflexive and temperamental-calm. Factor 7, an ethical factor, has the following items loading on the dimension: honest-dishonest and loyal-disloyal. Factor 8, an affiliative factor, has the following items loading on the dimension: accessible-inaccessible and understanding–not understanding (*comprensivo-incomprensivo*).

Interestingly, La Rosa's (1986) work, among other studies, included a correlation with my original scale of affiliative obedience (Diaz-Guerrero, 1972). All but one of the factors of his self-concept correlated significantly with affiliative obedience, and Factors 1, 2, and 6 were highly significant. It is clear that the order, categorization, and content of this Mexican self-concept should not fail to impress at least Anglo-North Americans as being patently idiosyncratic.

CONCLUSION

It is evident from the contents of this chapter that indigenous psychologies must be pursued. By postulating tenets and delineating goals of a discipline to be labeled *ethnopsychology*, the founding of such a scientific endeavor is advanced. The consistent presence across Mexican groups and pervasive influence of the HSCPs in crucial domains of cognitive and personality functioning, as well as in so many other social science variables, is substantial evidence to support Tenets 6, 7, 8, and 9 of an ethnopsychology. The above discussion has demonstrated partial fulfillment of all the goals of Mexican ethnopsychology listed in this chapter. Furthermore, in addition to the ethnopsychological endeavors of the staff and graduate students in the Graduate Division of Social Psychology at the National University, work is in progress to establish in Mexico a two-year master's degree on research in ethnopsychology.

REFERENCES

Berry, J. W. (1974). Canadian psychology: Some social and applied emphases. *Canadian Psychologist, 15,* 132-139.

Berry, J. W. (1978). Social psychology: Comparative, societal and universal. *Canadian Psychological Review, 19,* 93-104.

Chavez, E. A. (1901). Ensayo sobre los rasgos distinctivos de la sensibilidad como factor del caracter mexicano. *Revista de la Instruccion Publica Mexicana, 5*(2-3), 58-64, 88-93.

Diaz-Guerrero, R. (1952). Teoria y resultados preliminares de un ensayo de determinacion del grado de salud mental, personal y social del mexicano de la ciudad. *Psiquis, 2*(1-2), 3-56.

Diaz-Guerrero, R. (1961). *Estudios de psicologia del mexicano.* Mexico City: Antigua Libreria Robredo.

Diaz-Guerrero, R. (1967a). The active and the passive syndromes. *Revista Interamericana de Psicologia, 1,* 263-272.

Diaz-Guerrero, R. (1967b). Sociocultural premises, attitudes and cross-cultural research. *International Journal of Psychology, 2*(2), 79-87.

Diaz-Guerrero, R. (1972). Una escala factorial de premisas historico-socioculturales de la familia mexicana. *Revista Interamericana de Psicologia, 6,* 235-244.

Diaz-Guerrero, R. (1973). Interpreting coping styles across nations from sex and social class differences. *International Journal of Psychology, 8*(3), 193-203.

Diaz-Guerrero, R. (1974). La mujer y las premisas historico-socioculturales de la familia mexicana. *Revista Latinoamericana de Psicologia, 6*(1), 7-16.

Diaz-Guerrero, R. (1975). *Psychology of the Mexican: Culture and personality.* Austin: University of Texas Press.

Diaz-Guerrero, R. (1976). *Hacia una psicologia social del Tercer Mundo* (Cuadernos de Humanidades No. 5). Mexico City: Universidad Nacional Autonoma de Mexico.

Diaz-Guerrero, R. (1977). Culture and personality revisited. *Annals of the New York Academy of Sciences, 285,* 119-130.

Diaz-Guerrero, R. (1979). Origines de la personnalite humaine et des systemes sociaux. *Revue de Psychologie Appliquée, 29*(2), 139-152.

Diaz-Guerrero, R. (1982a). Fuentes de ansiedad en la cultura mexicana. *Ensenanza y Investigacion en Psicologia, 8*(1), 65-75.

Diaz-Guerrero, R. (1982b). *Psicologia del mexicano.* Mexico City: Trillas.

Diaz-Guerrero, R. (1982c). The psychology of the historic-sociocultural premises, I. *Spanish Language Psychology, 2,* 283-410.

Diaz-Guerrero, R. (1984a). La psicologia de los mexicanos: Un paradigma. *Revista Mexicana de Psicologia, 2*(2), 95-104.

Diaz-Guerrero, R. (1984b). Tristeza y psicopagologia en Mexico. *Salud Mental, 7*(2), 3-9.

Diaz-Guerrero, R. (1985). Holtzman Inkblot Technique (HIT): Differences across Mexican, Mexican-American and AngloAmerican cultures. In E. E. Roskam (Ed.), *Measurement and personality assessment* (Vol. 8, pp. 247-259). Amsterdam: North-Holland.

Diaz-Guerrero, R., & Emmite, P. L. (in press). *Innovaciones en educacion: Un analisis de sistemas de las habilidades basicas en la educacion.* Mexico City: Imprenta de la Universidad Nacional Autonoma de Mexico.

Diaz-Loving, R., & Andrade-Palos, P. (1984). Una escala de locus de control para ninos mexicanos. *Interamerican Journal of Psychology, 18*(1-2), 21-33.

Gomez-Robleda, J. (1948). *Imagen del mexicano.* Mexico City: Secretaria de Educacion Publica.

Gomez-Robleda, J. (1962). *Psicologia de mexicano: Motivos de perturbacion de la conducta psico-social del mexicano de la clase media.* Mexico City: Universidad Nacional Autonoma de Mexico, Instituto de Investigaciones Sociales.

Hofstede, G., & Bond, M. H. (1984). Hofstede's culture dimension: An independent validation using Rokeach's Value Survey. *Journal of Cross-Cultural Psychology, 15,* 417-433.

Jahoda, G. A. (1979). A cross-cultural perspective on experimental social psychology. *Personality and Social Psychology Bulletin, 5,* 142-148.

Jahoda, G. A. (1984). Do we need a concept of culture? *Journal of Cross-Cultural Psychology, 15,* 139-151.

La Rosa, J. (1986). *Escalas del locus de control y autoconcepto: Construccion y validacion.* Unpublished doctoral dissertation, Universidad Nacional Autonoma de Mexico.

Nowicki, S., & Strickland, B. R. (1973). A locus of control scale for children. *Journal of Consulting and Clinical Psychology, 40,* 148-154.

Osgood, C. E., Suci, G., & Tannenbaum, P. H. (1957). *The measurement of meaning.* Urbana: University of Illinois Press.

Ramirez, M., III. (1983). *Psychology of the Americas: Mestizo perspectives on personality and mental health.* New York: Pergamon.

Rohner, R. P. (1984). Toward a conception of culture for cross-cultural psychology. *Journal of Cross-Cultural Psychology, 15,* 111-138.

Segall, M. H. (1984). More than we need to know about culture, but are afraid not to ask. *Journal of Cross-Cultural Psychology, 15,* 153-162.

Szalay, L. B., & Brent, J. (1967). The analysis of cultural meaning through free verbal associations. *Journal of Social Psychology, 72,* 161-187.

Triandis, H. C. (1977). Cross-cultural social and personality psychology. *Personality and Social Psychology Bulletin, 3,* 143-158.

Triandis, H. C. (1978). Some universals of social behavior. *Personality and Social Psychology Bulletin, 4,* 13-16.

Triandis, H. C., Vassiliou, V., Vassiliou, G., Tanaka, Y., & Shanmugan, S. B. (1972). *The analysis of subjective culture.* New York: John Wiley.

4

ECOLOGICAL-SOCIAL MODEL OF GREEK PSYCHOLOGY

JAMES GEORGAS

A focus on the indigenous psychologies of different nations is perhaps inevitable at this stage of cross-cultural psychology. The first stage of development of cross-cultural psychology focused on detecting differences on some psychological variable between two cultures (Jahoda, 1980) and the ensuing interest of psychologists was perhaps partly motivated by the example set by anthropology in demonstrating the seemingly infinite variations wrought by cultures. The second stage of development, in which cross-cultural psychology still finds itself, is concerned with the methodological and theoretical issues of establishing cultural universals and specifics unique to a culture or set of cultures. The search for universals across cultures, exemplified by the factor-analytic approach of Hofstede (1980), Triandis et al. (1986), and many others, focuses on a key concept or grand theme common to all the cultures studied, such as individualism-collectivism, and specifies the position of each culture on the dimension, as well as relationships between the variable and other independent and/or dependent variables. And yet, even when functional relationships are established, one must still explain how and why they occur in each culture.

I believe that the salient issue in cross-cultural psychology at this stage of development is the problem of interpretation or explanation. That is, how are we to interpret psychological data from two or more ethnic groups in a way that is meaningfully related to the idiomorphic ecological and social factors of each ethnic group, but also related to universal ecological and social factors?

A clarification of the terms *ecological, social, nations,* and *ethnic* is necessary at this point. *Ecology* refers to components of the physical environment and organismic variables, as well as the results of technology fed back from traditional behavior (Berry, 1975). *Social* refers to the institutions of the culture, such as economic, political, education, and religious institutions, as employed by sociology. The term *nations* refers to the geographic delineation of a nation-state, such as Greece or the United States. Finally, *ethnicity* refers to the national heritage (including language and culture) of a group of people within a homogeneous nation such as Greece or within a heterogeneous nation such as the United States, with many ethnic groups. *Idiomorphic* refers to the specific ecological, social, and cultural patterns that characterize a specific nation or ethnic group.

A perusal of articles in any cross-cultural journal, such as the *Journal of Cross-Cultural Psychology,* and specifically the discussion sections, in which the authors attempt to interpret their results in terms of more than "Cultures A and B were high on variable X, and cultures C and D were low," will convince the reader that the search on the part of the author for interpretations that might explain the similarities or differences between the nations in terms of ecological, social, or cultural factors are meager and somewhat arbitrary. In other words, interpretations of the similarities or differences between cultures often reflect the phenomenon of serendipity, in that amorphological or conceptual explanations for similarities or differences often seem to just pop into authors' minds. Similarly, we often select different nations for cross-cultural studies because we intuitively expect they will differ ecologically and socially, and thus culturally.

Thus the focus on indigenous psychology reflects a return to the basics in cross-cultural psychology, in that psychologists should specify the ecosocial structure of their cultural world, the elements of which play determining roles in shaping psychological phenomena. That is, I do not believe that indigenous psychology is another name for national character, but that it should focus on the ecological and social elements that determine psychological phenomena. And I would argue that the ultimate solution is an explicit working model of the ecosocial system of ethnic groups or, expressed in a different way, a model of classification of ethnic groups in terms of ecological and social variables. In this way, cross-cultural researchers, in either selecting nations or interpreting the data, could specify the ecosocial units that characterize each ethnic group.

Up to now, as the reader may have irritably noticed, I have deliberately avoided using the term *culture.* As Rohner (1984) explains, *culture* has two definitions within anthropology. The cultural realists argue that culture is behavior: regularly occurring organized modes of behavior in technological, economic, religious, political, familial, and other institutional domains. The cultural nominalists, on the other hand, view culture as a symbol system, an ideational system, a rule system, a cognitive system—in short, as a system of meanings. The cultural nominalists have viewed the construction of a theory of culture as manifestly impossible, and indeed many believe that the essence of anthropology lies in its idiomorphic approach to culture. Segall (1984), in responding to Rohner's suggestion that cross-cultural psychology follow the road of the cultural nominalists, suggests that the search for the conceptualization of culture be abandoned and that cross-cultural psychology search for whatever ecological, sociological, and cultural variables might link with established variation in human behavior. Segall further advocates using, as a heuristic framework, the concept of "nonprescient adaptiveness of behavioral change," which is related to the work of Berry (1975, 1976, 1979, 1980) and D. T. Campbell (1975; Campbell & Naroll, 1972) and would be applied as follows:

> Start with an expectation that any behavioral pattern found anywhere has evolved over a time period, and that the pattern in question is in place because it somehow fit its environment . . . it is very likely an adaptive pattern. I would have us ask for any such pattern: In what way does this behavior fit? With what other features of the natural and social environment is it consistent? What functions might it serve? How does it contribute to the probability of long-term survival of the group in its place? (Segall, 1984, p. 160)

Thus Segall would focus on those ecological and social factors that are functionally related to behavior.

I would agree with Segall that what is needed in cross-cultural psychology at the present time is not a theory of culture, as defined by the cultural nominalists, but a working model, a system of classification, that would categorize ethnic groups in terms of ecological and social variables. A model for an ecological theory of human development has been developed by Bronfenbrenner (1977). Triandis (1980) has referred to five levels of ecosocial systems. The most differentiated ecosocial theory has been elaborated by John Berry (1976, 1979), whose model refers to (a) the ecology of the environment, (b) cultural adaptations to the ecology, (c) biological adaptations to the ecology, (d) the acculturation to changes in the preceding three factors, and (e) the effects of variations in the preceding four factors on psychological differentiation.

AN ECOLOGICAL AND SOCIAL MODEL

The proposed ecological and social working model (Georgas, 1988), or system of classification, contains three basic concepts: ecological factors,

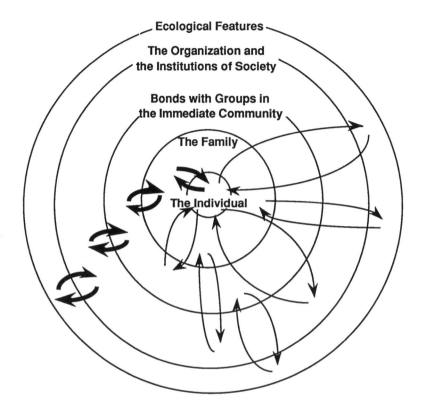

Figure 4.1. Topological Representation of the Model

social institutions, and group interactions. These three concepts are subdivided into the five basic elements of the model (see Figure 4.1).

The *ecological factors* consist of features of the physical environment (mountains, plains, climate) and the human-made environment (demographic patterns, oikistical patterns or the patterns of towns and cities, and so on) that can play determining roles in shaping the subsistence patterns, types of social institutions (Berry, 1979), significant in-groups, types of family organization, and so on.

The *organization and institutions of the society* comprise the subsistence system, the political and judicial system, the educational system, religion, and means of mass communication. Berry (1979) refers to the sociopolitical system, Bronfenbrenner (1977) refers to the macrosystem, and Murdock and Provost (1973) refer to institutional values. These variables could be quantified according to their functional relationships to psychological differentiation, perhaps based on dimensions from political science (Rummel, 1972, 1976), such as national wealth, authoritarian power, energy production, and system of national government.

The *bonds with groups in the immediate community* include the degree and quality of contact with significant groups within the immediate community, such as students, coworkers, neighbors, judges, the police, teachers, clergy, and friends. Bronfenbrenner (1977) refers to this as the microsystem; Triandis (1980) calls it the intraindividual system. An important distinction should be made between the institutions of society and the bonds with representatives of these institutions, in regard to the degree of influence in shaping values, attitudes, cognitions, behavior, and so on. This recalls Toennies's (1961) distinction between gemeinschaft and gesellschaft. *Gesellschaft,* or society, refers to an imaginary and mechanical structure, or an artificial construction of an aggregate of human beings. *Gemeinschaft,* on the other hand, refers to the real and organic life of the immediate habitat, and to the many contacts of human beings found in kinship, in the proximity of dwellings, the communal fields, and the contiguity of holdings in the immediate neighborhood, and finally to friendships. The local neighborhood or small village, with its policeman, may have a greater influence on the psychological differentiation of the person than does the institution. The concept of justice, for example, may be more likely to be shaped by the behavior of the local policeman in a large city, who is perceived as distant, punishing, unapproachable, or by the policeman in a small village, who is a friend and approachable, than by some abstract cognitive categorization call law enforcement.

The family is placed in a separate category from groups in the immediate community because of its critical role in the socialization of the child (Minturn & Lambert, 1964; Whiting & Whiting, 1975). It is a universal finding that the family is the primary source of influence in the socialization of the child and the child's most significant source of day-to-day stimulation, for at least the first five years of life. The type of family—nuclear, extended, one-parent, polygamous—also profoundly affects psychological differentiation.

The final element in the model is *the individual,* or, more specifically, psychological variables such as cognition, personality, emotions, learning, values, and the like, as well as biological variables. These five elements refer to the structure, or static, part of the model. There is another dimension, the diachronic, that explains how the structure changes during a specific time period, and how its current structure is related to the traditional structure. The diachronic or time dimension serves as a means of identifying chronological invariances, that is, functional relationships between ecosocial variables and psychological differentiation that have remained relatively invariant across time periods. These chronological invariances can be contrasted with those functional relationships that have changed owing to acculturation.

AN ECOSOCIAL ANALYSIS OF THE HELLENES

This section will present an analysis of Greek indigenous psychology in terms of the ecosocial diachronic model outlined above (Georgas, 1988). The presentation of the ecological and social phenomena of the Greek culture will provide a theoretical structure with which the cross-cultural psychologist can understand the psychological data and make comparisons with other cultures. In regard to the diachronic analysis of Greece, I have depended on accounts from various Greek historians (Sfyroeras, 1975; Vakalopoulos, 1980; Zakynthinos, 1976) to isolate from the history of modern Greece incidents and descriptions pertaining to the ecological system, the subsistence system, and institutions such as education, law, and religion. As indicated above, my purpose was to isolate the chronological invariances and the effects of acculturation, which can in turn affect the functioning relationships with psychological variables, in this case, values.

A brief sketch of the past 200 years of the history of the Hellenes will focus on those peak historical events and periods that influenced recent invariants and changes in the ecological and social variables in Greece.

At the end of the eighteenth century, the Hellenes were but one of many ethnic groups, with distinct language and culture, within the Ottoman Empire, which had captured Byzantium or New Rome, the head of the Orthodox church, and the antipod to the capital of Catholicism in Rome. The dissolution of the Byzantine Empire had the effect of isolating the Hellenes from the profound cultural, religious, and economic changes that took place in southern and northern Europe during the Renaissance. However, that both the Greek language and the Orthodox church were able to survive within the Ottoman Empire was the result of a number of factors. The Ottoman rulers, who were essentially warriors, were faced with administering a variety of ethnic groups of diverse languages, religions, and cultures within an empire that ranged from North Africa through the Middle East, encompassing all the Balkans and reaching at one point the bastion of Vienna. Proselytizing was not part of the Muslim religion, and this had the effect that the peoples of this vast empire were not assimilated into one homogeneous culture. Because the Ottomans realized that the administrators of the former Byzantine Empire were capable of undertaking many bureaucratic tasks, and because the Orthodox church was administered by the Hellenes, the Hellenic language became necessary and the predominant means of communication within the Ottoman Empire, which led to its perpetuation. The Orthodox religion, and the church itself, was tolerated under the condition that it did not foment insurrection within the empire; when rebellions did occur, they were stamped out ferociously by the Ottomans, but this had the opposite effect of creating heroes and martyrs. However, despite the lack of a nation-state of Hellas or Greece, the continuity of the identity of Hellenism was maintained.

In the meantime, the profound social and economic evolution taking place in Europe during this period did not leave the Hellenes completely untouched. The Renaissance in Italy during the sixteenth and seventeenth centuries led to the renewal of interest in the ancient Greek classics, and Hellenes from Venice reintroduced the written language and culture to the Hellenes within the Ottoman Empire through secret schools. The withdrawal of Venice from the eastern Mediterranean during the latter part of the eighteenth century, together with the opportunities afforded to enterprising sailors and merchants during the Napoleonic wars, resulted in Hellenes engaging in trading and merchant shipping throughout the Mediterranean, a historic means of subsistence that continues up to the present. At the end of the eighteenth century, the Ottoman Empire was in a period of decline. Aided by the interest of philhellenes such as Lord Byron, and because England, Russia, and France were at odds with the Ottoman Empire, the Hellenes revolted in 1821, and within a decade had established an independent nation, which was under the influence of both the German states and the British Empire for the next 100 years. However, what are today the island of Crete and all of northern Greece were not given up by the Ottomans until the early part of this century.

Up to the 1930s, industrial development in Greece, in contrast with northern Europe, was meager and primarily met domestic needs. Greece was mostly a nation of peasant farmers, fishermen, herders, and merchants. At the end of World War II, a terrible civil war erupted in Greece that did not end until 1950. But during the 1950s Greece began to industrialize, albeit tardily in relation to other European nations devastated by war. Rapid industrialization led to demographic changes as young people left their agricultural pursuits in the small villages to go to urban centers such as Athens. From the mid-1950s to the present there have been profound changes at all levels of the ecological and social structure. These changes, together with the chronological constants, will be discussed next.

The Ecological Features

The ecological features of Greece, according to the model, are separated into geographic features, oikistical features, and climate. The characteristic geographic features of Greece are its mountains, the hundreds of islands scattered throughout the Ionian, Aegean, and Cretan Seas, and its few fertile plains. The characteristic oikistical and demographic features of Greece consist of small, isolated communities in the mountains and on the many islands and relatively large cities on the plains, by natural ports on the mainland and on the islands. Because communication and travel between isolated communities in the mountains was in the past very difficult, it resulted in their necessarily becoming autonomous and self-sufficient; as Segall (1984) might call it, they demonstrated "nonprescient adaptiveness of behavioral change." Even in present-day Greece, travel between some islands occurs only once a week or less. During the Ottoman rule, many Hellenes fled the exposed communities in the plains and by the sea after punitive military expeditions or to protect themselves from brigands, thereby establishing small communities in the mountains that, because of their isolation, offered natural protection.

In regard to functional relationships between Greece's oikistical features and personality traits, it is of interest that historians have ascribed different personality traits to inhabitants of the plains and those of the mountains. In the austere and harsh conditions of the mountains,

> survival required hard work, which had as a result the development of physical and mental traits, and the creation of different types of personality traits. Under these harsh conditions, the families returned to a more primitive type of life, to herding and small crop agriculture. The mountain people adapted by developing the personality traits of the insurgent, the indomitable, who refused to compromise with authority, and who became a brigand in order to survive. (Sfyroeras, 1975, pp. 145-146)

Travelers to Greece during the eighteenth century referred to inhabitants of the plains as "stolid, submissive, unable to take initiatives"; inhabitants in the mountains and the islands were described as "lively, rebellious, flexible, open to every opportunity which might better their lives" (Tsoukalas, 1977, p. 118). Vakalopoulos (1980) refers to descriptions of mountaineers as having "attitudes of superiority, with confidence in their abilities . . . hardworking and intelligent, but unstable, changeable, cunning, rancorous, and separated into factions" (p. 305).

Although small communities are still in existence in Greece, they are populated mainly by the elderly and are no longer autonomous as in the past. In 1981 almost 40% of the Greek population was concentrated in the two large urban areas of Athens and Thessaloniki. The migration from the small communities to the large urban centers began in the 1950s and reached its peak in the 1970s.

The Mediterranean climate is moderate, without extremes as in tropical or polar regions. On the other hand, crop failures, decimation of herds of animals, and earthquakes have been frequent occurrences.

The Organization and
Institutions of the Society

Economic Organization. The ecological features of Greece shaped specific types of subsistence patterns that remained unchanged for hundreds of years. The plains, essentially broad valleys between mountains, permitted the cultivation of crops. Cities in the plains and ports on the mainland or on the islands became trading and mercantile centers. In the mountains, the ecology was amenable only to herding of goats and sheep and to vine and olive cultivation. Fishing was the standard mode of subsistence in communities by the sea, together with merchant shipping. During the past 20 years, the traditional forms of subsistence patterns have given way to increased industrialization and services related to tourism. In 1983, 30% of the working population was engaged in agriculture, forestry, or fishing, 28.6% in industry, and 41.4% in services. Figures such as these make comparisons between different nations meaningful.

Political Institutions and Legal System. The geographic features of Greece, as discussed previously, are functionally related to the establishment of many small, isolated, and economically self-sufficient communities. The history of Greece indicates that effective political control over such communities, communication with which was extremely difficult, was almost impossible (Zakynthinos, 1976). Thus the ecological features played a significant role in the development of self-government within these isolated communities, together with a considerable degree of autonomy. For example, the Ottoman rulers must have realized that effective political control over these thousands of small communities would have required a military presence well beyond their manpower capacities. The situation for the cities on the accessible plains and the coasts was different, and the Ottomans concentrated their forces on controlling these larger centers.

Thus the Ottomans were most likely forced by ecological conditions to permit partial self-government of the scattered mountain communities, with the provision that the communities pay their taxes. The system of taxation, as old as the Byzantine Empire, was adopted by the Ottomans; this consisted of taxation of the community as a whole, not of individuals or heads of households. The political organization of each community consisted of a president and a board of councillors, elected by the community members, who were responsible for the administration of the community and for assigning to each family its share of the community tax burden. As will be discussed later, this feature of relative autonomy and self-government, in which each community essentially set its own traditions, customs, and the right to judge its own members according to local "laws," was a critical factor and an invariant that profoundly affected the Greek's social perceptions of law, fairness, government, and suspicion of central government that have continued until the present time.

After the independence of Greece in the early 1800s, a monarchy with a German prince as king was the form of government, with an elected Greek legislature. During the early part of this century, the monarchy was rejected, brought back by plebiscite, rejected, brought back by plebiscite, and rejected again in 1973. These changes were also related to a series of military coups, the most recent from 1967 to 1974. Greece became a member of the European Community in 1981, and as such its present political system is similar to that of other members of the community, with relatively strong control by the central government.

The Educational System. The education of youth during the past 200 years in Greece passed through the same stages as in the European Community, but at a slower rate. The direct training of youth by the family, to learn the skills of the farmer or the fisherman, characterized the method of education in the isolated communities of Greece during Ottoman rule. During the seventeenth century, the renewed interest in Aristotle and Plato in Italy was partially instigated by Greek scholars in Venice and other centers of learning. Greek scholars reintroduced the written language and the rich literature of the Greek classics through secret schools throughout Greece. The creation of the modern Greek state in the early nineteenth century was accompanied by the establishment of an organized educational system, modeled on the European system.

One of the highest values of the traditional agricultural family was to send at least one of the sons to the university. At the present time, the structure of the Greek educational system is similar to that of other European countries, with six years of elementary education, six years of secondary education, and university education. Nine years of education are compulsory. Approximately 90% of the population is considered literate.

Religion. Perhaps the most important single influence during the Ottoman rule in maintaining the language and the identity of the Hellene was the Orthodox church. The clergy acted as teachers of the language and the culture to the young, were arbitrators within the small communities, were sometimes elected to the board of councillors, and often were the only literate members of the community. In addition, the church and the clergy were often the leaders of insurgences against the Turks, and thus became martyrs and symbols of opposition. The church played a major role in the revolution against the Ottomans.

At the present time, 95% of the population are nominally Greek Ortho-dox, although the proportion of people attending church regularly in the ur-ban areas is probably around 10%.

Mass Communications. The ecology of Greece and the abundance of small, isolated communities had the important effect of limiting the amount of contact with the outside world and thus restricting the amount of informa-tion available to the inhabitants. The communities on the exposed plains, near the large ports and merchant centers, and on the islands, with their mer-chant fleets, were exposed to more sources of information and foreign influ-ences than were the inhabitants in the mountains. On the other hand, the lack of communication with the outside world had the effect of preserving the Greek language and culture.

The full effect of the mass media, and its most important medium, televi-sion, has reached the isolated villages only within the past 10 to 15 years. The nationwide road network, which was begun during the 1950s, has re-sulted in virtually all areas of present-day Greece being accessible. The re-cent increase in tourism has resulted in people from isolated villages being exposed to foreign influences, and has played a strong role in the accultura-tion of Greece.

Bonds With Groups in the Immediate Community

The quality and quantity of bonds with groups in the immediate commu-nity, or in Toennies's gemeinschaft, is the first element in the model, which is based primarily on concepts and data from social psychology. People be-long to different in-groups, which vary according to the structure of the society. Complex societies have more in-groups than do simple societies. Collectivistic societies also have fewer in-groups than do individualistic societies, as Triandis (1993) notes. He further elaborates the types of rela-tionships characteristic of in-groups in collectivistic societies, such as un-questioned attachment, distrust of out-groups, perception that in-group norms are universally valid, automatic obedience to in-group authorities, and distrust and unwillingness to cooperate with out-groups. These concepts can be used ultimately to classify cultures along this dimension (Triandis et al., 1986).

The small, isolated, autonomous community is an invariant in the Greek historical ecosocial model. Greek historians agree that the characteristic po-litical organization of the small Greek community, together with its tradi-tions and behaviors, extend backwards to ancient Greece. It is likely, as previously discussed, that ecological features of Greece were determining factors in the development of the policy of tax collection of both the Byzantine and Ottoman empires. Effective control of the isolated communities by the central government was impossible under the conditions of poor communication. Thus the isolated communities had a large measure of autonomy and self-government, which led to collectiveness and solidarity against any outsider. Giannoulopoulos (1975) describes the typical types of bonds:

> The community was closed and highly suspicious of any outsider who might attempt to involve himself and possibly influence changes in civic affairs. Any violation of traditional ethical standards or religious customs, as well as local prohibitions, provoked the reaction and sanctions of the entire community. The members of the community were judge, jury and punishers of those who violated their customs, whatever was the law of the central government. The collective responsibility of the community members, the respect for life, the respect of one's honor and one's property, institutions collectively supported by the community, were carefully protected. The fair distribution of the tax burden among the community members, the right to elect their own leaders, the right to choose their teachers, the right to reject their priest, were rights carefully nurtured and guarded. (p. 141)

On the other hand, the intragroup relationships, the relations among factions composed of different families within the community, were not characterized by unity and were often hostile and destructive. As Giannoulopoulos (1975) describes:

> The same community system which nurtured collective responsibility as a protection against outside intervention by the Ottomans, enclosed within itself the causes of complaints, disputes, factionalism, and the division of the community into factions. The assignment of the amount of taxes by the elected councilors was often unfair, which led to complaints and disputes. Thus, self-interest, ambitions and animosity divided the leaders and many of the families into factions. (p. 141)

At this point, one can make certain speculations about the functional relationships between ecological features, social institutions, small isolated communities, and the psychological characteristics of Greeks. The ecological features of Greece favored the creation of small isolated communities. Because of poor communication with these communities and the resultant inability of a central government to control them effectively, they were most likely forced to permit a considerable degree of self-government and autonomy in exchange for the payment of taxes. Communities elected their leaders and developed their own customs, traditions, and informal judicial system, which were often at variance with the laws of the central government. Within the isolated communities there was a system of collective responsibility and solidarity against outside threats, but also frequent internal dissension and fractionalism. This ecosocial framework might well explain certain psychological concepts of Greeks.

Triandis and Vassiliou (1972) have explained that there is no concept of "fairness," in the Anglo-Saxon sense, in Greece. The social perceptions of "justice" and "fair play" among Greeks even at the present time are shaped by the community, with the result that laws and the judicial system are sometimes perceived as hostile inventions of the central government.

The industrialization and urbanization of Greece during the past 20 years has resulted in different psychological characteristics of younger people compared with older people in the villages, but also differences between inhabitants of small communities and urban centers. In large urban centers such as Athens, the bonds with groups in the immediate community, or the neighborhood, are quite different from those in the traditional small community.

The Family System

Anthropological holocultural studies have found evidence for functional relationships between ecosocial variables and family types (Levinson & Malone, 1980). There is a curvilinear relationship between societal complexity and family type so that both the least and most complex societies have small, nuclear families (McNett, 1973). Specifically, in small hunting and gathering societies and in large industrialized societies the nuclear family predominates, whereas in agricultural societies the extended family is typical (Blumberg & Winch, 1972; Nimkoff & Middleton, 1960; Osmond, 1969). In addition, Chu and Hollingsworth (1969) have found evidence based on 531 societies that the extended family has a higher level of social stratification than the nuclear family (Nimkoff & Middleton, 1960).

In line with the above structure, the characteristic Greek family type was extended, which is an invariant according to our definition. At the present time, the nuclear family is predominant in Athens and a few of the large urban areas, although there are still strong traces of extended family relationships. The extended family system was probably functional in agricultural societies because many hands are needed for the cultivation of the land. However, in traditional Greece, the extended family was also characteristic of fishermen, of merchants, and indeed throughout the society. Perhaps the most cogent description of the functional relationship between social factors and the structure of the Greek family was made by a traveler through Greece, Thiersch, in 1833:

> Because there never was a central government which was able to control or protect the people, one had to search elsewhere for protection and support. The most natural and secure support was found in the family, whose members, including second cousins, are nowhere so united and so willing to help each other than in Greece. The isolated individual has to ally himself with some group. He becomes a follower, or a leader of a group. In this case, a prominent person has a group of followers dependent on him, who call on him, who ask his advice, who execute his wishes, who protect their common interests, always being careful to be worthy of his esteem and his trust. This is the nature of the many groups in Greece. . . . Rather than being astonished regarding this, one must recognize in this system, the course and the natural and necessary organization of a political society which was left to its own devices for survival.

Thiersch's description of the functioning of the groups in the Greek society is remarkably similar to the definitive analysis of the Greek in-group by Triandis and Vassiliou (1972), who show that the Greek in-group is composed of more than the extended family, but includes such people as best man at the wedding, the godfather, in-laws, and friends, with the basic criterion that they show concern and support during times of need. The appropriate behaviors toward members of the in-group are cooperation, protection, and help, whereas appropriate behaviors toward members of the out-group are competition and hostility (Triandis, Vassiliou, & Nassiakou, 1968). Also, one of the key central values of the in-group, which encompasses many other values, is *philotimo* (Triandis & Vassiliou, 1972; Vassiliou, 1966; Vassiliou & Vassiliou, 1973). *Philotimo* can be loosely translated as "honor," but typical responses (Vassiliou, 1966) suggest that it has a special meaning for the Greek in-group—that is, "to give to others," "to be correct in fulfilling your obligations," "to sacrifice yourself for others," "to respect others." The functional relationships between the in-group in the small isolated community and the development of a key value such as *philotimo* are obvious here.

The close bonds, the interdependence, the mutual obligations, and the unity of the Greek extended family have been described by anthropologists, sociologists, and psychologists (interested readers should see J. K. Campbell, 1964; Campbell & Sherrard, 1968; Doumanis, 1983; Dragonas, 1983; du Boulay, 1974; Friedl, 1963; Katakis, 1976, 1981, 1984; Nassiakou, 1977; Lee, 1966; Peristiany, 1965; Pipinelli-Potamianou, 1965; Polemi-Todoulou, 1981; Safilios-Rothschild, 1967; Tsoukalas, 1977).

Family Values

The focus of this section is on how the family values of Greeks have changed in relation to changes in the ecosocial model. This can be described, according to Berry's (1979, 1980) model of acculturation, as the accommodation of the values of Greeks to changes in the ecosocial system. Thus it is important for purposes of interpretation of any observed changes in values to specify which elements of the ecosocial model are presumably determining factors.

On the one hand we have the ecosocial model of traditional Greece, which has been described above, as the baseline measure or the reference point, against which any changes are measured. A sample representative of inhabitants from this ecosocial setting can be found in small isolated villages in Greece, particularly those older in age. Their children, because of exposure to elements of the model such as education and mass communication, would be expected to have acculturated more than the parents. On the other hand, we have the ecosocial model of acculturated Greece, reflecting the changes during the past 30 years. Inhabitants of Athens would represent the forefront of acculturation, particularly the younger generation. The older generation in Athens would represent a mixed sample, including those who were born in Athens and those who moved from small communities to Athens.

The diachronic invariants of the traditional ecosocial model and the most important elements of the ecosocial model that have changed during the past 30 years and are characteristic of Athens are presented in Table 4.1.

In regard to the ecological features, the diachronic invariants of the traditional model are the geographic features, which determined the formation of many small isolated communities in the mountains and on the numerous islands. The changes characteristic of Athens are demographic and resulted from migration from the isolated communities to Athens, resulting in large urban areas.

In regard to economic activities, the invariant subsistence patterns of the small communities, influenced by the geographic features, resulted in most of the population engaging in agriculture, fishing, herding, trading, or merchant shipping. The economic activity of present-day Athens is primarily industrial and service oriented, so that the individual works in a nonfamily setting, and thus the interdependence of the agricultural family is no longer functional.

Political institutions and the legal system have also undergone change. The years of Ottoman rule, even after the establishment of the modern Greek state, resulted in attitudes of distrust of central government. The effective autonomy of isolated communities led to active involvement and control of local government, as well as to established local customs. The political or-

Table 4.1 Diachronic Invariants of the Traditional Ecosocial Model and Elements of the Model That Have Changed During the Past 30 Years in Athens

Diachronic Invariants	Changes: Athens
Ecological features: small isolated communities in the mountains and on the numerous islands	Migration from isolated communities to Athens
Economic activity: agriculture, fishing, herding, trading, and merchant shipping	Population engaged in industry and services
Political institutions: distrust of central government, active involvement in and control of local government, established local customs	Central government, without active involvement in day-to-day political activities
Education: increase in years of schooling	Increase in years of schooling
Mass communication: lack of contact with the outside world, distrust of strangers	Free contact with many groups, television
Bonds with groups in the immediate community: power of the in-group, collectivist type	Depersonalization, power of collectivist in-group lessened, many in-groups
Family: extended, with cooperation, interdependence, mutual obligations, self-sacrifice, group identity	Nuclear, individualist

ganization characteristic of Athens and indeed all of Greece at the present time is strong central government, without active involvement in day-to-day political activities.

In regard to education, there has been an increase in years of schooling for all children, both those from isolated communities and those in Athens.

The forms of mass communication characteristic of isolated communities resulted in lack of contact with the outside world and distrust of strangers. In present-day Athens there is free contact with many groups, and the influx of television has resulted in the inflow of information.

Bonds with groups in the immediate community of the traditional small isolated communities were characterized by the power of the in-group, composed not only of the members of the extended family, but of in-laws, distant relatives, and others bonded together through acts of aid in times of crises and through a complex system of mutual obligations. Thus the in-group in the small communities of Greece is essentially collectivistic (Triandis & Vassiliou, 1972) in nature. The quality of life in the urban neighborhood in Athens is similar to that in many large urban areas, with the same problems of depersonalization. The power of the traditional in-group has been lessened, and the individual is able to join a variety of in-groups characteristic of complex societies, such as clubs and political parties.

In regard to family, the type of extended family found in Greece was similar to those found in agricultural communities, in which the psychological characteristics of cooperation, interdependence, mutual obligations, self-sacrifice, and group identity were functional. The characteristic type of family in Athens is nuclear, although there are still traces of living arrangements of the extended family type, in which relatives, or children and parents, might live in different apartments in the same or nearby buildings.

ACCULTURATION OF
FAMILY VALUES IN GREECE

The findings concerning acculturation of family values are based on two studies. One involved a sample composed of 417 university students, 227 from small communities from throughout Greece and 190 students either born or raised in Athens (Georgas, 1989). The second involved a sample of 678 subjects, members of 226 three-person families, consisting of father, mother, and son or daughter, average age 18 (Georgas, 1991). Of these families, 110 were from Athens and 116 were from small communities.

Family values were measured with a 64-item questionnaire that included items such as "The father should be the head of the family." The word *should* was used in almost all of the statements so as to emphasize the normative aspect of values. The responses were on a 5-point scale: agree, somewhat agree, not certain or don't know, somewhat disagree, disagree. Items were scored so that 1 was toward the traditional value direction.

The 64 values were factor analyzed in both studies with the PA 2 method, with iteration, and rotated according to the varimax criterion. Only factor loadings of .40 or greater were interpreted. Separate factor analyses were conducted for Athens and for the small communities in both studies.

Perhaps the strongest factor that emerged from these studies was named Hierarchical Father-Mother Roles. This factor was common to all of the subsamples, although in some samples (e.g., fathers and mothers from small communities; Georgas, 1991) it ranked first in terms of percentage of explained variance, whereas with Athenian students it ranked lower (Georgas, 1989). This factor referred to the traditional roles of the extended family, in which father was the head of the family, acted in an authoritarian manner, and controlled the finances, and the mother was submissive, conciliatory, a

Table 4.2 Means of University Students ($N = 417$) From Athens and Small Communities According to Gender on Factor Hierarchical Father-Mother Roles

	Gender	
	Males	Females
Athens	4.22	4.50
Small communities	3.68	4.33

Table 4.3 Means of Fathers, Mothers, and Offspring ($N = 678$) From Athens and Small Communities on Factor Hierarchical Father-Mother Roles

	Athens	Small Communities
Offspring	4.02	3.79
Mothers	3.12	2.47
Fathers	2.90	2.19

Table 4.4 Means of Family Roles and Gender of Offspring on Factor Hierarchical Father-Mother Roles ($N = 678$)

	Gender Offspring	
	Sons	Daughters
Offspring	3.57	4.05
Mothers	2.83	2.74
Fathers	2.64	2.36

housewife, and cared for the children. On the other hand, an examination of the mean ratings on this factor indicated that Athenian students (Georgas, 1989) rejected these traditional roles, as did small community students (Table 4.2) and 18-year-olds (Georgas, 1991) from both Athens and small communities (Table 4.3). As would be predicted from the model, small community fathers, who are still functioning within the traditional ecosocial framework (Georgas, 1991), strongly approved of these values, as did their wives, whereas Athenian mothers and fathers were in a transitional stage of not being certain (Table 4.3).

In regard to the effects of gender (Table 4.4), the results further indicated that sons were more traditional than daughters (Georgas, 1991). Fathers and mothers of daughters were more traditional than fathers and mothers of sons.

Finally, correlations of hierarchical mother-father roles between the off-spring and mother and father indicated that the male offspring correlated higher with fathers than did female offspring (Georgas, 1991). This latter finding suggests that the son identifies with the father's position regarding these hierarchical mother-father roles, whereas there is little correlation be-tween the father's and the daughter's position.

These findings can be interpreted in terms of the ecosocial model outlined above. In the Greek extended family, the hierarchical family roles were strictly defined (du Boulay, 1974; Friedl, 1963; Triandis & Vassiliou, 1972). The father was the *pater familias,* an authoritarian who made the important decisions in the family, controlled the finances, and had high social power (French & Raven, 1959). Mother's role was to care for the children. In Athe-nian nuclear families with fathers employed in the professions, the father's social power was diminished in relation to the mother's (Safilios-Rothschild, 1967). Child-rearing practices involved all the members of the extended family taking an active role, whereas in the nuclear family, the mothers, with help only from the fathers, raised the children (Doumanis, 1983). Thus the results suggest that the fathers and mothers from small communities still ascribe to the values associated with these traditional roles, because the types of eco-nomic activities in which they are involved—agriculture, fishing, and so on —still functionally support the structure of the extended family system. On the other hand, their children, during this study about 18 years of age, who have broken out of this traditional mold in that they have attended secondary school, are working and thus have sources of income independent of their fathers', are in the process of acculturation. On the other hand, the sons, although disagreeing with the hierarchical father role, still identify with it more than do the daughters. Also, the fact that Athenian parents are uncertain about the traditional hierarchical roles suggests the effects of ecological and social changes, specifically the type of economic activity in the nuclear fam-ily—that is, the nuclear family in Athens does not tend to be interdependent in the economic sphere; for instance, the father works in a factory, the mother in a shop, the son goes to school, the daughter works in an office.

Another factor that emerged from these studies was named *philotimo,* referring to this key value that controls the interdependent relationships and obligations of the in-group (Triandis & Vassiliou, 1972; Vassiliou, 1966; Vas-siliou & Vassiliou, 1973). The value *philotimo* emerged in the same factor with values that referred to maintaining good relationships with relatives, economic support of the offspring by the parents, obligations of the children toward parents and relatives, and expectations that children should respect grandparents, should help in the home, and so on. The means of this factor were in the direction of agreement for all of the samples, although there were some differences. For example, small community students were more in agree-ment than were Athenian students. However, interesting differences emerged in regard to the factor analyses of the separate samples. The content of the factor *philotimo* in the Athenian university students was restricted to relationships among members of the nuclear family. They did not include some obligations of the children toward the family, nor did the maintenance of good relationships with relatives appear in this factor. But most important, this factor did not emerge at all in the offspring, aged 18, from either Athens or the small communities. This suggests that although the values associated with *philotimo* are still an integral part of older people in the small communities and even in Athens, and among the university students from small communities, among the Athenian university students *philotimo* is not embedded within the context of the extended family or the in-group, and that for the 18-year-olds of the new generation, this key value has disappeared. The explanations can be found within the ecosocial model.

Other findings also emerged from these two studies (Georgas, 1989, 1991). However, the overall findings suggest that the transition of the Greek society from an agricultural, fishing, herding, and mercantile economic society, with many small, autonomous, isolated communities, characterized by an extended family system and a broad in-group, with predominantly collectivistic values, to a services and industrialized society, with large urban centers, characterized by nuclear families and many in-groups, is accompanied by the gradual adoption of individualistic values.

CONCLUSIONS

The purpose of this chapter has been to argue that during the current stage of development of cross-cultural psychology there is a need for a model—at this stage a temporary system of classification—that will permit the categorization of ethnic groups in terms of ecological and social variables. Such a model would lead to a more systematic means of searching for functional relationships between ecological and social variables and the psychological variables that either are common to ethnic groups or differentiate between them. Perhaps it is necessary at this stage that cross-cultural psychology abandon the definition of *culture* as idiomorphic to a specific ethnic group and as impossible to generalize to the construction of a theory of culture, as has been argued by the cultural nominalist branch of anthropology (Rohner, 1984). Berry's ecosocial model represents an approach to the construction of a working model that would permit the generalization of findings in cross-cultural psychology.

This chapter has presented the structural elements of such a model, consisting of ecological factors, social institutions, bonds with groups in the immediate community, and the family, together with a diachronic analysis of changes in the structure of the model. The context of application of the model, in this case, has been Greece, and the psychological phenomenon studied has been the family values of Greeks. Interpretations of the determining factors underlining the findings in these studies have been based on this explicit ecosocial model. Similar analyses could be performed for all the "indigenous psychologies" presented in this volume so as to permit the classification of different ethnic or national groups in terms of this common structure and to permit the interpretation of the psychological phenomenon studied in terms of the determining factors both within and between these national or ethnic groups.

REFERENCES

Berry, J. W. (1975). An ecological approach to cross-cultural psychology. *Netherlands Journal of Psychology, 30,* 51-84.

Berry, J. W. (1976). *Human ecology and cognitive style: Comparative studies in cultural and psychological adaptation.* New York: John Wiley.

Berry, J. W. (1979). A cultural ecology of social behavior. In L. Berkowitz (Ed.), *Advances in experimental social psychology.* New York: Academic Press.

Berry, J. W. (1980). Ecological analyses for cross-cultural psychology. In N. Warren (Ed.), *Studies in cross-cultural psychology.* London: Academic Press.

Berry, J. W. (1983). The sociogenesis of social sciences: An analysis of the cultural relativity of social psychology. In B. Bain (Ed.), *The sociogenesis of language and human behavior.* New York: Plenum.

Blumberg, R. L., & Winch, R. F. (1972). Societal complexity and familial complexity: Evidence for the curvilinear hypothesis. *American Journal of Sociology, 77,* 898-920.

Bronfenbrenner, U. (1977). Toward an experimental ecology of human development. *American Psychologist, 32,* 513-531.

Campbell, D. T. (1975). On the conflict between biological and social evolution and between psychology and moral tradition. *American Psychologist, 30,* 1103-1126.

Campbell, D. T., & Naroll, R. (1972). The mutual relevance of anthropology and psychology. In F. L. K. Hu (Ed.), *Psychological anthropology.* Cambridge, MA: Schenkman.

Campbell, J. K. (1964). *Honour, family and patronage: A study of institutions and moral values in a Greek mountain community.* Oxford: Clarendon.

Campbell, J. K., & Sherrard, P. (1968). *Modern Greece.* London: Ernest Bern.

Chu, H., & Hollingsworth, J. S. (1969). A cross-cultural study of the relationship between family types and social stratification. *Journal of Marriage and the Family, 31,* 322-327.

Doumanis, N. (1983). *Mothering in Greece: From collectivism to individualism.* New York: Academic.

Dragonas, T. (1983). *The self-concept of preadolescents in the Hellenic context.* Unpublished doctoral dissertation.

du Boulay, J. (1974). *Portrait of a Greek mountain village.* Oxford: Clarendon.

French, J. R. P., & Raven, B. (1959). The bases of social power. In D. Cartwright (Ed.), *Studies in social power.* Ann Arbor: University of Michigan Press.

Friedl, E. (1963). *Vassilika: A village in modern Greece.* New York: Holt, Rinehart & Winston.

Georgas, J. (1988). An ecological social model: The case of Greece. In J. W. Berry, S. H. Irvine, & E. B. Hunt (Eds.), *Indigenous cognition: Functioning in cultural context.* Dordrecht, Netherlands: Martinus Nijhoff.

Georgas, J. (1989). Changing family values in Greece: From collectivist to individualist. *Journal of Cross-Cultural Psychology, 20,* 80-91.

Georgas, J. (1991). Intrafamily acculturation of values in Greece. *Journal of Cross Cultural Psychology, 22,* 445-457.

Giannoulopoulos, I. (1975). Koinotites [Communities]. In *History of the Greek nation* (Vol. 11). Athens: Ekdotiki Athenon.

Hofstede, G. (1980). *Culture's consequences: International differences in work-related values.* Beverly Hills, CA: Sage.

Jahoda, G. (1980). Theoretical and systematic approaches in cross-cultural psychology. In H. C. Triandis (Ed.), *Handbook of cross-cultural psychology: Vol. 1. Perspectives.* Boston: Allyn & Bacon.

Katakis, C. (1976). An exploratory multi-level attempt to investigate intrapersonal and interpersonal patterns of twenty Athenian families. *Mental Health and Society, 3,* 1-9.

Katakis, C. (1981). The concept of purpose and its relatedness to entropy control: Implications for preventive and therapeutic interventions. *Mediterranean Journal of Social Psychiatry, 2,* 16-19.

Katakis, C. (1984). *Of tris tautotites tis ellenikis oikogeneias* [The three faces of the Greek family]. Athens: Kedros.

Lee, D. (1966). *Rural Greece.* Athens: Institute of Child Health.

Levinson, D., & Malone, M. J. (1980). *Toward explaining human culture.* New Haven, CT: HRAF.

McNett, C. W. (1973). Factor analysis of a cross-cultural sample. *Behavior Science Notes, 8,* 253-257.

Minturn, L., & Lambert, W. W. (1964). *Mothers of six cultures.* New York: John Wiley.

Murdock, G. P., & Provost, C. (1973). Measurement of cultural complexity. *Ethnology, 12,* 379-392.

Nassiakou, M. (1977). *Prosdokies tis meteras, noimosyni tou paidiou kai kinitro epitihias* [Mother's expectations, intelligence of the child, and achievement motivation]. Unpublished doctoral dissertation.

Nimkoff, M. F., & Middleton, R. (1960). Types of family and types of economy. *American Journal of Sociology, 66,* 215-225.

Osmond, M. (1969). A cross-cultural analysis of family organization. *Journal of Marriage and the Family, 31,* 302-310.

Peristiany, J. G. (1965). *Honour and shame: The values of Mediterranean society.* London: Weienfels & Nicolson.

Pipinelli-Potamianou, A. (1965). *Personality and group participation in Greece.* Athens: Center for Mental Health and Research.

Polemi-Todoulou, M. (1981). *Cooperation in family and peer group: A study of interdependence in a Greek island community.* Doctoral dissertation, Bryn Mawr College.

Rohner, R. P. (1984). Toward a conception of culture for cross-cultural psychology. *Journal of Cross-Cultural Psychology, 15,* 111-138.

Rummel, R. J. (1972). *Dimensions of nations.* Beverly Hills, CA: Sage.

Rummel, R. J. (1976). *National attributes and behavior.* Beverly Hills, CA: Sage.

Safilios-Rothschild, K. (1967). A comparison of power structure and marital satisfaction in urban Greek and French families. *Journal of Marriage and the Family, 29,* 345-349.

Segall, M. H. (1984). More than we need to know about culture, but are afraid not to ask. *Journal of Cross-Cultural Psychology, 15,* 153-162.

Sfyroeras, B. (1975). Somata antistaseos tou ellenismou [Resistance groups in Hellenism]. *History of the Greek nation* (Vol. 11, pp. 140-151). Athens: Ekdotiki Athenon.

Thiersch, F. (1833). *De l'etat actuel de la Grece.* Leipsig.

Toennies, F. (1961). Gemeinschaft and gesellschaft. In T. Parsons, E. Shils, K. Naegele, & J. Pitts (Eds.), *Theories of society* (Vol. 1, pp. 191-201). Glencoe, IL: Free Press.

Triandis, H. C. (1980). Introduction. In H. C. Triandis (Ed.), *Handbook of cross-cultural psychology* (Vol. 1). Boston: Allyn & Bacon.

Triandis, H. C. (1993). *Culture, self-ingroup relationships, and social behavior.* Manuscript submitted for publication.

Triandis, H. C., Bontempo, R., Betancourt, H., Bond, M., Leung, K., Brenes, A., Georgas, J., Hui, C. H., Marin, G., Setiadi, B., Sinha, J. B. P., Verma, J., Spangenberg, J., Tousard, H., & de Montmollin, G. (1986). The measurement of the etic aspects of individualism and collectivism across cultures. *Australian Journal of Psychology, 38,* 257-267.

Triandis, H. C., & Vassiliou, V. (1972). An analysis of subjective culture. In H. C. Triandis (Ed.), *The analysis of subjective culture.* New York: John Wiley.

Triandis, H. C., Vassiliou, V., & Nassiakou, M. (1968). Three cross-cultural studies of subjective culture. *Journal of Personality and Social Psychology, 4*(Suppl.), 1-42.

Tsoukalas, K. (1977). *Exartisi kai anaparagogi* [Dependence and reproduction: The social role of educational mechanisms in Greece, 1830-1922]. Athens: Themelio.

Vakalopoulos, A. E. (1980). *Historia tou neou Hellenismou* [History of the new Hellenism] (Vol. 5). Athens: Thessaloniki.

Vassiliou, G. (1966). *Diereunesis metavleton ypeiserhomenon eis tin psychodynamikin tis hellenikis oikogeneias* [Exploration of factors related to the psychodynamics of the Greek family]. Athens: Athenian Institute of Anthropos.

Vassiliou, V., & Vassiliou, G. (1973). The implicative meaning of the Greek concept of philotimo. *Journal of Cross-Cultural Psychology, 4,* 326-341.

Whiting, B., & Whiting, J. W. M. (1975). *Children of six cultures: A psycho-cultural analysis.* Cambridge, MA: Harvard University Press.

Zakynthinos, D. (1976). *The making of modern Greece from Byzantium to independence.* Oxford: Oxford University Press.

5

BETWEEN WEST AND EAST

Humanistic Values and Concerns in Polish Psychology[1]

PAWEL BOSKI

ASSUMPTIONS FOR
INDIGENOUS PSYCHOLOGY

A symposium on indigenous psychologies held during the Eighth International Congress of Cross-Cultural Psychology illustrated two possible meanings of that term, and hence two theoretical approaches. In the first, *indigenous* psychology is equivalent to "folk" or "lay" psychology held by ordinary people in a given culture; as such, it should be contrasted with the scientific discipline of psychology as cultivated by academic researchers and professional specialists. (Here the situation is no different from the distinction between "native medicine" and "scientific medicine.") The second meaning lays emphasis on national or cultural specificity of *scientific psychologies* in various countries.[2]

As this domain of reflection and/or research is a new one in our discipline, it seems particularly proper to agree on its frontiers. Consequently, it is my contention that the distance between the referents denoted in the two definitions is large enough to justify their conceptual separation, rather than to cover them with one term and continue with the present conceptual confusion. Analysis of lay or ethnic "worldviews" should—in my opinion—be called *ethnic cognition,* and has long been a focus of interest among cross-cultural psychologists. Next, I propose that the term *indigenous psychology* be limited to meta-analyses and comparisons of various national, regional, or cultural systems of academic (scientific) psychologies, with the aim of discovering theoretical, methodological, or value-related specificity. The conceptual distinction proposed here has not gone unnoticed by others who apply the term *indigenous* also to Western psychology (Berry, Poortinga, Segall, & Dasen, 1988, chap. 16).

The postulate of conceptual separateness does not, however, deny the importance of analyzing mutual influences between ethnic cognition and indigenous psychology within a given culture. It is an interesting question to ask, for instance, to what extent the theories and research themes undertaken by Nigerian psychologists, or by their American counterparts, are influenced by beliefs and practices held in their respective cultures. In other words, ethnic cognition will be seen as one of the sources for indigenous psychology, be it European, African, or North American.

I will now specify some conditions that I consider critical for any indigenous psychology:

$$IPsy = IP * (CV + IS).$$

This formula reads: Indigenous psychology is a function of *indigenous problems* (IP), typical for a given national/cultural/regional entity, and *cultural values* (CV) plus *intellectual styles* (IS), which characterize the ways in which those problems are approached and solutions are sought. The symbolic format of this statement is intended to facilitate the reader's encoding and memory, rather than to suggest a literal mathematical function.

Indigenous Problems

By *indigenous problems* one could understand, after Berry (1976), those ecological features of a given national/social territory that have direct bearing on psychological processes of the local people. Berry's approach, however, has been applied to comparative studies of psychological processes in pretechnological societies, and it needs some extension to suit our purpose of analyzing psychology systems in developed countries. Accordingly, *indigenous problems* are defined here as those modes of cognitive/emotional adaptation, coping/defensive strategies, and life-styles that are specific for the large segments of a given society and determined by its natural environment, dominant technology, the present sociopolitical reality, and its historical context.

Some examples may illustrate the above definition. "Effects of malnutrition and/or a polygamous family on child development" are specific indigenous problems for most Africans and their psychologists. Malnutrition, in particular, is a result of food shortages and of low-quality (protein) diet, which in turn are related to complex climatic and sociocultural factors. At the other end of the spectrum, overeating and obesity have become indigenous problems for North American people and their psychologists. Here again, abundance of food, eating habits, and life-styles in the United States (such as heavy reliance on automobiles for transportation) are the key indigenous causes of the problem. Similarly, the effectiveness of various techniques of advertisement and persuasion on attitude change (e.g., "foot-in-the-door" or "door-in-the-face") will attract the attention of many American social psychologists, as the indigenous phenomena of their market-oriented society. But to their colleagues from other parts of the world where advertising techniques are not practiced, these concepts and research the behind them will remain totally exotic.

In the existing literature, an excellent analysis of indigenous problems/ conditions that determined the shape taken by American indigenous psychology by the turn of century is that by Boring (1950), in his *A History of Experimental Psychology*. Boring notes that although most first-generation American psychologists had been the students of Wundt, their transplantation of German introspectionist psychology to the New World must have failed, as it did, because it was not suited to the local conditions. American society, built of uprooted immigrants, was integrated around a single theme: "individual freedom for individual economic success," often called "American dream" ideology. It needed a psychology of action, of adaptive responses to the local environment, and of individual differences. That is how functionalism and behaviorism were born while contemplative psychology of consciousness died out.

The assumption of indigenous problems creates restrictions on levels of generality in psychological laws and justifies diversification of our discipline; yet, at first glance, it does not seem to be peculiar to psychologists only. Also in the natural sciences, biologists study certain species that belong to, say, tropical or circumpolar regions; similarly, geologists search for minerals and rock deposits specific to some parts of the globe or perhaps to a given planet only. In all these examples problems have some temporal-spatial delineation. Yet biologists and geologists researching their rare species or fossils could hardly be called indigenous scientists, because the theories and methods they apply are most likely regarded as universal. In other words, the *etic* versus *emic* debate (Berry, 1969), so fundamental for psychology and other social sciences, does not seem to be of any relevance to the natural sciences.

It is of course easy to imagine, or to give concrete examples of, psychologists equipped with etic hypotheses, traveling to more or less exotic places in an attempt to test them, with expectations of finding universals or discovering specificities. In such cases they would not differ much from their colleagues in the natural sciences, and we would be equally reluctant to call them and their studies indigenous. Moreover, as such scientific excursions are usually performed by Western or Northern psychologists, carrying their own theoretical instructions and methodological tools as well as ignorance about the local culture, one can often hear a justified outcry among "local" psychologists that the visitors "do not understand indigenous problems," "present a distorted view of reality," and so on (which, to be fair, does not seem to restrain these critics from making direct adaptations of foreign tests for their own research or applied endeavors). Such reactions are difficult to imagine in the natural sciences.

The above examples illustrate a more general argument that is of central importance for this chapter: Indigenous problems constitute a necessary but by no means sufficient condition for delineating the field of indigenous psychology. For that task to be completed we have to consider cultural values (CV) and intellectual styles (IS).

Cultural Values

As has been pointed out, psychological phenomena are ecoculture relative: Some are peculiar just to a specific culture and do not exist elsewhere; some have different contextual mechanisms and forms of manifestation (expression). But cultures also present stores of values regarding both everyday activities and intellectual styles, including philosophies and approaches to scientific endeavor. Hence certain theoretical paradigms in psychology may gain great popularity in one socionational milieu, yet wither in another.

Cultural values select and frame the problems relevant in a given society. Briefly, psychologists may differ, as they do in their personal philosophies, on such dimensions as pragmatic effectiveness versus humanist values. In the first instance a psychologist would favor a behaviorist approach to learning or therapy, in the other he or she would opt for a phenomenological school of thought. When Berry (1984) contrasts the American "melting pot" with the Canadian multicultural ideology toward immigrants, he is talking of indigenous differences in cultural values and national policies regarding the otherwise identical problem of absorbing large numbers of new North Americans. The degree to which academic psychologists are actively involved in the sociopolitical problems of their societies is also regulated by value expectations regarding intellectuals and their work: "ivory tower" versus "social responsibility."

It is a classical Marxist thesis that researchers (in social sciences especially) cannot escape their value-ideological commitments. Hence the best one can do is to be aware of one's "indigenous" options and choices in this respect.

Intellectual Style

Finally, intellectual style is a preferred epistemology or methodology that may characterize psychologists from a given national/cultural/regional entity. Examples include experimentation versus correlational methods; clinical studies versus laboratory designs; rationalism versus empiricism. These oppositions are real not only in terms of individual preferences among various researchers (within-group variance), but also as group differences; for instance, psychologists in the Third World countries generally are not in favor of laboratory experimentation (to say nothing about the obvious technological difficulties they face in this respect).

Psychology as a discipline—at least its social branches—belongs to what late nineteenth-century philosophers of science called *Geisteswissenshaften* (Dilthey, 1924/1977), as opposed to natural sciences. Later, sociologists such as Weber (1904/1949) and Znaniecki (1935/1967, 1969) postulated that social studies be conducted by applying the principle of a *humanist coefficient,* that is, with an ultimate goal of *understanding* human phenomena from the inner perspective of experiencing actors, rather than by trying to *explain* events, which is characteristic of the natural sciences. That humanist (or phenomenological) epistemology is close to the emic/etic distinction in cross-cultural psychology (Berry, 1969) and has obvious "indigenizing" consequences, as well as strong anti(neo)positivistic tones, criticizing the latter's claims to universality and hierarchical-reductionist order of sciences. What is of direct importance at this point is the proposition that the humanist or neopositivist epistemologies may be more or less evenly spread out in a given "intellectual territory," contributing to the definition of indigenous psychology of that land.

It is my hope that the above discussion has sufficiently clarified the proposed conditions for conceptualization of indigenous psychology. As to the relations among the three components in the above equation, the asterisk suggests that indigenous problems may be assessed objectively and independent of cultural values (e.g., objective criteria for "malnutrition" or "obesity"). But such "orthogonality" would not be the intended conclusion. Another possibility should also be seriously entertained, that phenomena may appear as problems only when filtered through certain cultural values and intellectual styles (e.g., because of widespread poverty and a different value system, obesity is not a problem in West Africa, but a symbol of wealth and status).

POLISH INDIGENOUS PSYCHOLOGY

Before setting off to develop a model of indigenous Polish psychology, two other remarks may be of some use. The first addresses the issue of accuracy and its criteria: I will be presenting a *prototypical* model of Polish psychology, one that maximizes the number of "family resemblances," hence it should not be seen as falsified by any exemplars fitting in less than perfectly.

The second point is of a more personal character. I was trained in the Polish intellectual tradition, and I obtained my Ph.D. at the University of Warsaw. Yet, during those early formative years or later, I would not have been able to write on indigenous Polish psychology "from within." This has been made possible only owing to my long period of work abroad, first in Nigeria, where I interacted with African, Asian, and Western colleagues, most of them educated in the United Kingdom or the United States; it was there that I first experienced my coming from a different background. Later, during my peregrination through Canada and the United States, that feeling of intellectual identity became an even better defined and sharper cognitive insight. Here is how I see it.[3]

Indigenous Problems

It is not easy to decide on one or a few psychological problems that will stand for an indigenizing *differentia specifica* of a given country; obviously, such problems must be entrenched in historical-social realities of that country. Still, it is my contention that in the case of Poland, the main theme for psychological theorizing and research can be phrased as follows: *interactions and conflicts between the individual and the social system* (the latter including nation, political system, school, and family). This theme could be further specified with three problems:

1. struggle for conditions of individual and national autonomy against threats of internally and externally superimposed systems
2. integration and identification of the individual with the social system(s)
3. effectiveness of social and individual efforts in organized, productive activities

The first two of these are antithetical and reflect the split within the conditions of human living in Poland: individualism, mistrust, and opposition on one hand; nationalistic feelings and "togetherness" or collectivism on the other. The third is seen as a desirable consequence after finding a constructive *modus vivendi* for the former two (it is within the focus of the current reformatory process in the Polish economy).

There are both historically remote and more recent origins of this Polish phenomenon. A short flashback to the past will tell us of the traditions of the earlier unparalleled "golden freedom" (often anarchic and corrupt) enjoyed by the noble class until the end of the eighteenth century. Then came the partitions that swept the sovereign state from maps for 123 years (1795-1918). Those historical circumstances helped to instill hate and mistrust toward external oppressive powers, but also toward any type of government and system of laws. Rebellion was considered the highest national virtue, and 20 years of the Second Republic (1918-1939) were not enough to change that orientation, particularly as the country was torn apart with many social and ethnic conflicts. The years of World War II (1939-1945) witnessed a period of armed resistance and struggle for survival; but again, the military effort was far from integrated, a consequence of deep political divisions. The past 42 years (1945-1987) have marked the once imposed and continuous rule of the Communist party (Staub, Bar-Tal, Karylowski, & Reykowski, 1984). Its programs and strategies of building a society of real socialism in Poland have never enjoyed popular support, which led to another troubled period of cyclic crises and deepening breakdowns in mutual relations between society (nation) and the state symbolized by that Communist party. Hence, facing adverse and threatening conditions, Poles have trained themselves in disobedience, unruliness, and disorganized behavior, but paradoxically, all that was intended to serve individual as well as national survival.

The last element of the triad, that of effective effort in the sphere of economic production, found its manifestation in the *positivist ideology* (openly rival to the romantic themes) in the second half of the nineteenth century, but has failed to shape the social life ever since, because a series of external and internal crises have continuously prevented workable solutions to the first two problems.

The important point arises, whether and to what extent have the abovementioned historic circumstances been reflected in theoretical and research topics undertaken by Polish psychologists? Answering this question positively, one should first observe that the leading orientation in Polish psychology during the past two to three decades has been that of personality and social behavior (Lukaszewski, 1974; Obuchowski, 1970; Reykowski, 1979; see also Derlega & Grzelak, 1982; Staub, Bar-Tal, Karylowski, & Reykowski, 1984). I will concentrate mainly on Reykowski's (1977, 1978, 1979, 1982, 1983, 1984) theory of personality and prosocial behavior, which has been the most influential in Poland and is also perhaps the best known to the outside world. The most prominent aspect of Reykowski's *regulatory theory of personality* is its emphasis, first, on mental representations of self and other social objects as cognitive (iconic and semantic) structures and, second, on their regulatory consequences for egocentric (self-oriented) versus prosocial (helping, altruistic) behavior and for personality change.

There are a number of noticeable differences between Reykowski's theory and many models of prosocial behavior in American psychology. First is the already mentioned link with personality structure, rather than situational social behaviorism; second, Reykowski always considers egocentric orientation as an alternative to altruism, which is a continuation of Znaniecki's (1935/1967) earlier distinction between selfishness and sociability; third (and most important) is his classification of personality mechanisms of helping. Analyzing studies done by American colleagues, Reykowski (1979, 1982) argues that many of them fall into categories that he calls "ipsocentric" (pseudoprosocial) and "endocentric" (activated by self-related considerations). In his view, genuine but neglected (by others) mechanisms of prosocial personality orientation consist of *personal standards generalization,* (endocentric motivation) and *intrinsic* (exocentric motivation) (1979, p. 40).

We shall consider these in more detail, including research examples. The hypothesis of personal standards generalization (PSG) rests on the following reasoning: (a) An individual has cognitive representation of self-related states that he or she considers normal or ideal; (b) when the individual detects a discrepancy between these states and current events, motivation is generated for him or her to improve his or her position vis-à-vis these standards or to restore them; (c) psychological distance (or similarity) to self is the key dimension that people locate others on; and (d) to the extent that another person is perceived as similar to self, that person's state of need (distress, emergency) will generate the same type of motivation as if the observer's self was affected. This type of prosocial motivation is called generalization of personal standards, and its gradient follows the Pavlovian principle of stimulus gradient generalization (Reykowski, 1979, p. 163). In other words, the closer the other to self, the stronger the tendency to respond to the other's needs as if they were one's own.

The effect of similarity is well known in the studies on interpersonal attraction (Byrne, 1971), and it can be extended into the domain of helping: We like those similar to us and hence we help them. Reykowski's theory, however, reaches out beyond that reasoning; specifically, it postulates that research should start with analyzing self-related affects and cognitions before moving to examining the issue of similarity. Reykowski's PSG hypothesis was tested in studies by Karylowski (1975). In his experiment, subjects' measures of self-esteem and interests were first taken, and then they were shown a profile of a "partner's" interests on the same scales. The partner's profile was manipulated so as to provide a high versus low level of similarity; based on such manipulation, level of liking for that fictitious person was measured. Next, subjects went through a period of working for self and for that apparent partner. Karylowski's study produced two important findings: (a) Self-esteem is a moderator of the similarity → attraction relationship—that is, only those who like themselves like those who are similar to them; (b) similarity leads to increased helping and is not moderated by self-esteem, or is independent of self/other-liking path. In brief, similarity demonstrated a strong direct effect on helping but only an interactive effect (depending on self-esteem) on liking. In his discussion of Karylowski's findings, Reykowski (1979, p. 148) interprets them in favor of the PSG mechanism, as not reducible to the attraction paradigm theory.

Self-structure and self-generated motivation are not the only mechanisms regulating prosocial behaviors of humans. Our cognitive system contains representations of many other objects (physical, individual persons, social institutions). Reykowski extends his theorizing concerning self to these representations: Standards of their real or ideal (value laden) states may generate motivation if discrepancies are noticed. This leads to an important theoretical hypothesis of prosocial orientation originating independently and without mediation of self-structure and self-esteem concerns. This line of Reykowski's theorizing proves to be rich in research implications, by suggesting that the potential of prosocial behavior may be enhanced with "switching-on" and "switching-off" techniques, that is, by concentrating attention on representations of other objects or by similar manipulations related to the self (see Reykowski, 1979, pp. 266-280; 1984). Empirical evidence concerning the effects of the "off-self" concentration on enhanced readiness for prosocial behavior (perception of others' problems, offering solutions) is provided by Jarymowicz (1979). The most interesting test of Reykowski's theorizing should be credited again to Karylowski (1982, 1984), who proposed a distinction between *endocentric* (self-esteem mediated) and *exocentric* (selfless, "pure," altruistic) mechanisms of helping. Karylowski gathered two types of data in support for his theory-derived hypotheses. First, he designed a semiprojective technique called the Prosocial Motivation Inventory (PMI), intended to measure endocentric versus exocentric reasons (justifications) for helping others. With the PMI he found that adolescent subjects who scored high in endo- versus exocentric altruism had different socialization experiences: Mothers of endocentric girls, in their socialization techniques, frequently resorted to the child's moral self and guilt feelings; mothers of exocentrics reported more other-oriented inducements. Second, in experimental demonstrations, Karylowski (1982, 1984) found that self-focused attention generally diminished the altruistic orientation, except for endocentric individuals who held prosocial norms highly relevant for their self-esteem.

Interest in the self, in Polish psychology, has not been limited to the problem of its inhibiting or (sometimes) promoting role in prosocial orientation. I have researched extensively the dimension of psychological distance. In a series of studies, I found that ethnicity and task outcome were the dimensions of self-other similarity that affected attributional style (egotism) and evaluative perception of the actor (Boski, 1983, 1988b). In a different context, I used similarity between self and a national prototype as a measure of immigrants' acculturation and identity (Boski, 1991).

Finally, as a possible "counteraction" to emphasizing similarity and egocentrism, some recent works have concentrated on such aspects of self as individuality and need for uniqueness (Jarymowicz, 1984), freedom (Kofta,

1984), autonomy, and sense of self-directedness (ongoing projects in Rey-kowski's laboratory).

The question the reader may be asking at this point can be stated as fol-lows: Is the connection between the Polish dilemma of individualism versus togetherness and the above representative research topics on prosocial be-havior and self-structure well and convincingly proven? Or can one even perhaps argue that the correspondence is at best, remote? In the sense that Reykowski's theory is abstract, and most of the studies that emerged from it are experimental, the rationale for raising such questions or doubts is well understood. I have not been able to find appropriate research examples that would be closer to individualism and prosocial solidarity during any of the political crises that have shaken Polish society since World War II. Obvi-ously, bringing the current political problems into the laboratory or taking them to the streets as field studies would be equally as interesting as politi-cally unwise. And, after all, theoretically oriented psychology has justifiable ambitions to formulate principles that will transcend dramatic current events. My contention is that the enormous concentration of Polish psychology on prosocial orientation and on self is not coincidental. How could it be just a coincidence that such theories have been born in a country where personal sacrifice for supreme national values and personal dignity, and not economic profit or prosperity, has been a rule modeled and passed from generation to generation during the past 200 years? And in a country where costs and eco-nomic categories in general (always present in American models of helping!) have traditionally been held in low esteem?

Finally, although we do not have studies on helping among Solidarity members or self-centeredness among Communist party members, there are important general or essay-type contributions of Polish psychologists to cur-rent sociopolitical problems. I will leave the analysis of psychologists' po-litical involvement to the closing part of this chapter and concentrate on another theoretical problem that has received professional attention: person-ality change. Again, personality change is hardly mentioned by American psychologists in other than clinical contexts. The situation is essentially dif-ferent in the work of Polish psychologists, obviously reflecting dramatic social change that all living generations of Poles have witnessed and experi-enced during their lifetimes. Hence personality change has been an inherent part of Reykowski's regulatory theory (as well as of Lukaszewski's and Obuchowski's writings). In a paper devoted to that topic, Reykowski (1983) proposes a conceptual framework for analyzing personality change in re-sponse to social change. His basic assumption has been that social change causes a strain upon a person's stabilized cognitive network, including his or her values, meanings, and expectations. Depending on its scope and impact in relation to the prevailing "systems of individual meanings," social change may be assimilated, may destabilize the personality system, or may lead to positive changes. In the last case, Reykowski differentiates between an adaptive (external) change, construction of a parallel (alternative) personality, and "deep" change, which entails restructuring of an individual's cognitive (semantic) system. Without going into a detailed discussion of this proposition, it would be proper to note that the theoretical outline of personality change has obvious affinity to the already discussed mechanisms of helping behavior. Similarities can be seen at two levels of analysis: a "shallow" one, where quasi-prosocial actions correspond to assimilative-behavioral change; and a "deep" personality level, where intrinsic prosocial motivation corresponds to restructuring of the individual's semantic system.

One might wish that Reykowski's conceptual opening would initiate systematic studies on personality configurations and changes in the Poland of today. So far, unmatched in this respect is Floryan Znaniecki's (1935) classic *Ludzie terazniejsi a cywilizacja przyszlosci* (Contemporary People and Civilization of the Future), where the author compares "people of work," "well-behaved people," and "people of leisure"—corresponding to the main social strata of pre-World War II Poland. But even without further documentation the above analysis should be sufficiently convincing as to the importance of "personality in social context" as a distinct subject matter in Polish psychology, reflecting fundamental problems of that society.

The theme of efficient and organized behavior is perhaps less represented in theoretical works of Polish psychologists. It is important, however, to mention here the tradition of the Lvov-Warsaw school of logic and philosophy and the names of its two representatives, Kotarbinski and Tomaszewski. The first was not a psychologist, but a philosopher with interests mainly in the fields of logic, methodology, and ethics. The discipline of *praxiology,* which Kotarbinski (1965) originated, was designed as a metatheory of organized action: goal efficient and cost-effective. In the field of psychology, Tomaszewski (1963) proposed a similar type of *theory of action,* which postulated human behavior structured in molar units, called "tasks." (I will return to Tomaszewski's work later, in the discussion of cognitive style and epistemology in Polish psychology.) It should also be added that the concept of task has been central in the already discussed personality theories of Reykowski, Obuchowski, and Lukaszewski. Reykowski (1976), at the earlier stage of his work on prosocial behavior, made a distinction between *allocentric* and *sociocentric* types; the former characterizes activity organized around satisfying needs of another person, whereas the latter is conceived as a task formulated and executed within the framework of a social institution. The concept of a prosocial task refers to its superordinate role in integrating "molecular" behavior. Obuchowski (1977), on the other hand, theorized about hierarchical tasks, which organize a person's life within a time perspective stretched into the future. Such tasks form conditions for stability and autonomy of personality. Obuchowski contrasted such a mode of personality functioning with the one where a person operates within the context of concrete, here-and-now tasks, and is controlled or swayed by changing situations.

As this chapter is being written at a time when radical economic and sociopolitical reforms are being introduced, it may be hoped that in the coming years we shall witness even greater involvement on the part of Polish psychologists, as they share in solving the above-discussed indigenous problems of their society.

Cultural Values: Catholic and Marxist Humanism

Humanism is the ethical system to which all orientations of Polish sociocultural life subscribe, particularly those of the Catholic tradition but also the Marxist ideology (so far as it tries to dissociate from Stalinist deformations). Here also, the correlated nature of indigenous problems and social values is clearly seen: Prosocial functioning, personal autonomy, and change are not only manifestations of the problems of Polish society, translated into the language of academic psychology. There is definitely a valuation process associated with them, such that individual self-directedness and prosocial orientation are positive accomplishments of humanist values, whereas alienation or egocentrism create reasons for humanist concern.[4]

Christian humanism in its Polish version is usually called *personalism,* with the roots in Thomas Aquinas's philosophy and Roman Catholic doctrine. An outstanding representative of this orientation, during his academic career, was Karol Cardinal Wojtyla, who continues that line of social ethics in his teachings and encyclicals as Pope John Paul II. Although personalism conceives the ultimate fulfillment of human nature in its spiritual relationship with God, its social ethics emphasizes inalienable rights of human beings to live in sociopolitical conditions where freedom and dignity, as well as communal values, are preserved. In its critical terms, Catholic personalism is aimed against all kinds of political oppression and economic exploitation, and also against materialistic consumerism, be it of Eastern or Western origin.

Socialist humanism is a rival ethical doctrine in Poland. It was born after the fall of Stalinism in 1956, and professed by philosophers who considered themselves or were considered by the party apparatus as "Marxist-revisionists" (Kolakowski, Schaff, Fritzhand, Suchodolski, and others). Socialist humanism claims its origins in the writings of the young Marx (e.g., "The Economic-Philosophical Manuscripts," 1844). Its main slogan is "Full emancipation of human persons from all kinds of alienation." In the not very remote past of the late 1960s, Polish "Marxist-revisionists" showed intellectual and personal courage in analyzing various forms of alienation, not only in the Western capitalist, but also in socialist type of society. Today, even the top official authorities make attempts at declaring support for humanist values, to the extent that General Jaruzelski has coined the term *socialist personalism.*

With the above ideological background, it should not be surprising that Polish psychology in general can be called a *humanist psychology.* Here again studies on altruism can serve as the best illustration of this thesis. No one will perhaps contest the idea of positive valuation associated with prosocial behavior, but there is more than that in the context of works centered on Reykowski's theory. In his monograph on prosocial motivation and personality, Reykowski (1979, pp. 69-84) shows that Marxist philosophy should be seen as one of the inspiring sources of the current psychology of prosocial orientation. First of all, Marxism strongly emphasizes social and historical aspects of "human nature" shaped and changed by social relations; the latter are determined by ownership of the means of production and the type of production relations resulting from that ownership (Lange, 1963, chaps. 1, 2). In this approach, no question concerning human egoism or altruism can be answered in general, but always in reference to a specific socioeconomic formation. For instance, the capitalist mode of production is characterized by private ownership of the means of production and by production relations of capital and hired labor. Individualistic or egoistic motives (profit motive, exploitation, and so on) are seen as inherent to the system, vital for continuation and survival of the capitalist economy; economic determinism of human actions overrides the person's "good intentions" or altruistic tendencies. Hence the theory postulates a "structural inhibition" to prosocial behavior in capitalist society. Marxism (in its nondogmatic forms) allows, however, for social awareness being more than a reflection of actual social reality: Ideology may create ideal standards and motivation to change the present order of things. Socialist ideology and political programs based on it are the evident examples of this thesis. The content of socialist ideal standards is definitely prosocial, antiegoistic. One could thus conclude that a particular interest in the psychology of prosocial orientation can be derived from the humanist values of socialist ideology; this thesis certainly offers a broadened contextual account as to how Reykowski's "Warsaw school of prosocial motivation" was born.

Other aspects of humanism will require more elaboration now. The most convenient way to start is to recall a conceptual opposition, particularly meaningful in the American context, between *behaviorism* and *humanism* (symbolized, for instance, in controversies between Skinner and Rogers). Consequently, let us look at behaviorism from that ethical perspective. Not coincidentally, one of Skinner's books bears the title *Beyond Freedom and Dignity* (1971). Here, behaviorism is not concerned with those and other human values as perceived and experienced phenomenologically. Radical behaviorism (Skinnerian version) is interested in efficient external control of human behavior (Skinner, 1974), whereas its modified, "revisionist" version would replace the above with internal control, that is, competence and efficacy (Bandura, 1986). The behaviorist framework is a psychological extension of ethical pragmatism or utilitarianism, and a related concept of "enlightened self-interest"; it represents the heart and soul of the "American life-style." A reference to Boring's (1950, pp. 505-508) analysis of functionalism (predecessor of behaviorism) as a manifestation of American indigenous psychology, in response to the values of a pioneer, individualistic, and success-oriented country, is again relevant at this point. Contrary to that, "humanism" has been placed at the periphery of American culture, and "humanist psychology" is hardly recognized in its academic circles.

Looking back to the Polish scene, we find that behaviorism, because of its antihumanist nature as well as some epistemological characteristics discussed in the next section, did not make its mark in the history of Polish psychology. It is possible, but only to a limited degree, to conceptualize prosocial acts within the behaviorist tradition: They will then appear as instrumental to obtaining individualistic rewards. Prosocial behaviors motivated by instrumentality and exchange principles are rightly called *pseudoprosocial* (Reykowski, 1979, p. 40). It is only on the ethical grounds of humanism that mechanisms of helping such as Reykowski's off-self ideal standards could have originated. The applied problems of "making our world more prosocial" can also be differentially addressed in this context. The behaviorist guideline, "Ensure that doing positive things to others is profitable or equitable to the actor," would not be accepted in the Polish situation on ethical grounds. Instead, enhancing or facilitating access of ideal standards (off-self objects related) has become the goal in experimental research and for practical tasks. The last illustration shows a relative independence of indigenous problems and values. The problem of enhancing prosocial solidarity can be approached in either a behaviorist or a humanist way—the decision depends on value choices.

No other applied field better documents the antibehaviorist, humanist nature of Polish psychology than clinical psychology does, particularly the theory and practice of psychotherapy. An essential feature of Polish approaches to psychotherapy today is its tight connection with theories of personality, which formulate its goal as constructive, deep changes in the personality (references to Reykowski's and Obuchowski's works are appropriate here). In other words, it is not a specific behavior that is the root problem, and that should be modified in order to improve the patient's psychological adjustment, but his or her personality structure, that is, the patient's cognitive representations and affective attachments, as well as modes of interaction (communication) between self and others. Hence it is an insight-cognitive type of psychotherapy, and its humanist values can best be appreciated in rejection of behavioral therapy as a "shallow" and "manipulative" technology. A number of colleagues deserve to be mentioned as proponents of the outlined approach, including Mellibruda, Jankowski, and Grzesiuk. On the research side, Grzesiuk (1978, 1979) has been studying pathology of interpersonal communication. She has been investigating healthy or *partnership* versus disturbed or *nonpartnership* (egocentric) styles of interactions in normal and clinical populations. The therapeutic process, in her framework, is regarded as a means of experiencing one's (or a people's) destructive communication patterns and working toward a partnership style.

It should be further said that the experiential, interaction-oriented style of clinical psychology characterizes university teaching programs, starting at the undergraduate level. There, students admitted to the clinical specialization first spend many hours in training groups as clients and later as cotherapists under a teacher-clinician's supervision. This type of program is practically unknown in North America, and it reflects the role attributed to the quality of the clinician's personality and communication skills as the main diagnostic and therapeutic factors. On the other hand, behavior modification approaches and technologies are given marginal attention in clinical programs offered at Polish universities. The conclusion we may reach here is this: The theory and practice of psychotherapy in Poland implement the humanist value system of the society, to strengthen the individual's dignity in intra- and interpersonal integration.

It is not surprising that the Western schools of psychotherapy currently enjoying highest popularity in the Polish clinical community are Rogers's person-oriented therapy, Gestalt therapy (Perls), transactional analysis (Berne), and various versions of psychodynamic or existential systems. Those movements with emphasis upon self-actualization, free expression, spontaneity, and existential being have been more successful in Poland than in the United States, where they have remained labeled as counterculture and regarded with intellectual suspicion. Rogers, in his *A Way of Being* (1980), reflects that nowhere else did he receive such enthusiastic reception as in Poland. If he had had the background information provided here, he would not, perhaps, have been as surprised as he was. Because of Polish intellectual and ethical tradition, not only had behavior therapy or modification never before been given serious thought or practiced in clinical settings, but the individualistic-anarchistic character of the California-born humanistic psychology appealed to the needs of many Poles, disillusioned with their political situation. A classical Rogerian incongruence has emerged for millions between their reality of experienced facts and phony ideology served by the Communist party, the so-called success propaganda of the 1970s.

Yet, it should be clear from the above discussion that the humanist character of Polish psychology has much deeper roots in fundamental social values and intellectual traditions of the land, compared with the esoteric character of the American humanistic psychology of Rogers and Perls, which lacks sound theoretical reflection and never grew above the level of counterculture. On the contrary, Polish psychology is inherently humanistic by being anchored in the core value system of its culture. The one-sided individualism in American versions of self-actualization has also been criticized by Reykowski (1979, pp. 61-69) and contrasted with Polish/European humanism, which emphasizes equally the values of other individuals (partners, fellow citizens, humans).

Intellectual Style or Preferred Epistemology

Two points that characterize Polish intellectual style and articulate themselves in psychology are hypothetical-deductive rationalism and a sharp distinction between natural sciences and humanities/social sciences, with psychology belonging to the latter category.

Methodology, perhaps more than anything else, is the unifying ground in scientific endeavor. Yet, there is a variability in epistemological approaches to psychology, particularly in the relationship between theory and empirical data. Relevant in a general sense and useful for present purposes is the distinction, introduced by Popper (1968), between two modes of theory construction: *hypothetical-deductive* ("top-down") versus *empiricist-inductive* ("bottom-up"). Both have had traditions in European philosophy, the former being associated with Continental rationalism and the latter with British empiricism (and then with American pragmatism). The hypothetical-deductive strategy can be characterized by a relative dominance of theory over data and falsification as a principle of testing. Inductive empiricism is much more data oriented and cautions against unjustified theoretical speculations. In Polish social sciences, the Popperian hypothetical-deductive strategy has gained high acceptance over the much criticized inductive empiricism (Malewski, 1974).

Current cognitive (and social cognitive) theories of perception, memory, or thinking can be seen as examples of the hypothetical-deductive strategy becoming a paradigm in psychology. The role of hypothetical constructs is highly emphasized there (such constructs as prototype and schema). On the other hand, behaviorism, social learning, and trait-psychometric approaches are obvious examples of data-oriented empiricism. Skinnerian operant behaviorism and Catellian factor-analytic studies both considerably reduce the scope and role of theorizing, although they very much differ in concrete methods of data collection: experimentation versus psychometry. Skinner, in particular, has best exemplified the methodological postulates of radical neopositivism, which wanted theoretical statements to be nothing but short-hand notation of empirical procedures and observations.

Depending on one's criteria of evaluation, much of Polish psychology's weakness or strength has to do with its tilt toward theory at some expense of data. This comes as a consequence of an antibehaviorist stand and of older mentalistic traditions. If we take again Reykowski's theory as a representative example, many constructs will be found where empirical interpretation (partial operationalization) is complex: "Regulatory mechanisms of social behavior," "categories of social object coding," "network of cognitive representations," "position of self in cognitive system," and "intrinsic prosocial motivation" are just some of his basic theoretical terms. The distance between the language of theory and that of empirical description is equally large in Obuchowski's (1970) distinction between *concrete* and *hierarchical* codes of functioning, and in Lukaszewski's (1974) cognitive dimensions of personality.

Observation and personal experience show that the just-discussed features of Polish psychology may create problems of communication with psychologists who are more down to earth in the matter of theorizing. But that is very much in the Polish style: When facing a dilemma between well-established but simple data and an interesting but only hypothetical relationship, choose the latter and call the former "shallow" or "superficial."

Apart from the preference for the hypothetical-deductive mode of theorizing, the richness of theoretical constructs and "intervening variables" in Polish psychology should be related to its humanist and nonnaturalistic orientation. It comes as a consequence of the thesis reiterated here (at the risk of being repetitious) that Polish psychology has never been influenced by behaviorism, but defined itself as a *Geisteswissenshaft.* From the university professor to the student taking a course in introductory psychology, there is consensus that psychology is a science of human consciousness, affective and cognitive processes, and purposeful action, but not a science of "living organisms' behavior."

Once again, a comparison with North American psychology, which so often "sets the standards" for others, seems appropriate. Boring's observation that adaptability and evolution are the key concepts and guidelines for American psychology is as relevant today as it was 100 years ago. A society that is factually and ideologically "young" programatically shunned the cultures and traditions of Old Worlds (of any other continent), offering a "melting pot" instead. The symbolic refrain is that cultures are "idiosyncratic

uniforms" of no utilitarian value and that they constrain individual entre-
preneurship. Humans stripped of their cultures appear as "human animals,"
and as such become one among many other species of interest for psychologists. Consequently, biological explanations of human behavior, even in
social psychology, abound in the United States (e.g., sociobiological approaches to helping, aggression, leadership). The Polish, and perhaps European, perspective is dramatically different. On the premises of qualitatively
different human brain structures and uniquely human sociocultural environments, human psychology has been developed, with cognitive/semantic representation and affective experience of the world as its key features.

A short historical sketch of the discipline in Poland may be helpful for a
better understanding of these phenomena. Psychology, as it was conceived
and practiced at German and Austrian universities in the late nineteenth century, came to Polish academic institutions with little delay. The first laboratory, modeled after Wundt's, was established by Heinrich in Krakow in 1897.
It was, however, Twardowski, head of philosophy at the University of Lvov
from 1895 to 1938, who is considered the founding father of Polish psychology (see Misiak & Stautd, 1954, chap. 12). Twardowski was a student of
Brentano, and clearly more interested in psychology of "acts" than of
Wundtian experimentation on elementary "contents" (sensations). In contrast with the German type of introspectionism, with its roots in physiology,
Polish psychology of consciousness had stronger links with epistemology
and logic. That was again owed to Twardowski, the originator of the "Lvov-
Warsaw school." That school produced such influential philosophers/
logicians as Ajdukiewicz, Lukasiewicz, Ossowska, and Kotarbinski on one
hand, but parallel to them were psychologists Witwicki, Kreutz, Baley, and
Tomaszewski. That is why the first generation of Polish psychologists was
more interested in higher mental processes of thinking, reasoning, and representation than in Wundtian sensationism. On the same grounds, *Gestalt
psychology* was known and appreciated before World War II. To summarize,
the first half of this century saw Polish psychology born and growing as a
science of human consciousness, and particularly that of higher mental processes, studied by introspectionist methodology.

That situation was brought to an end soon after World War II, but not as
much by the war itself as by the political events of the Communist takeover
and the Stalinist period of 1948-1956. Those years profoundly affected all
aspects of Polish academic life. Psychology in its previous form was banned,
departments were closed, and the only tolerated activity in the field became
that of Pavlovian conditioning (behaviorism), more as an ideological tool
than as a creative science. Not surprisingly, with the advent of a post-Stalinist
thaw, there was a strong "reactance" tendency against Pavlovism, but equally against American behaviorism of those days. Two examples will illustrate

this thesis. The first is on the negative side and concerns the work of Konorski (1969), himself a student of Pavlov, whose studies on the integrative function of the brain, although highly acclaimed, were never considered as a psychological theory because they were largely based on animal studies. The other example from the early 1960s is Tomaszewski's (1963) theory of action, already mentioned. Tomaszewski, himself a student of Twardowski, was earlier an articulate critic of introspectionism (for its increasing irrelevance and methodological dead ends). But later, he equally rejected the molecular and mechanistic S→R type of psychology. Instead, he postulated that human behavior be analyzed and studied in a molar paradigm: T→O—that is, task→outcome. Tomaszewski postulated S→R chains within a task activity, but it was the latter that he considered a superordinate, goal-oriented, and awareness-intentional structure. Tomaszewski's theory of action was an original fusion of introspectionism and early cognitive psychology. Tolman and particularly Miller, Galanter, and Pribram (authors of *Plans and the Structure of Behavior,* symbolized by the TOTE scheme) were his favorite psychologists on the American continent. Also, as shown earlier, a theory of action was convergent with praxiology, a "methodology of efficient action," developed by Kotarbinski. With time, Tomaszewski's interests evolved into problems of consciousness, acquisition, and structure of knowledge (Tomaszewski, 1976).

Besides his theoretical influence, Tomaszewski personally played the role of an intellectual mentor to a number of students, and through them he was able to establish a paradigm or school of psychology comparable only to that of Twardowski, a half century ago. Those who belonged to that school became themselves active researchers in the 1960s and 1970s, covering a number of areas defining the field of modern psychology: cognitive and psycholinguistics (Kozielecki, Kurcz), social-personality (Reykowski, Fraczek, Lukaszewski), and psychophysiology (Strelau). All of these leading figures in today's Polish psychology claim allegiance to Tomaszewski's theory of action.

The legacy of Tomaszewski's conceptual framework can be traced most directly in the works of Kozielecki, a highly reputed cognitive psychologist. Kozielecki (1981) mathematized Tomaszewski's theory of action in the domain of risk taking, decision making, and thinking. Although the experimental part of his work has strong affinity with American models of risk, utility, and expectation, he is first of all a theoretician with a rigorous background from the Polish school of mathematics and logic. Moreover, his psychological decision theory is broad in theoretical scope and applications, comprising some research problems traditionally belonging to personality (e.g., level of aspiration, plans, goals, and self), and clinical psychology (e.g., clinical diagnosis/judgment). Not surprisingly, Kozielecki's interests have recently turned to even broader domains, such as theory/philosophy of science, religion, and the psychology of intellectuals.

It may be noted that continuation of the Lvov school of rationalism in Kotarbinski's praxiology and Tomaszewski's theory of action appears as the Polish version of pragmatism. One may also ask whether this version of psychology is compatible with its humanist character, so strongly emphasized before. The key element providing the link between the two is again Tomaszewski's concept of *task*. Human actions are structured in tasks, some impersonal (e.g., achievement) and some interpersonal (e.g., prosocial). All, however, are cognitive structures that integrate values, goals, and intentions at the level of individual consciousness; at the same time, tasks also integrate individual actors with other performers in a social system of superordinate tasks.

ON "BEING" AND "DOING": SOCIAL ROLES OF PSYCHOLOGISTS IN POLAND

In his analysis of social roles played by the men of science, Znaniecki (1965) proposes a typology related to such activities as creation, systematization, continuation, and implementation of scientific knowledge. But academicians work and live outside their ivory towers of pure science. In each society, scientists and academicians form a distinct social group: the intellectual elite. Yet, there are reasons to believe that the role of that group may vary from one society to another. In Poland, the role and status ascribed to *intelligentsia* has been unique indeed; theirs has been the role of storing, upholding, and transmitting national values and the raising of national conscience (Chalasinski, 1946; Szczepanski, 1966). Intellectuals as spiritual leaders were of particular importance for national survival during the periods of subjugation to external powers. But as such historical periods are not remote and internal crises shake the nation's present days, intellectuals could not retreat to more neutral roles of professional experts only, as seems to be the case in the West. Hence university professors often speak out as moral arbiters and present their own points of view and perspectives on current national affairs. In comparison with their colleagues in the West, and in North America in particular, Polish intellectuals are much more politically active. There are, of course, examples of Western individuals playing prominent roles in the world of academia and politics elsewhere, but except for political science there seems to be a separation between the two. For Polish professors, in contrast, it is the rule, rather than the exception, to write for daily or weekly newspapers, to present views on television programs, to sit on expert panels or advisory committees, to be elected to provincial councils or to the national Parliament, to hold ministerial positions, or to be vocal members of the opposition. Psychologists are among them too. They say more than their research data reveal; they do not refrain from essay types of analyses on such issues as "psychological mechanisms of political crisis: trust and accountability"; "political alienation of the state-party authorities"; "conditions for the dialogue between the state authorities and opposition"; "working toward national cohesion and agreements"; "psychological factors on economic reforms"; "does real socialism contradict the laws of psychology?"; and "the elected or the outcasts: reflections on immigration of Polish intellectuals."[5] The name of the often-mentioned Professor Reykowski is well known to the reading public, but so are Kozielecki, Obuchowski, and others. Equally active are applied psychologists, particularly in the fields of school/educational and clinical psychology.

Hence we can conclude that the humanistic nature of Polish psychology is revealed not only in its being about people, but in its being for the people.

IMPLICATIONS AND CONCLUSIONS

What is the broader context for analyses such as the one attempted in this chapter, on national indigenous psychologies, their potential uses and implications? First of all, a claim for indigenous psychologies is a logical derivation from two more fundamental premises: (a) cultural and (b) historical determinism of human psychological processes. The first defines the domain of cross-cultural psychology as an established subdiscipline in contemporary psychology. The other premise can be exemplified in some psychologists' historical meta-analyses on the status of our discipline (Gergen, 1973, 1984). The argument goes, given that psychological phenomena differ along synchronic and diachronic orders, theoretical thinking and research on them must bring different results also. In short, by proposing the idea of indigenous psychology one has to take a position in defining our discipline as a cultural and historical science. Moreover, because science itself is a social activity within a cultural/historical context, its focus and angle of concentration depend on values and epistemological styles of a given place and time. Hence the postulate to extend the emic characteristics of ordinary cognition to scientific endeavor called indigenous psychology.

On the other side of this coin, by taking such steps one must decide against psychology defined as a natural science. The latter implication for academic/professional identification is serious indeed; it would be a gross distortion of reality to declare that either cross-cultural or historical social psychology is widely recognized or in the "mainstream" of our science. The standard position, at least on the domineering American stage, is to ascribe psychology the status of a natural science.

Realism should counsel us to avoid extremes, and a realistic assessment of psychology cannot deny universal principles in basic processes (cognition, emotions, development) in our *Homo sapiens* species. Hence a formula of selectivity appears as the most satisfactory heuristic: The impact of cultural and historical factors, defined by symbolic meaning and values, should be most pronounced in the domains of social functioning. Consequently, indigenous aspects of national/regional psychologies should be most obvious in social psychology and negligible in physiological psychology.

The construction of Polish indigenous psychology has followed that instruction: It has concentrated almost exclusively on its social branches and some general, paradigmatic principles. That was the reason for leaving aside such highly influential work as Jan Strelau's (1983) theory of temperamental traits and their physiological mechanisms (which has a number of points tangential with Eysenck's basic dimensions of personality). Construing a model of indigenous psychology along the three proposed components (problems, values, and intellectual styles) is not different from the goals set by sociology of science (knowledge): to document the influence of social factors in the process of knowledge formation and its final results. Such a type of meta-analysis has the task of enhancing scientific self-awareness and stands in its own right. Yet potential benefits of such autoreflection can be broader: to control the dangers of academic ethnocentrism, and also to guide cross-cultural studies by testing the limits of generalizations obtained from studying (apparently) indigenous problems with the tools of indigenous approaches.

The present chapter has met its objectives to the extent that it adds to Polish psychologists' self-awareness and to other readers' sense of their indigenous contrasts.

NOTES

1. The paper in its present format was completed in 1987. In the last six years, events of historical scale have taken place in Poland and the whole region of Central-Eastern Europe: the collapse of communism and the beginning of transformation toward a new political and economic system. These changes, I believe, do not make the main theses of my paper outdated but demand a broadened perspective. If edited today, the text would have to integrate such phenomena as: psychologists participating politically in the transition period, appearance of political psychology as a new domain of scientific inquiry, or psychologists in a market economy.

2. Among those presenting at this symposium, the proponents of indigenous psychology defined as ethnic lay psychology were Joseph Trimble, Rogelio Diaz-Guerrero, and Denise Jodelet. The second approach, conceiving of the field of indigenous psychology as tantamount to cultural specificity of national schools of academic psychology was present in papers by Durganand Sinha, John Berry, E. Sampson, and me.

3. Earlier drafts of this chapter were read by my colleagues at the University of Warsaw in Poland and by others living outside of the country. I wish to express my special gratitude to Dr. Lidia Grzesiuk, who, on my behalf, asked many Polish psychologists to share with me their opinions about the text; she then collected them and sent the feedback to me. It was a time-consuming and uneasy job, but very helpful for me, who—living abroad—may have missed some important works, references, and above all the zeitgeist of the most recent years. The following persons were willing to share their views with me: Professor T. Tomaszewski, Professor S. Mika, Dr. K. Skarznska, and Dr. Grzesiuk. Professor J. Reykowski sent me words of encouragement, writing that "the type of work you have undertaken is unprecedented in Polish psychology." Also, Dr. J. Karylowski, now at the University of North Florida, showed a similar interest and made supportive comments.

4. This text is being written in the United States, and as this country serves as a source of immediate contrasts, it should be noted that the term *humanism* is very rarely used in this society; when it is, it is often specified as *secular humanism,* a doctrine that is seen as in opposition to fundamentalist Christian Protestantism. All such associations would be highly misleading. Polish humanism is a part of the great European tradition that originated in ancient Greece and in modern times has been present philosophically since the Renaissance.

5. What is even more important, Reykowski was the politburo member during the last year of the Communist Party existence. He was the chief political negotiator during the Round Table Talks with Solidarity (February-April 1989), which led to peaceful transition to the post-Communist era.

REFERENCES

Bandura, A. (1986). *Social foundations of thought and action: A social-cognitive theory.* Englewood Cliffs, NJ: Prentice-Hall.

Berry, J. W. (1969). On cross-cultural comparability. *International Journal of Psychology, 4,* 119-128.

Berry, J. W. (1976). *Human ecology and cognitive style.* New York: Halsted.

Berry, J. W. (1984). Multicultural attitudes and education. In R. J. Samuda, J. W. Berry, & M. Laferrière (Eds.), *Multiculturalism in Canada.* Toronto: Allyn & Bacon.

Berry, J. W., Poortinga, Y., Segall, M. H., & Dasen, P. (1988). *Cross-cultural psychology: Research and applications.* New York: Cambridge University Press.

Boring, E. G. (1950). *A history of experimental psychology* (2nd ed.). New York: Appleton-Century-Crofts.

Boski, P. (1983). Egotism and evaluation in self and other attributions for achievement-related outcomes. *European Journal of Social Psychology, 13,* 287-304.

Boski, P. (1988). Cross-cultural studies of person perception: Effects of ingroup/outgroup membership and ethnic schemata. *Journal of Cross-Cultural Psychology, 19,* 287-328.

Boski, P. (1991). On becoming a Canadian or remaining a Pole: Change and stability of national self-identity among Polish immigrants in Canada. *Journal of Applied Psychology, 21*(1), 41-77.

Byrne, D. E. (1971). *The attraction paradigm.* New York: Academic Press.
Chalasinski, J. (1946). *Geneza inteligencji polskiej* [On the origins of Polish intelligentsia]. Warsaw: Cztelnik.
Derlega, V., & Grzelak, J. (Eds.). (1982). *Cooperation and helping behavior: Theory and research.* New York: Academic Press.
Dilthey, W. (1977). *Descriptive psychology and historical understanding.* The Hague: Martinus Nijhoff. (Original work published 1924)
Gergen, K. J. (1973). Social psychology as history. *Journal of Personality and Social Psychology, 26,* 309-320.
Gergen, K. J. (1984). An introduction to historical social psychology. In K. J. Gergen & M. M. Gergen (Eds.), *Historical social psychology.* Hillsdale, NJ: Lawrence Erlbaum.
Grzesiuk, L. (1978). Interpersonalne komunikowanie sie jako przejaw postaw spolecznych [Interpersonal communication as a means of social attitudes expression]. In J. Reykowski (Ed.), *Teoria osobowosci a zachowania prospoleczne* [Theory of personality and prosocial behaviors]. Warsaw: PAN.
Grzesiuk, L. (1979). *Style komunikacji interpersonalnej* [Styles of interpersonal communication]. Warsaw: PWN.
Jarymowicz, M. (1979). *Modyfikowanie wyobrazen dotyczacych 'ja' dla zwiekszania gotowosci do zachowan prospolecznych* [Modification of self-referent images to increase readiness for prosocial behaviors]. Wroclaw: Ossolineum.
Jarymowicz, M. (1984). *Spostrzeganie wlasnej indywidualnosci* [Perceiving one's individuality]. Wroclaw: Ossolineum.
Karylowski, J. (1975). *Z badan nad mechanizmami pozytywnych ustosunkowan interpersonalnych* [Studies on the mechanisms of positive interpersonal orientations]. Wroclaw: Ossolineum.
Karylowski, J. (1982). Two types of altruistic behavior: Doing good to feel good or to make others feel good. In V. Derlega & J. Grzelak (Eds.), *Cooperation and helping behavior: Theory and research.* New York: Academic Press.
Karylowski, J. (1984). Focus of attention and altruism: Endocentric and exocentric sources of altruistic behavior. In E. Staub, D. Bar-Tal, J. Karylowski, & J. Reykowski (Eds.), *Development and maintenance of prosocial behavior.* New York: Plenum.
Kofta, M. (1984). Freedom of choice and moral behavior. In E. Staub, D. Bar-Tal, J. Karylowski, & J. Reykowski (Eds.), *Development and maintenance of prosocial behavior.* New York: Plenum.
Konorski, J. (1969). *Integracyjina rola mozgu* [Integrative function of the brain]. Warsaw: PWN.
Kotarbinski, T. (1965). *Praxiology: An introduction to the science of efficient action.* Oxford: Pergamon.
Kozielecki, J. (1981). *Psychological decision theory.* Dordrecht, Netherlands: D. Reidel/Polish Scientific Publishers.
Lange, O. (1963). *Political economy* (Vol. 1). New York: Pergamon.
Lukaszewski, W. (1974). *Osobowosc: Struktura i funkcje regulacyjne* [Personality: Structure and regulatory functions]. Warsaw: PWN.
Malewski, A. (1974). *Studia z metodologii nauk spolecznych* [Studies in methodology of social sciences]. Warsaw: PWN.
Misiak, H., & Stautd, V. M. (1954). *Catholics in psychology: A historical survey.* New York: McGraw-Hill.
Obuchowski, K. (1970). *Kody orientacji i struktura procesow emocjonalnych* [Orientation codes and the structure of emotional processes]. Warsaw: PWN.

Obuchowski, K. (1977). Autonomia jednostki a osobowosc [Individual autonomy and personality]. In J. Reykowski, O. Owaynnikowa, & K. Obuchowski (Eds.), *Szkice z psychologii emocji, osobowosci i motywacji* [Essays in the psychology of emotions, personality, and motivation]. Warsaw: Ossolineum.

Popper, K. R. (1968). *The logic of scientific discovery.* London: Hutchinson.

Reykowski, J. (1976). Nastawienia egocentrycrne i nastawienia prospolezne [Egocentric and prosocial orientations]. In J. Reykowski (Ed.), *Osobowosc a spoleczne zachowanie sie ludzi* [Personality and human social behavior]. Warsaw: KiW.

Reykowski, J. (1977). Osobowosc w perspektywie rewolucji naukowo-technicznej [Personality in the perspective of scientific-technological revolution]. In T. M. Jaroszewskj (Ed.), *Prezemiany osobowosci w spoleczenstwie socjalistycznym* [Personality transformations in a socialist śociety]. Warsaw: KiW.

Reykowski, J. (1978). Podstawowe mechanizmy regulacji spolecznego zachowania sie czlowieka [Fundamental regulatory mechanisms of human social behavior]. In J. Reykowski (Ed.), *Teoria osobowosci a zachowania prospoleczne* [Theory of personality and prosocial behavior]. Warsaw: PWN.

Reykowski, J. (1979). *Motywacja, postawy prospoleczne a osobowosc* [Motivation, prosocial attitudes and personality]. Warsaw: PWN.

Reykowski, J. (1982). Motivation of prosocial behavior. In V. G. Derlega & J. Grzelak (Eds.), *Cooperation and helping behavior: theory and research.* New York: Academic Press.

Reykowski, J. (1983). Osobowosc wobec przemian spolecznych i technologicznych: Szkic problematyki [Personality and the process of sociotechnological changes: An outline of problems]. In J. Jarymowicz & Z. Smolenska (Eds.), *Poznawcze regulatory funkcjonowania spolecznego* [Cognitive regulators of social functioning]. Wroclaw: Ossolineum.

Reykowski, J. (1984). Spatial organization of a cognitive system and intrinsic prosocial motivation. In E. Staub, D. Bar-Tal, J. Karylowski, & J. Reykowski (Eds.), *Development and maintenance of prosocial behavior.* New York: Plenum.

Rogers, C. R. (1980). *A way of being.* Boston: Houghton Mifflin.

Skinner, B. F. (1971). *Beyond freedom and dignity.* New York: Knopf.

Skinner, B. F. (1974). *About behaviorism.* New York: Knopf.

Staub, E., Bar-Tal, D., Karylowski, J., & Reykowski, J. (Eds.). (1984). *Development and maintenance of prosocial behavior.* New York: Plenum.

Strelau, J. (1983). *Temperament, personality, activity.* New York: Academic Press.

Szczepanski, J. (1966). *Studia nad inteligencja polska* [Studies on Polish intelligentsia]. Warsaw: PWN.

Tomaszewski, T. (1963). *Wstep do psychologii* [An introduction to psychology]. Warsaw: PWN.

Tomaszewski, T. (1976). Wiedza jako uklad reproduktywno-generatywny [Knowledge as a reproductive-generative system]. *Psychologia Wychowawcza* [Educational Psychology], *33,* 145-159.

Weber, M. (1949). *Methodology of the social sciences.* Glencoe, IL: Free Press. (Original work published 1904)

Znaniecki, F. (1935). *Ludzie terazniejsi a cywilizacja przyszlosci* [Contemporary people and civilization of the future]. Lvov-Warsaw: Ksiaznica Atlas.

Znaniecki, F. (1965). *The social role of the man of knowledge.* New York: Octagon.

Znaniecki, F. (1967). *Social actions.* New York: Russell & Russell. (Original work published 1935)

Znaniecki, F. (1969). *On humanistic sociology.* Chicago: University of Chicago Press.

6

PSYCHOLOGICAL THOUGHT WITHIN THE SYSTEM OF RUSSIAN CULTURE

B. F. LOMOV
E. A. BUDILOVA
V. A. KOLTSOVA
A. M. MEDVEDEV

Psychological knowledge, the ideas, concepts, and theories of psychological realities, constitute important components of a culture. Myths, songs, proverbs, literature, political and medical treatises, and philosophical and religious texts from the past have added to, and elaborated upon, the vast store of psychological knowledge. Reflected in all spheres of spiritual life is the psychological picture of the world with its moral and ideological components, which has played and continues to play an important role in shaping the major features and directions of a culture.

Culture, as a sphere of spiritual life of a society, is a product of development influenced by various economic, social, and political structures. Although culture is a common phenomenon for all humankind, it is incarnated in unique national forms. It cannot be considered as a sum total of features discriminating one nation from others. It is a system for reproduction of a spiritual world of an ethnicity that forms the basis for the integrity of its existence. Culture supports continuity, successions of the development of what Humboldt called "the individual form of human spirit, the nation." Every culture is characterized by a unique set of concepts, images, a system of values, and a specific type of perception of the world.

National peculiarities of culture undoubtedly affect the way scholars from different nations have come to interpret the objectives of psychology. Different systems of culture may favor the development of specific scientific directions and the formation of dominant orientations in scientific research. The combination of sociocultural conditions that constitutes the medium for psychological ideas has a concrete historical configuration and nourishes the national features of these ideas. Psychology, like other sciences, is bound to historical processes and is full of the spirit of a given epoch. Moreover, psychological science as a component of the integral whole, the culture, develops in agreement with general cultural regularities, its own regularities being a component of this systemic whole.

What are the peculiarities of Russian psychological science as a sociocultural phenomenon? What new features may one expect to discover by analyzing the development of psychological thought within the context of Russian culture? The search for answers to these questions is complicated by insufficient studies of Russian culture in general ("Kompleksnaya Programma," 1988) and the history of Russian psychology in particular. Let us try to single out some general features of the development of psychological knowledge of Russian culture.

How may we characterize Russian culture? It is an open culture. It has its roots not only in Slavic and proto-Slavic cultures, but also in Byzantine culture, in the cultures of antiquity, in Scandinavian cultures, and in the cultures of Eastern nomads. The first Russian state was a multinational state. Beside the Eastern Slavic tribes, it was formed of Ugro-Finnish and Turkic tribes.

HISTORICAL BACKGROUND

The early Russian princes were known as the Varangians. For several centuries the Russians fought against the Eastern tribes (Huns, Rechenegs, Polovetzs, Tartars), and yet Russian literature bears no trace of contempt for these peoples (Likhachev, 1982). We should point out that the old Russian literature is full of feeling for the integrity of the world, combined with a deep sense of patriotism. Old Russian scribes never failed to place events in historical perspective. They would either begin a narrative with a reference to major events in world history (the Creation, the Flood, the Tower of Babel) or build the story into the world history immediately (e.g., write the narrative as a part of a major historical text; Likhachev, 1987, p. 13).

Beginning in the eleventh century, the authors of the old Russian texts considered the problems of the genesis and the essence of the mind; its properties and role in the psychological life of an individual; the composition of the senses; memory and its features; individual and developmental differences; the problems of character, of "self-government," and of the will; the passions; and the genesis of dreams. In the fifteenth century an attempt was made to build up a system of psychological terms based exclusively on the autothonic (Russian) lexicon (*Is Istorii Russkoy Psikhologii,* 1961, pp. 31-32).

The Russian "all-responsiveness" (F. M. Dostoyevski), a national feature of the Russian character since the old days, precluded any ethnic or spiritual self-isolation, national supremacy, or discord. Dialogue, synthesis, and mutual enrichment are typical of Russian culture.

The concept of "Sacred Russia" itself has no message of ethnicity. The Moscovian state was open to all who were willing to join the Orthodoxy (Averintsev, 1988). The glory of the Russian culture is shared by Trivolis (a Greek), Cyprian (Bulgarian), Krizhanich (Chorvat), Derzhavin and Karamzin (Tartars), Valikhanov (a Kazakh), and many representatives of other peoples. The receptivity of the Russian culture, its ability to incorporate the gains of other national cultures without changing its essence, is a major feature of traditional Russian thought. Radical changes in Russian society, such as the adoption of Christianity, the reforms of the seventeenth century through the nineteenth century, and the October Revolution of 1917, reveal the strength of the tradition. Arnold Toynbee, an outstanding historian of the twentieth century, wrote in a letter to Soviet academician N. I. Konrad, "Your country is composed of such a great number of peoples speaking so many different languages and inheriting so many different cultures that it appears to be a model of the whole world" (*Problemy Istorii I Teorii Mirovoy Kultury,* 1976, p. 160).

For this reason, it was only logical that the scientific tradition of *Völker-psychologie* (ethnopsychology) gained autonomy. The advent of *Völkerpsychologie* is usually dated to 1859, when Moritz Lazarus and Hayim Steinthal founded the *Zeitschrift für Völkerpsychologie und Sprachwissenschaft* (Journal of Ethnopsychology and Linguistics) and to 1863, to the "Lectures on Human and Animal Soul" by Wilhelm Wundt. These ideas were further developed in Wundt's 10 books of the *Völkerpsychologie.*

Yet a little earlier, speaking at the Second Annual Meeting of the Imperial Russian Geographic Society on November 29, 1846, N. I. Nadezhdin (1804-1856) described the principles of what he called "psychological ethnography" as a branch studying psychological properties of peoples and national characters. Under his guidance, a program for sociopsychological studies was developed. Several thousand copies of the program were distributed in the departments of the Geographic Society all over Russia. The program was oriented to the study of ethnopsychology in relation to life conditions, cast of mind of an ethnic group, culture, psychological properties, psychological peculiarities of family relations, and rearing children (Budilova, 1983, 1988).

It should be noted that Nadezhdin's idea of building the "psychological ethnography" was influenced by all the developments of Russian psychological thought (Medvedev, 1988). The old Russian chronicles begin with the *Povest Vremennykh Let* (Narrative of the Times, beginning with the twelfth century). It recognized that peoples and tribes "have their own customs and laws of their fathers and their own habits" (*Polnoe Sobranie Russkikh Letopisey*, 1926, p. 12). The everyday life, customs, and habits were accumulated in the folklore, in the poll-tax books, in the instructions for *voivodes* (commandant of an army, governor of a province in old Russia), and in numerous narratives by travelers. Up until the eighteenth century, ethnic psychological knowledge developed quantitatively rather than qualitatively (i.e., facts of psychological peculiarities of the tribes and peoples earlier unknown accumulated with the development of the Russian state). The transfer of ethnopsychological knowledge into the sphere of science occurred in the eighteenth century, together with a new stage of development of Russian culture.

The state reforms of Peter the Great signaled an epoch of rapid cultural development. In accordance with Peter's *ukase* (edict), special foundations were set up to promote scientific knowledge. Among these were the St. Petersburg Academy of Sciences, the university, the *Kunstkamera* (the first scientific museum), the academy library, and several scientific cabinets (laboratories). The Academy of Sciences became the center of Russian science. It made arrangements for several expeditions to Siberia, the Far East, and the Far North of Russia. The duration of these travels was normally several years, and the participants were many. Among the biggest was the Great Northern Expedition (1733-1743). The St. Petersburg Academy worked out detailed research programs and questionnaires to collect data. The reports and diaries of the travelers and numerous other observations were compiled, describing the customs, habits, and national psychological peculiarities of the peoples inhabiting the Russian Empire.

Among the authors of the first questionnaire was an encyclopedist, a fellow of Peter the Great, V. N. Tatischev (1686-1750), who considered knowledge of people's habits no less important in the case of war than knowledge of the enemy's fortifications (Tatischev, 1979, p. 92). Tatishchev saw the practical advantages of psychology. He supported the exploration of all aspects of human activity and tried to incorporate psychological knowledge into education and socialization.

The name of a great Russian scientist, M. V. Lomonosov (1711-1765), is closely connected with the Academy of Sciences. Lomonosov's works pushed forward a number of scientific disciplines in Russia. He produced no special psychological works, but in his work in numerous scientific areas he had to tackle psychological problems (Koltsova & Vklad, 1986). Proceeding from the materiality of the world and its ongoing change and development, Lomonosov looked for a material basis of the soul. According to Lomonosov, ideas and concepts are reflections of the order of things, the way they are in the world, whereas the brain is the receptacle of ideas, the main regulator and the governor of human actions. Ideas generated by the objective world arise in human activity. Lomonosov considered actions and passion to be the main motivational forces of mind. According to Lomonosov (1983), any reasonable intention without an action is dead, dull, and futile (vol. 7, p. 320). Russian psychological thought inherited Lomonosov's approach to an individual as to a personality in action. Lomonosov's psychological ideas played an important role in making psychology a branch of science, including ethnopsychology. Lomonosov made an attempt to study the historical genesis of formation of the national character of the Russian people and tried to prove the common genesis of several tribes on the basis of comparison of their customs and ways of life.

RELIGION AND SCIENCE
IN THE RUSSIAN CONTEXT

Another peculiarity of Russian culture that can be traced back to all spheres of spiritual life is the coexistence and development of two alternatives in the ideological content and directions of thought (e.g., scientific thinking and idealistic religious thinking). One can hardly understand the development of psychological thought within the system of Russian culture, the regularities of the development connected with the spiritual tradition, and the historical way of Russia without due consideration of interaction between the secular and the religious constituents. Christianity in its Orthodox version contributed greatly to the cultural development of Russia. Unfortunately, for a long time historical studies of Christianity in Russia have been scarce, with propaganda substituted for scientific investigation. Some specialists point to the absence of comprehensive historical studies of the Orthodox church in Russia. Without such studies the picture of the historical life of the country is incomplete and impoverished in all its socioeconomic, political, and cultural aspects (Klibanov, 1988).

We may consider at least two aspects of the problem of interaction between religious and psychological thought. First is the impact of religious concepts of man (his place in the world, the spiritual essence) upon the emergence of psychological ideas. A Russian psychologist, A. I. Galich (1783-1848), for example, put forward a task to construct a sort of "humanology."

He developed an anthropological conception that explained psychological phenomena on the basis of data from natural sciences and at the same time comprised a concept of a "vital force" built into humans by God (Galich, 1834). Second, the Church has accumulated for centuries a very rich psychological account of the formation of conscience, the psychological state of individuals, and the formation of group behavior.

The priests have been able to relieve emotional tension in the believers who come to confess their sins. Why do people feel relieved after confession even though they are not necessarily helped or advised directly? According to P. A. Florensky (1914), the spiritual pastors help them to recognize the state of disagreement, discrepancy, or disintegration of spiritual life. It is not that "I do," but "something is being done to me." It is not that "I live," but that "something is happening to me" (p. 174).

The Orthodox tradition has developed several systems of psychological training and self-regulation. They are as rigorous as the well-known psychological traditions of Zen Buddhism, Confucianism, and Taoism. The hermits and monks of the Russian monasteries were skilled in the techniques of "sobering" the mind and heart, of "looking into" the mind and conscience, and of the concentration of spiritual forces. The use of these techniques not only changed ethical orientations but enabled the religious to build up a specific type of personality, with prescribed psychological characteristics.

All these modes and techniques of "the inner making," as the monks called the training, were thoroughly elaborated and tested. At the end of the fifteenth century an outstanding priest named Nil Sorsky (1433-1508) wrote the *Monastery Statutes,* an encyclopedia combining philosophy and psychology that contained the instructions on monasticism and asceticism (*Nila Sorskogo Predanie Ustav,* 1912).

In the beginning of the second half of the sixteenth century "the outer making" took the upper hand. This type of asceticism was based on mortification of the flesh through strict fasting, exhausting vigils, carrying chains, and the like. The inner making, based on the knowledge of the psychological states of the ascetic, was pushed to the periphery of religious life. The process of revival of "the Saint Fathers' Wisdom" began in the eighteenth century. In the nineteenth century the well-known Optima Pustyn monastery reigned supreme (Averintsev, 1988). People from all over the country came to Optima Pustyn to get advice from the monks. The monastery was visited by I. V. Kireyevsky, F. M. Dostoyevski, V. S. Solovyev, A. K. Tolstoy, L. N. Tolstoy, and many other people who wrote about Russian culture.

The reforms initiated by Peter the Great had a major impact on the Church. The Church became a part of the state. The control of science, the management of education, and education in primary and high schools became new functions of the Church. The Church itself also had special educational institutions, the seminaries and the academies. These institutions educated the clergy, from country priests to professors of theology who held chairs of philosophy in ecclesiastic and secular educational institutions.

As a result, the Church owned powerful tools of information dissemination. It controlled a network of periodicals, magazines for believers, confessional and philosophical journals, and collections of works of ecclesiastic academies. In addition, it published many religious books in Russia.

The ecclesiastic education system lodged psychology under the discipline of philosophy. In the middle of the nineteenth century, theologians lectured on philosophy and psychology in the universities of St. Petersburg, Moscow, Kiev, and Kazan. They wrote the first textbooks on psychology.

Among the theological sciences a special discipline was worked out, the moral Orthodox theology that dealt with the problems of social psychology and developmental psychology. The clergy were specially trained in psychology and mastered psychological methods that could be used with groups and individuals. In the 1830s, following the instructions of the director, Father Innokenty, the Kiev Ecclesiastic Academy adopted a special program for research in the teaching of psychology. This psychological knowledge was intended to prepare pastors for their practical activities. Work headed by Father Theophan had the objective of elevating the level of psychological education to equal the level of European scientific standards and at the same time enabling clergymen to fulfill their duties in the most efficient way.

DEVELOPMENT OF PSYCHOLOGY IN RUSSIA

Unlike in Western Europe, where the emphasis on individualism led to secularization of culture and lessening of the influence of the church, the process in Russia developed within the framework of religious tradition. The Church continued to play a very important role in every aspect of life.

The specific feature that permits discrimination between the genuine old Russian texts and translated ones is the latter's tendency to combine the teaching of the fathers of the Church with scientific knowledge and practical expertise (Gavriushin, 1988). For example, the *Tolkovaya Paleya,* which is attributed to the thirteenth century, is a treatise on the creation of the world that combines the history depicted in the Bible with scientific judgments. The theological understanding of the human mind is illustrated with an empirical description of mental life. The story of the creation of man by God is supplied with a description of the composition of the human body. Speaking about the anatomy and physiology of the brain, the author insists that it is the brain that "sees everything" (perceives sensory data) and "gives thoughts" to the heart and the soul. Thus the thought becomes a product of processing the external impressions in the brain, though earlier the author stressed that the soul obtains wisdom from God (*Paleya Tolkovaya Po Spisku,* 1892-1896).

In the second half of the nineteenth century and the twentieth century psychological thought in Russia made a great leap forward. In addition to the conditions common for Western European, American, and Russian science that emphasized the development of experimental psychology, Russia saw one special event that had an impact upon the cultural life of the country, determined the direction of further development of psychology, and prompted the creation of the first Russian experimental psychological laboratories. This was I. M. Sechenov's teaching on the functioning of the brain, his program of the construction of psychology as science, with the introduction of objective methodology and experimental studies.

The Sechenov program was based on his teaching of brain functioning, described in his well-known work, *The Reflexes of the Brain* (1863/1965). Sechenov analyzed the mind in connection with the material world and human activities in it. This connection was also conceived of as a connection between the mind and the brain, the mind considered to be a function of the higher department of the nervous system that regulates human activities. Having reviewed and changed the existing schemes of the reflex activity of the nervous system, Sechenov devised a scheme incorporating psychological components, from elementary sensitivity up to thinking. The studies of emergence and development of different levels of psychological processes and related levels of human actions were becoming the subject matter of psychology.

The teaching by Sechenov and his work on propagation of psychological knowledge raised great interest in society. Many discussions followed publication of Sechenov's program of the development of psychology. His public lectures on psychology were a great success. Being a physiologist, Sechenov, according to the existing rules, could not teach students in psychology. Yet, beginning in the 1860s it was he who determined the direction of the development of Russian psychological thought.

In his public lectures Sechenov discussed his *Element of Thought* and other works. The newspaper *Sankt-Peterburgskie Vedomosti* (St. Petersburg News) of February 16, 1877, reported, "The novel subject of the well-known scientist I. M. Sechenov, his great popularity as a talented lecturer, has attracted so many listeners that one could hardly find a vacant place in the spacious Auditorium of the Pedagogical Museum." Many outstanding Russian scientists, writers, actors, and artists came to listen to Sechenov's lectures, among them I. S. Turgenev, V. V. Stasov, A. F. Koni, and M. Gorki. After Sechenov moved to Moscow, he continued to lecture for the general public. The *Russkie Vedomosti* (Russian News) (1889, issue 344) commented on his first lecture in the Doctor's Club: "More than 300 listeners enlisted to participate. Beside the quantity, the quality of the audience was outstanding. Among those present there were many Moscow University professors and famous Moscow physicians. The audience met Sechenov with lasting applause."

The polemics between Sechenov and K. D. Kavelin, who was a professor of state and law, a member of the Geographical Society, and director of the society's research program on "psychological ethnography," touched upon the questions of the subject matter and the objectives of psychology. Sechenov expressed his point of view in regard to the message of discussion in the article "Who Should Work How in Psychology?" Psychological discussions developed in Moscow and at Kazan University. Newspapers and magazines gave substantial coverage to the discussion in articles, summaries, and pamphlets.

Publication of every new psychological book by Sechenov was a big event in the country's cultural life. A well-known psychologist, N. E. Vendensky, Sechenov's disciple, recalled that familiarity with *The Reflexes of the Brain* was considered to be necessary for every educated person in Russia in the second half of the nineteenth century. A book by Sechenov titled *The Psychological Studies* is included in V. I. Lenin's private collection of books now preserved in the Kremlin.

Russian literature also took great interest in psychology. This was reflected in writers' attitudes toward psychology and their depiction of the inner world of the individual. Nineteenth-century Russian literary creations were a peak of portrayal of human mental life.

The attitudes of writers toward Sechenov and his theory were varied. His views were met in different ways, but Sechenov's ideas about human mental activities and the personality of the scientist raised tremendous interest. L. M. Tolstoy followed the controversy between Sechenov and Kavelin and discussed the problems in a letter to N. N. Straklov, a pamphleteer.

In the 1880s, Tolstoy discussed the freedom of the will in a dispute at the Moscow Psychological Society. In Tolstoy's novel *Anna Karenina*, Stiva Oblonsky, who has a weakness for everything that comes into fashion, recalls a family quarrel and thinks of "the reflexes of the brain" on an unhappy occasion. Chapter 7 of the novel contains a philosophical discussion of the freedom of the will and his disagreement with the postulation of a strictly caused determination of human activity. Tolstoy used the concepts connected with *The Reflexes of the Brain* throughout *Anna Karenina*; he compared his thought with Sechenov's line of thinking.

Dostoyevski's letters testify to his attention to the psychological discussions. He emphasized the great talent of Sechenov; the scientist's name is often mentioned in Dostoyevski's notebooks. Dostoyevski's novels contain many ideas about the essence of mental life that were generated in the contemporary atmosphere of psychological discussions; his own private collection of books included *The Reflexes of the Brain.* In Dostoyevski's *The Brothers Karamazov,* disputes between the characters often reflect the psychological disputes.

The community of views of Sechenov and M. G. Chernyshevsky and later the literary critics of his novel *What Is to Be Done?* shared the opinion that Sechenov was a prototype for Kirsanov, M. A. Bokova (Sechenov's wife) was a prototype for Veral Pavlovna, and P. I. Bokov for Lophukhov. This opinion is often a motive of memoirs; the students of Chernyshevsky's literary heritage discuss it very widely. We can hardly support the idea of a direct connection between fiction and realistic life, but it is likely that Chernyshevsky could have had in mind the relations among Sechenov, Bokova, and Bokov, who were his close acquaintances. In a rough copy of the novel, Chernyshevsky (1975) wrote, "All that is essential in my novel are the facts that occurred in the life of my good acquaintances" (p. 713). M. E. Saltykove-Schedrin, in his reviews and pamphlets, often defended the teachings of Sechenov.

Russian theater workers also disseminated Sechenov's psychological works. In a rough copy of an article, A. N. Ostrovsky, a playwright, discusses acting on the stage in the light of the reflexive theory of psychological activity. The founder of the Moscow Art Theatre and famous Russian producer K. S. Stanislavsky kept Sechenov's *Reflexes* among his books; the copy in his collection includes many notes written by the producer himself. In his own works Stanislavsky developed Sechenov's views in regard to the nature of mind as connected with acting. According to Stanislavsky, an actor should unify the two sides of the role he or she plays, the psychological and the physical.

In Russia the development of psychological experimentation was fostered by medical psychiatrists. The first Russian experimental psychological laboratory was created in 1885 in the Kazan University Hospital. The founder of the laboratory was V. M. Bekhterev, an outstanding researcher, neurologist, and psychiatrist, and a follower of Sechenov. When Bekhterev was elected full professor of the Military Medical Academy in Petersburg, he founded another experimental psychological laboratory in the Academy Hospital. At the same time a number of new laboratories were opened in hospitals of Moscow (directors S. S. Korsakov and A. A. Tokarsky), in Kiev (A. I. Sikorsky), in Kharkhov (P. I. Kovalevsky), in Yuriev, now Tartu (V. F. Chizh), and in Odessa (N. N. Lange).

The staff members of the first Russian psychological laboratories considered their missions to be the search for experimental evidence that the mind is a function of the brain and the objective study of the dependence of perceptual images on outer stimuli. Many experiments were done to study the brain locations of epidermal, muscular, visual, and acoustic sensations, and their thresholds.

The Bekhterev laboratories conducted combined morphological, physiological, and psychological experimental research. They studied the influence of external and internal conditions on human voluntary movement, the acquisition of skills, and the impact of movements on other movements. This work was aimed at elucidation of the influence of psychological factors upon different functions of an organism in order to find the objective indicators of their changes in the experimental process. Bekhterev emphasized the determination of human sensations by the objects of the external world that act on the brain by means of the sensory organs. Thus he shared this view of Sechenov. The experimenters proved that the qualitative differences in sensations are determined by the qualities of the stimuli. They directed their conclusions against the dominant contemporary teaching on the specific energy of sensory organs, thus supporting Sechenov's view of peripheral sensors as transformers of external energy. The psychological laboratories published the results of their experiments in medical journals. Doctors who worked in the laboratories usually combined their psychological work with clinical practice.

Some years later, in 1901, A. P. Nechaev organized in Petersburg a laboratory that was the first to conduct experimental studies in child and pedagogical psychology. The laboratory staff included teachers who conducted psychological experiments in schools. They organized psychological laboratories in schools in Petersburg and other cities. This connection with pedagogical practice predetermined Nechaev's success and popularity. Nechaev and his coworkers became organizers of the first all-Russian congresses of pedagogical psychology in 1906 and 1909. In fact, these were the first congresses of psychologists, and they went beyond the framework of pedagogical psychology.

A great role in the cultural life of Moscow was played by the Moscow Psychological Society in 1885 under Moscow University. Professor M. M. Troitsky, the founder of the society and its first chairman, was chair of philosophy at the university. The second chairman was N. Y. Grot. The Psychological Society united lecturers on philosophy who specialized in psychology and other university professors. Several psychiatrists working in psychological laboratories also joined the society, as did the Moscow psychological laboratories. The Moscow Psychological Society promoted open discussions and celebrations that were visited by a wide circle of Moscow intellectuals, cultural workers, and others. In 1889 the society began publishing the journal *Voprosy filosofii i psikhologii* (Questions of Philosophy and Psychology), which provided multifaceted coverage of spiritual life, philosophy and psychology, psychological approaches to art and literature, and the problems of morals and ethics. The journal published reports and lectures and also covered the discussions held in the Psychological Society.

During the first decades of the twentieth century psychology in Russia was becoming more vibrant. Some new psychological educational and research institutions were created. In 1907 Bekhterev organized the Psychoneurological Institute in St. Petersburg. G. I. Chelpanove organized the Psychological Institute of Moscow University in 1912.

These were the times of methodological crisis in European and American psychology. The situation was reflected in journals and discussed at international psychological congresses. Psychology in Russia also faced the phenomenology of crisis, but with many peculiar features. The psychologists trained before the revolution came to dissension on methodological issues. Those who used objective methodology in experimental studies opposed the defenders of subjective methodology. Those with scientific orientation opposed the university professors of philosophy.

Postrevolutionary Soviet Russia proclaimed new principles of cultural life based on Marxism. Psychologists tried to find solutions to their methodological problems on the basis of the dialectical materialism of the Marxist philosophy.

The works of Lenin played an important role in consolidating the materialist tendencies in Soviet psychology. Among these works *Materialism and Empirio-criticism* contains a nosological analysis of the essence of conscience and mind as subjective images of the objective world. The process of reflection is considered not as "a mirrorlike act" but as a process of an actively organizing human being. To the extent that human existence is social existence, the process of activities includes manifold multiqualitative relations with the social world. Thus the mental world becomes socially determined. Social determination of mind in Soviet psychology is conceived of in terms of "activity," "communication interaction," and "social relations."

The peculiar feature of Soviet psychology is its homogeneity, the unity of methodological principles. It is based on a system of general psychological principles, concepts, and categories, among which the pivotal principles are those of determinism, of the unity of conscience and activity, and of mediation of mental phenomena by personality.

However, this homogeneous basis gave birth to different scientific schools characterized by different subject matters, different conceptual preferences, and dominant directedness toward practical or theoretical problems. The works of these schools are well known both in the former USSR and around the world. They include the works of the Rubinstein school; Vygotsky's sociohistorical school; Lenotiev and Luria's activities approach; Ananiev's work on the conceptual direction of integrative knowledge; Uznadze's psychology of the set; Myasischev's psychology of relations; Smirnov and

Zinchenko's studies of memory; Teplov, Nebylitsin, and Merlin's studies of individuality; and the studies of psychological phenomena in communication and the systems approach formulated and conducted in the Institute of Psychology of the USSR Academy of Sciences.

The advent of *perestroika* in the USSR stimulated the growth of scientific and general interest in the combination of ideas connected with the concept of culture. The processes developing in Russian society lead toward a better in-depth understanding of a specific role of spiritual continuity, including the progress of science. The history of psychology acquires a new dimension as a substantial component of the history of culture.

REFERENCES

Averintsev, S. S. (1988). Vizantia i Rus.: Dva tipa dukhovnosti [Byzantium and Russia: Two types of spirituality]. *Novy Mir, 7.*

Budilova, E. A. (1983). *Sotsialno-psikhologicheskie problemy v russkoi Nauke* [Socio-psychological problems in Russian science]. Moscow.

Budilova, E. A. (1988). Psikhologicheskie issledovaniya russkogo geograficheskogo obschestva: Uzuchenie traditsii i nauchnykh shkol v istorii sovetskoi psikhologii [Psychological studies of the Russian Geographical Society]. In *Studies on traditions and scientific schools in the history of Soviet psychology.* Moscow.

Chernyshevsky, N. G. (1975). *Chto delat?* [What is to be done?]. Leningrad.

Florensky, P. A. (1914). *Stolp i utverzhdenie istiny. Opyt pravoslav noi teoditsei v dvenaddtsati pismakh* [The pillar and the consolidation of the truth: An experience of the Orthodox theodicy in twelve letters]. Moscow.

Galich, A. I. (1834). *Kartina cheloveka* [The image of man]. St. Petersburg.

Gavriushin, N. K. (1988). Drevnerusskiy traktat o "chelovecheskom estestve" [The old Russian treatise on human nature]. *Priroda, 1.*

Is istorii russkoy psikhologii [Excerpts of the history of Russian psychology]. (1961). Moscow.

Klibanov, A. I. (1988). Vremena menyaiutsya, i my—s nimi [Times are changing—we too]. *Druzhba Narobov, 6.*

Koltsova, V. A., & Vklad, M. V. (1986). Lomonosova v razvitie otechestvenno psikhologicheskoy nauki [Lomonosov's contribution to the development of Russian psychology]. *Psikhologicheskiy Zhurnal, 7*(6).

Kompleksnaya programma po istorii kultury narodov SSSR [The combined program of studies in the history and culture of the people of the USSR]. (1988). *Istoria SSR, 1.*

Likhachev, D. S. (1982). S dobrom i mirom [Good and peace]. *Literaturnoye obozreniye, 12.*

Likhachev, D. S. (1987). *Velikiy put: Stanovlenie russkoy literatury XI-XVII rekov.* Moscow.

Lomonosov, M. V. (1950-1983). *Polnoe sobranie cohineniy* [The collected works]. Moscow-Leningrad.

Medvedev, A. M. (1988). K voprosu of genezise etnicheskoy psikhologii [Remarks on the question of genesis of ethnic psychology]. In *Metodologicheskiye i teoreticheskiye problemy sovremennoy psikhologii* [The problems of methodology and the theory of modern psychology]. Moscow.

Nila Sorskogo predanie i ustav [The narrative and statutes]. (1912). St. Petersburg.

Paleya Tolkovaya po spisku, sdelannomy v Kolomne v 1406 g./Trud uchenikov N.S. Tikhomirova
[The Paleya Tolkovaya, by the hand-written copy made at Kolomna in 1406. The works by
N. S. Tikhomirov disciples]. (1892-1896). Moscow.

Polnoe sobranie russkikh letopisey [A full collection of Russian chronicles]. (1926). Vol. 1,
No. 1. Leningrad.

Problemy istorii i teorii mirovoy kultury [Problems of history and theory of world culture].
(1976). Moscow.

Sechnov, I. M. (1863/1965). *Reflexes of the brain.* Cambridge, MA: MIT Press.

Tatischev, V. N. (1979). *Izbrannye Proizvedeniya* [Selected works]. Leningrad.

7

TRADITIONAL AND MODERN PSYCHOLOGIES IN COMPETING CULTURAL SYSTEMS

Lessons From Iran 1978-1981

FATHALI M. MOGHADDAM

The purpose of this chapter is to review a number of important lessons to be learned from the recent experiences of psychology in Iran. Although both Third World and Western psychologists are showing greater concern for the status of their discipline in developing countries (e.g., Blackler, 1983; Connolly, 1985; Moghaddam, 1987; Moghaddam & Taylor, 1985, 1986; Rosenzweig, 1982, 1984; Russell, 1984; Sinha & Holtzman, 1984), there is a need for more discussion and information exchange on the challenges facing psychologists attempting to move toward indigenous Third World psychology.

The literature on psychology in the Third World can be usefully placed into four categories. First, there are accounts of the state of psychology in particular Third World countries, such as Turkey (LeCompte, 1980), the Philippines (Lagmay, 1984), and China (Shum, 1985), and in particular regions of the Third World, such as Africa (Wober, 1975) and South America (Ardila, 1982). These accounts tend to emphasize the historical development of modern psychology in a particular country or region; they are mainly descriptive and contribute little directly in terms of theoretical or critical assessment of psychology in the Third World.

AUTHOR'S NOTE: An earlier version of this chapter was presented at the Eighth International Congress of Cross-Cultural Psychology, Istanbul, Turkey, July 1986. I am grateful to R. Lalonde, W. E. Lambert, D. M. Taylor, M. P. Zanna, and anonymous reviewer(s) for comments made on an earlier draft.

A second category consists of studies that attempt to demonstrate how modern psychology can contribute to Third World development. Examples in this category include Bennett and Watangia's (1983) work on primary health care and Kingsley's (1983) work on technical training.

Third, there are discussions that attempt to provide a theoretical framework within which to review critically the state of psychology in the Third World. For example, Moghaddam and Taylor (1985) have introduced the concepts of "dual perception" and "parallel growth" to argue that psychology in the Third World tends to be limited to the modern sector and divorced from the traditional sector of developing societies, and that Third World psychology centers tend to have few concrete ties with each other, but to be influenced by prestige "model" centers in the developed world.

A fourth category involves critical evaluations of avenues for the development of a potentially more effective psychology for the Third World. Discussions that fall into this category seem to be increasing (see Connolly, 1985; Moghaddam, 1987; Sinha & Holtzman, 1984), perhaps as a reaction to the overzealous exportation of psychology from developed to developing countries.

However, there is a need for at least a fifth approach, that would focus upon the problems facing Third World psychologists in their attempts to evolve an indigenous Third World psychology. There is a severe shortage of critical accounts by indigenous Third World psychologists about their experiences of trying to move toward a psychology *in* and *of* the Third World (Berry, 1978). In particular, such accounts should aim to identify topics that most urgently need to be addressed in future research by students of indigenous Third World psychology. This chapter is intended to help fill this gap.

The following section provides an outline of the larger context in which indigenous Third World psychologists work. An important feature of this context is the presence of competing cultural systems: the first modern and imported, the second traditional and indigenous. The discussion then focuses upon the development of modern psychology in Iran and the reactions of Iranian psychologists in the period 1978-1981 to the challenges facing them after the revolution of 1978. The experiences of the "Iran experiment" suggest four areas that urgently need to be addressed by researchers: first, the training of Third World psychologists; second, institutional support for psychology in the Third World; third, cooperation among Third World psychologists; and fourth, possible limits to extending Western psychology to the traditional sector of Third World societies.

COMPETING CULTURAL SYSTEMS
AND THE ROLE OF THIRD WORLD ELITES

Third World societies have been experiencing a cultural invasion from the developed world, the roots of which lie in the historical relationship between colonies and colonial powers. The influence of colonization has been felt by Third World societies in diverse ways. At one level, the economies of such societies became shaped by, and dependent upon, the needs of colonial powers. The experiences of India present a relevant example. As Menon (1980) notes:

> The encouragement of cash crops such as sugar, jute, indigo, and cotton in place of food met the needs of European industries for raw materials, but it left the populations of the colonies ever more vulnerable. The consequences were grim: during the 200 years that the British were in India, the country suffered the worst series of famines in its millenial history. (p. 9)

The same vulnerability is demonstrated by Third World countries, such as Iran and Mexico, that have become heavily dependent upon oil revenues and have suffered as a result of changes in the needs of Western economies and the subsequent fluctuations in oil prices.

However, the influence of colonial power extends beyond the economic sphere. Mainly by influencing the culture of Third World elites, the colonial powers have fundamentally influenced the cultural systems of the colonies. The important role that elites have had in shaping Third World societies has been fairly extensively documented, for example, in analyses of the roles of elites in India (Carter, 1974) and the People's Republic of China (Scalap, 1972), economic development, Lipset and Solari's (1967) studies of elites in South America, and also studies of elites in the Middle East (see Zartman, 1980). An important characteristic of Third World elites is their tendency to be Westernized and to enjoy life-styles that are more similar to those of middle- and upper-class Westerners than to the traditional sectors of their own societies. At the same time, being more Westernized and having a Western education legitimates the dominant position of the elite in the Third World.

However, it is not only in the Third World that there exist major cultural differences between social classes. For example, in an extensive cross-national study of parents' child-rearing values, Lambert and his associates demonstrated that social class is a more important variable accounting for fundamental cultural differences than is ethnicity (see Lambert, 1987; Lambert, Hamers, & Fraser-Smith, 1979).

A Westernized cultural system has evolved in the modern sector of Third World societies supported by the modern industrial sector and Western social sciences. The modern industrial sector was developed mainly in response to the needs of the developed world. Similarly, the Western social sciences that have been imported to Third World societies reflect the needs, intellectual or otherwise, of developed rather than developing societies. However, traditional cultural systems survive in the traditional sectors of Third World societies, supported by traditional industries and the social and psychological knowledge provided by traditional religions and philosophies. For example, an integral belief system about human behavior is enshrined in Islam and has a particularly strong influence in the traditional sector of Iranian society.

The modern and traditional sectors of developing societies are supported by "modern" and "traditional" psychologies. In this context, the term *modern psychology* refers to the Western science of psychology. The term *traditional psychology* refers to the systems of beliefs and understandings about human behavior that exist in Third World societies, derived mainly from traditional philosophies and religions. In many instances, these distinct psychologies will have contradictory explanations. For example, modern psychology tends to interpret dreams in terms of an individual's history. Thus an important feature of Freudian analysis involves the unraveling of past events generally, and childhood experiences in particular, through the interpretation of dreams. By contrast, in the cultural context of Islamic Iran the tendency is to interpret dreams in terms of an individual's future. Thus the contents of dreams are analyzed with the purpose of finding clues about future behavior and events, rather than past ones.

Traditional and modern cultural systems can be said to be in a state of competition in Third World societies insofar as there are forces attempting to extend or maintain the influence of each. *Modernization, Westernization,* and *industrialization* are all terms that have been used to refer to the general movement toward the extension of modern cultural systems. This movement has been spearheaded by Western-educated elites.

In summary, modernization in the Third World has involved the growth of a modern sector that is technologically and culturally very different from the traditional sector. The cultural system dominating this modern sector is primarily Western and imported. The social sciences generally, and psychology in particular, serve to support this modern sector, through providing a conceptual framework for interpreting events and behavior that is compatible with the Western life-styles of Third World elites and their adopted Western models. The growth of modern psychology in Third World countries such as Iran should be viewed in the light of these broad historical developments.

THE GROWTH OF
MODERN PSYCHOLOGY IN IRAN

It was not until the 1960s that Western psychology was imported into Iran on a large scale. Although psychology had been introduced as an independent subject in the curriculum of the National Teachers College before World War II, it was in 1959 that the first department of psychology was established in Iran (see Ayman, 1976, for a discussion of the history of modern psychology in Iran). By the mid-1970s, courses leading to a bachelor's degree in psychology were offered at ten Iranian institutions, and more specialized courses leading to a master's degree in psychology were offered at five institutions. Applied psychology outside the universities also experienced growth, particularly in the area of psychological tests and measurements (Ayman, 1976, p. 207). The Psychological Association of Iran was established in 1968, and a Persian-language *Journal of Psychology* appeared quarterly, including both translations of Western research material and some original work carried out by Iranian psychologists.

After World War II the United States was the single most important foreign nation influencing affairs in Iran, and this was reflected by the shape of the psychological knowledge being imported into Iran. Although ex-colonial powers such as Great Britain and France still exerted considerable influence on Iranian affairs, it was to the United States that the majority of Iranian psychologists looked, particularly in terms of "prestige models" to copy. Iranian universities adopted the U.S. "credit" system and generally modeled themselves on U.S. institutions. Almost all Iranian psychologists received their advanced training in Western universities, with the United States being the most important training ground.

Among the Iranian psychologists listed in the second edition of the *International Directory of Psychologists* (Duijker & Jacobson, 1966), 39.1% received their highest level of formal training in the United States, 43.5% in various European countries, and 17.4% in Iran. Among those listed in the third edition of the *Directory* (Jacobson & Reinert, 1980), 50% received their highest degree in the United States, 41.7% in various European countries, and 8.3% in Iran.

The influence of the United States was also important in the area of applied psychology. For example, psychological testing and vocational guidance were probably first introduced to Iran through the U.S. Technical Operations Mission (see Ayman, 1976, p. 207).

The rapid importation of modern psychology into Iran was assisted by a policy of large investments in the area of higher education and social science "research centers." Investments at the level of primary education, from which the majority of Iranians benefited, remained low compared with those in higher education, from which an affluent minority tended to benefit. For example, in 1974 expenditure levels in higher education per student by the United States and by Iran were at fairly similar levels: $2,582.40 and $2,061.20, respectively. In the same year, however, expenditures in primary education per student by these two countries were highly dissimilar: $1,792.20 in the United States and $119.10 in Iran (see Orivel, 1981, pp. 122-125). This relatively large investment in higher education by Iran was matched by an enormous effort to extend social science research institutions (see Tavassoli, 1976, p. 16).

However, the development of modern psychology in Iran was severely hampered by what Moghaddam and Taylor (1985) have termed parallelism and dualism. *Dualism* refers to the existence of two sectors, one modern and the other traditional, that coexist in the same society. Although the main sources of dualism are technological, in the shape of a modern industrial sector superimposed on the traditional economy of a Third World society, dualism also results in very different social perceptions evolving in the modern and traditional sectors. In the case of Iran these differences were dramatic and probably played a major role in bringing about the social and political upheavals of the late 1970s. More specifically, there was severe dislocation between the life-styles, social perceptions, and aspirations of modern and traditional Iranian sectors. Modern psychology remained mainly within the bounds of the modern sector and divorced from the traditional sector of Iranian society. *Parallelism* refers to the development of different institutions in the same society that have few or no concrete cooperative links with each other, but are dependent upon institutions outside that society. For example, psychology departments in Iran tended to have few concrete links with each other, but to be highly dependent upon prestigious psychology centers in the West.

CHALLENGES FACING IRANIAN
PSYCHOLOGISTS AFTER THE REVOLUTION

The revolution of 1978 was accompanied by a widespread feeling that there should be greater efforts toward "indigenization" in almost all areas of Iranian society. Universities and other academic institutions became a major focus for this indigenization effort, with the social sciences generally and psychology in particular being prime targets. Probably the most serious critics of modern psychology in Iran proved to be university students, as well as a significant number of faculty members. The demand was made for a "non-

Western" psychology that would more directly meet the intellectual and material needs of Iranian society.

During the period of 1978-1981, Iranian psychologists experienced a dramatic change in the value system influencing teaching and research in psychology. Prior to the revolution, academic links with Western psychology centers had enjoyed high status, whereas those with Iranian psychology centers were ascribed relatively low status. Similarly, psychological research reported in a Western language, preferably English, and appearing in North American or European journals enjoyed very high status compared with research reported in Persian and published in Iranian or Third World journals. This value system also influenced teaching styles, so that teachers introduced Western terminology into the classroom and relied almost completely upon Western theories and concepts to explain human behavior.

Most important, the topics and research examples chosen for discussion were generally adopted from the context of Western societies and tended to reflect the concerns of Western researchers.

After the revolution, Western psychology no longer enjoyed high status according to the new dominant value system. Iranian psychologists found themselves being evaluated by a new set of rules, according to which indigenization rather than Westernization was positively valued.

The new value system demanded that psychology be strictly applied in orientation, and that it be directly relevant to major problems faced by the Iranian masses, a significant proportion of whom tended to have traditional life-styles and to be economically poor, illiterate, and rural dwelling. The new value system did not deny the possibility of psychological universals, but it regarded "pure research" as a luxury that Third World countries cannot afford. What was seen to be needed for Iran was a science of behavior that would directly tackle the major problems of the most deprived sectors of society and help bring about improved living conditions.

It would probably be fair to say that a significant number of Iranian psychologists made a serious effort to meet the challenge of indigenization. However, a number of factors severely restricted the efforts of these generally well-intentioned individuals. Some of these factors were related to the internal politics of Iran at the time and the restrictions imposed upon the work of psychologists. However, restrictions arising out of the dualism and parallelism that characterized modern psychology in Iran were probably of even more fundamental importance.

Dualism

The three major problems arising as a result of dualism concerned, first, the training received by Iranian psychologists in the West; second, teaching and research instruments available to Iranian psychologists; and third, the "separation" of Iranian psychologists from the traditional sector of Iranian society, in the sense that their teaching, research, and professional practice tended to be oriented toward, and more in tune with, the modern sector.

Most Iranian psychologists had received their advanced training in the West. The courses they followed in Western universities were designed to meet the needs, intellectual or otherwise, of Western societies. In particular, the research questions that students studied were derived from the Western context and were designed to tackle issues that were seen to be relevant and important from that context, such as human-computer interactions, managerial stress, single-parent families, and alcoholism. By contrast, issues that might have higher priority in a Third World context might include illiteracy, the extended family, learning in impoverished environments, and psychological processes involved in "modernization."

In addition, the training received by Iranian psychologists in the West prepared them to conduct research using the equipment, trained human resources, and subject populations—in short, the general infrastructure—supporting psychological research in the West. For example, Iranian psychology students carrying out psychological research in a Western university would have at their disposal the advice and support of experts in their areas of specialization, sophisticated experimental equipment, laboratories, extensive library and computing facilities, as well as a subject population generally familiar with, and sympathetic toward, scientific research. Upon returning to Iran, these students would typically find that the most important elements of this support structure were missing. There would be few, if any, colleagues knowledgeable about their areas of specialization. Furthermore, experimental equipment and laboratory space would be scarce, library and computing facilities would be relatively limited, and the subject population would be generally unfamiliar with scientific research. In short, the situation in which they now found themselves was devoid of all or most of the facilities that they had learned to depend upon.

Another problem that arose as a result of the "inappropriate" training received by Iranian psychologists in the West concerned career expectations. During their studies in the West, Iranian psychologists learned about a career structure and a system for performance evaluation that was not in harmony with the state of affairs in Iran. They learned that academic staff are evaluated first and foremost according to research performance. They began to appreciate that publications matter, but that publishing in some journals has higher status than publishing in others. They learned that research grants are important, but that the prestige associated with receiving grants from some sources is higher than that associated with others. Also, they came to know about "prestige" psychology centers that have an important influence in shaping modern psychology. In short, they acquired the values of Western academic psychology, together with its particular jargon—"soft money," "tenure track," and the like. However, success as an academic in a developing country such as Iran is not necessarily helped by the adoption of the value system of Western academia, or by the knowledge that *soft money* refers to limited-term funding that is usually intended for research purposes, or that a having a tenure track position means that there is the possibility of landing a permanent appointment somewhere down the line.

Upon returning to their own society, Iranian psychologists were confronted with a career structure and system of evaluation that was very different from that of the West, although lip service was often paid to the Western system. In Iran, teaching skills rather than research performance had priority. Also, psychologists achieved career advancement mainly by serving as consultants for educational, industrial, or military concerns, or by landing key government posts, or by rising in university administration.

Differences between the performance evaluation systems of Western countries and Iran meant that Iranian psychologists had to reorient themselves when they returned to work in Iran. Typically, they returned to Iran full of plans about research projects and publications, to find that they were now being evaluated on a different basis and that institutional support for "Western-style" research was not available. The first practical challenge they faced was that of teaching anything between 10 and 25 hours a week, on topics that were often far removed from their areas of specialization. The result was that some Iranian psychologists joined the "brain drain" to the West (i.e., they joined the tens of thousands of highly educated developing world persons who move to industrialized countries annually, as immigrants, refugees, or so-called guest-workers), the majority gave up the idea of research completely, and only a small minority continued to conduct research in Iran.

The inappropriate nature of the training received by Iranian and other Third World psychologists in the West has meant that, from an economic perspective, this training has probably been more beneficial to Western societies than to Third World societies. In most cases, Third World students receiving training in the West act as the labor force for carrying out research projects, the results of which are of little or no direct assistance to their own societies. In some instances, Third World psychologists continue in this role as what Warwick (1980, pp. 321-322) has referred to as "hired hands" and as the "providers of raw data" for Western psychologists after they return to their own countries. This process is, in effect, an extension of the wider economic relationship between Third World and Western powers:

The territories of Africa, Asia and Latin America were developed as append-
ages of the economies of the ruling countries. They still largely retain their
original characteristics of providers of essential primary commodities in exchange for manufactured goods supplied by the industrially developed countries. (Menon, 1980, p. 66)

Second, efforts toward an indigenous Iranian psychology were hampered
by the nature of the teaching and research instruments available to Iranian
psychologists. Psychology textbooks were either direct translations of Western texts or prepared almost exclusively using Western resources. Very little
effort was made by writers to include examples of research carried out by
Iranian and other Third World psychologists. The outcome of this situation
was that after the revolution teachers suddenly found themselves confronted
with little or no teaching material that was suitable according to the new
dominant value system.

The lack of teaching materials reflecting the needs of Iranian society
rather than the West can be partly explained by referring to the training of
Iranian psychologists in the West. As part of this training, students were generally required to demonstrate competence in specialized areas of Western
psychology. In very few, if any, instances were students encouraged to explore the state of modern psychology in their own countries. The reason for
this is partly because Western psychologists supervising the research of Iranian psychologists, and Third World psychologists generally for that matter,
tend to be unaware of the state of psychology in the Third World. Also, research supervisors generally require their students to undertake research projects in areas that are directly related to their own areas of specialization.
Such areas tend to reflect the needs of Western rather than Third World
societies.

Third, Iranian psychologists found that their efforts to extend modern
psychology to the traditional sector of their own society was hampered by
fundamental cultural rifts. These rifts are part of the dualist character of
Third World societies and, in this context, they concern the value system
underlying modern psychology and influencing Western-trained Iranian psychologists. For example, there have developed in the traditional sector of
Iran a number of religious ceremonies that function in a similar manner to
what is termed *group therapy* in the West. One such ceremony is the *Rowzeh,*
which involves a small group of people being guided through a number of
activities by a group leader (*Rowzeh-khan*). Among the psychological outcomes of these activities tend to be intense emotional discharge and a decrease in stress levels. However, such ceremonies belong to the traditional
sector and have generally remained far removed from the work of Western-

trained clinical psychologists. Consequently, their potential clinical uses are still essentially unexplored.

Parallelism

As a consequence of the parallelism characterizing modern psychology in Iran, Iranian psychologists attempting to move toward an indigenous psychology have been confronted by three major problems. First, there is a lack of research tradition involving cooperation among Iranian psychologists and between Iranian psychologists and other Third World psychologists. Such cooperation is essential, because the sharing of experiences and ideas among researchers confronted by similar challenges in the Third World will undoubtedly pave the way toward greater progress in indigenous Third World psychology. Second, there has been a tendency to look toward the West when seeking solutions to problems, rather than trying to achieve solutions by exploiting indigenous resources. Third, there has been a lack of knowledge about the research activities of colleagues in Iran and in other Third World countries.

Parallel growth has tended to hinder the development of group cooperation among Iranian psychologists and between Iranian psychologists and other Third World psychologists. Upon returning to Iran after their training in the West, most Iranian psychologists tended to retain strong links with psychologists in the West, but to neglect colleagues in Iran and in other Third World countries. The larger social structure, together with the value system influencing the work of psychologists, tended to encourage the strengthening of links with the West, rather than links within the Third World. One important consequence of this was that a strong tradition of cooperation among Iranian psychologists within Iran, or between Iranian psychologists and other Third World psychologists, had not evolved.

Parallelism led Iranian psychologists to look toward the West for new orientations in teaching and research, rather than looking toward indigenous needs and resources. This situation arose partly as a result of a lack of knowledge about the activities of other psychologists in Iran and in other Third World countries. Also, Iranian psychologists had not developed the confidence required to seek new orientations through reliance upon indigenous resources. This problem persisted after the revolution, with much duplication and wasted effort resulting. For example, the task of developing an undergraduate psychology program that more effectively reflects Iranian needs was simultaneously taken up by most psychology departments in Iran in the postrevolution period, with almost no collaboration between departments. At the time, I was teaching at both Tehran University and the National University of Iran, and became aware of two different committees at these universities, both attempting to develop a new psychology curriculum, but neither having much contact with each other or with any of the other similar committees springing up in different universities.

A similar problem of duplication has existed since the prerevolution era with respect to the translation of terminology, with numerous authors preparing their own lists of "Persian equivalents" for Western psychology terms (Ayman, 1976, p. 208). This problem was exacerbated by the fact that Iranian psychologists tend to be trained in various Western countries, according to diverse academic traditions, and thus translate texts from different Western languages.

IMPLICATIONS AND CONCLUSION

During the years 1978-1981, Iranian psychologists made a serious endeavor to prepare the way toward an indigenous Iranian psychology. They were confronted, however, with many problems, the most important arising out of the dualism and parallelism characterizing modern psychology in Iran. The experiences of Iranian psychologists during this difficult period suggest four major issues that need to be addressed by researchers: first, the training of Third World psychologists; second, institutional support for psychology in the Third World; third, cooperation among Third World psychologists; and fourth, possible limits to extending modern psychology to the traditional sectors of Third World societies.

The training of Third World psychologists in Western universities has generally been undertaken with little regard for the special needs of Third World societies. The general attitude of both Western teachers and Third World students has tended to be that the best policy is for Third World psychologists to experience the same "high-quality" training as Western psychologists. However, the "appropriateness" of this training for Third World psychologists needs to be assessed more closely (for a more in-depth discussion of "appropriate training" for developing world psychologists, see Moghaddam & Taylor, 1987). It would be particularly constructive to conduct such an assessment in relation to the skills required by Third World psychologists to function effectively as researchers and practitioners in their own societies, and to contribute to indigenous Third World psychology. The Western training received by Iranian psychologists seemed to be in important ways inappropriate to meet the challenge of indigenization.

Second, how can the training of Third World psychologists be better designed to take into consideration the kinds of institutional support available for research and practicing psychologists in their own Third World societies? As psychologists in Iran found when they were cut off from Western sources after the revolution, and as most Third World psychologists who return to work in their own societies discover, the successful utilization of indigenous resources generally requires a different set of skills. Training that would emphasize indigenous support systems would also ultimately strengthen these systems and decrease reliance upon the West.

Third, more attention needs to be given to the problem of how to strengthen ties among psychologists in the Third World. A number of important steps have already been taken in this direction by the International Union of Psychological Science, the International Council of Psychology, the Interamerican Society of Psychology, the International Association of Cross-Cultural Psychology, UNESCO, and other international bodies. However, the traffic in psychological knowledge and expertise still tends to be between Third World and industrialized nations, rather than between countries within the Third World. One outcome of this situation in Iran was that there had hardly developed a tradition of cooperation between psychologists in Iran, or between Iranian psychologists and other Third World psychologists. The present pattern of communication among psychologists around the world tends to hinder the development of indigenous Third World psychology and to maintain or strengthen the dependence of Third World psychologists on the West.

Fourth, although cross-cultural psychologists have given some attention to the issue of adapting research methodology to meet the needs of different cultural contexts (e.g., see Triandis & Berry, 1980), there is a need for more discussion on the possible limits of extending modern psychology to the traditional sectors of Third World societies. For example, to what extent is it feasible or useful to extend clinical services to traditional sectors of Third World societies where there already exist "tradition-supportive" psychologies, mainly based upon religious beliefs and value systems?

Finally, a word of caution is required regarding some possible consequences of developing indigenous Third World psychology: The value system underlying such a psychology might in important ways contradict the value system underlying Western psychology. For example, polygyny is regarded as useful and necessary in certain circumstances by some Islamic groups in Iran, as well as in other Muslim countries. Of relevance to this is a study carried out in Nigeria with the explicit purpose of creating positive and open-minded attitudes toward polygyny (Ugwegbu, 1982). From a Western perspective, it would seem contradictory to talk about "open-minded attitudes toward polygyny" while research that adopts such a goal would probably be judged "unethical." However, the development of indigenous psychologies in the Third World will necessarily highlight and test certain values implicit in Western psychology, and this could have positive consequences for all of psychology.

REFERENCES

Ardila, R. (1982). Psychology in Latin America today. *Annual Review of Psychology, 33,* 103-122.

Ayman, I. (1976). Iran. In V. S. Sexton & H. Misiak (Eds.), *Psychology around the world* (pp. 204-211). Monterey, CA: Brooks/Cole.

Bennett, M., & Watangia, K. (1983). Primary health care: New challenges for applied psychologists. In F. Blackler (Ed.), *Social psychology and developing countries* (pp. 177-187). Chichester: John Wiley.

Berry, J. W. (1978). Social psychology: Comparative, societal and universal. *Canadian Psychological Review, 19,* 93-104.

Blackler, F. (Ed.). (1983). *Social psychology and developing countries.* Chichester: John Wiley.

Carter, A. T. (1974). *Elite politics in rural India.* Cambridge: Cambridge University Press.

Connolly, K. (1985). Can there be a psychology for the Third World? *Bulletin of the British Psychological Society, 38,* 249-257.

Duijker, H. C., & Jacobson, E. H. (1966). *International directory of psychologists* (2nd ed.). Assen, Netherlands: Royal Vangorcum.

Jacobson, E. H., & Reinert, G. (1980). *International directory of psychologists* (3rd ed.). Amsterdam: North-Holland.

Kingsley, P. R. (1983). Technological development: Issues, roles and orientations for social psychology. In F. Blackler (Ed.), *Social psychology and developing countries* (pp. 131-153). Chichester: John Wiley.

Lagmay, A. V. (1984). Western psychology in the Philippines: Impact and response. *International Journal of Psychology, 19,* 31-44.

Lambert, W. E. (1987). The fate of old-country values in a new land: A cross-national study of child rearing. *Canadian Psychology, 28,* 9-20.

Lambert, W. E., Hamers, J., & Fraser-Smith, N. (1979). *Childrearing values: A cross-national study.* New York: Praeger.

LeCompte, W. A. (1980). Some recent trends in Turkish psychology. *American Psychologist, 35,* 745-749.

Lipset, S. M., & Solari, A. (1967). *Elites in Latin America.* New York: Oxford University Press.

Menon, B. P. (1980). *Bridges across the South.* New York: Pergamon.

Moghaddam, F. M. (1987). Psychology in the three worlds: As reflected by the crisis in social psychology and the move toward indigenous Third World psychology. *American Psychologist, 42,* 912-920.

Moghaddam, F. M., & Taylor, D. M. (1985). Psychology in the developing world: An evaluation through the concepts of "dual perception" and "parallel growth." *American Psychologist, 40,* 1144-1146.

Moghaddam, F. M., & Taylor, D. M. (1986). What constitutes an "appropriate psychology" for the developing world? *International Journal of Psychology, 21,* 253-267.

Moghaddam, F. M., & Taylor, D. M. (1987). Toward appropriate training for developing world psychologists. In C. Kagistcibasi (Ed.), *Growth and progress in cross-cultural psychology* (pp. 69-75). Lisse, Netherlands: Swets & Zeitlinger.

Orivel, F. (1981). Fresh obstacles facing policies aimed at reducing educational inequalities. In UNESCO (Ed.), *Planning education for reducing inequalities* (pp. 111-128). Paris: UNESCO.

Rosenzweig, M. R. (1982). Trends in development and status of psychology: An international perspective. *International Journal of Psychology, 17*, 117-140.

Rosenzweig, M. R. (1984). U.S. psychology and world psychology. *American Psychologist, 39*, 877-884.

Russell, R. W. (1984). Psychology in its world context. *American Psychologist, 39*, 1017-1025.

Scalap, R. A. (Ed.). (1972). *Elites in the People's Republic of China.* Seattle: University of Washington Press.

Shum, J. C. (1985). Psychology as an academic and applied science in China. *Bulletin of the British Psychological Association, 38*, 405-409.

Sinha, D., & Holtzman, W. H. (Eds.). (1984). The impact of psychology on Third World development [Special issue]. *International Journal of Psychology, 19*(1).

Tavassoli, G. A. (1976). Social sciences in Iran. In UNESCO, *Social sciences in Asia I: Bangladesh, Iran, Malaysia, Pakistan, Thailand* (Reports and Papers in Social Sciences 32). Paris: UNESCO.

Triandis, H. C., & Berry, J. W. (Eds.). (1980). *Handbook of cross-cultural psychology* (Vol. 2). Boston: Allyn & Bacon.

Ugwegbu, D. (1982). Effectiveness of self-persuasion in producing healthy attitudes towards polygyny. In I. Gross, J. Downing, & A. D'Heurle (Eds.), *Sex role attitudes and culture change* (pp. 151-155). Dordrecht, Netherlands: D. Reidel.

Warwick, D. P. (1980). The politics and ethics of cross-cultural research. In H. C. Triandis & W. W. Lambert (Eds.), *Handbook of cross-cultural psychology* (Vol. 1, pp. 319-371). Boston: Allyn & Bacon.

Wober, M. (1975). *Psychology in Africa.* London: International African Institute.

Zartman, W. I. (1980). *Elites in the Middle East.* New York: Praeger.

8

DIVERSIFICATION OF AMERICAN INDIANS

Forming an Indigenous Perspective

JOSEPH E. TRIMBLE
BEATRICE MEDICINE

At one time the United States and its people were likened to a melting pot of different racial, ethnic, religious, and national groups, and rightly so, given the influx of hundreds of groups over the course of 500 years or so. Within the past two decades, however, numerous social critics have been suggesting that an American character has yet to emerge from the mixing of culturally diverse groups. What exists today is a country held together by certain political and economic orientations and a distinctive flair for technology in a quilted framework of many diverse ethnic lifeways. One of those groups, the American Indian, is the core subject of this chapter.[1]

The intent of this text is to examine critically the extent to which the subjects of the field of psychology exist within the context of culturally unique groups. More to the point, do psychological principles, as advocated and professed by this seemingly American-dominated profession, exist in one form or another within the *ethos* (lifeways) and *eidos* (thoughtways) of indigenous peoples? If they do, then the field of cross-cultural psychology may not be necessary. But if they do not, the field has far more problems than

AUTHORS' NOTE: We wish to thank Barbara Means Adams and Alberta Arviso for their assistance in providing material for portions of this chapter. The senior author also extends his gratitude to the Triethnic Center for Prevention Research at Colorado State University and the National Institute of Drug Abuse for support provided through Grant P50 DA 07074. Correspondence concerning the chapter should be addressed to Joseph E. Trimble, Center for Cross-Cultural Research, Department of Psychology, Western Washington University, Bellingham, WA 98225-9089.

most would be willing to admit. We would argue that in its present form the current knowledge base of psychology cannot be effectively generalized to the American Indian. Moreover, by creating a term such as *ethnopsychology* to account for variations owing to culture, the scientist-practitioner would be imposing an array of completely inappropriate interpretations. In a word or so, traditional-oriented American Indians, regardless of their linguistic and lifeways differences, do not have a single, unifying concept that offers a thorough understanding of the human mind. Hence attempting to use conventional psychological tenets to identify and describe Indian affective and behavioral patterns can only result in flawed interpretations.

SOCIAL SCIENCE SHAPES AN IMAGE

The American Indian has been the subject of seemingly countless research efforts, conducted predominantly by educational researchers and anthropologists. Within the past three decades, psychiatrists, psychologists, and social workers have devoted considerable attention to investigating the psychosocial correlates of the behavior and personality of America's aboriginal people. Kelso and Attneave (1981) compiled some 1,360 articles on Indian mental health topics, and Mail and McDonald (1980) list 969 citations dealing exclusively with alcoholism among Indians. A review of the citations from both bibliographic sources reveals that the vast majority refer to American Indians in a generic, collective manner and give little attention to their extraordinary and complex diversity. The tendency to view American Indians in a collective manner is the source of one of the major problems in formulating an indigenous psychology and, consequently, creates a sensitive methodological problem.

Historically, it would be difficult to identify the source of the tendency for social and behavioral scientists to view American Indians in a collective manner. It mirrors, however, the tendency among European colonizers to gloss all aboriginal peoples. Moreover, a finger could be pointed in the direction of the anthropological school of culture and personality, which emphasized the unique cultural life-styles of particular indigenous groups and their distinctive personality styles. Typically, followers of this school gathered information on a tribe's customs and living patterns and then used that information to infer the existence of a prevailing collective character. Ruth Benedict's interpretive work on the Zuni of the southwestern United States and the Kwakiutl of Vancouver Island in the Pacific Northwest are illustrative. Benedict built her cultural descriptions on the Nietzchean duality of "Apollonian" and "Dionysian" to isolate modal characteristics among the two native groups. For the Kwakiutl, Benedict (1959) argued, "They valued all violent experience, all means by which human beings may break through the usual sensory routine, and to all such experiences they attributed the highest value" (p. 80). In speaking about Indians of the Northwest Coast, Benedict also referred to them as Dionysian, even though she admitted that "they had a culture of no common order" (p. 173). To the contrary, Benedict characterized the Zuni as people taken by moderation, sobriety, and conforming; she found them ritualistic and collective-oriented. The effect of Benedict's formulation had long-lasting repercussions in anthropology, especially for the culture and personality school's emphasis on the configurational approach.

Other examples of anthropological attempts to identify a core, unifying personality structure abound. In commenting about Kaska "ethos," Honigmann (1949) suggested that they were people of strong emotional constraint, emotionally inhibited in interpersonal relationships, apathetic, and distrusting of others. And speaking about the Teton Sioux, Macgregor (1970) stated that "in this environment the basic personality has become almost schizophrenic between desires to gain status and role outside the reservation and to enjoy warm, stable and positive interrelations by remaining at home" (p. 99). Erik Erikson's (1939) work, too, on the Pine Ridge reservation in South Dakota was equally configurative and reflected the focus on a modal personality pattern.

In a text intended for use in Indian boarding schools, the psychologist-educator John Bryde boldly titled his work *Modern Indian Psychology.* Bryde attempted, through historical and psychological analysis, to portray the personality of Siouan-speaking peoples (i.e., Dakota, Lakota, and Nakota) in collective terms. Making extensive reference to psychoanalytic theory, Bryde attempted to impose etic-grounded concepts on the life-styles and characters of a reasonably diverse people and with little regard for the extensive variations indicative of the Sioux.

Glossing Over an Ethnic Group

An abundance of examples from the personality and culture school could be cited to illustrate further the research and writing style. The style erroneously attempted to characterize an identifiable common cultural group as though they were single-minded, as evidenced by a unique personality style. To an extent the approach persists, especially in comparative research, where one finds study after study contrasting Indians with whites, blacks, Hispanics, Asian Americans, and other Indian groups. Descriptions of the respective sample populations are usually presented in global terms, without comment on the enormous amount of variability particular to the group in question (see Trimble, 1991). To punctuate the contention, Forbes (1990) points out that "one of the strange things about the Americas is that ethnic and racial categories are extremely arbitrary and are unevenly applied" (p. 23).

The argument, with a slight twist, can be extended to certain anthropologists and psychiatrists who have seen key informants as exemplars of their tribes. "Any member of a group," stated anthropologist Margaret Mead (1953), "is a perfect sample of the group-wide pattern on which he is acting as an informant" (p. 6). Any scholar knowledgeable of recent criticisms of Mead's research in the Manoan Island group of Samoa is painfully aware of the pitfalls associated with this approach (see Freeman, 1984). The presumed isomorphic relationship between a key informant and the ethos and eidos of a distinct culture is simplistic, artificial, and woefully unrepresentative. Moreover, attempts at capturing and portraying a modal character rule out the rich diversity provided by distinct lifeways and thoughtways within and between group differences. Results generate copy for wonderful narrative nonfiction but bestow little justice on the rigors of scientific inquiry.

To add substance to the argument that the study of an indigenous psychology of American Indians is not only fostering a pseudoetic but may well be impossible, it would be useful to provide some definitions. As most scholars know, the term *American Indian* is an imposed ethnic category with little relevant meaning. At best it is a generalized gloss that was originally foisted upon the Arawak, a now extinct tribe once indigenous to islands off the southeastern coast of the United States, by Spanish and Italian explorers and colonists.

Somehow, and no one is really certain why, the category continued to be used to the extent that almost all indigenous, native peoples of the Western Hemisphere are referred to as Indians. You hear and see it everywhere— Canadian Indians, Mexican Indians, Indians of Central America, Brazilian Indians, Indians of the Central Plains. For better or worse, the term has become institutionalized and even accepted by the native peoples themselves.

Tribal-Specific Definitions

Tribal groups had names for themselves and indeed linguistic-specific names for other tribal groups. Tribes with such names as Lakota, Cheyenne, Navajo (Dine), and Hopi referred to themselves as "human beings" or "the people." Within tribes, bands such as "those with burned thighs" or "those who plant near the water" and moieties such as "Eagle" or "Raven" were given more specific names to refer to some unique characteristic. In addition, tribes such as the Lakota referred to other tribes according to their physical features and characteristics—the Cheyenne were referred to as *Sihivena* (people with a shrill voice), the Winnebago as *Hotanke* (loud voice people), and the Navajo as *Sna-hde-hde-ha* (those with striped blankets). Such distinctions were typically ignored by American colonialists, historians, and novelists, leaving the world with the erroneous impression that American Indians were a distinctive but singular lot. It appears that it is more convenient to gloss a group than to deal with the discrete entities within it.

Within the past decade or so efforts to replace the term *American Indian* with *Native American* were initiated by Indian activist groups, aided by conscientious liberal sympathizers and by universities and colleges in their affirmative action policies and considerations. The effort died rather suddenly when Indian political groups such as the National Congress of American Indians (NCAI) and the National Tribal Chairman's Association (NTCA) recognized that many descendants of early colonialists could indeed consider themselves natives, as their ancestors have been in America for about 400 years. Despite the stance taken by the NCAI and NTCA, many non-Indians insist on using the term *Native American*. In the state of Alaska, indigenous peoples are referred to as Alaska Natives and nonindigenous folks are native Alaskans—the distinction is clear, and most abide by the encompassing categories.

Government Attempts at a Definition

For logistic and political reasons, the federal government, through the Bureau of Indian Affairs (BIA), found it necessary to provide a legal definition of an American Indian, the only ethnic group in the United States that is afforded this distinction. The definition has undergone numerous revisions in the past 100 years or so, but currently the BIA defines an American Indian as a person whose American Indian blood quantum is at least one-fourth and who is a registered or enrolled member of one of the 300 or more federally recognized tribes. The hard-and-fast criteria eliminated many people of American Indian background who affiliated in one form or another with one of some 60 federally nonrecognized tribes, ones that in many cases never signed formal treaties with the government or were part of scattered small groups in the Northwest and Southwest parts of the United States.

Some recognized or "treaty" tribes do not agree with the BIA criteria and have developed their own specifications. Some have lowered the blood quantum criterion to one-eighth and even one-sixteenth; a few have increased it to one-half. One tribe in Oklahoma in the late 1960s opened its rolls to anyone who could prove ancestral ties—the specificity of blood quantum was not viewed as an important criterion.

For some American Indians the BIA's restricted definition is not representative of the range of Indian life-styles and levels of identification. The U.S. Bureau of Census and Department of Education (DOE) each developed their own criteria. The Census Bureau allows each citizen to declare his or her ethnic origin on the basis of the group with which he or she most identifies—in a word, the criterion is self-enumerative. The criteria developed by DOE are probably more pragmatic and perhaps closer to reality. After conducting an extensive survey among Indian people throughout the United States, DOE staff generated some 70 distinct definitions. After a careful review of the results, DOE decided on a definition that closely resembles BIA criteria but provides more latitude for tribal-specific criteria, regardless of federal status.

Government definitions are developed largely to determine who is eligible for services provided by treaty arrangements and congressionally mandated programs. The definitions do not include the extent to which an individual follows tribal custom and tradition or the degree to which he or she professes an ethnic identification. Francis Svennson (1973), a political scientist of American Indian background, recognized this when she stated that being Indian "is a state of being, a cast of mind, a relationship to the Universe. It is undefinable" (p. 9). Yet this definition, too, may cause difficulties in those concerned with emerging "New Age" philosophies and the search for an indigenous identity.

Interaction and Validation Styles

Among most American Indians just being federally recognized and fitting the definitional criteria of the BIA and DOE are not sufficient. For many, it is vitally important to glean a sense for the way one lives and subscribes to traditional and readily identifiable life-style patterns. As a consequence, when two strangers meet and it is apparent that both possess distinctive physical characteristics—dark straight hair, dark brown eyes, brown skin, high cheekbones, broad nasal structure, and other distinguishing features—they seek to elicit information from each other to substantiate degree of ethnic affiliation. Using a nesting procedure, one will ask, "Where are you from?" "What tribe do you belong to?" "Who are you related to?" in an effort to generate some commonly shared knowledge. If one or the other doesn't quite fit the physical stereotype, the conversation may well turn to identifying which parent or grandparent was non-Indian and what the person's blood quantum might be. This is usually a delicate subject, so it is often handled rather carefully. If all of the information appears authentic and genuine, the conversation may lapse into one in which each shares stories about presumed common life experiences. Often the conversation takes on a form of "homeland centrism," where the daily, contemporary life-style of the individual's origins is emphasized over traditional tribal customs and traditions. Hence Indians from reservations are likely to discuss socializing influences more indicative of contemporary lifeways "back home" than to give attention to classic tribal customs. In a very subtle way the conversation is designed to provide evidence that the participants are not only American Indians by definition but that they have the experiences to back that up—experiences that demonstrate that they identify with their ethnic origins.

Ethnic group validation and confirmation dialogues vary considerably from one tribe to another. Among the members of the Navajo (Dine) Nation in the American Southwest, two individuals who meet each other for the first time will follow a highly stylized, almost ritualized, dialogue that is guided by strict protocol. Typically, the first speaker (usually the one who appears to be the elder) will begin by introducing him- or herself, by name, in the Navajo language. The introduction is followed by an identification of the speaker's maternal clan, then the paternal clan, followed by the maternal grandfather's clan and then the paternal grandparents' clan. Then the speaker will identify up to four different clans that belong to his or her maternal side of the family—these clans are usually not stated until the maternal clan is first identified. The speaker then identifies whether he or she comes from the eastern or western side of the vast Navajo reservation—the distinction is important because there are some distinct and unique linguistic differences between the two sides. Finally, the first speaker will mention something that is distinctive about a parent or grandparent, such as "My grandfather is known for horses." The second speaker follows the form in the exact order presented to him or her. The two speakers then may continue the introductory dialogue until they have mutually identified their kinship and clan connections with one another. Once this is done, the conversation can then—and only then—lapse into other topics of mutual interest.

Even though there are a generalized set of definitions and colloquial efforts to promote further clarification of ethnic origins, American Indians make up an extraordinarily diverse and complicated ethnic group. According to the 1990 U.S. Census there are close to 2 million American Indians and Alaska Natives in a national population of more than 260 million people. And there may well be many more, as many Indians either refuse to participate in the census or do not want to be identified as Indians for a multitude of personal and social reasons. There are well over 450 identifiable tribal units, some having as few as four or five remaining enrolled tribal members. The Navajo of New Mexico and Arizona is the largest tribe, with more than 170,000 members listed on the rolls.

Similarity and Dissimilarity

The diversity among American Indians is compounded by the fact that more than 60% are of mixed background, the result of miscegenation and intermarriage among African American, Euro-American, and Hispanic populations. Many "breeds," or people of mixed marriages, are not considered "ethnically pure" by some American Indians and non-American Indians alike and hence are not viewed as characteristically American Indian in terms of knowledge of traditional mores and folkways. Of course, this assumption is blatantly fallacious as many "breeds" are often much more "native oriented" than many so-called pure Indians—blood quantum is certainly not an accurate gauge of ethnic affiliation and knowledge of traditional lifeways. Nonetheless, this fallacy serves as a convenience for both native and nonnative populations.

Viewed in acculturative terms, American Indians represent the full range of acculturative status, from native or tradition oriented to fully acculturated. For many, English is a second language, and for many more proficiency in English as well as the tribal dialect is rather prevalent. Berry, Trimble, and Olmedo (1986) point out that individuals vary in terms of their response to the acculturative process and that "not only will groups and individuals vary in their participation and response to acculturative influences, some domains of culture and behavior may become altered without comparable changes in other domains" (p. 297). Acculturation is an uneven process, hence individuals and groups are not uniformly affected by cultural and psychological phenomena. For American Indians, too, the process of psychological acculturation is not only uneven but extraordinarily variable across individuals and tribes. Not all American Indians are alike, which makes the selection of respondents and key informants a delicate and complicated process.

The native and tribal-specific lifeways and thoughtways are extraordinarily complex and variegated. Consider, for example, that there are some 100 distinct languages, each with its structural and functional variations, still in use today. Embedded in the languages are highly stylized classification and grammatical rules. And, as one might expect, the linguistic rules direct the ordering of lexicons that are used to describe social and behavioral patterns and styles. In this domain, the tribes have developed distinct lexicons to describe illnesses and sicknesses, particularly those of the mind and spirit—the psychiatric literature often refers to these descriptions as culture-bound disorders (Trimble, Manson, Dinges, & Medicine, 1984).

Manson, Shore, and Bloom (1985) interviewed 36 informants from the Hopi Nation of Arizona concerning their understanding of illnesses. The researchers asked their informants to generate responses to the question,

Table 8.1 Hopi Illness Categories

Elicited Responses and Interpretations: "What are the sicknesses or things that can be wrong with people's minds or spirits?"

- *wu wan tu tu va/wu ni wu* (worry sickness)

  dysphoria with mood swings, low self-esteem, lack of control over oneself and the surrounding environment, constant worry, anger, partial loss of memory, visual and auditory hallucinations, exhaustion, insomnia, poor appetite, dizziness, increased physical complaints, argumentative behavior

- *ka ha la yi* (unhappiness)

  cognitive disorientation, thoughts about death, limited memory loss, tearfulness, inability to sleep, loss of appetite, complaints about physical health, loneliness, desire to die

- *uu nung mo kiw ta* (heartbreak)

  acute sadness over unrealized expectations or disrupted interpersonal relationships, feelings of ineffeectiveness, sleep loss, exhaustion, physical complaints

- *ho nak tu tu ya* (drunkenlike craziness) (with or without alcohol)

  psychological agitation, worry, anger, wide mood swings, cognitive disorientation, visual and auditory hallucinations, constant argumentativeness

- *qu vis ti* (turning one's face to the wall)

  disappointment, withdrawal, loneliness, despondency with death thoughts, suicidal ideation, anger, argumentativeness

SOURCE: Adapted from Manson et al. (1985).

"What are the sicknesses or things that can be wrong with people's minds or spirits?" Table 8.1 shows a summary of their findings. Essentially, the query elicited five tribal-specific illnesses that have intrinsic meaning to the Hopi—the translations of the names for the illnesses certainly follow the kinds of behavior thought to be indicative of psychopathological disorders across many cultures.

The linguistic elicitation process used by Manson et al. lends some understanding to the style members of a particular tribe use to view illnesses and sicknesses that affect the spirit or mind. The five Hopi categories illustrate that a worldview exists that does not fit conventional psychiatric nosology. To attempt to match each Hopi concept categorically with a clinical concept would be foolhardy and an insult to the contextual nature of the Hopi language. Tribal-specific linguistic elicitation procedures can substantiate the notion that indigenous concepts exist to describe extreme variations in human behavior. The elicited terms and categories, however, must be interpreted and understood within a tribe's worldview.

The principal tribal bands of North and South Dakota, the Sioux or Teton Lakota, have several lexicons in their language to describe people whose behavior is somewhat atypical. However, there is no linguistic evidence available to suggest that the Sioux rely on categories or taxonomic hierarchies to distinguish people on an "abnormal" or psychopathological gradient. In general, especially for the more traditionally oriented, the Sioux place a high premium on the process of self-actualization—one's behavioral and emotional state is achieved through one's own initiative, influenced, in part, by aspects of the spirit world. Moreover, an individual's achieved psychological state is contextual and emerges as a consequence of situations and contexts that are intertwined with all aspects of behavior. Descriptions of Siouan character, therefore, must be attributed to self-attainment, the social context or situation, and the influence of spiritual entities.

To illustrate the point, we provide several examples from the Teton Lakota language. *Witko* can be used to refer to someone who is crazy, deceptive, tricky, or unconventional; it can also mean "one who has no values" or "loss of mind." *He wichasa ki ozula witkoko he* translates to mean "that man is very crazy"—*ozula* can mean "very" as well as "full," thus the *wichasa* (man) can be "filled with craziness." A person who is described as *gnaskinvan* is one who is "foolish-like crazy"—one in this state often babbles or mutters seemingly unconnected words. But some people who babble may be referred to as *iwakan*—the babbling or use of words in a disconnected, even backward, way may be attributed to some physiological problem or to a sacred, spiritual source. If the attribution is spiritual, then the person may be referred to as *heyoka*, which can mean "foolish" or, more loosely, "clown" (some Lakota object to this translation, preferring "contrary").

To refer to someone as *heyoka*, however, connotes much more than the term implies. The connotation is that the person has a special power achieved principally through dreams about thunder and lightning (the thunderbirds). A *heyoka* protects the people from lightning and storms and "his capers, which make people laugh, are holy." He is "somebody sacred, funny, powerful, ridiculous, holy, shameful, visionary." A *heyoka* "has more power than the atom bomb" (Lame Deer & Erdoes, 1973, pp. 225ff.). It is not uncommon to refer to someone who is *heyoka* as one who is also *witko*.

Those who exhibit unusual or odd behavior also can be referred to as *sicawachin* (those who scream out of emotional duress), *wasilkigla* (a person made irritable by a prolonged or chronic physical ailment), or *awaicihtani* (one experiencing a sense of guilt). Emotional scars are often attributed to the concept of *kisleya*. Those who are the victims of *kisleya* are intimidated through shaming or are shamed by someone else. The phrase *michica ki wayatka pi s?a cha istelmava pi* translates, "My children are drunks and they shame me." Shaming has a deep psychological meaning for the Lakota and can provoke profound emotional feelings that can lead to soul loss. Some actually experience extreme *kope* (a variant of paranoialike fear) because they are concerned that their kin will bring shame (soul loss) upon them.

Often people are made spirit sick through *hmunga,* which is a form of sorcery that can lead to soul loss; the term is similar to *takpe,* which means that one is in danger of spirit attack. Someone who is *wosihyagle* experiences bad luck through a wicked, evil (*sica*) source or a curse. Similarly, someone who is experiencing *wacingnun* is one who is considered to be bewildered and has an unconnected soul that is wandering around. Often one will hear someone say *mathaca ki mayaza,* which can mean "My soul is weary," yet *yaza* also can mean "pain," "ache," or "hurt." One's weariness, pain, or ache can be the result of *hmunga* and it can also mean that one is sad, tired, sleepy, and weary as a consequence of personal and social circumstances. The meaning, and therefore the translation, of *mathaca ki mayaza* is contextual and an achieved state.

Attempts to identify tribal-specific lexicons about illnesses can promote an understanding of the way the people give meaning to variations in human behavior. But linking, categorizing, or matching the lexicons according to conventional psychiatric classifications serves no one. Ethnoscience is an emerging area of interest that pushes for more culture-specific understanding, yet this fashionable perspective presumes almost unwittingly that indigenous peoples categorize human phenomena in much the same way everyone does. Indigenous populations may use categories and taxonomies, however, their linguistic rules may dictate procedures that vary considerably from one group to the next.

METHODOLOGICAL CONSIDERATIONS

The range of diversity among Indians creates some interesting sampling and methodological problems. In general, in selecting Indian respondents for psychological study, most researchers rarely go beyond a first-level nesting procedure—that is, they identify their sample as either reservation or urban. A few rely on a second-level nesting procedure in which they mention tribal affiliation, and fewer still mention tribe, blood quantum, and location of residence within a community. In many studies American Indian respondents are typically identified on the basis of physical characteristics. The more the respondent fits the physical stereotype, presumably the more authentic the sample and hence the more reliable and representative. To assure an authentic sample, many researchers include a proportionally imbalanced subset of elders.

Elders are often considered to be far more representative of a tribal culture and "Indianness" than are youth. Such sampling approaches are presumptuous and most likely do not capture the deep-structured cultural dimension that many researchers seek in their research efforts. Conventional sampling approaches used in American Indian research may capture a portion of the diversity and be representative of the collective status of contemporary Indians, but what does the research model tell us about cultural influences, lifeways, and cognitive organization? To what extent can results be generalized to tribes and to Indians in general? Probably not much. Small wonder, then, that a good deal of the research yields results with overlapping variances and small mean effects. Overlapping variances imply that those who fall into the same distribution are culturally similar. They also imply that those who fall in the overlapping portion reflect characteristics indicative of the contrast group. To the contrary, those from the contrast cultural group who fall on the alleged American Indian distribution may be assumed to be "Indian" when in fact they may not be.

Given the diversity of American Indians and current sampling issues, what can one do to capture more accurately the indigenous psychological and situational characteristics of Indian tribal units? More precisely, can an *emic* be identified given the above-stated circumstances?

Ethnic Identity and Hierarchical Nesting

As a start, the researcher should consider the importance of compiling an inventory of the nature of the unit of analysis (see Berry, 1985). The investigator then should carefully explore the concept of a unit's ideas about ethnic identification, focusing on their cognitive orientation and values expressions from a cognitive-behavioral orientation. Determining ethnicity provides researchers with data that enable them to establish more compact homogeneous subgroups. Identifying value orientations, in addition, provides data that reveal the extent to which a respondent endorses traditional indigenous values against those more representative of a dominant culture or the one serving as the major acculturating agent. Presumably a native-oriented, nonacculturated individual would endorse and act out native-oriented values, and one who expressed the least ethnic identification would espouse values more in line with the group to which he or she affiliates. Once data are accumulated on the two variables, the researcher can then proceed to conduct tribal-specific and comparative cross-cultural studies by introducing other variables of interest. Furthermore, data on the two variables would extend the nesting procedure to at least a fourth level, assuming a relatively homogeneous sample of members from a particular tribe or for the generalized category of American Indian.

The *hierarchical nesting* respondent identification procedure results in a rather subjective interpretation of ethnicity and value orientation. In fact, the method comes close to the main premises of symbolic interactionism, which are (a) "humans act toward things on the basis of the meanings that the things have for them"; (b) "the meaning of the things is derived from, or arises out of, the social interaction that one has with one's fellows"; and (c) "the meanings are handled in, and modified through, an interpretative process used by the person in dealing with the things he encounters" (Blumer, 1969, p. 2). In more specific terms, ethnicity and expression of values are centralized meanings particular to the individual and therefore have intrinsic importance in their own right.

The main premise of symbolic interactionism closely resembles Triandis's (1972) notion of subjective culture, however, he takes a more collective rather than an individual approach. "By subjective culture," Triandis says, "we mean a cultural group's characteristic way of perceiving its social environment" (p. 3). The variables of the subjective culture approach are essentially attributes of cognitive domains and are analyzed by extracting consistently generated responses that form a map outlining the group's characteristics.

Neoidiographic Ethnic Identity

Use of both perspectives comes close to the emergent thinking of the *neoidiographic* approach, a term probably first introduced by Zavalloni (1980). This approach actually emphasizes the person element in the person × situation schema advocated by the interactional school of personality. The importance of a neoidiographic perspective, as suggested by Mischel (1973), lies in the manner in which an individual *interprets* and *internalizes* lifeways and converts them to thoughtways. Zavalloni emphasizes that neoidiographic data take the form of "psychological processes that are idiosyncratic and individual rather than central tendencies in an aggregate" (p. 109). Data, therefore, take the form of *idiosyncratic cognitive productions* such as those elicited by free-association procedures.

It can be argued that ethnic identification is a subjective experience designed "to express affiliation, allegiance or oneness" with a preferred group (Casino, n.d., p. 16). Equally important is the notion that ethnic identity is contextual and that it "is a product of social *transaction* insofar as one assumes an ethnic identity by claiming it and demonstrating the conventional signs of membership. A claimant is always subject to the response of others who may concur with or deny the claim" (Casino, n.d., p. 18; emphasis added).

Efforts at establishing ethnic identity typically occur at an *exonymic* level (Casino, n.d.), where the researcher presents a set of fixed attitudelike statements to the respondents. Often the ethnic identity scale resembles a pseudoetic set of items. What emerges is an outsider-produced, *exonymic,* level of identity, and not the respondent's *autonymic* definition. Ethnic actors indeed embody an ethnic consciousness (Klineberg & Zavalloni, 1969) that is closely aligned with the culturalogical elements of the group with which they affiliate. The ultimate test, of course, is "the authentic union of personal identity (the autonym) with communal identity" (Casino, n.d., p. 17). Therefore, it is logical to assume that a concordance would exist between the *autonymic* and the *exonymic* where the importance is placed on the individual's own categories and intentions for self-identification. Yet it would be foolhardy to assume that the individual's criteria would not line up with those of the group— often, however, the criteria developed by researchers do not align with the group's criteria and hence may well be conceived as *pseudoexonymic.*

Nesting the ethnic identity of an individual from a neoidiographic process and following the symbolic interactionist approach can serve to refine the identification of American Indian samples. It makes sense, then, that identifying respondents merely on the basis of outward physical appearances and their present places of residence is hardly useful in establishing an *authentic* representation of the cultural or tribal group in question.

Neoidiographic ethnic identification involves more than merely nesting subjects in a hierarchical scheme. More often than not, individuals will use rather *ethnolocal* speech patterns and gestures to promote the authenticity of their claims. If outward physical appearances do not mesh, or there is the sense that the other party doubts the identity claim, ethnic actors will tend to exaggerate and give emphasis to mannerisms and speech idiosyncracies known to be particular (or peculiar) to the group in question. Such emphasis of ethnolocal mannerisms often occurs when people from the same ethnic group gather in geographic areas other than their homelands or communities of common origin. The somewhat stylized ritual can be referred to as *situational ethnicity*; ethnic actors take the occasion to reaffirm their ethnicity, often to the dismay and puzzlement of outsiders. Including these ethnicity-specific mannerisms in a measure of ethnic identification, although a worthy research effort in its own right, would be awkward, time-consuming, and possibly redundant.

Ethnolocal Value Orientation

A more suitable companion to the measurement of ethnic identity involves a measure of ethnolocal value orientations. The logic of this recommendation rests in part with the notion that "values refer to orientations toward what is considered desirable or preferable by social actors. . . . they express some relationship between environmental pressures and human desires" (Zavalloni,

1980, p. 74). Advocates of the symbolic interactionist perspective further emphasize the importance of values, as "the glue that holds a society, as the controlling regulator that brings and keeps the activities in a society in orderly relationship, and as the force that preserves stability in a society" (Blumer, 1969, p. 74). Triandis (1972) takes this idea one step further by maintaining that values are reflected in specific types of behavior exhibited by individuals.

Zavalloni (1980, p. 90) does not see values as central tendencies of a society, and argues that they should not be invoked as explanations of the causes of social behavior. Values, at their best, are an *emergent* product of social interaction. Therefore, in the course of their transactions actors will display behavior presumed to be desirable and preferable.

There is a growing body of evidence suggesting that value orientations are indigenous and particular to ethnic groups, and that within groups values may be interpreted and enacted within individuals (see Triandis, 1972; Trimble, 1982; Zavalloni, 1980). That being the case, it makes sense to identify ethnicity-specific values and link them with symbolic expressions of ethnic identity. Given that the ultimate test of identity involves an authentication of one's personal identity with that of the community, it is logical to assume that value expression, too, would be subject to authentication. For example, if an ethnic actor claims an identification with an Eskimo community in Alaska, then most assuredly the actor would value generosity, a value central to transactions among village residents—if the actor gave an indication to the contrary, he or she would likely be suspect (despite outward physical appearances) and probably be accused of thinking and acting like a white man. Ethnic actors may be convinced that they are every bit what they say they are, yet the resonance of their ethnic claims may be undermined if their behavior is discordant with the preferred and valued behavior of the ethnic community.

Does the discordance between identification and communal preferred value expressions imply that the actor is seen as a less acceptable member? For American Indians and Alaska Natives it depends on who you talk to and who is making the judgment. Most often, but not always, the judgment of traditional elders may be final.

The value orientations of American Indians have received some attention in the past decade or so. Bryde (1972) identified and compiled a contrasting set of American Indian and non-Indian American values based on information he obtained from numerous informants, primarily from the Siouan bands in North and South Dakota:

- *Present oriented versus future oriented:* American Indians live in the present. They are not concerned about what tomorrow will bring, but enjoy now. Non-Indians live for tomorrow, constantly looking to and planning for the future.

- *Lack of time consciousness versus time consciousness:* Many tribal languages have no linguistic equivalent for time consciousness. For Indians there is always time to accomplish what must be done, even if tasks are not completed today. The lives of non-Indians, on the other hand, are governed almost entirely by time. Those who are prompt are respected and those who are not are usually rejected and reprimanded.

- *Generosity and sharing versus personal acquisitiveness and material achievement:* American Indians get in order to give. The one who gives the most commands the most respect. By contrast, non-Indians are judged by what they have, so that material achievement means acquiring many possessions, which in turn carry the hope of social mobility.

- *Respect for age versus emphasis on youth:* American Indians respect persons who have knowledge of the people and the world around them. Older American Indians are respected for their wisdom and knowledge. The non-Indian society places a greater importance on youth, an emphasis seen daily on television and in politics, for example.

- *Cooperation versus competition:* American Indians learn to get along with others and to value working with others. In the American Indian group there is conformity, not competition. Non-Indians believe that competition is essential. Progress results from competition, and lack of progress may be synonymous with lack of competition. Every aspect of daily living in the non-Indian culture is quite competitive.

- *Harmony with nature versus conquest over nature:* Nature, in the American Indian view of the world, is indivisible, and a person is only a part of that one thing. American Indians accept the world and do not try to change it. Non-Indians attempt to control the physical world, to assert mastery over it—the more control over nature, the better.

Zintz (1963, p. 175) provides another list of values drawing comparisons between Anglo-Caucasian and Pueblo groups from the southwestern United States:

Pueblo	*Anglo*
harmony with nature	mastery over nature
present time orientation	future time orientation
explanation of natural phenomena	scientific explanation for everything
follow the old ways	climb the ladder of success
cooperation	competition
anonymity	individuality
submissiveness	aggression
work for present needs	work to get ahead
sharing wealth	saving for the future
time is always with us	clock watching
humility	win first prize if at all possible
win once, but let others win also	win all the time

The contrasting lists of values identified and developed by Bryde and Zintz closely follow the early work of Kluckhohn and Strodtbeck (1961). Specifically, the latter researchers investigated the value orientations of five communities in the American Southwest; the Zuni and Navajo tribes were part of the sample. Their extensive work led to the identification of five common human problems that the five groups shared and for which the groups differed in value orientations about the solutions.

An examination of the Bryde and Zintz lists reveals remarkable similarities given the distinctive lifeways and thoughtways of Plains Indians and those from the southwestern part of the United States. Both, however, reflect an etic assessment, and future research should build on indigenous-grounded perspectives. In an attempt to shed some insight on a portion of the etic problem, Trimble (1982), using an open-ended sentence completion format, found that Indian and non-Indian students attending the same small high school in southeastern Oklahoma differed significantly in their value expressions. In another study, Trimble (1982) surveyed 791 Indians from five separate areas of the United States and found strong agreement for seven value dimensions. Hence there is some evidence that a generalized value orientation does exist for American Indians and that they do differ, however slightly, from the dominant culture. Brown (1969) points out that essential American Indian values, especially among the Plains Indians, have persisted despite the encroachment of more dominant American lifeways. Admittedly, more research is needed on the subject, as the body of literature is rather scant.

SUMMARY AND IMPLICATIONS

What then are the implications for promoting an investigation of ethnic identification in tandem with value expressions among American Indians? First, we believe anthropologists, psychologists, psychiatrists, and sociologists who do research on Indians need to abandon their reliance on a broad ethnic category. By itself, the term *American Indian* is vacuous and provides little in the way of cultural specificity. Furthermore, when data gathered on American Indians are compared with those from other ethnic populations the meaninglessness of the findings are enhanced. In the main, use of ethnic glosses in comparative cultural research may well serve to perpetuate negative stereotypes as little credence or attention is given to the diversity particular to the groups in question.

Second, use of ethnic identifiers and preferred value expressions would be useful in expanding our knowledge of the acculturative process. Often, researchers use acculturative measures as a means for identifying ethnic affiliation. Not only is the emergent result a pseudoetic finding, but it seems to deny the respondent the opportunity to express his or her subjective sense of identification, the autonym. Use of neoidiographic approaches would place the measure of acculturation in a more realistic perspective, where ethnic identification and preferred behaviors would have central importance. More than that, ethnic actors who profess a subjective belief in their common descent do so because of the need to propagate and maintain group formation and cohesion.

Finally, use of ethnic identification and values orientations via the route of symbolic interactionism could result in a clearer and more concise understanding of the ethos and eidos of American Indian groups. Eventually, the result of adding additional psychological and sociological variables could lead to a formulation of an indigenous psychology that is sensitive to the unique lifeways and thoughtways of native populations.

NOTE

1. The term *American Indian* is an ethnic gloss (see Trimble, 1991). It is a term imbued with political and social considerations and is used in this chapter to refer to the aboriginal population of the United States. American Indians, or Indians, in fact, constitute a complex array of more than 300 distinct tribes or nations currently residing in the United States, among whom at least 100 different languages are spoken.

REFERENCES

Benedict, R. (1959). *Patterns of culture.* Boston: Houghton Mifflin.

Berry, J. W. (1985). Cultural psychology and ethnic psychology: A comparative analysis. In I. Reyes Lagunes & Y. Poortinga (Eds.), *From a different perspective: Studies of behavior across cultures* (pp. 3-15). Lisse, Netherlands: Swets & Zeitlinger.

Berry, J. W., Trimble, J. E., & Olmedo, E. (1986). Assessment of acculturation. In W. J. Lonner & J. W. Berry (Eds.), *Field methods in cross-cultural research* (pp. 291-324). Beverly Hills, CA: Sage.

Blumer, H. (1969). *Symbolic interactionism: Perspective and method.* Englewood Cliffs, NJ: Prentice-Hall.

Brown, J. E. (1969). The persistence of essential values among North American plains Indians. *Studies in Comparative Religion, 3,* 216-225.

Bryde, J. (1967). *Modern Indian psychology.* Aberdeen, SD: Bureau of Indian Affairs.

Bryde, J. F. (1972). *Indian students and guidance.* Boston: Houghton Mifflin.

Casino, E. S. (n.d.). *Introduction to ethnicology: Ways of talking about ethnicity.* Unpublished manuscript, Honolulu, HI.

Erikson, E. H. (1939). Observations on Sioux education. *Journal of Psychology, 7,* 101-156.

Forbes, J. (1990). The manipulation of race, caste and identity: Classifying AfroAmericans, Native Americans, and red-black people. *Journal of Ethnic Studies, 17*(4), 1-51.

Freeman, D. (1984). *Margaret Mead and Samoa.* New York: Penguin.

Honigmann, J. J. (1949). *Culture and ethos of Kaska society* (Yale Publications in Anthropology 40). New Haven, CT: Yale University Press.

Kelso, D., & Attneave, C. (1981). *Bibliography of American Indian mental health.* Westport, CT: Greenwood.

Klineberg, O., & Zavalloni, M. (1969). *Tribalism and nationalism.* The Hague: Mouton.

Kluckhohn, F. R., & Strodtbeck, F. L. (1961). *Variations in value orientations.* New York: Harper & Row.

Lame Deer, J., & Erdoes, R. (1973). *Lame Deer: Seeker of visions.* New York: Simon & Schuster.

Macgregor, G. (1970). Changing society: The Teton Dakotas. In E. Nurge (Eds.), *The modern Sioux: Social systems and reservation culture.* Lincoln: University of Nebraska Press.

Mail, P. D., & McDonald, D. R. (1980). *Tulapai to Tokay: A bibliography of alcohol use and abuse among Native Americans in North America.* New Haven, CT: HRAF.

Manson, S., Shore, J., & Bloom, J. (1985). The depressive experience in American Indian communities: A challenge for psychiatric theory and diagnosis. In A. Kleinman & B. Good (Eds.), *Culture and depression* (pp. 331-368). Berkeley: University of California Press.

Mead, M. (1953). National character. In A. L. Kroeber (Ed.), *Anthropology today.* Chicago: University of Chicago Press.

Mischel, W. (1973). Toward a cognitive social learning reconceptualization of personality. *Psychological Review, 80,* 252-283.

Svennson, F. (1973). *The ethnics in American politics: American Indians.* Minneapolis: Burgess.

Triandis, H. C. (1972). *The analysis of subjective culture.* New York: John Wiley.

Trimble, J. E. (1982). Value differences and their importance in counseling American Indians. In P. Pedersen, J. G. Draguns, W. J. Lonner, & J. E. Trimble (Eds.), *Counseling across cultures* (pp. 201-226). Honolulu: University of Hawaii Press.

Trimble, J. E. (1991). Ethnic specification, validation prospects, and the future of drug use research. *International Journal of the Addictions, 25*(2A), 149-170.

Trimble, J. E., Manson, S., Dinges, N., & Medicine, B. (1984). American Indian concepts of mental health: Reflections and directions. In P. Pedersen, N. Sartorius, & A. Marsella (Eds.), *Mental health services: The cross-cultural context* (pp. 199-220). Newbury Park, CA: Sage.

Zavalloni, M. (1980). Values. In H. C. Triandis & R. W. Brislin (Eds.), *Handbook of cross-cultural psychology: Vol. 5. Social psychology.* Boston: Allyn & Bacon.

Zintz, M. V. (1963). *Education across cultures.* Dubuque, IA: William C Brown.

9

DEVELOPING A
FILIPINO PSYCHOLOGY

VIRGILIO G. ENRIQUEZ

The history of psychology in the First World has been interpreted as moving toward the goal of universal knowledge. It has separated from philosophy and consciously modeled itself after the natural sciences. First World psychology has been partial to "universal" findings and scientific values of replicability, verifiability, and generalizability. In a sense, universality is the motive behind the series of systematically replicated experiments, from rats to humans, from the laboratory to the field.

American psychologists are no longer contented with studying white Anglo-Saxon sophomore university students. They are now interested in blacks, Hispanics, and other minority groups. Filipino psychologists similarly have gone beyond the convenience of captive university classes and air-conditioned Makati offices. They have gone to the field themselves. Just like their colleagues in anthropology and linguistics, the psychologist, Filipino or otherwise, now occasionally faces the discomfort of "mud huts and mosquitoes."

Although field research in Third World countries may not always be welcomed sociopolitically, it is probably a turning point in providing a much broader data base. It should be stressed, however, that a broader data base is far from adequate for assuring a global psychology unless alternative perspectives from non-Western psychologies are put to use. In fact, there is a need to rewrite the history of psychology with due consideration to Asian thought, experience, and perspectives.

PHILOSOPHICAL ISSUES
IN INDIGENOUS PSYCHOLOGY

The need for the cultural validation of supposedly universal concepts and methods moves us away from the political overtones of the term *indigenization* and leads us to consider more fundamental human issues. In the area of cross-cultural psychology, Serpell (1977) poses the issue as revolving around "*appropriate* ways of describing and explaining the behavior of human beings" (p. 4; emphasis added). It can be argued that this use of the word *appropriate* advisedly takes the issue out of the exclusive arena of psychological and scientific disputations and puts it back where it belongs (i.e., the philosophy of values).

A growing number of social scientists have been wary of the inappropriateness or even patent inapplicability of Western models in the Third World setting. It is ironic that most of the people who express this kind of concern are precisely the social scientists from Third World countries who were trained in the West or in the Western tradition. Reservations range from a call for local adaptation or modification of Western models to outright charges of intellectual dependence and academic imperialism. However, some Third World social scientists acknowledge the problems, but shrug them off on the grounds that there are no suitable alternative indigenous models and concepts to use. In addition, there are those who see nothing at issue at all because they are convinced that any departure from the Western approach is blasphemy at the altar of science.

Issues along this line are not limited to Third World countries. They are also found in the West, as can be gleaned from Graumann's (1972) report as past president of the German Society of Psychology on the state of German psychology. Graumann noted O'Connell's (1970) perception of "a relatively uncritical dependence on American psychology" as "thriving in Germany today." Graumann found this hard to deny, because "at least 50% (or even more likely 80%) of all psychologists in the world live in the U.S.A. and a similar high percentage of the more than 20,000 yearly psychological publications are written in English" (p. 129).

A similar observation can be made on the state of psychology in Japan, an economic giant and an Asian member of the First World, if not of the Western world, by affinity. Hoshino and Umemoto's (1986) report on Japanese psychology is indeed a description of the status of Western (particularly American) psychology in Japan. Except for localized exceptions such as the work on indigenous psychology in Kyoto, indigenous Japanese psychology is mainly handled by anthropologists, philosophers, and humanists.

The American dominance in psychology needs to be reexamined, not only because of the notable achievements outside of North America that have been ignored due to language barrier (for example, Soviet psychology), but more so because of the invaluable resource lodged in otherwise ignored national psychologies, particularly those of the Third World. Western psychologists themselves who rally under the banner of "cross-cultural psychology" have argued for a universal psychology as contrasted with psychology based on generalizations from studies done in industrialized countries. The arguments are forceful and the sentiments real, but a "cross-cultural psychology" will remain a promise as long as indigenous psychologies are untapped because of language and culture barriers.

One must challenge the unstated bias in O'Connell's (1979) concern for the German dependence on American psychology and Graumann's measure for reacting to this concern. By *psychologist,* these writers apparently meant one who has an academic degree in psychology. A strict adherence to the union-card criterion of being a psychologist would of course exclude not only a sizable number of eminent thinkers in the Western tradition and scholars who obtained their degrees in history or anthropology in the specialized West, but also the unwritten but no less real psychologies of peoples who may not even have a tradition of publishing journal articles in psychology to speak of. The validity of unwritten psychologies does not depend on the extent and manner of their articulation.

Graumann's statistics on publications also imply a high regard, if not reverence, for the printed or written word. In this mode of thinking, one immediately looks away from cultures with unwritten languages and almost unconsciously looks up to the university-trained psychologist.

Figure 9.1 suggests an alternative model aimed at developing a global psychology through a cross-indigenous perspective. In this model, the different cultures of the world are tapped as sources of cultural knowledge. The resulting pool may then be called cross-cultural knowledge. More aptly, it is cross-indigenous knowledge, to distinguish it from the kind of cross-cultural knowledge derived from an application of the psychology of industrialized countries to data gathered from the Third World (see Figure 9.2).

SIKOLOHIYANG PILIPINO:
TOWARD THE DEVELOPMENT
OF INDIGENOUS FILIPINO PSYCHOLOGY

Given the colonial background of Filipino psychology, and considering the Great Cultural Divide as East meets West in the development of psycho-

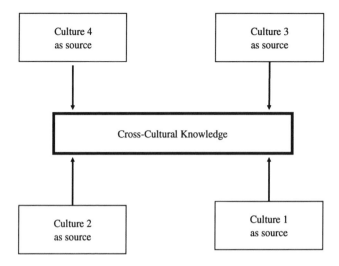

Figure 9.1. Toward a Global Psychology Through a Cross-Indigenous Perspective
NOTE: The direction of arrows indicates indigenization from within.

logical thought in the Philippines, a movement has evolved in the Philippines emphasizing the following dominant themes: (a) identity and national consciousness, specifically looking at the social sciences as the study of humankind and *diwa* (consciousness and meaning), or the indigenous conception and definition of the psyche, as a focus of social psychological research; (b) social awareness and involvement as dictated by an objective analysis of social issues and problems; (c) national and ethnic cultures and languages, including the study of traditional psychology, called *kinagisnang sikolohiya* by Salazar (1983); and (d) bases and application of indigenous psychology in health practices, agriculture, art, mass media, religion, and so on, but also including the psychology of behavior and human abilities as demonstrated in Western psychology and found applicable to the Philippine setting.

The movement has three primary areas of protest. First, as a *sikolohiyang malaya* (liberated psychology), the movement is against a psychology that perpetuates the colonial status of the Filipino mind. The psychology of *pagbabagong-isip* is seen as a step toward the decolonization of the Filipino psyche through "reawakening" as a stage in the development of national consciousness. Second, the movement is against the importation, and imposition, of psychology in the Third World that has been developed in, and is appropriate to, industrialized countries. Thus *sikolohiyang pang-industriya* (industrial psychology) is reconceptualized as an aspect of *sikolohiyang pangkabuhayan* (livelihood/economic psychology). As a consequence, a

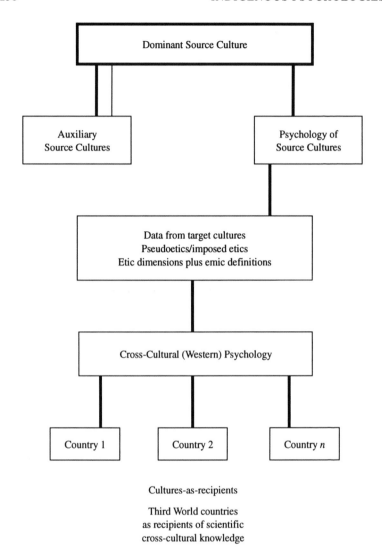

Figure 9.2. Schematic Diagram of Uninational Dominance in Psychology: Indigenization From Without

shift in theoretical and research focus also led to a change in the application of psychology toward serving the underserved. Within the Philippines this meant a move from the cities to the rural villages. Third, as a *sikolohiyang mapagpalaya,* the movement is against a psychology used for the exploitation of the masses.

The new consciousness, labeled *sikolohiyang Pilipino,* has emerged through the use of local languages as a tool for the identification and rediscovery of indigenous concepts. Filipino language is seen as the appropriate medium for the delineation and articulation of Philippine realities together with the development of a scientific literature that embodies the psychology of the Filipino people.

Sikolohiyang Pilipino can be explained through a metaphor: the difference between a *tao sa bahay* (person in the house) and a *taong-bahay* (a house person). A *tao sa bahay* may be someone who just passed by, a visitor who is not voluntarily or necessarily interested in staying in the house. But a *taong-bahay* is a permanent dweller and has a role in his or her house. *Sikolohiyang Pilipino* is like a house person as it focuses on indigenous developments in the field of psychology from the Filipino perspective. It is most commonly understood to mean the psychology of Filipinos: their character, their values, and their *paninindigan* (principles). *Sikolohiyang Pilipino* refers to psychological theory, knowledge, method, and application developed through the Filipino culture (Enriquez, 1976).

San Buenaventura (1983) has identified three major goals or *kaganapan* (realization, fulfillment, or completeness) of *sikolohiyang Pilipino.* They are *pagsasakatutubo* (indigenization), *pagka-agham* (science), and *pagkapilipino* (appropriateness to the Filipino identity). Rood (1985) sees the goal of *sikolohiyang Pilipino* as being made up of three interrelated tasks: the development of indigenous psychological concepts, the utilization of indigenous research methods, and the creation of a more authentic and appropriate social scientific psychology.

Filipino national scientist Alfredo V. Lagmay (1984) is clear in his stand that *sikolohiyang Pilipino* should evolve on the basis of a "total approach." By "total," Lagmay refers to the fact that although the method is objective and scientific, the approach undeniably involves the total human being, including human judgment and human values. As an analogy, engineers' knowledge and their technical ability to build a bridge do not constitute an end. The "total" approach also includes the question, For whom are you building the bridge? Ventura (1980) summarizes this orientation as follows:

> A reader of Philippine psychology literature will immediately note that the decade of the seventies was marked by a concern for indigenization, a recognition of language as a basic variable in personality, social psychology and testing, a broadening of the data base of Filipino psychology through a concern for studying individuals in their natural social setting, rediscovering of the ties of Filipino psychology with other fields of study, and greater involvement, on a nation-wide level, of Filipino social scientists in the development of the literature of Filipino psychology. In the University of the Philippines, the interest

in indigenization brought about research on Philippine psycholinguistics, Filipino concepts and cognition, and master's theses which utilized language as a major variable (Ventura, 1973; Lazo, 1974; Alfonso, 1974). Along with this recognition of the importance of language came a consciousness of the limitations and sometimes emptiness of Western theories and methods. Students became more critical about the Western orientation in research and in the classroom. Mangulabnan (1977) referred to this as *metodong angat-patong* (literally, "lift-pile" method) and aptly described the uncritical acceptance and use of Western theories and strategies.

Sikolohiyang Pilipino does not advocate that foreign theories should be discarded on the grounds of their origin. Uncritical rejection is just as dangerous as uncritical acceptance of Western theories. *Sikolohiyang Pilipino* calls for the exercise of care in the adoption of foreign theories. Bonifacio (1980) explains:

> [We have to] exercise care in using them [Western theories] because the actual sources of such explanations are very different from ours. While it is true that no one in any society is exempt from psychological problems, we have to underscore the fact that the sources of such problems differ greatly from one society to another.

Sikolohiyang Pilipino need not be caught in the debate between the nomothetic and the ideographic. It is not even a choice between the nomological and the hermeneutic. It is enough to realize that science is not value free and that culture is a context for the scientific enterprise. Indigenous psychology does not aim to create a psychology applicable only to the indigenous culture. More accurately, indigenous psychology aims to develop a psychology based on and responsive to the indigenous culture and realities.

IN SEARCH OF CORE FILIPINO CONCEPTS

The task of identifying key concepts for understanding people's minds, personalities, or behaviors is a difficult task. In this section I will identify existing, meaningful, and lexicalized concepts in the Filipino language. These concepts can be the key for understanding Filipino social psychology.

Language is not merely a tool for communication. Meaningful concepts for understanding a culture are most often identifiable in the culture's own language. Existing literature abounds with such concepts as *amor propio, bahala na, pakikisama, hiya, utang na loob,* and *kapwa.* These concepts, however, function as mere labels, with very little research and understanding of their deeper significance and content. Moreover, indigenous Philippine terms most often found in American-oriented English-language research are drawn primarily from the Tagalog language of Central Luzon (*bahala na, ningas kugon,* and so on). A smattering of concepts are occasionally plucked from different regions of the country (e.g., *mahay* and *gaba* from Cebuano), but as a whole, the analysis and interpretation of Filipino values are substantially keyed to a foreign language and perspective.

The token use of Filipino concepts and the local language has led to the identification of some supposedly Filipino national values. Among the frequently mentioned values are *hiya* (shame), *pakikisama* (yielding to the leader or majority), *utang na loob* (gratitude), *amor propio* (sensitivity to personal affront), and *bayanihan* (togetherness in common effort). Some regional values that have been recognized include *maratabat* (a complex combination of pride, honor, and shame), *balatu* (sharing of one's fortune), *ilus* (sharing surplus food), *kakugi* (meticulousness and attention to detail), *patugsiling* (compassion), *kalulu* (empathy), *hatag gusto* (generosity), *paghiliupod* (faithfulness in need or plenty), and *pagsinabtanay* (fidelity with one's promises) (Elequin, 1974).

The emphasis in this kind of research, then, apparently, is the search for the English equivalent of the indigenous term. The label is fitted, squeezed, and pushed into the mind-set concomitant to the foreign equivalent. The term's real significance in the Philippine context is diminished if not entirely lost. More sinister still, by lifting the indigenous term from its milieu and slapping it on a supposed value, the researcher can attach whatever significance he or she may wish to assign to the latter. In the hands of a Western-oriented researcher whose motivation in doing the research may concededly be academic, such privileges may, unwittingly, be supportive of oppressive ends.

The inappropriateness of this dangerous approach to the study of Filipino values can best be seen in the concepts most often treated and highlighted in research of this ilk: *hiya, utang na loob,* and *pakikisama.* Many social scientists have studied these as separate values and in isolation from all others. Moreover, popular writers, taking their cue from these studies, often situate these values at the very seat of the Filipino's personality.

The alternative is to provide a systematic analysis of concepts that are indigenous to the Filipino culture. The three concepts of *hiya, pakikisama,* and *utang na loob* are such a triad, whose legs emanate from a single trunk, the actual core value of the Filipino personality. This core value has been identified as *kapwa.* Thus surface values are not free-standing values that anyone can assume at will. The core value must be cultivated and understood first before the full meaning of the surface values can become apparent and appreciated. These concepts emphasize a strong sense of human relatedness.

Interrelatedness of individuals can be considered the basic unit of analysis. Filipino language is rich with conceptual terms that describe and delineate various forms of interrelatedness.

In earlier work, I identified eight different levels of interrelatedness in Filipino language (Enriquez, 1985, p. 262):

1. *pakikitungo* (transaction/civility with)
2. *pakikisalamuha* (interaction with)
3. *pakikilahok* (joining/participating with)
4. *pakikibagay* (in conformity with/in accord with)
5. *pakikisama* (being along with)
6. *pakikipagpalagayan/pakikipagpalagayang-loob* (being in rapport/understanding/acceptance with)
7. *pakikisangkot* (getting involved with)
8. *pakikiisa* (being one with)

These concepts are the basis of interrelatedness and, more important, the basis of human interactions. The eight levels range from "the relatively uninvolved civility in *pakikitungo* to the total sense of identification in *pakikiisa*" (p. 262).

For example, in the language of food, there are several different meanings for sharing among the Filipino Bulacan middle class. The language is divided into two categories: one for the "outsider" and one for "one of us." For the *ibang-tao* (or the "outsider" category), there are three levels: *pakikitungo* (level of amenities), *pakikibagay* (level of conforming), and *pakikisama* (level of adjusting). For the *hindi ibang-tao* or "one of us" category, there are two levels: *pakikipagpalagayang-loob* (level of mutual trust) and *pakikiisa* (level of fusion, oneness, and full trust).

There is a superordinate concept that embraces both the "outsider" category and "one of us" categories. It is *kapwa* (roughly translated as "fellow being"). The concept of *pakikipagkapwa* encompasses all levels in both categories, and is considered to be a most important psychological term. It is not a superficial level of interaction, but refers to "humaneness to its highest level."

The closest English equivalent of *kapwa* is "others." However, the Filipino word *kapwa* is very different from the English word *others*. The English word denotes a boundary between self and other; it is an exclusionary term. *Kapwa*, however, is an inclusionary term, emphasizing the unity of the self with others. In the English language, *others* is used in contrast to *self*, and suggests the recognition of the self as a separate and distinct identity. *Kapwa*, in contrast, recognizes shared identity.

Kapwa arises from the awareness of shared identity with others. As I have noted elsewhere, the *ako* (ego) and *ibasa-akin* (others) become integrated as one in *kapwa* (Enriquez, 1985). Thus the saying *Hindi ako iba sa aking kapwa* (I am no different from others) can be comprehended. Once *ako* starts to distinguish self from others, the *kapwa* is in effect destroyed.

> *Pakikipagkapwa* is much deeper and profound in its implications. It also means accepting and dealing with the other person as an equal. The company president and clerk in an office may not have an equivalent role, status, or income but the Filipino way demands and implements the idea that they treat one another as fellow human beings (*kapwa-tao*). (Enriquez, 1985, p. 267)

The use of indigenous language can lead to the identification of an underlying precondition to the existence of surface values. This is the concept and value of *pakiramdam* (shared inner perception, feeling for another). The function of this value is to act as the processor, the pivot, that spins off the surface values from the core value of *kapwa*. A person without *pakiramdam* cannot possibly have *pakikisama* and *utang na loob*. Similarly, one cannot expect *hiya* from someone who has no *pakiramdam*.

Perhaps I can best illustrate this value system using the popular Filipino conception of the *masamang tao* ("bad" or "evil" person). The *masamang tao* can be characterized as one who does not exhibit the accommodative values of *hiya, utang na loob,* and *pakikisama*. The denial or absence of each of these accommodative values is labeled: (a) the *walang pakikisama* (one inept at the level of adjustment), (b) the *walang hiya* (one who lacks a sense of *karangalan,* or honor/propriety), and (c) the *walang utang na loob* (one who lacks adeptness in respecting a shared dignity, *karangalan* and *kagandahang-loob*).

The person characterized as *walang pakiramdam* is of course worse off than any of the three "evil" characters above mentioned. It is definitely unfortunate, to put it mildly, to be afflicted with such an inadequacy. This particular sad state is captured in one Filipino word: *manhid* (numb, or absence of feeling). Such a character pales in comparison, however, beside one who is *walang kapwa*.

One argument for the greater importance of *kapwa* in Filipino thought and behavior is the shock or disbelief that the Filipino registers when confronted with one who is supposedly *walang kapwa(-tao)*. If an individual is *walang pakisama,* others might still say, "He will eventually learn," or "Let him be, that's his prerogative." If a person is *walang hiya,* others say, "His parents should teach him a thing or two." If a person is *walang utang na loob,* others might advise, "Avoid him." But if a person is *walang kapwa tao,* people say,

"He must have reached rock bottom," or "*Napakasama na niya*" (He is the worst).

The surface values can vary cross-culturally. Even the relative importance attached to the pivotal value of *pakikiramdam* is determined by cultural imperatives. Not so with *kapwa*. In the Philippine value system, *kapwa* is at the very foundation of human values. This core value then determines not only the person's personality but his or her very personhood or *pagkatao*. Without *kapwa*, one ceases to be a Filipino and human.

This basic concept reaffirms the integrity of every individual regardless of his or her status. It refers to treating everyone with dignity and respect, not because they earned it or deserve it, but because they are fellow human beings:

> Aside from the socio-psychological dimension, *pakikipagkapwa* has a moral and normative aspect as a value and *paninindigan* (conviction). Situations change and relations vary according to environment. For example, *pakikipagkapwa* is definitely inconsistent with exploitative human transactions. (Enriquez, 1985, p. 267)

These basic ideas are socialized at a very early age in the family. The family builds the foundation of individual character and morality. It serves as a vehicle for preparing a child to participate in his or her own culture. It is the locus where children learn to incorporate these basic values. As Guthrie (1968) notes:

> If there is one aspect of Philippine life that impresses a western observer it is the role of the family in the life of the individual. Filipinos inculcate a strong sense of a family loyalty which spreads beyond the nuclear family of parents and children. Family obligations extend to cousins several times removed, to in-laws and to others who are made a part of the family by such ceremonies as sponsors at a marriage or a baptism. (p. 55)

Guthrie further comments that the extended family is the basic unit in the Philippines. Within the extended family, there is mutual sharing of resources and good fortunes, and at the same time despair and disappointments are also equally shared.

THE CROSS-INDIGENOUS METHOD

The development and utilization of indigenous viewpoints can no doubt be approached in a number of ways. More important, these viewpoints occur at many levels and cut across many disciplines. What appears to be an isolated development in a particular discipline in a particular country usually proves to be part of an overall pattern. This observation obtains with greater impact in Third World countries, where lines dividing disciplines are not nearly as sacred as they are in the West.

An example of a possible approach to *indigenization from within* is outlined in Figure 9.3. To be sure, there are many ways through which indigenization from within can occur. It may also be implemented as a policy (or as a strategy, depending upon native commitment to the idea) in a variety of ways. What seems to be workable in one Third World culture may not necessarily be effective or workable in another.

Various approaches can be developed. Identification of key concepts followed by semantic and lexical elaboration need not be an element of indigenization from within in every discipline or country. What is essential are the source and direction of culture flow. Figure 9.3 shows the contrast between an example of indigenization from within and indigenization from without. The perspectives motivating either type of indigenization can even be working at cross-purposes. In fact, the term *indigenization from within* can be viewed as semantically anomalous. The term is proposed only as a convenient tool for the task of showing the difference between the development of Third World cultures in their own terms as a natural process and indigenization as seen by people who habitually perceive Third World countries as recipients and targets of culture flow.

The cross-indigenous method calls for a multilanguage/multiculture approach based on indigenous viewpoints (Enriquez, 1977). Even if it is granted that the use of a foreign language and culture does not distort social reality in the indigenous culture, it still makes a great deal of sense, for scientific and not maudlin reasons, to use the local languages and cultures as sources for theory, method, and praxis. As Alfonso (1977) puts it, the exclusive use of a supposedly international language "can lead to the neglect of the wealth of indigenous concepts and methods embodied in a language more meaningful to the culture." She argues that "developing and following a Filipino orientation in the conduct of research and teaching in psychology is not inconsistent with the goals of psychology as a science in search for universalities but rather a contribution to it." In fact, the cross-indigenous method better assures generalizability of findings precisely because several languages and cultures are used as sources and bases. The findings of Western-based psychology as applied in research and practice in a Third World country using a Western language and orientation can very well be artifacts of the language and the method.

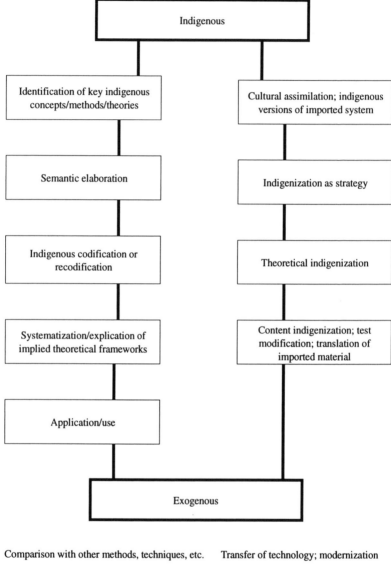

Figure 9.3. Indigenization According to Source and Direction of Culture Flow

Indigenous Methods

Indigenous methods may of course be motivated by the search for universals. Jacob and Jacob (1977), in another but similarly motivated context, put it as follows:

> The variables affecting human relations may differ radically across national cultures, so that studies within one country will not provide adequate evidence for universal generalizations about social dynamics. At least one cannot tell without conducting comparative studies in a number of differing cultural situations. (pp. 86-87)

Jacob and Jacob were ahead of their time. They are quite right in saying that "common tools and techniques are essential for successful comparative research, and they must be relevant to the circumstances being investigated" (p. 87). However, such tools and techniques have to be identified and refined. Even the "simple" task of asking questions can have a variety of parameters to make its use in one situation in the same culture different from its use in another—more so if you have a number of cultural settings involved. Even assuming that the questions are "the same" (after a series of translations, back translations, calibration according to functional equivalence, contextualization, and so on), the answers may lend themselves to a variety of interpretations.

Although people find it easy to appreciate indigenous concepts, they show initial puzzlement when "radical cultural relativists" tell them about indigenous methods. It is excruciatingly hard to liberate oneself of ethnocentric bias, especially when "your way" has been adopted and used in many situations throughout the world. In any case, it can be reasonably argued that simply because the questionnaire has evolved into a technology or even an industry in the United States, it does not follow that it should be used in the Third World. Simply because the methodology of the interview has been tossed about and refined (in certain particular ways) in the West (from research to therapy), this does not mean that Third World researchers and therapists should learn to conduct interviews in the Western way (see, for example, de Vera, Montano, & Angeles, 1975; Feliciano, 1965; Santiago, 1975). Phillips (1973), for example, does not even raise the secondary question of appropriateness and applicability in other cultures in his book *Abandoning Method,* where he challenges the use of interviews and questionnaires in sociological research. He calls attention to the more basic questions of validity and data accuracy.

In the Philippines, equally challenging are the development and application of local, and therefore culturally meaningful, innovative methods. It is not enough for the *katutubong pamamaraan* (indigenous method) to respond to the canons of science. The actual development and implementation of the method should also be sensitive to the situation and needs of the Philippines as a Third World country. The method should by all means be objective, but the approach should be *total*. Multiple operationalism is a value, but the pitfalls of reductionism are not to be ignored. Beyond the objective are a number of subjective constraints weighed against the imperatives of methodological objectivity. Filipino psychologists have long known that methods can be objective, subjective, and even projective, but they should always be appropriate. A *katutubong pamamaraan* in the Philippine context is not just culturally sensitive and appropriate, it is people oriented.

The "collective indigenous methods" described below were developed through processes of threshing out research problems, data collection, interpretation, and use of research findings through community dialogues. The myth of research expertise as the monopoly of American-trained specialists was gradually eroded.

Pagtatanung-tanong

Pagtatanung-tanong (asking around) is derived from the Filipino word *tanong*, which means "asking a question." It has been identified as an indigenous research method in Philippine social science research. The repetition of *tanong* in *tanung-tanong* means that the question is asked several times of different informants, thus increasing the reliability of the response. It also means that the people involved in the *pagtatanung-tanong* are aware that other informants are available, and thus any individual informant is not particularly burdened by the question. Someone else may answer the question or perhaps provide additional details, allowing an air of casualness to lighten the interaction. The informant never feels that he or she is being grilled or put under investigation.

Pagtatanung-tanong can be time-consuming at the start of the research, but patience can pay off in the end in the form of useful leads on where to focus the research. The researcher is able to gather otherwise inaccessible data because of the development of trust and rapport. A lot of hours are spent exchanging questions, feelings, and ideas. Regardless of the cultural setting, a research method should be accepted as natural and appropriate to the particular cultural group or subculture under study.

Pagtatanung-tanong as a research method is essentially a cross between surveys and informant interviewing. The cultural source of a culturally appropriate indigenous research method does not entail a claim that the method works exclusively in that particular culture. In her discussion of the usefulness of *pagtatanung-tanong* in cross-cultural studies, particularly among ethnic minority groups, Pe-Pua (1990) identifies four major characteristics of this method. First, it is participatory in nature. The informant has input into the structure of the interaction in terms of defining its direction and in time management. The structure is not predetermined by the researcher, as in the interview. Whereas the interview favors a listing of questions in the form of a schedule, whether tentative or final, this arrangement is not advisable in *pagtatanung-tanong*. Second, the researcher and the informant are equal in status. In fact, the researcher usually finds him- or herself in a "mutual interview," sometimes answering as many questions as he or she is asking. Third, it is appropriate and adaptive to the conditions of the cultural group. Although the interviewer favors one-to-one interaction in *pagtatanung-tanong,* it is better to start with a group of informants, if the informants so desire, in order not to invite suspicion or offend the prevailing group/cultural norms and values. Fourth, it is integrated with other indigenous research methods in the particular cultural context. *Pagtatanung-tanong* can be part of a systematic field observation together with *paali-aligid* (casing) and *pakikisalimuha* (social interaction as a research method).

Paali-aligid as an indigenous method generally serves to prepare the ground for actual *pakikisalamuha.* The cooperation of a *tulay* (bridge or medium) makes it possible for the researcher to reach a higher level of interaction with the participants. The use of the local language helps to establish rapport with the participants and their relatives. A researcher may be an outsider to the subculture under study, but can be considered an insider from the perspective of shared language and culture.

Paali-aligid as a casing activity is characterized by a fair amount of hesitancy and fascination. The *paali-aligid* approach is recommended in studies involving people who may distrust the researcher. *Paali-aligid* does not involve any direct exchange or contact with the people in the possible areas of research.

Pakikisalimuha and Levels of Interaction

In a site, a researcher needs gradually to direct interaction with the research subjects/participants in their "natural habitat," on the basis of prior *pagtatanung-tanong* and *paali-aligid.* On the basis of *pagmamasid-masid* (casual but studied observation) and *pakikiramdam* (sensitivity to interpersonal cues), the researcher decides to proceed with the interactive phase of the research, called *pakikisalamuha.* The use of tape recorders, camera, and other instruments for documentation purposes can be most effective, depending upon specific group and cultural norms.

Social interaction can be rather superficial, such as interaction at the level of amenities. The researcher can be very civil and polite. A cultural group may be ready to accept him or her as a visitor or as a compatriot or as an outsider. A deeper level of interaction is made possible through a series of intermediaries.

Pagdalaw-dalaw: Establishing and Maintaining Empathy

Participation in the activities of the community is essential in establishing and maintaining contact with research participants, their friends, and their relatives. Participation is primarily oriented toward socially desirable activities. "Talking story," listening to a friend/community member play the guitar, watching a boxing bout, and playing basketball on the neighborhood court may prove to be ideal ways of establishing rapport and camaraderie. With younger adolescents, learning how to dance street jazz routines can help pave the way to acceptance, perhaps not as one of them but as an older relative.

SUMMARY AND CONCLUSION

I have attempted in this chapter to provide an indigenous psychology developed within the Filipino cultural perspective. My goal has been to articulate a conceptual framework that is relevant to the Filipino culture, and toward this end I have systematically described some Filipino concepts. Indigenous methods have also been evolving from fieldwork. These methods have evolved out of necessity—they served practical purposes (i.e., entering into a community and earning trust). They are also imperative for helping researchers to gain a more reliable and valid understanding of the phenomena under investigation.

These conceptual and methodological advances need to be seen as a source of cross-cultural knowledge. They need to be compared and contrasted with similar or related studies in other cultures. Such cross-indigenous comparisons can lead toward the discovery of true universals.

REFERENCES

Alfonso, A. B. (1977). *Towards developing Philippine psychology: Language-related issues in teaching and research.* Paper prepared for the Fourth Conference of the Asian Association of National Languages, University of Malaysia, Kuala Lumpur.

Bonifacio, M. F. (1980, October 23). *Kamalayang Etniko at Pambansang Pananagutan* [Ethnic consciousness and national responsibility]. Presidential address, *Ika-anim na Pambansang Kumperensya sa Sikolohiyang Pilipino,* Bicol State University.

de Vera, M. G., Montano, A., & Angeles, E. A. (1975). *Ang metodo ng pagtatanung-tanong* [The method of *pagtatanung-tanong*]. Unpublished manuscript, University of the Philippines, College of Arts and Sciences.

Elequin, E. (1974). Educational goals, aims and objectives. Report of a study by a working group in Asia. Unesco-Nier Regional Programme for Education Research in Asia. National Institute for Educational Research.

Enriquez, V. G. (1976). Filipino psychology: Perspective and direction. In L. F. Antonio, E. R. Reyes, R. E. Pe, & N. R. Almonte (Eds.), *Proceedings of the First National Conference on Filipino Psychology.* Quezon City: Pambansang Samahan sa Sikolohiyang Pilipino.

Enriquez, V. G. (1977). Toward cross-cultural knowledge through cross-indigenous methods. *Philippines Journal of Psychology, 12,* 9-16.

Enriquez, V. G. (1985). *Kapwa*: A core concept in Filipino social psychology. In A. Aganon & S. M. Assumpta David (Eds.), *Sikolohiyang Pilipino: Isyu, Pananaw at Kaalaman* [New directions in indigenous psychology]. Quezon City: National Book Store.

Feliciano, G. D. (1965). The limits of Western social research methods in rural Philippines: The need for innovation. *Lipunan, 1,* 114-128.

Graumann, C. F. (1972). The state of psychology, I. *International Journal of Psychology, 7,* 123-134.

Guthrie, G. M. (1968). *Six perspectives on the Philippines.* Manila: Bookmark.

Hoshino, A., & Umemoto, T. (1986). Japanese psychology: Historical review and recent trends. In G. Blowers & A. Turtle (Eds.), *Psychology moving east: The status of Western psychology in Asia and Oceania.* Boulder, CO: Westview.

Jacob, B. M., & Jacob, P. E. (1977). The diplomacy of cross-national collaborative research. In K. Kumar (Ed.), *Bonds without bondage.* Honolulu: East-West Center.

Lagmay, A. V. (1984). Western psychology in the Philippines: Impact and response. *International Journal of Psychology, 19,* 31-44.

Pe-Pua, R. (1990). *Pagtatanung-tanong*: A method for cross-cultural research. In V. G. Enriquez (Ed.), *Indigenous psychology: A book of readings.* Quezon City: Philippines Psychology and Research Training House.

Phillips, D. L. (1973). *Abandoning method.* San Francisco: Jossey-Bass.

Salazar, Z. A. (1983). The ethnic dimension: Papers on Philippine culture history and psychology [Special issue]. *Ang Tambuli* (Counselling Center for Filipinos, Caritas Association for the City of Cologne), *1.*

San Buenaventura, M. (1983). *Philosophical basis of Filipino psychology.* Unpublished master's thesis, University of the Philippines, Quezon City.

Santiago, C. E. (1975). Ang kahulugan ng pagkalalake sa mga Pilipino. Sikolohiyang Pilipino: Mga Piling Papel. Papel Blg. 4, Serye ng mga papel sa pagkataong Pilipino, Nobyembere. [Filipino psychology: Selected papers no. 4, Series of readings in Filipino personality.]

Serpell, R. (1977). *Cultural validation of psychology* (Working paper for the Emic/Etic Study Group, Cross-Cultural Researchers' Project). Honolulu: East-West Center.

Ventura, E. (1980). *Filipino psychology: Some recent trends and developments.* Unpublished manuscript, University of the Philippines.

10

LATIN AMERICAN PSYCHOLOGY AND WORLD PSYCHOLOGY

Is Integration Possible?

RUBEN ARDILA

Psychology has developed in all the countries of the world, from those included in the capitalist industrialized world (the so-called First World) and those in the communist world (Second World) to those in the developing world (Third World). It is considered that present-day psychology has given special attention to problems of the First World and shares First World assumptions about science, humankind, and nature. The enormous advance of psychology in the United States has influenced the development of the discipline all over the world. Nevertheless, there exist important problems to be studied in other parts of the world. The Third World (Latin America, Asia, and Africa) has made important contributions to psychology that have not received enough acknowledgment. In this chapter I will refer mostly to Latin America, but will place the work in the context of the Third World in general. I will indicate ways that psychology can contribute to the comprehension and solution of problems associated with underdevelopment, such as the best use of human resources, achievement motivation, education, psychological aspects of poverty, relationships between health and behavior, and early learning. Finally, I will discuss the change in "cosmovision" required for the integration of the psychologies of the First, Second, and Third Worlds.

INTERNATIONAL PSYCHOLOGY

Psychology is above all an Anglo-Saxon phenomenon. It is conceived in English, thought about in English, written about in English, and takes into consideration problems relevant to Anglo-Saxon culture. Approximately 93% of the literature noted in *Psychological Abstracts* is written in English. Without a doubt, English has become the dominant language of science in general, not only of psychology. The United States is the nation in which most science is produced; more than half the scientists in all disciplines, not only psychology, live in the United States.

This dominance would be acceptable and would be an interesting phenomenon if it not were for certain implications. As I have indicated, above and in previous work, psychology takes into consideration problems relevant for Anglo-Saxon culture, not for other cultures (Ardila, 1982a, 1982b, 1984, 1986). It focuses on such features as evolutionism, operationalism, pragmatism, and empiricism.

Approximately 97% of the references found in psychology articles are to works published in English. This means that those who write in German, French, Spanish, and other languages must read and quote works written in English and not works in their own languages. It is most often the case that psychologists in non-English-speaking countries read about their colleagues' work in English. An article by a Spanish professor written in English is read more often by Spanish people than an article by that same professor originally written in Spanish. These points have been documented by several researchers, including Baldauf (1986) Marín (1985), Moghaddam and Taylor (1986), Ramírez (1983), Russell (1984), and Sinha and Holtzman (1984).

Important aspects are surely being left aside with this excessive emphasis on English and on Anglo-American psychology. Are there perhaps other ways of looking at psychological problems? Are there aspects of psychology that have been developed in other parts of the world and deserve greater attention? There is no doubt that the answer to both these questions is yes.

On one hand, it would be useful to have one international language and also integrated *concepts, methods,* and *goals* in psychology. Some researchers have attempted to provide such a framework (see, e.g., Ardila, 1988; Staats, 1983). The problem, however, is that findings, theories, and concepts derived from non-Anglo-American sources are not taken into account. The dominance of Anglo-American psychology (in terms of its achievements, influence, and the entrenchment of its scientific, technological, and professional perspective) has completely overshadowed advances made in other parts of the world.

Because the average psychologist speaks English, psychology journals published in other languages have difficulty establishing themselves. The main examples are the *German Journal of Psychology* for works originally published in German, *French-Language Psychology* for works in French, and *Spanish-Language Psychology* for works in Spanish. It is important to point out that only the first of these journals has survived. The other two had ephemeral lives. Marín (1985), who was the editor of *Spanish-Language Psychology*, writes:

> Several psychologists in the Americas and in Europe have maintained that the only way of diffusing their investigations internationally is when they are published in English and preferably in journals published in the United States. This idea is based on the fact that most psychologists in the world are English speakers and monolingual. If a certain ethnocentrism is added to the former phenomenon, the reason for the phenomenon mentioned before is easily explained. (p. 13)

He comments further:

> On more than one occasion one has heard a colleague say that the only way for his works to be known and quoted is to write them in English. This phenomenon is frequent not only among Latin Americans but also among Europeans who speak French or German, as can be seen from the discussions on the theme that have occupied the publications of several international associations of psychology. (p. 15)

Currently, English is the main mode of communication in psychology, analogous to the use of Latin during the Middle Ages. Those for whom English is not their first language have to dedicate a lot of time and effort to read in English, write their articles and books in English, and present results of their investigations in English. This time has to be deducted from time that otherwise would be dedicated specifically to research work (see Baldauf, 1986, for a detailed analysis of this problem, with quantitative data).

The problem is not only linguistic. It has to do with a "cosmovision," with a philosophy of research, and with the selection of issues for investigation. Psychology primarily studies issues that are relevant to the First World. Race, for example, is not an important subject in the Third World, but poverty and unemployment surely are. The psychological literature contains innumerable works on racial prejudices and very few on themes that are not directly relevant to the First World. This situation led me to point out in an earlier work that "in spite of our efforts to created a science that is universal, culture-free, and beyond the boundaries of time and space, psychology is still very much culture-bound" (Ardila, 1982a, p. 323).

THE THIRD WORLD

The term *Third World* refers to much of Latin America, Asia, and Africa. This part of this world represents the largest percentage of people living on the planet. The people of the Third World, however, live in conditions of backwardness and misery. This world contains people who are illiterate, who live under conditions of malnutrition, and who have not been integrated into the twentieth century.

The individuals and cultures that make up the Third World are not homogeneous. Problems faced by Tanzania and by Argentina, however, have many points in common, as do the problems in other countries of the Third World. There also exist great differences between them, however.

There can be numerous scenarios for socioeconomic development. Such development has many parameters that relate to health, work, education, and quality of life. These aspects are well developed in the First World. In the Third World people still die from hunger; there is unemployment; modern medicine has not been able to eradicate common diseases that have already disappeared in other parts of the world. Quality of life is quite low, except for a small percentage of the population. Malnutrition, poor medical services, lack of employment, inadequate education, and inefficient economic, social, and political infrastructures are some of the basic problems.

The countries of the Third World do not represent Rousseau's ideal of the "noble savage." Many in the First World have idealized Third World countries as places where people live without pollution, in close contact with nature, and in humane family and sociopolitical structures. But the people of the Third World, living in conditions of backwardness and underdevelopment, are not happy. Third World countries need to develop while keeping an equilibrium between development and maintaining respect for human values.

PSYCHOLOGY AND UNDERDEVELOPMENT

Psychology is the study of an organism's behavior, *behavior* meaning everything the organism does or says. Psychology has always focused on behavior, the investigation of the way humans and other animals act. It is not the study of the psychological interior, but of behavior. Psychology is a discipline that is cultivated as a science and also as a profession in the First World. People in other cultures share the same origins of psychology, define their discipline in similar ways, and face similar problems.

The concept of behavior has widened to include not only muscular contractions and glandular secretions, but also cognition, affects, and goals. Thinking, planning for the future, reflecting on one's past, and being sad are examples of behavior. Broadening the boundaries of the concept of behavior has enabled psychology to be more inclusive.

In the Third World, psychology has been widely accepted. Numerous universities in Africa, Asia, and Latin America have founded psychology departments in the past decade. The psychology of the Third World puts greater emphasis on social relevance than does the psychology of the First or Second World. Basic research is not emphasized; concrete applications are.

In the Third World the emphasis of psychology is on applications, on solving problems that these countries face. Psychology can collaborate with other disciplines in comprehending and providing solutions to important problems of the developing world. The following seven areas are among the most important.

First is the use of *human resources*. Developing countries are inefficient; people work much but produce very little. Rules related to work schedules, employee motivation, monetary incentives, and organizational structure need to be reexamined. Organizational psychology has an important role to play in ensuring better use of human resources in the Third World.

Second, developing countries are not characterized by high *achievement motivation*. They are high in motives of affiliation and of power. McClelland (1961) and his collaborators applied their theory to the Third World and obtained interesting cross-cultural results. They found that achievement motivation is lower in the Third World than in the First. Although McClelland's theory has limitations, the study of achievement motivation and its implications is an important area of research.

Third, *education* in the Third World is traditional, repetitive, and impractical. It has limited applicability and usefulness. It cannot incorporate scientific or technological advances (see Bunge, 1982). Applied behavior analysis can improve education considerably in the developing world, making it more efficient, useful, and adapted to its current needs.

Fourth, most people in the Third World are living in *poverty*. Absolute poverty is common for wide sectors of the population. Nevertheless, people do very little to change this situation; they do not use the available resources. In earlier work, I proposed a psychology of poverty based on the concept of Seligman's *learned helplessness* (Ardila, 1979b). People consider their situation desperate, and they do not do anything to rise above it. They end up thinking that control of their lives is external and not internal, that life is not made by oneself but by others: government, God, luck, politics, and the upper classes.

Fifth, most behavior associated with *health and disease* can be modified. A person's life-style can predispose him or her to health or disease. Health is affected by abuse of alcohol, tobacco, and other drugs; by lack of physical exercise; by inadequate nutrition; by stress; and by pollution. The situation is rather complex in the Third World. The role of psychology for understanding and modifying behavioral factors associated with disease can be the first step in promoting healthy human development.

Sixth, the developing world is very *young*. In Latin America the average person is no more than 20 years old. Birthrates and death rates are high, despite programs promoting birth control and advances in medicine. Early stimulation and education for children are exceedingly important in the Third World (see Ardila, 1979a, 1990).

Finally, when a country develops, the life expectancy of its people increases, sometimes going from an average of 40 or 50 years to 60 years or more. With longer life expectancy, the number of *old people* in the population increases. In the Third World old people constitute only 6% of the population; in the developed world they make up 12%. The quality of life for the elderly needs to be improved in the Third World.

The above seven areas are those in which psychology can help the most in finding solutions to problems in the developing world. Because of the emphasis on the social relevance of psychological studies, it is highly likely that these areas will soon begin to receive the attention they deserve.

When insisting on social relevance, we must not forget that psychology is above all a *science*. If we are not objective, and if we do not use the most refined methods of measurement that the science has to offer, our findings are not going to be applicable. The fact that the Third World gives more importance to social relevance than to fundamental research does not negate the importance of basic research.

INTEGRATION

There exists a long history of reciprocal distrust and misunderstanding between the First and Third Worlds. This is reflected in diverse aspects of culture, among which is science. The condition exists in many disciplines, including psychology. Many psychologists of the First World consider that advances in psychology are limited to work done in the United States, Canada, England, and Germany. On the other hand, psychologists of the Third World have a great distrust for psychology from these countries, and they emphasize the necessity of the development of an autonomous psychology that studies problems specific to and relevant for the development of the Third World (see, for example, Diaz-Guerrero, 1977). The past several years have been specially important in this respect. The gap between psychology written in English and that written in other languages has been increasing instead of decreasing, and the insistence on a psychology relevant to the Third World is being heard more frequently.

It is important to understand that we can learn from each other. With more trips to foreign lands, with psychologists coming from all parts of the globe, concepts, methods, theories, and findings of Anglo-American psychology are relevant for other parts of the world. Through greater participation in international congresses, better knowledge about what is happening beyond our own frontiers, more extensive reading in languages different from our own, greater exchange of ideas and results of investigations with colleagues who have different cultural backgrounds, more intense organizing of international affiliations, and increased joint research ventures, we can create an *international community of psychologists.* Though efforts have been made in this direction, the goal is still far away.

The most important thing we must do is to change our attitudes and our cosmovision in a way that will allow each of us to become interested in others. We need to acknowledge that we can learn much from other cultures and consider that we all share the same planetary habitat, the same place in the cosmos, similar pasts, and very similar futures. When this *planetary conception* is accepted by psychologists, the barriers that exist for integrating the psychologies of the First, Second, and Third Worlds will finally be overcome. This will benefit us all.

REFERENCES

Ardila, R. (1979a). *Los orígenes del comportamiento humano.* Barcelona: Fontanella.
Ardila, R. (1979b). Psicología social de la pobreza. In J. O. Whittaker (Ed.), *La psicología social en el mundo de hoy* (pp. 399-418). Mexico City: Trillas.
Ardila, R. (1982a). International psychology. *American Psychologist, 37,* 323-329.
Ardila, R. (1982b). Psychology in Latin America today. *Annual Review of Psychology, 33,* 103-122.
Ardila, R. (1984). Factores socioculturales en el desarrollo de la psicología: el caso de America Latina. In H. Carpintero & J. M. Peiro (Eds.), *La psicología en su contexto histórico. Ensayos en honor de Josef Brozek* (pp. 41-49). Valencia, Spain: Universidad de Valencia.
Ardila, R. (1986). *La psicología en América Latina: pasado, presente y futuro.* Mexico City: Siglo XXI
Ardila, R. (1988). *Síntesis experimental del comportamiento.* Madrid: Alhambra.
Ardila, R. (1990). *Walden three.* New York: Carlton.
Baldauf, R. B. (1986). Linguistic constraints on participation in psychology. *American Psychologist, 41,* 220-224.
Bunge, M. (1982). *Ciencia y desarrollo.* Buenos Aires: Siglo XX.
Diaz-Guerrero, R. (1977). A Mexican psychology. *American Psychologist, 33,* 934-943.
Marín, G. (1985). Difusion internacional de la psicología iberoamericana: dimensiones del problema. *Revista Mexicana de Psicología, 2,* 12-19.
McClelland, D. C. (1961). *The achieving society.* New York: Free Press.
Moghaddam, F. M., & Taylor, D. M. (1986). What constitutes an "appropriate psychology" for the developing world? *International Journal of Psychology, 21,* 253-267.
Ramírez, M. (1983). *Psychology of the Americas.* New York: Pergamon.
Russell, R. W. (1984). Psychology in its world context. *American Psychologist, 39,* 1017-1025.
Sinha, D., & Holtzman, W. H. (Eds.). (1984). The impact of psychology on Third World development [Special issue]. *International Journal of Psychology, 19*(1).
Staats, A. W. (1983). *Psychology's crisis of disunity.* New York: Praeger.

11

INDIGENOUS PSYCHOLOGIES AND SOCIAL REPRESENTATIONS OF THE BODY AND SELF

DENISE JODELET

The aims of this chapter are to extend the concept of indigenous psychologies to numerous varieties of everyday psychological interpretation and to discuss the application of the social representation paradigm as an alternative to cognitive models. This paradigm allows for a complete account of the social psychological and cultural character of the construction of self- and other-related knowledge.

Since Heider's seminal work *The Psychology of Interpersonal Relations* (1958), social psychological research has focused constant and ever-increasing attention on "lay" or "naive" psychology, referring to commonsense knowledge or everyday understanding of oneself and others' behaviors. People are studied as "intuitive scientists," practicing psychology in a spontaneous manner without the support or basis of scientific information and training (Gergen, 1989; Gergen & Gergen, 1986). This concern with naive psychology is a focus of different research trends bearing on categorization (e.g., Rosch & Lloyd, 1978; Tajfel, 1982), attribution (e.g., Jones et al., 1972; Kelley & Michela, 1980), interpersonal knowledge, impression formation and implicit theories of personality, and self-perception (e.g., Bem, 1972; Bruner & Tagiuri, 1954; Chapman, 1967; Leyens, 1983; Passini & Norman, 1966; Shweder, 1980). This position has been reinforced since the "cognitive revolution" of the 1960s. Social cognition, which deals with how people perceive, process, and organize information about themselves and others, has become a dominant field in social psychology. But according to several social psychologists, this discipline, which produced some of the earliest and most appropriate approaches to cognition (Zajonc, 1980), now suffers from the shift toward a restrictive cognitivist perspective (Forgas, 1981; Gergen, 1989; Moscovici, 1982), losing its anthropological and social scientific character (Moscovici & Farr, 1984).

One of the consequences of this situation is that dominant models existing in psychology that are designed to account for everyday perception and understanding of people's behavior, traits, motives, and so on, overlook their cultural and social dimensions. Focusing on the intraindividual processing of information, studied in the vacuum of the laboratory, and compared with logical standards of rational reasoning, they most often tend to equate naive psychology with a lower or false form of scientific knowledge, insofar as it departs from the inference rules used by scientists. Forgetting Heider's (1958) advice to "bear in mind that these processes are within one encompassing situation" (p. 14), they neglect the social relationship and context within which naive psychology is embedded. They are thus led to ignore the collectively created and shared symbolic meaning systems that control this type of cognition (Pepitone, 1986).

Along with other social psychologists who criticize this cognitive reductionism, I assert in this chapter is that lay or naive psychology must treated as an "indigenous" one, even in cultures where scientific information is widely diffused via scholarly or mass media channels. The following six reasons support this assertion.

First, as everyday knowledge, naive psychology is socially regulated. It informs the construction of a social reality as shown by the work of phenomenologists, symbolic interactionists, and ethnomethodologists (see, for example, Berger & Luckman, 1966; Cicourel, 1973; Schutz, 1962). Second, with its commonsense dimension, it is a "cultural system," historically elaborated and regulated by historically defined norms of judgment (Geertz, 1983). Third, naive psychology belongs to the domain of "folk psychology," proposed by Wundt as one of psychology's two principal fields, which emphasizes the social aspects of mental processes (Farr, 1983). Its underpinnings are found in language, collective values, morals, customs, codes of behavior, and social conceptions of humankind that are specific to a given social group or cultural entity. Fourth, it bears the marks of social communication by which it is spread (Sperber, 1985). Thus it is a sort of "folk model" or "cultural model," defined in cognitive anthropology as a model of the world that is taken for granted, widely shared, and plays a role in understanding and action (Holland & Quinn, 1987). Fifth, it has social functions: the management of verbal and behavioral interactions with others and the mastering of social and personal life. Sixth, it is linked to the elaboration and expression of social identity and membership, and it depends on group links.

This claim and its implications have a twofold consequence for the study of lay psychology. First, it is necessary to take into account the social content as well as the context of this kind of knowledge, which is practical and deeply rooted in social life. This practical knowledge is based on world experience and oriented toward the mastering of this world by means of *declarative* (knowing that) and *procedural* (knowing how) knowledge, that is to say, through propositional statements on states of the world and practical, concrete manners to act on these world states. Second, this claim also necessitates a conceptual framework for coping with aspects related to the construction, circulation, and use of everyday-life psychology. Such a model is proposed by the "social representations" approach introduced by Serge Moscovici in 1961, which he further developed along with several other social psychologists in Europe (see Jodelet, 1989). This approach allows us to treat the "naive psychologist" not as an erroneous scientist, but as an "amateur" scientist. He or she is considered a fabricator of knowledge or a "mental craftsman." This also allows us to study different indigenous psychologies from the perspective of a common framework, thus permitting the analysis to transcend the specificity of each group. Such a framework leads to truly cross-cultural comparison, encompassing psychological processes, cultural values and beliefs, ecological and social constraints, and their interweaving. This perspective promises to advance the debate on universality/viability of psychological phenomena (Jahoda, 1982; Triandis, Halpass, & Davidson, 1973).

I will examine these two points successively. But first, let me begin with an anecdote that will facilitate the discussion of the shortcomings of cognitive models in accounting for indigenous psychologies, taking attribution theory as a prototypical case. While traveling by train in southern France, I was seated facing two women returning from the burial of a mutual friend. They seemed quite perplexed by the fact that there had not been any religious ceremony; even more so that this was apparently upon the request of the deceased. Consequently, these ladies were searching for an explanation of this fact. One of them proposed a hypothesis that seemed satisfactory:

It cannot be *him*. It *must* have been his wife's fault. Don't we have the saying "*Sans foi ni loi*" [Faithlessness is like lawlessness] and *he* was a regular, orderly, disciplined sort of man. Certainly, then, he *must* have had faith. Surely he had wanted a religious funeral.

Here we have an example of the reasoning of everyday-life psychology, which calls for a popular saying that will account for an unusual event and allows for the identification of a locus of responsibility. Our faithful travelers refuse to "blame" their friend or to besmirch the integrity of their memories of the deceased. They are thus obliged to find an explanation that conforms with their values. So they recall a proverb—that is, a principle of social regulation—drawing upon their own social background.

Would the models that formalize the causal explanation process such as those of scientific psychology be useful in analyzing this sort of reasoning? I don't think so. This is a case of finding the explanation for a given decision or behavior, as studied by attribution theory. It is a case of locating responsibility in one person (the deceased or his wife) as part of a personalizing process. But the logic used here is completely different from that described in social attribution or personalization processes. We can observe an interpretation following a deductive process based on a representation of humanity. This representation is carried through social communication, by a proverb from universal wisdom, and thus infused with value. This process illustrates how commonsense thinking works. Commonsense thinking, which we can equate with indigenous thinking, calls for an analytic model other than those normally evoked by psychologists.

These cognitive-type models postulate that all our psychological knowledge is composed of inferences based on the observation of the outside world and on information processed over the course of past experience. Needless to say, this vision of the lay psychologist as a scientist or statistician, functioning in a linear or mechanical way, cannot be appropriate to the degree of complexity involved in our interpretations of everyday understanding. Another aspect of this cognitivist perspective deserves mention: the use of singular and plural forms in the qualifying of psychologies. *Indigenous psychologies* is plural in form; one reason for this is that scientists conceive of indigenous psychologies and knowledge as being linked to group cultures that are considered unique and closed, without any possibility of community or communication between each other. On the contrary, *naive psychology* always appears in the singular form. Maybe scientists believe they are studying a universal rationality in their Western-world subjects. This ethnocentric rationality hypothesis joins the fundamental issue of variability/rationality raised in anthropology. Without entering into the debate, suffice it to say that this issue is quite relevant to the scientific status of indigenous psychologies (Pepitone & Triandis, 1987). What is particularly interesting about this vision is that it leads to a pessimistic portrayal of the rational lay psychologist. In order to overcome the contradiction implied in this portrayal of the rational lay psychologist, we must call for a more social approach.

Asch (1959) stresses the idea that the psychology of the specialist comes from lay knowledge. Heider wants us to observe the richness of this spontaneous psychology in order to learn from it. We are confronted with the paradox of treating as inferior something that is assumed to be itself the source of scientific knowledge. In their quest for universality and rationality, scientific psychologists fail in their analysis of commonsense psychology, applying schemata that ignore its many dimensions. And then having lost the true matter of the issue (which is social and symbolic), they postulate an inaccurate cognitive functioning. There is not one but many lay psychologies elaborated in ways that are specific to social groups or derived from more general backgrounds, be they ideological, scientific, or traditional. As indigenous psychologies, they are anchored in cultural or social contexts that ensure their practical validity, their cognitive specificity, whether or not they are "true" in a purely dualistic way.

If we look at the naive psychologist as depicted by numerous studies, he or she appears to be a "poor scientist," characterized by imperviousness to information, a tendency to seek behavioral confirmation of his or her conceptions of others, and a propensity to explain behavior by personal causes, as Moscovici (1982) points out. When, at the same time, scientists say that this knowledge is necessary for control over and mastery of the environment, we cannot avoid being astonished by the effectiveness of such erroneous and biased functioning, unless we recognize that this functioning is embedded in the process of a social construction of reality and that the world where information is selected and processed is itself shaped by social representations.

Here are two examples. The first concerns what Ross (1977) has called "the fundamental error," the tendency of observers to underestimate the role of situational factors in the explanation of others' behavior, thus relying on dispositional, internal traits—the case being the reverse for the actor. The generality of this bias is presented as reflecting a law of the human mind. Nevertheless, it has been shown that the search for personal explanations for events occurring to people can be easily related to historical, legal, ideological, and religious prompting of individual values and responsibility in Western societies. There is an "internality norm" (Beauvois & Dubois, 1987) that serves as a guideline for our judgments. This norm is not only linked to social desirability (Jellison & Green, 1981), it also expresses a social regulation within evaluative contexts and reflects the individualism dominant in Western culture. So attributing a personal cause instead of an external, situational one is not an error of logic, inherent to the poor scientist. On the contrary, such judgments are the result of correct application of premises given by our cultural background. In this sense, our psychological knowledge is derived from more general systems and changes according to the type of reference system involved.

Going further along this line of thinking, studies conducted in France and Switzerland have established that specific social groups are more inclined than others to make internal judgments that can be associated with a Manichean view of the social world. In matters of justice, conservative and conformist groups occupying established and wealthy positions, as well as some religious groups, explain criminality mainly by psychological factors and individual guilt, whereas leftist, upper-middle-class, and young people strongly advocate the role of social conditions of deviance (Robert &

Faugeron, 1978). According to studies on xenophobia, it appears that people who are against immigration for nationalistic reasons tend to see it as the result of voluntary choice owing to loss of solidarity with the native country. Inversely, people who oppose xenophobia for humanistic reasons emphasize economic constraints as a principal incentive for immigration (Windish, 1980).

Judgments of others as well as self-judgments are based on representations of human nature and society that express the interests, values, and norms of the group (large or restricted) to which we belong. Also intervening in this process is the expression of people's social identities. This is clear in the second example concerning implicit theories of personality. The matching of physical and behavioral traits and psychological characteristics or dispositions has been found to be dependent on the representation one has of personality. It has been found that this representation and the type of matching are susceptible to change between groups and over the course of time (Paicheler & Beaufils, 1984).

In a study of social representations of the body, I have shown that links between physical appearance and psychological characteristics are not recognized in the same manners among social groups that differ in the ways they manage their self-presentation (Jodelet, 1983). In brief, there is a drastic difference observed between those who have opportunities to care for their physical appearance (rendering it attractive and conforming to the norms of a well-trained body and pleasant look, as in the upper classes) and those who do not have such opportunities because of time and financial reasons (as in the lower and middle classes). Subjects were asked if physical aspects allowed inferences either on psychological traits, such as intelligence and character, or on health and moral states, or, finally, on social status and lifestyle. Upper-class subjects generally agreed that such inferences are possible, taking physical traits as good indicators of character, intelligence, and life-style, but not of social status. Subjects in the lower- and middle-class group rejected the possibility of these inferences, conceding that in a few cases bodily appearance reveals social status or state of health, but in no case does it indicate anything about psychological dimensions. Something of social identity and status acts to determine psychological reasoning according to the image one wants to present or defend in a social context more or less favorable for self-expression. The individual not only applies this reasoning to him- or herself, but also generalizes it with regard to others. Similar results have been found concerning ethnic and religious membership.

In earlier work, I found evidence of the dependence of body images and representations vis-à-vis cultural models and cultural change (Jodelet, 1984). I studied these images and representations by comparing two groups of subjects (men and women) interviewed at two different periods in history (1963 and 1975), situated around a period of social change at the end of the

1960s. It appeared that feminism and sexual liberation, diffusion of new corporal techniques, and psychoanalysis provoked a strong transformation in the feelings people had about their bodies. In 1975, people felt freer, more experience oriented, conscious of pleasure sensations, and conscious of their physical being. Conversely, for the group interviewed 15 years earlier, the relation to the body was distant and abstract, and bodily experience was limited to feelings of pain, tiredness, and illness. In terms of knowledge, the first group was interested in psychological and social factors affecting their state of well-being. The other group focused only on medical knowledge and normative principles concerning the body. These positions have an effect on the attention paid to health and illness, and are related to a normative stance. In the former group, subjects were preoccupied by moral and technical control of their bodies, adhering to norms of respectability and good presentation. The second group insisted on the necessity of keeping the body at ease rather than controlling its postures. If they did try to exercise control over their bodies it was in the name of their functional well-being, pleasure, or seduction. Adherence to one of these two norms is correlated to body feeling associated with either illness or pleasure and activity. The interiorization or refusal of a normative model suffices to change the bodily experience radically, from morbidity to an open and healthy relationship with the body.

Similar results were observed with reference to people's conceptions of their bodies' "capacity to resist illness" and their capacities to "control the influence of their mental state on the state of their body." According to a modernist conception, the body is autonomous, self-defensive, and regulated by a moral and psychological state of will. Those in this group oppose the effectiveness of medicine and reject the idea of a biological determinism on the state of their bodies. These conceptions are associated with a distant but rational relation with medical assistance. The other group is characterized as being medically dependent. These results illustrate the correlation between actions and representations that are sensitive to cultural change.

Even if one agrees with the existence of general processes and modes of reasoning in everyday-life "psychologizing," one can avoid considering neither the qualitative content on which these processes operate nor the social context within which they are embedded. There is no "pure" lay psychology, processed in a social vacuum. There are rather multiple lay psychologies nourished by different social elements: (a) the information resources available within a given social framework, (b) the values associated with the objects of focus of psychological thinking, (c) the projection of social identity connected with the social position of groups and individuals, and (d) the goal pursued through acquisition and application of a psychological knowing "that" and knowing "how."

When we pursue the exploration, interpretation, and prediction of our own or others' psychological states, traits, and behavior, three main features emerge. First, we use an arsenal of notions, criteria, and hypotheses that we share with others. This shared arsenal has a social origin and relevance, belonging to a common culture. Second, in using this arsenal we aim less at a speculative knowledge than at a concrete one. We try to orient our communications toward partners in interaction, to understand what is occurring to us in the course of our life span, or in response to our behavior. Knowledge of this sort needs to have concrete relevance to our social life. Third, as this arsenal is a practical knowledge, its functions have specific and direct impact on its construction and its application in everyday life.

Based on a common stock of knowledge, oriented toward fitting into our environment and structured by its functional relevance, lay psychologies cannot be isolated from social content and context. They must be treated as forms of social thinking. How can we proceed to weave together knowledge and its conditions? The trail is blazed in this direction by the approach of social thinking and commonsense knowledge in terms of social representations. The number of studies undertaken under this heading renders it difficult to give a strict definition of *social representation,* but I will try to cover what could be considered nowadays a consensual description and analysis of it.

Social representations are forms of social thinking used to communicate, understand, and master the social, material, and intellectual environment. As such, they are analyzed as products and processes of mental activity that are socially marked. This social marking refers to conditions and contexts where representations emerge, to communication by which they circulate, and to the functions they serve. This form of knowledge is construed in the course of social interaction and communication. It bears the mark of the subject's social insertion. Collectively shared, it contributes to the construction of a vision or version of reality that is common and specific to a social or cultural entity. This form of knowledge has practical aims and social functions. It operates as a system of interpretation of reality, serving as a guideline in our relation to the surrounding world. Thus it orients and organizes our behavior and communication.

In order to give a view of the conceptual analysis of the representational phenomena, I have tried to formalize this field of study, taking into account the numerous research contributions developed since the seminal work of Serge Moscovici. Figure 11.1 presents the different aspects and problems tackled by social representation studies that consider in different manners a threefold central question: Who knows and from what place? What is known and how is it known? On what object and with what effect?

Condition of Production and Circulation of SR   *Process and State of SR*   *Epistemological State of SR*

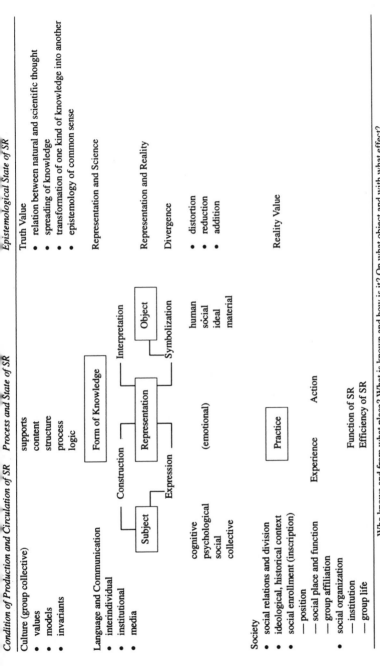

Figure 11.1. The Sphere of Study of Social Representations

At the center of the figure, a basic schema depicts the representation as a practical form of knowledge linking a subject to an object. The representation must always be studied as the representation of an object and a subject. The object can be in the material, social, human, or notional field. The nature of the representation is dependent on its specificity. Thus the representation is, along with its object, in a symbolic relation: It stands for its object and, at the same time, confers meaning upon it. These meanings are the result of an activity by which the representation appears as a construction made by the subject, expressing him- or herself. The subject may be either an individual or a group. Its representational activity is multifaceted: It can imply cognitive processes or psychological mechanisms (emotional investment, identity, motivation, and so on), but in all cases the social representation approach integrates the analysis of these processes and mechanisms of the social dimension with the social or cultural membership or participation of the subject. From this perspective, we must take into account the position of the subject in the social context or culture, the effect of social interactions and communication, or the influence of ideological trends pervading certain social groups. The social factors controlling the production and circulation of representational phenomenon are listed on the left side of the figure.

The upper right of the figure shows relations between lay and scientific knowledge. These relations have to do with scientific diffusion and vulgarization and with assimilation and transformation of scientific knowledge. This is a basic aspect to take into account in modern societies, where media channels ensure strong circulation of information. Now, turning to the practical functions of representations, we can find their root in everyday practices. They can act as versions of local theories defining a state of the world. As such they intervene, borrowing the expression of Bourdieu (1982), as "programs of perception," sculpting form out of the material, mental, or social environment.

Because a representation must be a representation *of* something, we must begin with an object socially valorized or controversial (a theory such as psychoanalysis or Marxism, an idea such as health or creativity, an event such as unemployment or nuclear hazard, and so on). We try to elicit the representation of this object by recollecting the system of beliefs, images, values, opinions, attitudes, semantic meanings, and behaviors associated with it. This system is analyzed in order to isolate a structural organization resulting from two main processes: *objectification* and *anchoring.* These processes reflect, at a formal and practical level, the social dimension involved in the construction of the representation.

Objectification explains the representation as a *selective construction, structuring schematization,* and *naturalization*—that is to say, as a cognitive whole that retains from the information provided by the external world a limited number of elements linked by relationships that form them into a structure responsible for organizing the field of representation and that is accorded the status of an objective reality. The process of anchoring comprehends a *grounding in the system of thought, allocation of meaning,* and *instrumentalization* of knowledge. This process explains how new information is first transformed and integrated into the ensemble of socially established knowledge and into the network of signification available to society for the interpretation of the real, and then reincorporated in the form of categories that serve to guide both understanding and action.

By the comparison of specific systems elaborated in different groups (the comparative study is crucial in this analysis), we are able to designate and reconstruct the social dynamics that lead to a representation characteristic of a given social situation or membership. Today, anthropologists make similar use of this notion. Social representations serve to account for the process by which, in a traditional society, interpersonal relations, power relations, and sex relations are articulated with the cultural order underlying the social organization. Representations of the person, the body, of health and illness appear as a means to particularize this cultural order for a given social entity. In the same way, we can read in social representations the expressions of a group, its values, needs, aspirations, taboos, and so on. We can also discover how a representation, with its anticipatory, legitimating, and rationalizing functions, serves the maintenance of social order and of intra- and intergroup relations.

In this manner, we can point out even at an individual level the existence of collective and shared contents of thought and social marking of cognitive activity. We can also demonstrate that this activity, a creative and generative one (designed to integrate and respond to novelty), is a process that assimilates information to an existing background. By this very mechanism, new data and the background itself are transformed.

I will now illustrate these points regarding psychological knowledge. Two examples will show how socially transmitted knowledge is used by individuals and groups to construe their interpretations of the psychological world. The first example of this process is Moscovici's study of the social representation of psychoanalysis. The diffusion of Freudian theory in society has provoked its transformation under the influence of surrounding values. The lay model of the theory identifies pathological symptoms with "complexes" resulting from "repression" situated between the opposite and conflicting forces of the "conscious" and "unconscious" mind. But in doing so, it eliminates an essential part of Freudian theory, the "libido," because of moral taboos regarding sexuality. At the same time and for the same reasons, psychoanalysis is rejected, as it is perceived to be emblematic of sexuality. Moreover, groups characterized by different cultural levels, political orientations, or religious doctrines give distinct meanings to the treatment, the patient, or the psychoanalyst, finding a way to incorporate the new science into their various preexisting mental systems. Thus for Catholics the treatment is analogous to confession and the analyst is perceived as a priest.

All these results allow the meandering of the scientific theory as it penetrates into the public sphere. One can also notice a fusion effect between old psychological notions and those taken from psychoanalysis. New concepts are used to interpret well-known psychological states and behavior: Blushing becomes the sign of a "timidity complex," submission to a professional hierarchy becomes the sign of "dependency on parental authority," and so on. In this venture the lay psychologist acts as an "amateur scientist," seeking to renew his or her knowledge to deduce and test clinical hypotheses. So on the one hand scientific knowledge becomes a lay knowledge. Is it not the fate of all scientific theory to become naive knowledge? On the other hand, lay psychology appears as a derivation from a scientific field, and not only as an algorithmic calculus based on direct observation.

I will now turn to another case of derivation, with the representation of mental illness in a peasant community in which there is a system of foster family care (Jodelet, 1991). Under the auspices of a psychiatric hospital, mentally ill patients, housed on farms, live and circulate freely among the population. Several aspects of the psychology developed by the peasants who live with the mental patients are of striking interest. For institutional reasons, the peasants do not have access to psychiatric information concerning the mental patients in the community. Obliged to interact closely with these patients, those in the peasant population were left to draw up their own theory of the significance of mental illness. In order to do so, they used data furnished by direct observation of the patients. They also borrowed from a core of traditional knowledge and notions, some of which are rooted in ancient beliefs and superstitions. Thus this peasant community fabricated a true form of indigenous psychology. Two types of illness are distinguished: one attacking the brain and another attacking the nerves. Whereas innocence is attributed to the first type, the second is perceived to be invested with a sort of natural violence, meanness, and sexuality. This model has existed from time immemorial and is found in different countries.

People imagine that the process at hand in both cases is analogous to the breakdown of natural liquids, such as blood or milk, as observed in daily farm work. One speaks of the "turning" (curdling) of the brain and nerves. With regard to the brain/nerves opposition, the causes of sickness are conceived differently depending upon the period of occurrence of the illness: childhood, adolescence, or adulthood. In the first case, the illness is perceived as caused by an innocuous brain deficiency. The second case indicates a dangerous affliction of the nerves and is attributed to "bad blood." In contrast, sickness declared during adulthood can only have an external cause, which is deduced from the value system of this rural group: All that goes contrary to local morality and life-style produces mental disorder (this includes urban life, noise, speed, schooling, and divorce).

Despite reassurances of noncontagiousness given by hospital personnel, peasants continue to think like their ancestors, believing that sickness is transmitted via bodily liquids (sweat, mucous, saliva). This belief has been reinforced by the introduction of psycholeptic drugs that redirect the illness exclusively toward the blood and the nerves. In order to protect themselves from contamination, the peasants elaborate certain rituals concerning physical contact with mental patients. They refuse to touch objects that have been in contact with the bodies of the patients, such as clothing and dishes. These objects must not be washed in the same water as those belonging to the host family. Within the family living space, they establish nontransgressible barriers. This segregation is extended to those who keep close proximity with and/or have friendly relationships with the mentally ill. The archaic representations help to recall the need to defend the group's identity and image by preventing the integration of the latter in private life. In this case, and for reasons of group survival, the rural population has shown itself to be a mental fabricator, using the cognitive elements at its disposal to derive a "knowing that" and a "knowing how."

An example concerning the knowing how (*savoir faire*) illustrates the subtlety of naive psychology. In order to familiarize the mental patients with household habits, the peasants have established a complex educational approach. For this they use handling techniques based on reinforcement: One acts on the patient through "tenderness" or through "fear," with a varied repertoire of incentive or dissuasive techniques. When confronted with unwanted behavior, one must first see if this behavior is susceptible to modification. This depends on the cause of the behavior: *education,* which itself suggests the possibility of correction; *mentality,* against which the peasants feel powerless, given the divergences between the patients' values and their own; the person's *character* and *illness.* Observation permits the peasants to distinguish these causes. For example, in order to choose between character or illness as a cause, one has to take into account how the patient relates to people. "Relating" behavior suggests a character trait, in contrast to illness, which causes the patient to withdraw in an autistic manner. Character is considered unchangeable, whereas illness is manageable. However, here too another criterion comes into play in the choice of technique. If one believes that the patient has a nerve problem, one will not use "fear" or "threat" techniques because of the danger of eliciting a violent automatic reaction. If the patient if "innocent," the punishment and reward repertoire can be used with more flexibility. This complex process mobilizes a whole theory concerning psychological functioning and effects of pathology on behavior, in order to choose an adequate and risk-free manner of relating to the mental patients. We see here that attribution processes rely on a set of conceptions of human nature, illustrating the remark of Farr and Moscovici (1984):

> The study of the mechanisms of attribution in isolation from the social contexts in which they normally operate is a serious impoverishment of the subject matter of social psychology. The antidote to this impoverishment is to study social representations as they operate in the social world outside the laboratory. (p. 24)

These findings give evidence that naive psychologies are the product of a long and subtle process of reflection and manipulation of notions taken up from diverse areas of daily life, tradition, and science. These psychologies are directly affiliated with indigenous psychologies. We must treat them as such and find the means to compare these various commonsense psychologies. In this way we are able to advance toward an anthropological psychology.

I would like to conclude by underlining how the social representation approach can contribute to this direction. This approach allows us to go well beyond interpersonal psychology, social perception, and so on. The social representation approach brings out whole knowledge systems, rooted in our cultural background and directly relevant for our daily life and *Dasein*. In this way we are able to understand adherence to a system of thought and persistence of beliefs. We can also link everyday-life psychology to a range of knowledge from other domains (traditional, social, medical, scientific) and follow the development and change in our interpretations of psychic life.

Moreover, the social representation approach allows a change in the treatment of indigenous psychologies, generally considered as by-products of closed cultural systems. Social representations do not provide us only with a means of articulating psychological constructs with their social and cultural foundations. Taking into account the social structures and relations that have an effect on the construction of specific groups' worldviews, they also allow us to escape from the risk of underestimating social aspects of cultural mental productions (Keesing, 1987). They also provide the means for comparing constructs among particular groups or cultures. Finally, the social representation approach is the key to examining transformations that affect indigenous psychologies because of intercultural contact, the diffusion of scientific knowledge, and the circulation of ideas that multiply the number of models available for thinking about the psyche.

I will close by asking the following questions: What if we, as researchers, were to study and compare the social representations of our own respective societies? Wouldn't this be a good way for the scientific community to communicate and enrich our own native and scientific psychologies?

REFERENCES

Asch, S. (1959). A perspective on social psychology. In S. Koch (Ed.), *Psychology: A study of a science* (Vol. 3). New York: McGraw-Hill.

Beauvois, J. L., & Dubois, N. (1987). The norm of internality and the explanation of psychological events. *European Journal of Social Psychology, 18,* 299-316.

Bem, D. J. (1972). Self perception theory. In L. Berkowitz (Ed.). *Advances in experimental social psychology.* New York: Academic Press.

Berger, P. L., & Luckman, T. (1966). *The social construction of reality.* Garden City, NY: Doubleday.

Bourdieu, P. (1982). *Ce que parler veut dire: Véconomie des échanges symboliques.* Paris: Fayard.

Bruner, J. S., & Tagiuri, R. (1954). Person perception. In G. Lindsey (Ed.), *Handbook of social psychology.* Reading, MA: Addison-Wesley.

Chapman, L. J. (1967). Illusory correlation in observational report. *Journal of Verbal Learning and Verbal Behavior, 6,* 151-155.

Cicourel, A. V. (1973). *Cognitive sociology.* Harmondsworth: Penguin.

Farr, R. (1983). Wilhelm Wundt (1832-1920) and the origin of psychology as an experimental and social science. *British Journal of Psychology, 22,* 289-301.

Farr, R., & Moscovici, S. (1984). On the nature and the role of representations in the self's understanding of others and of self. In M. Cook (Ed.), *Issues in person perception.* London: Methuen.

Forgas, J. P. (Ed.). (1981). *Social cognition; Perspectives on everyday understanding.* London: Academic Press.

Geertz, C. (1983). *Local knowledge; Further essays in interpretive anthropology.* New York: Basic Books.

Gergen, K. J. (1989). Social psychology and the wrong revolution. *European Journal of Social Psychology, 19,* 463-484.

Gergen, K. J., & Gergen, M. M. (1986). *Social psychology.* New York: Springer-Verlag.

Heider, F. (1958). *The psychology of interpersonal relations.* New York: John Wiley.

Holland, D., & Quinn, N. (1987). *Cultural models in language and thought.* Cambridge: Cambridge University Press.

Jahoda, G. (1982). *Psychological anthropology: An psychological perspective.* London: Academic Press.

Jellison, J. M., & Green, J. (1981). A self presentations approach to the fundamental attribution error: The norm of internality. *Journal of Personality and Social Psychology, 40,* 643-649.

Jodelet, D. (1983). La représentation du corps, ses enjeux privés et sociaux. In J. Hainard & R. Kaehr (Eds.), *Le corps en jeu.* Neuchatel: Musée d'Ethnographie.

Jodelet, D. (1984). The representation of the body and its transformations. In R. Farr & S. Moscovici (Eds.), *Social representations.* Cambridge: Cambridge University Press.

Jodelet, D. (Ed.). (1989). *Les repésentations sociales.* Paris: Presses Universitaires de France.

Jodelet, D. (1991). *Madness and social representations.* Berkeley: University of California Press.

Jones, E. E., Kanouse, D., Kelley, H. H., Nisbett, R. E., Valins, S., & Weiner, B. (Eds.). (1972). *Attribution: Perceiving the causes of behavior.* Morristown: General Learning Press.

Keesing, R. M. (1987). Models, "folk" and "cultural": Paradigms regained? In D. Holland & N. Quinn (Eds.), *Cultural models in language and thought.* Cambridge: Cambridge University Press.

Kelley, H. H., & Michela, J. L. (1980). Attribution theory and research *Annual Review of Psychology, 31,* 457-501.

Leyens, J. P. (1983). *Sommes-nous tous des psychologues?* Brussels: Mardaga.

Moscovici, S. (1981). Foreword. In P. Heelas & A. Lock (Eds.), *Indigenous psychologies: The anthropology of the self.* London: Academic Press.

Moscovici, S. (1982). The coming era of social representations. In J. P. Codol & J. P. Leyens (Eds.), *Cognitive approaches to social behavior.* The Hague: Martinus Nijhoff.

Paicheler, H., & Beaufils, B. (1984). *Les théories implicites de la personnalité: modè personnologique ou social.* Paris: Société Française de Psychologie.

Passini, F. T., & Norman, W. T. (1966). A universal perception of personality structure. *Journal of Personality and Social Psychology, 4,* 44-49.

Pepitone, A. (1986). Culture and the cognitive paradigm in social psychology. *Australian Journal of Psychology, 38,* 245-256.

Pepitone, A., & Triandis, H. C. (1987). On the universality of social psychological theories. *Journal of Cross-Cultural Psychology, 18,* 471-498.

Robert, P., & Faugeron, C. (1978). *La justice et son public: les représentations sociales du système pénal.* Paris: Masson.

Rosch, E., & Lloyd, B. B. (Eds.). (1978). *Cognition and categorization.* Hillsdale, NJ: Lawrence Erlbaum.

Ross, L. (1977). The intuitive psychologist and his short-comings: Distortions in the attribution process. In L. Berkowitz (Ed.), *Advances in experimental social psychology.* New York: Academic Press.

Schutz, A. (1962). The problem of social reality. In I. M. Natanson (Ed.), *Collected papers.* The Hague: Martinus Nijhoff.

Shweder, R. A. (1980). *Fallible judgment in behavioral research.* San Francisco: Jossey-Bass.

Sperber, D. (1985). Anthropology and psychology: Towards an epidemiology of representations. *Man, 1,* 73-89.

Tajfel, H. (1982). *Differentiation in social groups.* London: Academic Press.

Triandis, H. C., Halpass, R. S., & Davidson, A. R. (1973). Psychology and culture. *Annual Review of Psychology,* 355-378.

Windish, U. (1980). *Zenophobie.* Lausanne: L'Age d'Homme.

Zajonc, R. B. (1980). Cognition and social cognition: An historical perspective. In L. Festinger (Ed.), *Retrospective on social psychology.* New York: Oxford University Press.

12

INDIGENOUS ANALYSIS OF COLLECTIVE REPRESENTATIONS

A Korean Perspective

SANG-CHIN CHOI
UICHOL KIM
SOO-HYANG CHOI

Psychology emerged as an independent branch of science when Wilhelm Wundt established a psychological laboratory at Leipzig University in Germany (Boring, 1921). Wundt's students were influential in importing and transplanting psychology to the United States (Farr, 1983). In this new environment, psychology quickly took root and began to take on "indigenous *color* and *substance*" (Koch, 1985, p. 25). Psychology became naturalized in the land of individualism. Its basic foundations became intertwined with the basic assumptions of individualism. The general thrust of individualism is that "the subject matter of psychology is individual thought and action," and that "cognitive processes like remembering and reasoning can occur only in individuals" (Harré, Clarke, & De Carlo, 1985, p. 6). This marriage is most apparent in social psychology, as noted by Gergen (1985), Pepitone (1981), Sampson (1977), and Triandis (1987). These and other social psychologists are critical of individualistic assumptions and suggest the development of a more collectivist social psychology.

   The goal of this chapter is to examine the nature of Korean collective representations that are indigenous to Korean people. In order to accomplish this objective, we outline an alternative conceptual framework delineating the indigenous Korean perspective, specifically focusing on the nature of collective representations in Korean culture. We then provide four definitions of *group* that exist in the social psychological literature. These definitions serve as models for examining Korean collective representations. Next, we turn to an overview of social relations in Korean culture. In the final part of the chapter we present two empirical studies investigating the Korean concepts of *woori* (we, us) and *cheong* (human affection).

CONCEPTUAL FRAMEWORK:
AN INDIGENOUS APPROACH

The indigenous approach is adopted for analyzing Korean collective representations. The emphasis is on examining concepts or collective representations that exist in everyday language. The starting point of this research is similar to the *naive psychology* advocated by Heider (1958), who notes that naive understanding of interpersonal behavior is a good starting point for research: "The ordinary person has a great and profound understanding of himself and of other people which, though unformulated or vaguely conceived, enables him to interact in more or less adaptive ways" (p. 2). Heider assumes, however, that scientific analyses derived from these naive understandings are superior to lay versions.

Common sense is often purported to be nebulous and unreliable, but we reject this assumption in favor of the view that people's understanding of themselves and of their social worlds are extremely complex and sophisticated. If their understanding of the world were vague and unreliable, they could not function effectively in their environment (Harré et al., 1985). Concepts used in everyday language are lay versions of people's understanding of their human world. Although people do not have the means to describe and explain this complexity, most people are able to function effectively in a given culture. Wittgenstein notes that "the meaning of a word is its use in the language" (quoted in Budd, 1989, p. 21). A word has functional utility and communicative value for its users. It represents a version of social reality, a shared reality. Harré et al. (1985) suggest that common sense should be considered the "state-of-the-art" understanding of our human world. It is the task of psychologists to tap into the wealth of knowledge stored in the minds of people. Scientific psychology can then add to this knowledge base. Given that the collective understandings of these concepts are often implicit and not explicit, researchers need to clarify what these units mean, refer to, and symbolize. Researchers need to elaborate, organize, and systematize these understandings. The results of these refinements can then be verified by the participants themselves to assess the accuracy of the analysis.

The content of collective representations can be divided into two categories: cognitive knowledge and experiential knowledge. The focus of the current research is to examine experiences rather than cognition. Collective representations, such as *woori* and *cheong,* acquire their meaning through personal experiences. They contain affective, behavioral, and cognitive elements. By examining experiences, we can explore firsthand all three aspects of collective representations.

The collective representation of experiences needs to be differentiated from cultural products. Wundt, for example, examined cultural products, such as language, myth, and customs, as vehicles for understanding culture (Danziger, 1983). He did not examine human experiences, human interactions, and human affairs as they occurred. Cultural products are, however, one step removed from the phenomena themselves. Distortions and biases can enter into an analysis when one attempts to interpret the meaning and significance of cultural products. The focus of this chapter is the examination of human experiences that are salient and ongoing and that can be directly verified by the participants in a study.

There are limitations to the use of participants as expert informants. Participants may or may not be able to describe and explain accurately the meaning of their collective representations. This is the case because there are three levels of awareness: fully aware, capable of recognition but unaware, and unaware. Individuals at the first level are fully aware of their collective representations. They can easily recognize, articulate, and use a particular collective representation (e.g., social etiquette, rules for driving an automobile).

People at the second level can use and recognize particular collective representations without awareness of their underlying processes (e.g., grammar). Wittgenstein notes that we know how to use a language, but lack the ability to describe how we do it: "A description of the grammar of a word is of no use in everyday life; only rarely do we pick up the use of a word by having its use described to us; and although we are trained or encouraged to master the use of the word, we are not taught to describe it" (in Budd, 1989, pp. 4-5). Many psychological theories are of this nature, such as attribution theory, implicit personality theory, social comparison theory, and social exchange theory. When these theories are explained to people, they can readily recognize the basic ideas, but they are unable to articulate these theories themselves.

People at the third level are unaware of collective representations. According to Freud (1966), individuals are most often unaware of their own unconscious representations, such as the meaning of dreams, slips of the tongue, and forgetting. At the collective level, Jung (1964) suggests that people are incognizant of the collective unconsciousness. The contents are represented in "primordial images" or *archetypes.*

As researchers move away from the first level to the second and the third, they need to make a greater number of assumptions and inferences about the nature of the collective representations. This can result in a loss of validity. Interpretations can be significantly different from lay conceptions of collective representations. It is thus most appropriate to operate at the first level, where participants themselves can articulate and verify the meaning of their collective representations.

Another focus of this chapter is the examination of psychological attributes rather than physical, physiological, or biological attributes. The emphasis is on examining people's understanding of human nature and primary groups. Explanations of these representations should remain at the human level rather than be reduced to a physical, physiological, or biological level.

The final emphasis is on examining concepts that are salient and significant in a particular society. Ideas that are widely accepted and discussed should be investigated first. For this reason we have chosen the concepts of *woori* and *cheong*.

CONCEPTUAL ANALYSIS OF A GROUP

One of the most widely cited definitions in social psychology is as follows: "Social psychology attempts to understand and explain how the thoughts, feelings, and behaviors of individuals are influenced by actual, imagined, or implied presence of others" (Allport, 1968, p. 3). In this definition, the individual is the basic unit of analysis and other individuals serve as cues or stimuli for the focal person. Uichol Kim (1993) suggests that this definition represents the *aggregate mode* (see diagram A in Figure 12.1). This assumption allows experimentation in a laboratory setting to take place. In a typical experimental situation, other individuals or groups are introduced as stimuli (independent variables) and effects of such stimuli are observed in the behavior of individuals.

The basic assumptions of the above definition closely parallel the description of individualism. Spence (1985) defines individualism as "the belief that each of us is an entity separate from every other and from the group" (p. 1288). This belief can "lead to a sense of self with a sharp boundary that stops at one's skin and clearly demarks self from nonself" (p. 1288). Sampson (1977) similarly notes that "a predominant theme that describes our cultural ethos is *self-contained individualism*" (p. 769). It is defined by firm individual boundaries, personal control, and an exclusionary concept of the person (Sampson, 1988). Hsu (1983) uses "rugged individualism" to describe the same phenomenon. Kagitcibasi (1987) labels such a culture a "culture of separateness." The emphasis on individualism in the United States and Canada has been verified in numerous empirical studies (e.g., Bellah,

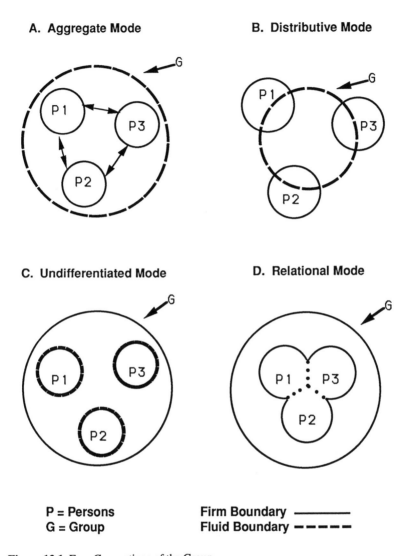

A. Aggregate Mode

B. Distributive Mode

C. Undifferentiated Mode

D. Relational Mode

P = Persons
G = Group

Firm Boundary ————
Fluid Boundary — — — —

Figure 12.1. Four Conceptions of the Group

Madsen, Sullivan, Swindler, & Tipton, 1985; Chinese Cultural Connection, 1987; Hofstede, 1980). This assumption, however, is considered limited for the understanding of collective phenomena such as self-regulating groups, institutions, and cultures (Gergen, 1985; Harré et al., 1985; Pepitone, 1981; Sampson, 1977; Triandis, 1987).

The second definition of a group emphasizes elements that are shared by members of a group; this can be called the *distributive mode* (see diagram B in Figure 12.1). It is similar to Sampson's (1988) "ensembled individualism." Compared with *self-contained* individualism, ensembled individualism is characterized by a more fluid boundary between self and other, a conception of self that is more inclusive and less exclusive, and an emphasis on control as in the field rather than in the individual (Sampson, 1988).

The social identity theory developed by Henri Tajfel (1981, 1982) and the social representation theory of Serge Moscovici (1981, 1984) are examples of the distributive mode. Social identity theory states that the individual is motivated to maintain a positive self-image. Self-image is composed of two elements: personal identity and social identities (Tajfel, 1981). Social identities are those attributes that are shared by members of a particular in-group.

A third perspective, labeled the *undifferentiated mode,* views a social unit as an entity in itself (see diagram C in Figure 12.1). A social unit is considered to be more than the mere sum of the individuals who constitute it. The current research on collectivism is representative of this perspective (Hofstede, 1980; Leung & Bond, 1984; Triandis, 1988). Triandis (1988) articulates collectivism as putting greater emphasis on four areas: (a) the needs and goals of the in-group rather than the individual, (b) social norms and duties rather than individual pleasure, (c) beliefs and values that are shared by in-group members rather than those that distinguish individual members, and (c) readiness to cooperate with in-group members rather than compete with them.

The *relational mode* focuses on the relationships among members of a particular group (see diagram D in Figure 12.1). Members of a group are bound by emotional glue such as *amae* (interdependence) in Japan and *cheong* in Korea. The relational orientation has been discussed by numerous researchers (see Kim, 1992, for a review). This mode will be further elaborated in the section below.

KOREAN CULTURE
AND SOCIAL RELATIONSHIPS

Confucianism has become a dominant philosophy that provides guidelines for virtually every aspect of Korean society (Han, 1974). Its teachings are deeply ingrained in the minds, thoughts, and behavior of Koreans (S. W. Lee, 1990; Pak, 1983). Within Confucian philosophy, human relationships occupy the central place (Chung, 1970). Liang Shu-Ming notes that in Confucianism "the emphasis is placed on the relation between particular individuals" (cited in King & Bond, 1985, p. 31). In addition to the Confucian influence, Korean culture traditionally has stressed the importance of human relations. D. S. Lee (1980) notes that Korean culture as a whole can be viewed as a "relationship culture."

Relationships among the individual, the family, society, and the world are best articulated in the writing of Confucius titled "Righteousness in the Heart" (in a chapter called "Great Learning," in *The Book of Rites*). He states:

> If there be righteousness in the heart,
> there will be beauty in character.
> If there be beauty in character,
> there will be harmony in the home.
> If there be harmony in the home,
> there will be order in the nation.
> If there be order in the nation,
> there will be peace in the world.

Confucius considered individuals to be linked in a web of social networks. The family serves as the most important prototype in human relations (King & Bond, 1985; S. W. Lee, 1990). For example, of the Five Cardinal Relations articulated by Confucius (between king and subjects, father and son, elder brother and younger brother, husband and wife, and between friends), three are based on family (King & Bond, 1985). S. W. Lee (1990) notes that "according to Confucianism, social relations are nothing more than an expansion of this family relationship" (p. 2).

Maday and Szalay (1976) empirically verified the importance of family in Korean culture in a study examining the psychological connotations of self. The four most important themes they found in Korean responses, in descending order, were (a) family and love; (b) ideals, happiness, and freedom; (c) hope, ambition, and success; and (d) money, material, and goods. These responses indicate that family, plus the love (*cheong*) that binds family members together, is the most important part of the Korean conception of self. The results from the Korean sample are consistent with other researchers' observations that Koreans are family oriented (H. J. Choi, 1965; Y. K. Kim, 1986; D. S. Lee, 1980; S. W. Lee, 1990).

American responses, in contrast, show a convergence around the individual. Maday and Szalay (1976) found that for Americans the four most frequent themes, in descending order, are (a) I, person, individual; (b) other people; (c) tiredness, loneliness, physical appearance; and (d) goodness, friendliness, sociability. Maday and Szalay note that the American conception of "me" focuses on the individuated self. Americans are detached from family members and are surrounded by strangers. There is an emphasis on negative emotions, such as tiredness and loneliness, rather than on the positive emotions found in the Korean sample, such as happiness, hope, and ambition.

Maday and Szalay (1976) note that Koreans and Americans relate to different sets of significant others. For Koreans, the family occupies the central place. Individual members need to contribute to the family's happiness and material success. Americans, on the other hand, need to prove their worth to strangers. Thus appearance, friendliness, and sociable behavior are emphasized.

Rohner (1984) and Rohner and Pettingill (1985) found similar contrasts when they compared the parent-child relationship in the United States and in Korea. In the United States, strict maternal control was perceived by adolescents as a manifestation of parental hostility, aggression, distrust, and overall rejection. This view is consistent with the fact that American parents, by and large, encourage independence and self-reliance (Kagitcibasi, 1987). Parental control is exerted when adolescents behave in inappropriate or disruptive manners. Parental control is antithetical to a warm and harmonious parent-child relationship.

In Korea, however, the results are reversed. Korean adolescents view parental control as an indication of warmth and lack of neglect. This result is consistent with the fact that parental involvement is an essential ingredient in Korean society. It is considered necessary to ensure success for one's children. Parental involvement is not viewed as control; it is an essential ingredient in academic, economic, and social success. Similar results have been obtained in a replication study involving Korean adolescents, Korean American adolescents, and Korean Canadian adolescents (Kim & Choi, in press).

The above results suggest that Korean culture as a whole can be viewed as emphasizing *relational plurality*. The two empirical studies described below provide empirical support for this contention. Two exploratory studies were conducted to examine Koreans' conception of a collective pronoun, *woori* (Choi & Choi, 1990), and an affective emotion that binds individual members to a group, *cheong* (Choi & Choi, 1991). These two concepts were chosen because they are ideal for an indigenous analysis.

STUDY 1: EMPIRICAL ANALYSIS OF *WOORI*

Woori in Korean denotes an inclusive group: we or us. It is a word used to denote a group of people (such as our family), an entity (such as our nation), and even possessions (such as our house). The term is most often used to denote a group of people. It has been the focus of extensive debate and discussion (S. C. Choi, 1976; S. H. Choi, 1990; K. T. Lee, 1985; Park, 1990; Yoon, 1987). Choi and Choi (1990) conducted an empirical study to examine the psychological connotations of the word *woori*. The study reported below is the first attempt to analyze the concept empirically.

Five questions were raised to elicit people's responses to *woori* and its psychological connotations in Korea and its equivalent counterpart, *we,* in Canada. The five questions were as follows:

1. Does the word *woori* [*we*] signify to you something other than a collective pool of individuals? If it does, what are the other associations?
2. What are your major "we-groups"?
3. Does your "we-membership" dwarf your personal, independent identity? If yes, to what extent?
4. Would there be any change in your perception if a person became a new fellow member of your we-group?
5. Is a we-membership bond essential or necessary for you to recognize, establish, or maintain a social relation with others?

Samples of university students from Seoul, Korea ($n = 60$), and from Edmonton, Canada ($n = 43$), were asked these questions. They were asked to free associate and provide their responses in an open-ended format. Topical themes were extracted from these open-ended answers. The results are presented, to the degree to which these topical themes emerged in the samples, in raw frequencies.

Results

For the first question (Does the word *woori* [*we*] signify to you something other than a collective pool of individuals?), 95% of the Korean responses could be categorized into five dominant themes. The most salient psychological connotation of *woori* was the affective bond shared by the members of a group in the Korean sample. Some 55% of the responses clustered around affective words such as "affection" (*cheong*), "intimacy," "comfort," and "acceptance." The second most frequent thematic category involved viewing the group as a unit or an entity. Words such as "oneness," "sameness," "bonding," and "of the same kind" (16%) were used to describe the group. The third category focused on "commonality" (13%), and the fourth clustered around "cooperation" (5%). The fifth category was simply an aggregate of individuals, "me and others" (5%).

For the Canadian sample, 90% of the responses could be categorized into three themes. The psychological connotations of *we* for the Canadian subjects contrasted sharply with the Korean sample. It referred simply to an aggregate of people. The most salient feature of *we* was a simple connotation of a loose cluster of individuals: "I and others," "two people," "people and me," "it just means a group of individuals" (60%). The second most frequent type of response was to view a group as "people who share same interest, hobbies, or perspective" (15%). The third theme emphasized "closeness," "intimacy," "belonging," "acceptance," and "togetherness" (15%).

For the second question (What are your major "we-groups"?), the answers for the two samples were very similar. Family emerged as the most frequent response (27% for the Korean sample, 28% for the Canadian sample), followed by friends (16% in the Korean sample, 21% in the Canadian sample), classmates (15% in the Korean sample, 14% in the Canadian sample), hobbies or interest groups (12% in the Korean sample, 5% in the Canadian sample), nation (6% in the Korean sample, 4% in the Canadian sample), and church (8% in the Korean sample, 4% in the Canadian sample). Relatives (8%) and girlfriends/boyfriends (3%) were also mentioned in the Korean sample. In the Canadian sample, work (4%) and roommates (3%) were also mentioned.

For the third question (Does your "we-membership" dwarf your personal, independent identity?), the vast majority of Korean responses (94%) affirmed the restrictive aspects of belonging to a group. Some 43% of the respondents noted that "we-membership" dwarfs personal and independent identity, and another 31% believed that it did so to some extent. The remaining 20% affirmed the restrictive aspect of belonging to a group, but also mentioned their willingness to accommodate or tolerate the inconvenience.

Further examination of the second part of the answer (If yes, to what extent?) for the Korean sample reaffirmed the idea that a group represents an *undifferentiated mode* in Korea. Of the clarifying responses, 31% indicated that individuals in a group have to follow the opinions or decisions made by the majority: 36% stated that it is necessary to concede to the group to maintain harmony, 23% noted that persons cannot express their own uniqueness or autonomy, and 10% indicated that involvement in a group can produce loss or waste of time.

The most frequent response for the Canadian sample indicated that groups were not restrictive to individuals' identity or autonomy (42%). Some 31% of the responses, however, affirmed some restrictive aspects of belonging to a group; 20% of the responses suggested that restrictions would depend upon the nature and size of the group.

For the fourth question (Would there be any change in your perception if a person became a new fellow member of your we-group?), the Korean responses acknowledged an increased personal closeness to a new member of a "we-group." The answers included the following themes: increase in closeness, intimacy, or affection (33%); attempt to promote harmony by understanding and accepting the person (25%); belief that a more favorable relationship will result (18%); discovery that the person is similar to oneself (7%); tendency to be more cautious (3%); and no change (8%).

The Canadian sample also acknowledged that knowing someone as part of the "we-group" would affect their perceptions of the person. Answers provided included the following themes: I'll come to know that the other persons, too, have the same interests, ideas, or perspective as me, and have commonality or similarity (41%); I will feel closer and more intimate (19%); I will make an effort to accept, like, understand, or accommodate the person (19%); the persons will still remain as independent individuals (10%); I will come to have more social interactions with the other person (7%); and others (4%).

For the fifth question (Is a we-membership bond essential or necessary for you to recognize, establish, or maintain a social relation with others?), 91% of the answers for the Korean sample stressed the importance of having an emotional bond between members of a "we-group." A total of 34% of the respondents indicated definite agreement. An additional 21% saw it as an essential factor, 23% viewed it as necessary but not essential, 13% viewed it as necessary to some extent, and 4% indicated that it was not necessary, but a facilitating factor. A final 4% of the responses indicated that it was not necessary.

Responses in the Canadian sample similarly indicated that the "we-membership bond" is a necessary component in social relationships, but to a lesser extent than in the Korean sample. The answers provided included the following themes: necessary, the presence of similarities or commonality are preconditions to any social relationship (35%); necessary to have a sense of acceptance, belonging, comfort, and intimacy (25%); not necessary (29%); being in a group, people can contribute to the society (4%); and others (6%).

Discussion

By examining the results from these five questions, one can begin to extract patterns in the two samples. The word *woori* elicits three major themes in the Korean sample: positive affects, oneness or wholeness, and the priority of the group over the individual. For the Korean sample the group takes precedence over individual members. The affective bond is the key that unites members of a group into a unified whole. This bond consolidates the members into a unit, and the characteristics of individuals are not mentioned as being important. The Korean responses suggest that the dominant form of a primary group in Korea is the relational mode followed by the undifferentiated mode.

The Canadian responses indicate that the majority of the respondents view a group as the aggregate mode and as a distributive mode. A group is simply an aggregate of plural individuals around the focal person *I*. The dominant response for the Canadian sample suggests that a group is a loose aggregate of individuals who most frequently serve as stimuli for the individual. Another common theme of *we* that emerged was the cognitive awareness of similarity shared by the members of the group. A group is often united by common interest or hobbies. Although the ideas of the undifferentiated mode exist, it is revealed in a minority of responses.

About a third of the Canadian respondents acknowledged that belonging to a group can be restrictive to one's autonomy. Because individuals in a group are either loosely aggregated or brought together by similar interests, they have the freedom to disassociate from the group when they deem it necessary. This can be more difficult for those in the Korean sample, where the relational mode and undifferentiated mode are emphasized. Collective aspirations and interests, and not those of the individuals, are upheld. In these modes, individuals need to subjugate, sacrifice, or align their interests with those of the group.

It is interesting to note that the primary groups are virtually identical in the two samples. Family, friends, and classmates are most frequently mentioned primary groups for both these university student samples. The difference between the two samples, however, lies in the type of relationship shared by the members of the group. The Korean respondents are merged into a collective unit through affective bonds. The Canadian respondents maintain their individuality, and they interact with members of a group. Thus the contrasting feature between groups in Korean and Canadian cultures is not in external criteria such as the type of a group, but in internal characteristics such as affective bonds that help to consolidate the group as an entity.

STUDY 2: EMPIRICAL ANALYSIS OF *CHEONG*

The second study examined the psychological connotations of an important affective bond, *cheong*. *Cheong* can be narrowly translated as "human affection," but its meaning is much broader. Prefixes can be added to *cheong*; for example, *moecheong* refers to an individual's love for his or her mother (*moe* is the word for mother), *incheong* means human compassion and sympathy (*in* means human), and *yeulcheong* means passion (*yeul* means heat).

Cheong develops from close attachment to persons, places, or things. The concept has been the focus of immense interest in the Korean social science literature (S. C. Choi, 1981; J. H. Kim, 1988; Y. K. Kim, 1986; Lee et al.,

1988; S. W. Lee, 1990; T. K. Lee, 1977; Y. R. Lee, 1986; Yoon, 1987), but had not previously been subject to empirical investigation.

Five open-ended questions were given to a sample of university students ($n = 36$) attending Chung-Ang University in Seoul, Korea (Choi & Choi, 1991):

1. The word *cheong* may incur some psychological associations. Write down your own ideas associated with how a person develops *cheong*.

2. When do you think a person can come to develop *cheong*? From your own experience, please write down experiences in which *cheong* has developed.

3. We often say in conversation that a person is full of *cheong*. What do you think are the characteristics of such a person? Write down some characteristics associated with such a person.

4. We often use the expression "It is hard to develop *cheong* with certain people." Write down behavioral characteristics of those people.

5. We use an expression that a person can lack *cheong*. Who would be such a person? Write down some psychological characteristics associated with such a person.

This study used the same procedure for extracting topical themes as was employed in the *woori* study described above. The results are presented to the degree to which topical themes emerged in the samples.

Results

In response to the first question, four features emerged. In order to develop *cheong* toward someone, one needs to spend a long time with that person, especially in one's childhood. The second feature is coresidence, living close to one another, and sharing both good and bad times together. The third feature is "human-heartedness," including elements such as warmth, comfort, and caring. The fourth feature is acceptance of the other person unconditionally, with complete understanding and trust. This means overlooking even the weaknesses and defects of the other person.

Cheong is shared among members of a primary group. The family is a prototypical example. It is natural that family members live together in coresidence for a long time. One's childhood is spent with family members. Within a family, members are encouraged to share with, to care for, and to trust in one another. The family serves as a model for all future relationships. Children are encouraged to develop similar relationships in other contexts, in school and later in life in the workplace. *Cheong* reflects relationship centeredness rather than person centeredness.

Responses to the second question, about the conditions necessary for *cheong* to develop, were very similar to those for the first question. Subjects listed time and coresidence as the most important factors. They also mentioned that long-term *woori* experience is necessary. Such experience is needed to develop a sense of relatedness characterized by intimacy, understanding, acceptance, frankness, and altruism. Experiencing and sharing joys, sorrows, troubled times, hard times, and problems together were also mentioned as important factors. These experiences are preconditions for the development of empathy.

For the third question, three features emerged to describe a person full of *cheong*: altruism, caring and tenderness, and "foolish kindness." The most important feature mentioned was willingness to help other people. Individuals full of *cheong* are not motivated by self-interest. Second, they readily show empathy and sympathy. They show considerable concern for other people's feelings, problems, and situations. The last feature emphasizes the overly simple, honest, sincere, unsophisticated, and uncalculating nature of *cheong,* to the extent that it might be considered foolish by others.

The fourth question concerned features that describe someone for whom it would be difficult to develop *cheong.* The characteristics mentioned were various: hypocritical, arrogant, selfish, calculating, indifferent, cool-headed, self-centered, independent, and perfectionist. The first five of these are negative descriptors, describing someone who is not genuine or sincere. The rest are not necessarily negative in content, but are characteristic of individualism (Sampson, 1988; Spence, 1985; Triandis, 1988). Respondents viewed people who are rational or perfectionist as being the type for whom they would have difficulty developing *cheong.* These features contrast sharply with a person full of *cheong,* where altruism, tenderness, concern, and foolish kindness are important.

In response to the last question, the characteristics of persons without *cheong* were given as follows: a person who has no sympathy for other people's pain and problems, a selfish person, a cool-headed person, and an apathetic person. These descriptions closely parallel the results of the previous question.

Discussion

Most Korean scholars consider *cheong* to be the fundamental basis of Korean emotionality (S. C. Choi, 1981; J. H. Kim, 1988; Y. K. Kim, 1986; Lee et al., 1988; S. W. Lee, 1990; T. K. Lee, 1977; Y. R. Lee, 1986; Yoon, 1987). *Cheong* by definition is primarily affective. It is not acquired directly, but circulates through an osmosis-like process to bind people together. For this reason *relational mode* emphasizes porous boundaries between group members. These porous boundaries allow *cheong* to flow naturally, without any impediments.

Cheong arises among close-knit family and friends who spend a long time together, living together in close quarters. The Korean mother-child relationship, *moecheong,* is the epitome of *cheong.* Characteristics that are associated with *cheong* are unconditionality, sacrifice, empathy, care, sincerity, and shared experience.

Cheong does not develop in contractual, commercial, or purely rational relationships. Someone without *cheong* can be described as being conditional, uncaring, selfish, cool, hypocritical, and apathetic. Someone without *cheong* can also be described as purely rational and logical. Such a person may also be self-reliant, independent, and autonomous.

GENERAL DISCUSSION

The results of the two studies suggest the existence of four types of groups: aggregate mode, distributive mode, undifferentiated mode, and relational mode. In the Canadian sample, groups were most often conceptualized as aggregate mode or distributive mode. In the Korean sample, the relational mode and the undifferentiated mode were most often mentioned.

Woori represents collective consciousness and *cheong* is the affective bond that consolidates *woori* members together. Both *woori* and *cheong* require that the people involved spend a long time together. Spending time together and coresidence allow group members to develop a trusting, sharing, and caring relationship. Time, coresidence, and shared experiences are preconditions for individual members to become consolidated into a collective unit. Individual members learn to be altruistic, sacrificing, and caring. This promotes relationship centeredness and group solidarity over individual interests. Individual members are encouraged to open their *ma-eum* (translated as mind, spirit, heart, or idea) to other members of the group. This allows *cheong* to flow and bind members together. Individuals who are hypocritical, selfish, apathetic, or rational are viewed as unwilling to or incapable of opening their *ma-eum* to others. They are labeled as lacking in *cheong* and may experience difficulty becoming part of the *woori* group.

It is often the case that an individual's interests can be in conflict with those of the group. Individuals are often requested to sacrifice their personal interests for the good of the group. Demanding personal sacrifice, however, is not the ideal solution. The ideal scenario involves a situation in which both individual and group goals are met and in harmony. This may mean that an individual needs to sacrifice his or her immediate personal interests for the benefit of the group. However, the group can provide resources and support that can be beneficial to the individual in the long run.

Although the results of the studies discussed here are interesting, they are exploratory. Further investigations are necessary to verify the findings of these two studies. Additional samples from different age groups, residential groups, and occupational groups should be employed to verify, refine, and extend the present results. Other related collective representations are needed to map out the complexity in human relationships understood by the Korean people. This chapter represents a first step toward this goal.

REFERENCES

Allport, G. (1968). Historical background of modern social psychology. In G. Lindzey & E. Aronson (Eds.), *Handbook of social psychology* (Vol. 1). Reading, MA: Addison-Wesley.

Bellah, R. N., Madsen, R., Sullivan, W. M., Swindler, A., & Tipton, S. M. (1985). *Habits of the heart: Individualism and commitment in American life.* Berkeley: University of California Press.

Boring, E. G. (1921). *A history of experimental psychology.* Englewood Cliffs, NJ: Prentice-Hall.

Budd, M. (1989). *Wittgenstein's philosophy of psychology.* London: Routledge.

Chinese Cultural Connection. (1987). Chinese values and the search for a culture-free dimension of culture. *Journal of Cross-Cultural Psychology, 18,* 143-164.

Choi, H. J. (1965). *Koreans' social character* (in Korean). Seoul: Minjosa.

Choi, S. C. (1976). Transition of the cultural value in Korea. In *Faculty research in Chung-Ang University.* Seoul: Chung-Ang University Press.

Choi, S. C. (1981). *The traditional thought of Koreans represented in Koran proverbs* (in Korean). Seoul: Na-He-Hall.

Choi, S. C., & Choi, S. H. (1990, July). *"We-ness": A Korean discourse of collectivism.* Paper presented at the First International Conference on Individualism and Collectivism: Psychocultural Perspectives from East and West, Seoul.

Choi, S. C., & Choi, S. H. (1991). Cheong: *The socio-emotional grammar of Koreans.* Unpublished manuscript.

Choi, S. H. (1990). *Communicative socialization processes: Korean and Canada.* Unpublished doctoral dissertation, University of Alberta, Edmonton.

Chung, Y. H. (1970). Comparative research on theories of emotion: With main emphasis on social emotion. *Korean Journal of Psychology, 1,* 77-90.

Danziger, K. (1983). Origins and basic principles of Wundt's *Völkerpsychologie. British Journal of Social Psychology, 22,* 303-313.

Farr, R. M. (1983). Wilhelm Wundt (1832-1920) and the origins of psychology as an experimental and social science. *British Journal of Social Psychology, 22,* 289-301.

Freud, S. (1966). *The psychopathology of everyday life.* New York: Penguin.

Gergen, K. J. (1985). Social psychology and the phoenix of unreality. In S. Koch & D. E. Leary (Eds.), *A century of psychology as science.* New York: McGraw-Hill.

Han, W. K. (1974). *The history of Korea.* Honolulu: University of Hawaii Press.

Harré, R., Clarke, D., & De Carlo, N. (1985). *Motives and mechanisms: An introduction to the psychology of action.* London: Methuen.

Heider, F. (1958). *The psychology of interpersonal relations.* New York: John Wiley.

Hofstede, G. (1980). *Culture's consequences: International differences in work-related values.* Beverly Hills, CA: Sage.

Hsu, F. L. K. (1983). *Rugged individualism reconsidered.* Knoxville: University of Tennessee Press.

Jung, C. (1964). *Man and his symbols.* Garden City, NY: Doubleday.

Kagitcibasi, C. (1987). Individual and group loyalties: Are they compatible? In C. Kagitcibasi (Ed.), *Growth and progress in cross-cultural psychology.* Lisse, Netherlands: Swets & Zeitlinger.

Kim, J. H. (1988). *Exchange of work and cheong* (in Korean). Seoul: Korean Anthropology.

Kim, U. (1993). Introduction. In U. Kim, H. C. Triandis, S. C. Choi, C. Kagitcibasi, & G. Yoon (Eds.), *Individualism and collectivism: Theory, method, and application.* Manuscript submitted for publication.

Kim, U., & Choi, S. H. (in press). Parent-child relationship and Korean culture. In P. Greenfield & R. Cocking (Eds.), *Cognitive development of minority children: Cultural continuities and discontinuities.* Hillsdale, NJ: Lawrence Erlbaum.

Kim, Y. K. (1986). *Koreans: Who are we?* (in Korean). Seoul: Ja-Yoo-Moon-Hwa-Sa.

King, A. Y. C., & Bond, M. H. (1985). The Confucian paradigm of man: A sociological view. In W. T. Tseng & D. Wu (Eds.), *Chinese culture and mental health.* New York: Academic.

Koch, S. (1985). Foreword: Wundt's creature at age zero and as centenarian: Some aspects of the institutionalization of "New Psychology." In S. Koch & D. E. Leary (Eds.), *A century of psychology as science.* New York: McGraw-Hill.

Lee, D. S. (1980). Traditional norms in family and problems of modern family (in Korean). In *Traditional values and establishment of new values.* Seoul: Institute of Korean Studies.

Lee, H. W., Lee, K. H., Park, J. M., Yoo, H. K., Hwang, I. C., Kim, M. J., & Jang, S. M. (1988). *The prototype of Koreanistic thought* (in Korean). Seoul: Jung-Shin-Moon-Hwa-Yon-Ku-So.

Lee, K. T. (1985). *The thought structure of Koreans* (in Korean). Seoul: Shin Won Moon Hwa Sa.

Lee, S. W. (1990, July). *Koreans' social relationship and Cheong space.* Paper presented at the First International Conference on Individualism and Collectivism: Psychocultural Perspectives from East and West, Seoul.

Lee, T. K. (1977). *The thought patterns of Koreans* (in Korean). Seoul: Moon-Ri-Sa.

Lee, Y. R. (1986). *New Koreans* (in Korean). Seoul: Moon-Hak-Sa-Sang-Sa.

Leung, K., & Bond, M. H. (1984). The impact of cultural collectivism on reward allocation. *Journal of Personality and Social Psychology, 4,* 793-804.

Maday, B. C., & Szalay, L. B. (1976). Psychological correlates of family socialization in the United States and Korea. In T. Williams (Ed.), *Psychological anthropology.* The Hague: Mouton.

Moscovici, S. (1981). On social representation. In J. P. Forgas (Ed.), *Social cognition: Perspectives on everyday understanding.* London: Academic Press.

Moscovici, S. (1984). The phenomenon of social representations. In R. M. Farr & S. Moscovici (Eds.), *Social representations.* Cambridge: Cambridge University Press.

Pak, C. H. (1983). Historical review of Korean Confucianism. In Korean National Commission for UNESCO (Ed.), *Main currents of Korean thought.* Seoul: Si-sa-yong-o-sa.

Park, S. H. (1990). *A social psychological study of the Koreans' we-hood-ness.* Unpublished master's thesis, Chung-Ang University, Seoul.

Pepitone, A. (1981). Lesson from the history of social psychology. *American Psychologist, 36,* 972-985.

Rohner, R. P. (1984). *Handbook for the study of parental acceptance and rejection.* Storrs: University of Connecticut Press.

Rohner, R. P., & Pettingill, S. M. (1985). Perceived parental acceptance-rejection and parental control among Korean adolescents. *Child Development, 56,* 524-528.

Sampson, E. E. (1977). Psychology and the American ideal. *Journal of Personality and Social Psychology, 35,* 767-782.

Sampson, E. E. (1988). The debate on individualism: Indigenous psychologies of the individual and their role in personal and societal functioning. *American Psychologist, 43,* 15-22.

Spence, J. (1985). Achievement American style: The rewards and costs of individualism. *American Psychologist, 40,* 1285-1295.

Tajfel, H. (1981). *Human groups and categories.* Cambridge: Cambridge University Press.

Tajfel, H. (1982). *Social identity and intergroup relations.* Cambridge: Cambridge University Press.

Triandis, H. C. (1987). Individualism and social psychological theory. In C. Kagitcibasi (Ed.), *Growth and progress in cross cultural psychology.* Lisse, Netherlands: Swets & Zeitlinger.

Triandis, H. C. (1988). Collectivism vs. individualism: A reconceptualization of a basic concept in cross-cultural social psychology. In C. Bagley & G. K. Verma (Eds.), *Personality, cognition and values: Cross-cultural perspectives of childhood and adolescence.* London: Macmillan.

Yoon, T. R. (1987). *Koreans* (in Korean). Seoul: Hyun-Am-Sa.

13

INDIGENOUS PSYCHOLOGY IN AFRICA

The Search for Meaning

MICHAEL O. A. DUROJAIYE

Twice in my career as a psychologist and in my life as an African the question has been put to me, "What about African psychology? Do you not have your own concepts and psychological processes?" The first time was in 1973 at Ibadan. The second time was in 1986 in Trinidad. On both occasions I was not ashamed to say that I did not know of any African psychological processes that are distinct from those found elsewhere in the world. I still do not know of any. I know of how psychology has been manifested and operationalized in Africa, and I know of psychology in Africa. The memory of my application for a Nigerian federal government scholarship in the late 1950s is still fresh. I was invited by the scholarship sponsors to attend an interview. There I was told that I had been invited so that I could be advised to desist from making applications every year to read psychology. I had applied every year for three years. The ebullient chairman said to me, "My son, you passed all your exams very well. You could have asked for a scholarship to study anything else and we would be pleased to give you a scholarship, but not for psychology. You see, we are still fighting against black magic and witchcraft, and we do not want anyone to go and study white magic and witchcraft."

Actually the chairman of the scholarship board was not as wrong as I thought then. In many respects indigenous psychology is characterized by a search into the cultural and traditional practices and identifying psychological principles that underlie these practices. But first, indigenous psychology presupposes indigenous psychologists to unravel the psychological principles behind the cultural and traditional practices. It makes sense therefore to describe the evolution of indigenous psychologists before describing indigenous psychological concepts and practices.

THE TRAINING OF AFRICAN PSYCHOLOGISTS

Before 1960, the only training opportunity in psychology for African scholars was through a postgraduate degree in education earned in English-speaking countries or through the *ecole normal superior* programs in French-speaking countries. By 1965, a handful of African scholars trained in the United Kingdom, France, Belgium, or the United States had returned to their countries, mainly to assume academic positions on the faculties of education in African universities. Teaching and research activities in psychology as a subject in its own right began as offshoots of teaching and research in education, social anthropology, or sociology in East, West, and Central Africa, with staff and financial support form the British and the French governments through their overseas development offices, and also from foundations, in particular the Ford and Carnegie Foundations in the United States. The activities of social science research institutes led to the establishment of departments of psychology in many African universities. An example is the University of Zambia, which established a Department of Psychology in 1968 as a result of the activities of the Rholes-Livingstone Institute of Social Research. Alistair Heron, a psychologist, became the director of that institute in 1963 and established the Human Development Research Unit in 1965. Among the aims of the unit were the following:

1. sponsorship of research programs to ascertain the extent to which psychological knowledge obtained through scientific research in Europe and the United States could be generalized to Central Africa
2. provision of locally derived data for use in dealing with social, educational, and planning problems of a rapidly developing country
3. provision of research bases for the teaching of psychology at the university

These objectives apply with equal force to the beginnings of psychology departments in all African universities, even though such clear statements of aims and such careful planning are difficult to find elsewhere. Today there are 14 departments of psychology in 10 African countries, with 5 in Nigeria alone. Many of the staff members in these departments of psychology are Africans. A great deal of effort is being expended to implement research and publication programs, but very few of these have actually been executed. In addition to a chronic shortage of research facilities, the effort is hampered by inadequate equipment, inadequate library facilities, insufficient financial grants for research, and overburdened staff with little time for research and the production of publications on psychology in Africa. One of the first departments of psychology was that at the University of Nigeria Nsukka in 1962.

PROFESSIONAL PRACTICE
OF PSYCHOLOGY IN AFRICA

In the past 10 years, with the increasing number of students who have completed psychology courses in the universities, the status of psychology has been improving. Far too little postgraduate work is done, however, to enable African psychologists to address themselves to interesting research and professional questions. Africans who graduate from departments of psychology often are not fully qualified to practice psychology or to engage in research. Without postgraduate training, psychology as a degree program is, in Africa as in most universities all over the world, a part of nonspecialist programs of basic university education. Graduates of departments of psychology therefore find themselves in the civil service or in commerce and industry in administrative positions. Only in rare cases are they employed in areas demanding skills in psychology, which is as it should be, because further professional training is necessary for such work.

A few universities offer postgraduate courses in guidance and counseling, clinical psychology and industrial psychology. Nigeria, Zambia, and Zimbabwe have created posts for clinical psychologists, educational psychologists, and industrial psychologists. Psychologists also work, in these and other countries, in schools and centers created by ministries of education for the purpose of giving guidance and counseling to school-age children. And psychologists are employed in testing for purposes of selection for educational and industrial training in many African countries. Educational ministries and examination bodies are the largest employers of psychology graduates. Graduates of other disciplines who have had postgraduate training in educational or other aspects of psychology are employed, together with psychology graduates, to carry out aptitude and ability testing for selection and training purposes, as well as for the assessment of achievement at the end of specific training programs.

Few clinical psychologists are employed in African countries, because there are as yet few qualified clinical psychologists who can make their need felt in local health services. In Zimbabwe and Nigeria, a handful of clinical psychologists are working in hospitals, but under adverse conditions. But with the growth of psychology departments and professional training facilities for psychology graduates, there may also come increasing demand for the utilization of psychologists' skills in industry, health services, education, and social services.

So it is that with the establishment of departments of psychology in many African countries and the employment of African psychologists in many public and private organizations and for different purposes and human concerns, in education, health, and industry, the personnel exist for exploration into indigenous psychology in Africa south of the Sahara and north of the Limpopo River.

The search for meaning in indigenous psychology in Africa antedated the evolution of indigenous psychologists. There were foreign psychologists who were concerned, among them Professor Gustav Jahoda, who before 1956 started the search for the meaning and functioning of psychology in Ghana. About the same time, the late Ombradane was working in French-speaking African countries. Other foreign psychologists worked through research and publications to unravel indigenous psychology in Africa. It is the ranks of these pioneers that the African psychologists joined from 1965 until the present time. The ranks are still swelling.

THE SEARCH FOR MEANING:
INDIGENOUS CONCEPT OF INTELLIGENCE

There are many indications that among the Yoruba the concept of intelligence has many facets. First, there is the admiration for the individual who in a discussion about any important issue of the day does more listening than talking—the "still waters run deep" type of person. Such an individual is believed to be taking in the issues under discussion, be they related to festival rites, marriage or funeral or naming ceremony; to a dispute about land or family matters; to political organization or chieftaincy rivalry; or to dealing with a husband or wife or child or other relation. Whatever the issue, the "wise" person listens patiently and speaks only when all views on the issue have been expressed.

Second, there is the respect given by the Yoruba to the person who, having heard all sides of an issue, can respond by placing the issue in its proper cultural context. This the person may do by relating analogous cases, showing how such issues were resolved in the past. The person may use proverbs to bring the matter into shape, or may simply recast other people's arguments, showing their strength and weaknesses and straightening the loopholes in their reasoning, at the same time paying the proper respect to these others' age, stature, status, and position in the society. The intelligent person takes pains to ensure that the criticism offered cannot be misconstrued as directed to a person; it is directed only to the views expressed. This much-admired individual is adept at handling ideas and proverbs while at the same time remaining unruffled by temper or excessive zeal for his own viewpoints. Rather, he is cheerful, somewhat apologetic, and pays respect to and acknowledges the elders each time he makes a statement that mere age would not have brought to his grasp.

Third, there are the different words used to indicate the components of the Yoruba concept of intelligence. For instance, there are different words for wisdom (*ogbon*), understanding (*oye*), planfulness (*eto*), knowledge (*imoran*), attentiveness (*ifokansi*), brains (*opolo*), and thoughtfulness (*ironu*); there are other words for ingenuity, creativity, originality, and discretion. Finally, there is a distinction made between constructive intelligence (*ogbon ewe*) and destructive intelligence, or skill in deception or cunning, which the Yoruba refer to as *ogbon arekereke.* The former is admired, the latter despised.

A preliminary investigation was therefore concerned with finding the components of a Yoruba definition of intelligence. Without imposing a definition and without giving any firm indication of what Yoruba equivalences of intelligence are, two situational cases were presented to 64 adult (32 men and 32 women) illiterate Yorubas in the rural areas of Ibadan. All 64 gave responses showing clearly that intelligence means many things (see Table 13.1). All 64 also despised cunning or destructive intelligence. There were no appreciable differences between males and females.

A CROSS-CULTURAL STUDY

Another study further explored the phenomenon of intelligence as conceived by two distinct African national groups who can be said to be truly two cultures.

Subjects

There were 240 subjects in all: 120 Yorubas and 120 Baganda. The 120 Baganda people consisted of 60 each from rural and urban settings, 30 males and 30 females from each setting. A similar sample of Yoruba subjects was drawn for this comparative study. My method was to present validated situations and then require subjects to say how they would describe a person in a particular situation.

Table 13.1 Yoruba Associations With the Concept of Intelligence in Two
Situations ($N = 64$)

	N	%
Description of a person who makes a useful tool		
an inventive person	60	93.8
a pacesetter	62	96.9
a resourceful person	64	100.0
a purposeful thinker	58	90.6
an ingenious person	56	87.5
an achiever	50	78.1
an imaginative person	58	90.6
an enterprising person	62	96.9
Most often used approach to problem solving		
When solving problems concerning local disputes, the intelligent person		
uses ingenuity and gentle persuasion by words	61	95.3
is courteous, friendly, and cheerful	64	100.0
makes an effort to bring about harmony and not to apportion blame	63	98.4
suggests a compromise solution	60	93.8
When solving problems concerning everyday events, the intelligent person		
makes a quick assessment of the situation	45	70.3
takes actions free of mistakes	57	89.1
takes action with care	64	100.0
makes verbal commentary that indicates previous experience	64	100.0
is purposeful	64	100.0
When solving problems concerning dealing with strange situations, the intelligent person		
shows caution	59	92.2
shows exploratory behavior	62	96.9
seeks counsel	64	100.0
shows deliberate action	60	93.8
is alert	64	100.0

An explanation of *validated situations* is called for. Both at the time of the 1968-1969 exploratory study and again before the investigation here reported was carried out, I received help from a group of 10 people in the particular areas from which subjects were drawn. These helpers might be described as "educated rural people." All of them are people who have traditional positions in their cultures and who maintain close links with rural and urban traditional practices. I held discussions with 10 such Yoruba elders and 10 such Baganda elders before deciding upon the situations to be used in the study. Thus each situation presented to the subjects was earlier judged by my consultants to require intelligence (*ogbon* or *opolo* for the Yorubas and *obugezi* for the Baganda).

The two situations presented were those used in the preliminary investigation of 1968-1969, with two questions added to the first situation. They are as follows:

1. Someone makes a very useful tool for use in the house or on the farm or for use in the improvement of any aspect of the economic activities of the community such as weaving, fishing, pottery. How would you describe such a person?

   How does he get this result?

   At what age is this usually possible?

2. Think of someone whose ways of solving problems you admire. Please tell me how he goes about solving problems:

   concerning local disputes

   concerning how to do things in everyday situations

   concerning dealing with strange events

   For each case, what would you say is responsible?

Results of the Investigation

Results confirm the results of the exploratory study carried out only among the Yorubas (see Table 13.2). The most striking features of these results, however, are the absence of any significant difference when rural and urban dwellers are compared for either Yorubas or the Baganda and, more important, the strikingly comparable data obtained for the Yorubas and the Baganda. In both cultures the age of occurrence of inventiveness is usually considered to be during early adulthood.

Discussion and Conclusion

The results of this investigation show that among the two African peoples studied the concept of intelligence has remarkable similarity. Both the Baganda and the Yorubas appear to associate many attributes with intelligence. Intelligence for them is a living concept that is manifested in the day-to-day performances of the people and in the ways they meet and solve everyday problems.

I am in agreement with Irvine (1970), who suggests that theories of intelligence are incomplete without reference to the centrality of affect and values that determine the directions that human abilities will follow in different

Table 13.2 Intelligence as Viewed by the Baganda and the Yoruba

	Baganda Sample (N = 120)				Yoruba Sample (N = 120)			
	Male		Female		Male		Female	
	Urban	Rural	Urban	Rural	Urban	Rural	Urban	Rural
One who makes useful tool								
is creative	10	6	4	4	8	12	8	6
is inventive	18	20	16	18	18	16	18	22
is useful	1	5	5	4	0	0	2	1
has brains	1	5	5	4	4	2	2	1
Such a person gets results through								
practice	22	20	18	20	20	22	18	20
having a flare	4	2	4	2	2	4	6	4
inborn	2	4	4	6	4	2	2	2
learning	2	2	4	2	4	3	4	4
Age when possible								
age 20 or after initiation into								
work	22	20	18	18	18	20	18	20
age 14—after circumcision	4	5	1	4	4	4	4	4
after marriage	4	3	8	6	4	4	4	3
on becoming a parent	0	2	3	2	4	2	4	3
In solving a local dispute, the intelligent person employs								
harmony	20	18	22	20	22	20	24	20
compromise	5	10	6	8	6	6	4	6
history, stories, and proverbs	5	2	2	2	2	2	2	4
An intelligent person solves everyday problems with								
knowledge	10	12	12	10	10	12	12	12
experience	5	4	6	6	8	8	6	6
thinking	15	14	12	14	12	10	12	12
An intelligent person deals with strange events by								
spontaneous action	6	8	8	6	8	6	8	8
insight	4	6	4	6	8	8	6	8
consultation	10	8	12	8	4	4	10	4
deep thinking	10	8	6	10	10	12	6	10
What is responsible for such behavior?								
brains	6	4	4	5	4	6	4	6
wisdom	4	4	6	7	5	9	9	5
practice	10	12	10	9	10	9	10	11
experience	4	4	4	3	3	2	3	2
knowledge	4	4	2	4	4	2	2	4
inheritance	2	2	4	2	4	2	2	2

societies. Read (1959) has shown the recognition of the value of practice in her study of the Bemba women, who say with great emphasis, "We teach and teach the girls" and "We make them clever." It is interesting that in the second study reported here, "practice" was unanimously mentioned as the way to become clever (see Table 13.2). It is similarly interesting that Irvine (1969) suggests that the Shona word *ngware,* which means caution, prudence, and wisdom, should be translated as intelligence. Table 13.2 here shows that to be a valid point. The emphasis given to "harmony" as a solution to problems relating to local disputes (see Table 13.2) has been noted by Vernon (1969), who quotes Jomo Kenyatta: "To the Europeans, individuality is the ideal of life; to the Africans, the ideal is the right relations with and behaviour to, other people," or, as Vernon says, "to achieve harmony."

In conclusion, this study is presented alongside others before it as an attempt to understand the concept of intelligence among Africans. It is the first I know of that compares people from East Africa with those from West Africa. The striking finding of similarity in the concepts of intelligence among these two African peoples so distantly separated is in my opinion a significant contribution that needs further investigation. Wober's (1974) finding that the Kiganda concept of intelligence is associated with "slow, careful, active, straightforward and sane" action (p. 974) is also supported.

Indigenous psychology will, to my mind, be unraveled to the extent that psychological concepts are identified and labeled from the indigenous peoples' expression of their understanding of specific behavior within their traditional and cultural daily lives. The view seems justified however, that indigenous psychology will succeed only in describing the specific indigenous contents and attributes of psychological phenomena. All human beings, by virtue of being species *Homo sapiens,* will have similar psychological processes. The labeling may represent different language usage, and the contents of peoples thoughts, learnings, and intellectual or social reactions may be different, but the processes and varieties of psychological entities are most probably the same. Human nature, human culture, and the uniqueness of each human being lead to the conclusion reached by such writers as Zaccaria (1967), that each person is in some ways like all other persons, like some other persons, and like no other person. Indigenous psychology can account only for cultural patterning that makes each person like some other person.

REFERENCES

Irvine, S. H. (1969). Culture and mental ability. *New Scientist, 42,* 230-231.

Irvine, S. H. (1970). Affect and construct: A cross-cultural check on theories of intelligence. *Journal of Social Psychology, 80,* 233.

Read, M. (1959). *Children of their fathers*. London: Methuen.

Vernon, P. E. (1969). *Intelligence and cultural environment*. London: Methuen.

Wober, J. M. (1974). Towards an understanding of the Kiganda concept of intelligence. In J. W. Berry & P. R. Dasen (Eds.), *Culture and cognition: Readings in cross-cultural psychology*. London: Methuen.

Zaccaria, J. S. (1967). Guidance implications of concepts from the field of culture and personality. *Personnel and Guidance Journal, 49,* 907-910.

14

BUDDHIST PSYCHOLOGY

A Therapeutic Perspective

PADMAL DE SILVA

Ancient systems of thought and religious traditions originating in early times have attracted considerable attention from modern scholars in recent decades. This attention has taken several forms, reflecting different but complementary kinds of interest. One is the historical interest that these systems and traditions naturally provoke. Another, slightly different and more exciting, interest has to do with the value of such study in the context of the history of ideas. Concepts and theories that appear to have been developed recently in a modern context may have parallels and antecedents that go back many centuries; this kind of prehistory of a modern notion adds a new dimension to one's perspective on the development of theories and ideas. And third, the study of ancient concepts and practices may focus on their practical relevance and value in the present day. In the case of a religious or other system that is still flourishing, this kind of endeavor can take the form of examining, from the standpoint of modern science, the validity and usefulness of some of its practices for specific purposes in today's world.

Buddhism has generated considerable interest among modern scholars from all of these perspectives. Although there has been a deep and relatively widespread interest among Western scholars in Buddhist philosophy from the time the Pali Text Society in London began to publish original canonical texts more than a hundred years ago, more recent years have witnessed a specific interest in the psychology of Buddhism. Before focusing on this, however, a few introductory paragraphs on Buddhism are in order.

AUTHOR'S NOTE: I would like to thank the Leverhulme Trust for a research award supporting my studies of Early Buddhist concepts and strategies of behavior change.

THE BUDDHA AND BUDDHISM

The Buddha (the word literally means "the fully enlightened one") lived in the foothills of the Himalayan mountain range in Northern India from 563 to 483 B.C. (For an excellent account of the Buddha's life, see Kalupahana & Kalupahana, 1982; useful accounts are also available in Nanamoli, 1972; Saddhatissa, 1976.) He was the son of King Suddhodana, who ruled the small kingdom of Sakya from the capital city of Kapilavastu, and Queen Mahamaya. The family belonged to the Ksatriya clan called Gautama. The prince, who was named Siddhartha, lived in royal luxury and comfort in his childhood and youth, but at the age of 29 he renounced his worldly life and set forth on a quest for the ultimate truth about the human condition. This was a time of great intellectual and spiritual interest and debate in Northern India, and Siddhartha went from one teacher to another, learning what each had to offer and trying out their teachings. He also experimented with his own ideas, including a period of severe austerity and self-mortification. The quest came to an end after six years, when he attained full enlightenment—that is, he became the Buddha.

From then on he traveled on foot in the vast territory of Northern India, expounding his teachings and establishing a community of monks, the *sangha.* He preached to diverse audiences, large and small, from all walks of life. At the time of his death at the age of 80, his influence was quite widespread; the community of monks was firmly established, and his teachings had become a major spiritual and intellectual attraction in those areas.

Buddhism spread very rapidly, in India, Sri Lanka, Burma, Tibet, Thailand, and further east, in parts of Indonesia, Japan, China, and Korea. The spread of the religion in various parts of the Eastern world also led, naturally, to modification and diversification, resulting in different schools and subschools with different traditions. The developments in the Far East led, eventually, to the Zen schools.

The teachings of the Buddha, and relevant background material, are found in what is referred to as the Buddhist canon, the original of which is in the Pali language. Later versions have been found in Sanskrit and Chinese, and indeed in other Asian languages, but the Pali canon is generally considered to be the most authentic and is the basis of the Theravada school of Buddhism, also referred to as Early Buddhism. The canon was put together at a council of monks shortly after the Buddha's death and was committed to writing in Sri Lanka in the first century B.C. (Saddhatissa, 1976). It consists of three parts, known as the "three baskets" (*Tipitaka*). These are the *Vinaya Pitaka,* containing the rules of discipline for the monks; the *Sutta Pitaka,* containing discourses of the Buddha on various occasions; and the *Abhid-*

hamma Pitaka, containing philosophical and psychological analyses that were finalized in their present form about 250 B.C., later than the material in the other two parts. (A full listing of the various parts of the Buddhist canon is available in Webb, 1975.)

The main teachings of the Buddha are contained in the Four Noble Truths (see Rahula, 1959; Saddhatissa, 1971):

1. Life is marked by suffering and is unsatisfactory (*dukkha*).
2. The cause (*samudaya*) of this suffering is desire, or craving.
3. This suffering can be ended (*nirodha*) via the cessation of desire or craving— this is the state of *Nibbana,* ending the cycle of births and deaths and all that goes with it.
4. There is a way (*magga*) to achieve this cessation, which is called the Noble Eightfold Path.

The Noble Eightfold Path is also called the Middle Path, as it avoids the extremes of a sensuous and luxurious life on the one hand and a life characterized by self-mortification on the other. (Both of these, it will be recalled, were experienced by the Buddha himself before his enlightenment.) The Middle Path is described as consisting of eight aspects: right understanding, right thought, right speech, right action, right livelihood, right effort, right mindfulness, and right concentration. The person who undertakes a life based on this path, renouncing all worldly attachments, hopes eventually to attain the *arahant* state, which may be described as a state of perfection; this marks the attainment of *Nibbana.* The *arahant,* upon death, ceases to be reborn, and thus the individual's cycle of suffering is fully extinguished. The attainment of the *arahant* state requires not only disciplined living but also concerted meditative efforts (see Katz, 1982).

The other main teachings of the Buddha include the negation of a permanent and unchanging soul (*anatta*) and the notion of the impermanence of things (*anicca*). Buddhism also excludes the notion of a God; there is no supreme being who rules, purveys, and controls everything. Each individual is his or her own master, and determines his or her own life and fate.

For the laity, the vast majority of people who did not renounce worldly life to devote themselves to the immediate quest for *Nibbana,* the Buddha provided a sound, pragmatic social ethic (see Tachibana, 1926). They were expected to lead a life of restraint and moderation, respecting the rights of others and being dutiful to those around them. Such a restrained and dutiful life was not only considered to be a necessary prerequisite of one's ultimate religious aim, but was valued as an end in itself. For example, the Buddha advised his lay followers to abstain from alcoholic beverages because indulgence could lead to demonstrable ill effects, such as loss of wealth, proneness to socially embarrassing behavior, unnecessary quarrels, disrepute, ill health, and eventual mental derangement. This empirical and pragmatic approach is a prominent feature of the ethical stance of Buddhism (see P. de Silva, 1983).

STUDIES OF BUDDHIST PSYCHOLOGY

The considerable interest shown by modern students in Buddhist psychology becomes entirely understandable when one realizes that there is a great deal of psychological content in Buddhism. Some parts of the canonical texts, as well as later texts, are examples of explicit psychological theorizing, whereas most of the others include psychological assumptions and much material of psychological relevance. For example, the *Abhidhamma Pitaka* contains a highly systematized psychological account of human behavior and mind (see Narada, 1968); the translation of one of the *Abhidhamma* books, the *Dhammasangani,* in fact bears the title *A Buddhist Manual of Psychological Ethics.* The practice of Buddhism, as a religion and a way of life, involves much in terms of psychological change. The ultimate religious goal of the *arahant* state reflects and requires major psychological changes. In addition, as can be seen from the previous section, the path toward the achievement of this goal, the Noble Eightfold Path, involves steps many of which can only be described as psychological (Katz, 1982).

Although the rapid popularization of Zen Buddhism in the West no doubt provided a special impetus for the relatively recent interest in the study of Buddhist psychology (see Hirai, 1974; Maupin, 1962; Sekida, 1975; Shapiro, 1978), quite independent of this several scholars had begun to appreciate, and to examine closely, the psychological aspects of Buddhism. Early studies into aspects of the psychology of Buddhism include Sarathchandra's monograph *Buddhist Psychology of Perception* (1958) and Jayasuriya's *The Psychology and Philosophy of Buddhism* (1963). These descriptive-expository studies were soon followed by publications that concentrated on specific aspects of Buddhist psychology and that attempted to compare them with modern psychological notions and/or to analyze Buddhist concepts in terms of theoretical frameworks derived from Western psychology. For example, Govinda (1969) analyzed the basic principles and factors of consciousness as found in the *Abhidhamma Pitaka,* and Johansson in 1965 offered an analysis of some fundamental psychological concepts of Buddhism (*citta, mano* and *vinnana,* all of which refer to different aspects of "mind") using a psychosemantic paradigm. He subsequently undertook a similar exercise for the concept of *Nibbana* (Johansson, 1969). He has also attempted a more ambitious exposition of the Buddhist theory of causality embodied in the notion of dependent origination (*paticca-samuppada*) from a modern psychological point of view (Johansson, 1979).

There are other examples, one of which is M. W. P. de Silva's (1973) study of the Buddhist and Freudian theories of motivation, in which he compares the three fundamental desires, or cravings, that are postulated as the major motivating forces in Buddhist psychology with corresponding Freudian notions. Thus Freud's libido is shown to be similar to *kama-tanha* (desire, or craving, for sensory gratification); *ego* to *bhava-tanha* (desire, or craving, for life, for continued existence); and *thanatos,* the so-called death instinct, to *vibhava-tanha* (desire, or craving, for nonexistence). Interestingly, a paper by Johansson also observes that the Freudian notion of ego defense mechanisms has a counterpart in the early Buddhist literature (Johansson, 1983).

In a recent paper Mannè-Lewis (1986) attempts to discuss the Buddhist concept of enlightenment (or perfection) in terms of the concepts of Western psychology. She argues that the Buddhist psychology of enlightenment provides a paradigm for a challenging new model that has relevance to modern psychology. In this discussion, two basic Buddhist psychological concepts, *sanna* and *sankhara,* which refer broadly to the perceptual and recognizing functions, respectively, in the texts, are seen as parallel to aspects of Kelly's personal construct theory. To quote: "*Sanna* may be [seen as] the process of forming elementary and basic constructs and hypotheses: *sankhara* is that of putting these together, concretizing them, in Kelly's terminology, into testable predictions" (p. 130). Mannè-Lewis also offers a Kellyan interpretation of the cognitive aspects of the state of enlightenment as follows: "All personal constructs have been eradicated, and there is a perfect correspondence between the mind of the perceiver and the phenomena perceived" (p. 136).

THERAPEUTIC RELEVANCE
OF BUDDHIST PSYCHOLOGY

Although studies such as the above are of much academic interest, it is the examination of the psychology of Buddhism from a therapeutic point of view that offers potentially valuable and exciting practical possibilities. The potential value of Buddhism for psychological therapy and mental health has been commented on by many authors (e.g., P. de Silva, 1984; Goleman, 1976; Mikulas, 1981; Walley, 1986). In the following sections, I will comment on several topics falling within this area.

This discussion will focus mainly on Early, or Theravada, Buddhism— that is, Buddhism as contained in the original Pali texts and the early Pali commentaries. The literature on which this chapter is based consists of the original Pali canon, the early Pali commentaries that were already in their present form by the fifth century A.D. (Malalasekera, 1928). Many of the general points I will make, however, are equally applicable to other schools and forms of Buddhism. It is perhaps worth mentioning that there is already a rapidly growing literature on other schools of Buddhism, especially Zen, from the standpoint of psychological therapy (e.g., de Martino, 1983; Reynolds, 1980; Shapiro, 1978).

Meditation

One aspect of Buddhist psychological practice that has already gained entry into modern psychological therapy is meditation. In the Buddhist texts, meditation is given pride of place as an essential part of the individual's religious endeavor. The aim of this endeavor, as mentioned above, is to reach a state of perfection, and personal development is an essential part of this quest. Whereas restrained and disciplined conduct is part of this training and preparation, meditation is considered a crucial ingredient.

In Buddhism, the individual's salvation or emancipation (i.e., the attainment of the state of perfection) is to be achieved through his or her own effort and striving. Neither the Buddha nor anyone else can do this for another; the Buddha can show the way, but the rest is essentially up to the individual. There is of course a role for a teacher, under whose guidance a disciple will learn to meditate and who will help with difficulties that may arise, but the actual work of meditation is to be practiced and developed by the person seeking salvation.

Two forms of meditation are prescribed in the classical texts, one called *samatha* (tranquility) and the other called *vipassana* (insight). Further forms of meditation have been developed in later forms of Buddhism, including various Tibetan and Zen techniques, but these two represent the earliest, and the original, Buddhist techniques, going back 2,500 years. For the sake of completeness, I should note briefly what these two forms of meditation consist of (for detailed discussion, see Solè-Leris, 1986; also see Nyanaponika, 1962).

The word *samatha* means tranquility or serenity. *Samatha* meditation is aimed at reaching states of consciousness characterized by progressively greater levels of tranquility and stillness. It has two aspects: the achievement of the highest possible degree of concentration and the progressive calming of all mental processes. This is done through increasingly concentrated focusing of attention, where the mind withdraws progressively from all external and internal stimuli. In the end, states of pure and undistracted consciousness can be achieved. The *samatha* meditation procedure starts with efforts at concentrating the mind on specific objects and progresses systematically through a series of states of *jhanas,* or mental absorption.

Vipassana, or insight, meditation also starts with concentration exercises using appropriate objects to focus on. In this procedure, however, once a certain level of concentration is achieved, so that undistracted mindfulness can be maintained, one goes on to examine with steady, careful attention, and in great detail, all sensory and mental processes. One becomes a detached observer of one's own activity. The aim is to achieve total and immediate awareness of all phenomena. This leads, it is claimed, eventually to the full and clear perception of the impermanence of all things and beings.

It is held that *samatha* meditation by itself cannot lead to enlightenment or perfection; *vipassana* meditation is needed to attain this goal. Whereas the former leads to temporarily altered states of consciousness, the latter leads to enduring and thoroughgoing change in the person's consciousness and paves the way for achievement of the *arahant* state.

The implications of the claims made in Buddhism for meditation for mental health in general, and for psychological therapy in particular, are clear. The meditative experiences of both types, when properly carried out and developed, could be expected to lead to greater ability to concentrate, greater freedom from distraction, greater tolerance of change and turmoil around oneself, greater ability to be unaffected by such change and turmoil, and sharper awareness of and greater alertness to one's own responses, both physical and mental. It would also lead, more generally, to greater calmness or tranquility. Although the ultimate goal of perfection requires a long series of regular training periods of systematic meditation, along with major restraint in conduct, the more mundane benefits of meditation should be available to serious and persistent practitioners.

From a therapeutic perspective, this means that Buddhist meditation techniques may be useful as an instrument, or strategy, for achieving certain psychological benefits. Primarily, meditation would have a role as a stress-reduction strategy, comparable to the more modern techniques of relaxation (Benson, 1975; Goleman, 1976). In fact, there is a substantial and growing literature in present-day clinical psychology and psychiatry that shows that meditation does in fact produce beneficial effects in this way (see Carrington, 1982, 1984; Shapiro, 1982). Studies of the physiological changes that accompany meditation have shown several changes to occur that together indicate a state of calmness or relaxation (Woolfolk, 1975). These include reduction in oxygen consumption, lowered heart rate, decreased breathing rate and blood pressure, reduction in serum lactic acid levels, and increased skin resistance and changes in blood flow. These peripheral changes are generally compatible with decreased arousal in the sympathetic nervous system. There are also certain central changes, as shown by brain wave patterns. The amalgam of these physiological changes related to meditation has been called the "relaxation response" (Benson, 1975). This kind of evidence clearly establishes the role of meditation as a relaxation strategy.

Meditation techniques have been used systematically for numerous clinical problems, mostly with useful results, but recent work has also moved toward the scientific evaluation of the efficacy of these techniques. Indeed, if meditation is to establish itself as a viable and worthwhile stress-control strategy in modern mental health care, the only way this can be achieved is through subjecting it to such systematic evaluation (see Woolfolk & Franks, 1984). The available data, using standardized training, show that systematically carried out meditation has definite value for certain problems with certain client populations. The problems for which meditation has been used in clinical settings include general stress and tension, test anxiety, drug abuse, alcohol abuse, and sleep problems (see Carrington, 1982, 1984; Shapiro & Walsh, 1984). Some recent research has also shown the usefulness of mindfulness meditation (a form of *vipassana* meditation; parallels are also found in other traditions, including Zen—e.g., Suzuki, 1970) training for the self-regulation of chronic pain (Kabat-Zinn, 1982; Kabat-Zinn, Lipworth, & Burney, 1985). It is interesting that the early Buddhist texts in fact contain specific references to the value of this form of meditation for the control of pain (e.g., *Samyutta Nikaya,* vol. 5). Similarly, the Buddha is also reported to have recommended meditation as a means of achieving trouble-free sleep (*Vinaya Pitaka,* vol. 1).

It is perhaps worth dwelling briefly, at this point, on the use of mindfulness meditation for pain control. Kabat-Zinn et al. (1985) report that 90 chronic patients who were trained in mindfulness meditation in a 10-week stress-reduction program showed significant improvement, as measured by various indices, in pain and related symptoms. A control group of patients who did not receive meditation training did not show such improvement. The researchers explain their rationale for selecting this strategy for the treatment of pain as follows: "In the case of pain perception, the cultivation of detached observation of the pain experience may be achieved by paying careful attention and distinguishing as *separate* events the actual primary sensations as they occur from moment to moment and any accompanying thoughts about pain" (p. 165).

It is this detached observation of sensations that mindfulness meditation, as described in the Buddhist texts, helps one to develop. This makes such meditation a strategy particularly well suited to pain control. It is significant that the references to pain control by mindfulness meditation in the original texts appear to make this very point. For example, it is stated that the venerable Ananda, the Buddha's personal assistant, once went to see a householder named Sirivaddha in the city of Rajagaha who was ill. Learning from the patient that he was in much pain, and that his pains were getting worse, Ananda counseled him to engage in the meditation of mindfulness. A similar episode is recorded with reference to another householder, Manadinna; Ananda once again offered the same advice. Another account is that of the monk Anuruddha, who fell quite ill. When some visiting monks asked him about his pain, his reply was that the pain-generating bodily sensations could not perturb him, as his mind was firmly grounded in mindfulness. The implication here is that meditation can reduce, or "block out," the mental aspect of the pain—that is, although the physical sensations of pain may remain intact, vulnerability to subjectively felt pain is reduced. The above accounts are all from the *Samyutta Nikaya,* which appears to maintain this position more explicitly in a different passage. It is worth quoting this at some length:

> The untrained layman, when touched by painful bodily feelings, weeps and grieves and laments . . . and is distraught. . . . But the well-trained disciple, when touched by painful bodily feelings, will not weep, nor grieve, nor lament . . . nor will he be distraught. . . . The layman, when touched by painful bodily feelings, weeps *etc.* He experiences two kinds of feeling: a bodily one and a mental one. It is as if a man is hit by one arrow, and then by a second arrow; he feels the pain of two arrows. So it is with the untrained layman; when touched by a painful bodily feeling, he experiences two kinds of feeling, a bodily one and a mental one. But the well-trained disciple, when touched by a painful bodily feeling, weeps not *etc.* He feels only one kind of feeling: a bodily one, not a mental one. It is as if a man is hit by one arrow, but not by a second arrow; he feels the pain of one arrow only. So it is with the well-trained disciple; when touched by a painful bodily feeling, he feels but one feeling, bodily pain only. (*Samyutta Nikaya,* Vol. 4)

The view of pain contained in this expository account is clear: Physical pain sensations are usually accompanied by psychological correlates, which are like added pain. The disciple who is trained (in mindfulness meditation), however, sees the physical sensation as it is, and does not allow him- or herself to be affected by psychological elaboration of pain. Thus the experience is limited to the perception of the physical sensation only. It is this account of pain that provides the rationale for the instances cited above, where those in pain were advised to engage in mindfulness meditation.

It is also been suggested, in the recent psychiatric and psychological literature, that meditation can have a useful function as an integrated part of a dynamic psychotherapeutic approach. Referring specifically to Buddhist mindfulness meditation, Kutz, Borysenko, and Benson (1985) discuss several ways in which such a combined approach would help. For example, the kind of psychological content that meditation of this type produces could provide useful raw material for psychotherapy sessions. With certain kinds of clients, such meditation could also help by enhancing their ability to discern and discuss their negative emotions. Kutz et al. also argue that, if a client engages in regular meditation, this would in effect be like extending therapy beyond the formal sessions with the psychotherapist, thus leading to both intensification and condensation of therapy. They stress that the combination of dynamic psychotherapy and mindfulness meditation is "technically compatible and mutually reinforcing" (p. 6). As both dynamic psychotherapy and meditation are ways of achieving personal psychological change and development, this proposed role for meditation in a modern psychotherapeutic context is not surprising (see Watts, 1963).

It must be stressed, however, that meditation techniques are not suggested here as a panacea for all psychological disorders. They were intended in Early Buddhism for self-development, and the texts refer, as seen above, to their additional beneficial effects in certain contexts and conditions. The point here is that the nature of the meditation endeavor and its results as part of a Buddhist's self-development suggest a useful role for it in therapy for certain psychological disorders, especially stress-related ones, and for the psychological aspects of certain physical conditions. The available clinical literature shows that this is often the case. Further studies, and particularly systematic and rigorously controlled trials, will in the future shed more light on what specific uses meditation can have in clinical therapeutic settings.

Behavioral Strategies

There is another aspect of Buddhist psychology that is of particular relevance from a therapeutic perspective. The literature of Early Buddhism contains a wealth of behavior change strategies, which can only be described as behavioral, used and recommended by the Buddha and his disciples. This is an aspect of Buddhism that had been neglected by modern researchers until very recently. It is only in the past few years that these behavioral strategies have been highlighted and discussed (see, e.g., P. de Silva, 1984, 1985). These strategies are remarkably similar to several of the established techniques of modern behavior therapy. Thus, if Buddhist psychology is akin to modern humanistic, transpersonal, and existential psychologies in view of its emphasis on the individual, his or her problems and anxieties, his or her predicament, and his or her development through personal effort (see Goleman, 1981), it also has a clear affinity to present-day behavioral psychology in view of these behavioral techniques. The ways in which the overall approach of behavior modification and that of Buddhism may be said to be broadly similar have been discussed by Mikulas (1978, 1981) in two important papers. Some areas of similarity highlighted by Mikulas include the rejection of the notion of an unchanging self or soul, focus on observable phenomena, emphasis on testability, stress on techniques for awareness of certain bodily responses, emphasis on the here and now, and wide and public dissemination of teachings and techniques. Given this broad similarity, and the general empiricist/experientialist attitude of Buddhism as exemplified by the *Kalama Sutta (Anguttara Nikaya,* Vol. 1), in which the Buddha advises a group of inquirers not to accept anything on hearsay, authority, or pure argument, but to accept only what is empirically and experientially verifiable, it is not at all surprising that specific behavior techniques were used and recommended in Early Buddhism. It is also entirely in keeping with the social ethic of Buddhism, which recognizes the importance of behavior conducive to one's own and others' well-being as a goal in its own right. When and where specific behavior changes are required, both in oneself and in others, these are to be effected using specific techniques.

The *behavioral* nature of these strategies needs to be stressed at this point. When a certain response needs to be altered, an attempt is made to change it at a behavioral level; that is, directly, by operating on the response itself, and not indirectly, via other means. This is precisely the approach of modern behavior therapy (e.g., Rimm & Masters, 1979; Wolpe, 1958, 1973). Behavior therapy distinguishes itself from other therapeutic methods by concentrating on the problem behavior directly, and at a behavioral level. There is no attempt to change the response in question indirectly, either through the exploration of assumed unconscious factors or through pharmacological agents acting through the nervous system. The problem behavior itself is operated upon. So it is with the behavioral strategies found in Early Buddhist literature. This is not to say that this is the only means of behavior change accepted or recommended in Buddhism. In fact, major behavior changes are expected to occur through personal development, including restrained conduct and systematic meditation training. On the other hand, quite independent of this overall personal development and the attendant religious goal, the Buddha and his disciples did not hesitate to resort to, or to advocate, direct and behavioral ways of changing responses where needed.

The range of behavioral strategies found in the literature of Early Buddhism is impressive (see P. de Silva, 1984). Indeed, when these are described using modern terminology and listed together, they look like the contents page of a modern behavior modification manual. These techniques include the following:

- fear reduction by graded exposure and "reciprocal inhibition"
- using rewards to promote desirable behavior
- modeling to induce behavior change

- stimulus control to eliminate undesirable behavior
- "aversion" to eliminate undesirable behavior
- training in social skills
- self-monitoring
- control of intrusive thoughts by distraction, switching/stopping, incompatible thoughts, and prolonged exposure
- intense, covert focusing on the unpleasant aspects of a stimulus or the unpleasant consequences of a response, to reduce attachment to the former and eliminate the latter
- hierarchical approach to the development of positive feelings toward others
- use of cues in behavioral control
- use of response cost to aid elimination of undesirable behavior
- use of a family member in carrying out a behavioral change program
- cognitive-behavioral methods (e.g., for grief)

Details of these, including references to the original texts, have been cited elsewhere and will not be repeated here (see P. de Silva, 1984, 1985, 1986). It will be useful, however, to provide an example of this behavioral approach in Buddhism and to indicate its similarity to modern parallels.

For the control of unwanted, intrusive cognitions, which particularly hinder meditative efforts and can therefore be a major problem for a Buddhist, several strategies are recommended. These include switching to an opposite or incompatible thought, ignoring the thought and distracting oneself, and concentrating intensely on the thought (for details and a fuller account, see P. de Silva, 1985). As can be seen, all of these bear close similarity to techniques used in modern behavior therapy for the problem of intrusive cognitions, especially obsessions. The first (switching to an opposite, incompatible thought) is basically no different from the thought-switching or thought-substitution technique described by Beech and Vaughan (1979), Marks (1981), Rachman and Hodgson (1980), Sturgis and Meyer (1981), and others. In this technique, the client is trained to switch to thinking a thought different from the unwanted intrusion. The Buddhist technique has the added refinement that the thoughts to be switched to should be both incompatible with the original one and wholly acceptable in their own right. For example, if the unwanted cognition is associated with lust, one should think of something promoting lustlessness; if it is associated with malice or hatred, one should think of something promoting loving kindness. The second Buddhist technique mentioned above (ignoring and distraction) is essentially similar to the distraction techniques advocated by modern therapists (e.g., Rachman, 1978; Wolpe, 1973). The client is instructed to engage his or her attention on a different stimulus or activity. The Buddhist texts also offer suggestions as to what distractions might be usefully employed; these include both physical and cognitive ones. For instance, one might recall a passage one has learned, concentrate on actual concrete objects, or undertake unrelated physical activity, such as darning one's garment. The third technique (concentration on the intruding thought) is similar to the modern technique of satiation/habituation training (e.g., Rachman, 1978; Rachman & Hodgson, 1980). Present-day therapists may instruct the client to expose him- or herself to the thought repeatedly and/or for prolonged periods of time. The Buddhist texts advise one to face the unwanted thought directly and continuously, concentrating on that thought and nothing else. Similar comparisons can be made between most of the other behavioral strategies found in the Buddhist texts and those established in present-day behavior therapy for similar purposes.

The importance of the presence of these techniques in the Buddhist texts is manifold. First, it reflects the fact that Buddhism is not concerned only with the individual's endeavors to achieve the ultimate religious goal by a process of self-development. As noted above, it also has something to offer in the area of day-to-day management of behavioral problems, often as a goal in its own right, for reasons of the individual's own and his or her fellow beings' benefit and happiness. Thus these techniques are applicable irrespective of whether one has committed oneself to a life devoted to the aim of personal development and, ultimately, of the state of *arahant*hood. Second, being clearly behavioral, these techniques are well defined, easy to use, and—above all—empirically testable. Indeed, the Buddhist approach is one of testing various strategies until an effective one is found. The main discourse that addresses the control of unwanted intrusive cognitions—the *Vitakkasanthana Sutta* of the *Majjhima Nikaya,* for example—offers the disciple five different techniques, each to be tried if the preceding one fails to produce the desired results. The Buddha's advice to the Kalamas on the importance of not accepting any view because of hearsay, authority, and so on, but only on empirical grounds, reflects and embodies this approach. Indeed, it will be recalled that the Buddha's own quest for enlightenment followed this empirical path; having tried out various methods and teachings available at the time, he rejected each of them as it failed to lead to his goal and eventually developed his own path (see Kalupahana & Kalupahana, 1982; Saddhatissa, 1976). Third, the techniques are for use on oneself as well as for influencing the behavior of others; examples are found of both types of uses.

In terms of psychological therapy, the relevance of this aspect of Buddhism is abundantly clear. A range of clearly defined techniques is available for use with common behavioral problems. The fact that these are similar to modern behavior therapeutic techniques in remarkable ways implies that their validity and utility are already established, as many of the latter have been subjected to rigorous clinical and experimental investigation (see Rachman

& Wilson, 1980). There is a strong case, too, for those Buddhist strategies that so far have no counterpart in modern behavior modification to be tested empirically, using rigorous clinical and experimental research methods. If grounds are found for considering them clinically useful, they can then be fruitfully incorporated into the repertoire of techniques available to the present-day therapist.

It can also be argued that these techniques will have particular relevance in the practice of therapy with Buddhist client groups. One of the problems that arises in using techniques derived from Western science with client populations of different cultural backgrounds is that the techniques offered may seem alien to the indigenous population. Thus they may not be readily accepted or, if accepted, compliance with therapeutic instructions may be poor. These cultural difficulties in therapy and counseling have been fully recognized in recent years (e.g., Draguns, 1981; Ward, 1983). On the other hand, if the techniques that are used and offered, although integral parts of a Western psychological system, are shown to be similar to ideas and practices that have been accepted historically by the indigenous culture, then they would have a greater chance of gaining compliance and success. Singh and Oberhummer (1980) describe how a behavior therapy program was successfully devised for a Hindu patient that included the Hindu religious concept of *karma yoga*. Similarly, therapeutic packages that include traditional Zen practices have been used successfully with neurotic patients in Japan (Kishimoto, 1985; see also Reynolds, 1980). It is likely that modern behavior therapeutic strategies will be more readily acceptable to Buddhist client groups if their similarities with those found in the early Buddhist literature, and the use of the same or similar techniques by the Buddha and his early disciples, are highlighted. The use of meditation techniques as a stress-reduction strategy with Buddhist groups in several places provides an example of this phenomenon. A case in point is the use of Buddhist meditation in a psychiatric setting in Kandy, Sri Lanka (P. de Silva & Samarasinghe, 1985).

Potential for Preventive Use

A further possible use of Buddhist psychology for therapeutic purposes lies in the area of prophylaxis, or prevention. Theoretically, there is much scope for this, both with Buddhist client groups and with others. Many Buddhist techniques appear to have a role to play in the prevention of certain kinds of psychological disorders. For example, training in meditation, leading to greater ability to achieve calmness and tranquility, can help enhance an individual's tolerance for the numerous inevitable stresses in modern life. It may be possible, in other words, to achieve a degree of immunity against the psychological effects of stress and frustration (see Meichenbaum, 1985, on stress-inoculation training). Further, training in mindfulness meditation can enable a person to develop the ability to be alert to, and to recognize, his or her own thoughts, feelings, anxieties, and worries as they arise, and to exercise some control over them. The facility and skill in self-monitoring that can be acquired with the aid of mindfulness meditation could provide a valuable means of self-control. The role of self-monitoring in the self-regulation of behavior is well documented (see Kazdin, 1974; Thoresen & Mahoney, 1974).

The overall self-development that Buddhism encourages and recommends also has a lot to offer for preventive purposes. For example, if people begin to learn not to develop intense attachments to material things and to those around them, they may be less vulnerable to psychological distress and disorders arising from loss, including abnormal and debilitating grief reactions. This is not to suggest that the total renunciation of all worldly comforts and attachments should be the goal of every person. Indeed, very few persons in today's world will want to renounce all material things and devote themselves to the attainment of personal perfection. The Buddha himself recognized that the majority of people would remain lay persons, with normal household duties and day-to-day activities end pursuits, and that only a relatively small number would renounce lay life completely, hence the prominence given in Buddhism to lay ethics (see Tachibana, 1926). On the other hand, some of the meditation exercises and other personal development endeavors found in Buddhism can potentially enable a person to develop an outlook on life and patterns of response that in turn will help him or her to cope with the problems of living with greater calmness and assurance and with reduced vulnerability to common psychological disorders. This kind of primary prevention is certainly worth exploring seriously.

Summary

To recapitulate, then, there are several ways in which Buddhist psychology can be of relevance to present-day therapeutic practice. First, it was noted that Buddhist meditation techniques have already begun to be used, and shown to be effective, for certain clinical problems. This practice is rapidly growing and is being investigated clinically and experimentally. Second, it was shown that Buddhism possesses an array of behavior change strategies, most of which bear striking resemblance to modern behavior modification techniques. The value of highlighting these similarities when such techniques are used with Buddhist client groups was stressed, as was the case for putting to clinical and experimental test those other behavioral techniques found in the Buddhist literature that so far have no modern parallels. Third, the substantial potential for the use of Buddhist techniques, meditation techniques and others, for psychological prophylaxis has been discussed. All in all, then, Buddhist psychology has a clear contribution to make to the practice of psychological therapy in today's world. Some use of it is already being made, but there is room for a much greater role.

BUDDHIST AND WESTERN PSYCHOLOGY

Finally, a few comments are in order on the relationship between modern Western psychology and Buddhist psychology. Relations between the scientific psychology of the West and indigenous systems of psychology can take many forms, ranging from totally independent existence to complete integration. Buddhist psychology, like other indigenous psychologies, is prescientific, but it is so only in the narrow sense, in that it developed prior to, and outside the context of, modern Western science. It offers clearly testable hypotheses and therefore can be brought within the realm of modern scientific inquiry. Further, as noted above, the overall stance of Buddhism is an eminently empiricist one (see Jayatilleke, 1963; also Mannè-Lewis, 1986), and the process of evaluating the notions and practices of its psychology is something that will be consistent with this stance. Such testing will not be alien to the spirit of Buddhism, which encourages inquiry and discourages dogmatic acceptance of theories and claims (see *Kalama Sutta,* cited above). Thus Buddhist psychology can make a contribution to modern scientific psychology without compromising its basic stance or that of the latter.

What are the chances of the successful integration of the two? Total integration between two independently developed systems of psychology, each quite sophisticated, does not seem to be either feasible or desirable. Modern scientific psychology will continue to evolve and grow, and in the process it will take in ideas, concepts, and techniques from all sources, for evaluation and—where evaluation has led to positive results—incorporation. It is likely that Buddhist psychology will continue to be one of the indigenous psychologies that will provide many such testable concepts and techniques, and thus contribute toward the further expansion and development of modern psychology. Beyond such interaction and influence, it is not plausible to assume that the two systems in their entirety will be, or can be, integrated. On the other hand, it is possible to envision that a limited integration between certain aspects of Buddhist psychology and certain parallel areas of modern psychology may fruitfully be accomplished. Mikulas (1981), for example, has argued for an integrated new system of behavior and behavior change, of which both Buddhism and behavior modification are subsets. Likewise, as noted earlier, some modern psychotherapists have argued for the integration of meditation with dynamic psychotherapy. Within the broad limits of psychology, it is indeed possible that such schools or areas of modern psychology that are able to derive much from or have much in common with indigenous psychologies may develop and flourish with such close interaction. There is, already, the transpersonal school of psychology, which incorporates a good deal of Buddhist and other ideas of personal development and enduring personal change (see Goleman, 1981). On this limited scale, close overlap and synthesis seem possible and are to be welcomed. In the broader context, indigenous psychologies are likely to keep interacting with modern Western psychology rather then achieving total integration with it. In this interaction, they will make contributions to both theory and practice in different areas, and with varying degrees of significance. Buddhist psychology, as we have seen, has already begun to make such a contribution, and it is likely to continue to do so in a major way in the future. It is safe to assume that this contribution will be particularly significant in the area of psychological therapy.

REFERENCES

Anguttara Nikaya (4 vols.). (1885-1900). (R. Morris R. & E. Hardy, Eds.). London: Pali Text Society.

Beech, H. R., & Vaughan, M. (1979). *Behavioral treatment of obsessional states.* Chichester: John Wiley.

Benson, H. (1975). *The relaxation response.* New York: Morrow.

Carrington, P. (1982). Meditation techniques in clinical practice. In L. E. Abt & I. R. Stuart (Eds.), *The newer therapies: A sourcebook.* New York: Van Nostrand.

Carrington, P. (1984). Modern forms of meditation. In R. L. Woolfolk & P. M. Lehrer (Eds.), *Principles and practice of stress management.* New York: Guilford.

de Martino, R. J. (1983). The human situation and Zen Buddhism. In N. Katz (Ed.), *Buddhist and Western psychology.* Boulder, CO: Prajna.

de Silva, M. W. P. (1973). *Buddhist and Freudian psychology.* Colombo, Sri Lanka: Lake House Investments.

de Silva, P. (1983). The Buddhist attitude to alcoholism. In G. Edwards, A. Arif, & J. Jaffe (Eds.), *Drug use and misuse: Cultural perspectives.* London: Croom Helm.

de Silva, P. (1984). Buddhism and behavior modification. *Behavior Research and Therapy, 22,* 661-678.

de Silva, P. (1985). Early Buddhist and modern behavioral strategies for the control of unwanted, intrusive cognitions. *Psychological Record, 35,* 437-443.

de Silva, P. (1986). Buddhism and behavior change: Implications for therapy. In G. Claxton (Ed.), *Beyond therapy: The impact of Eastern religions on psychological theory and practice.* London: Wisdom.

de Silva, P., & Samarasinghe, D. (1985). Behavior therapy in Sri Lanka. *Journal of Behavior Therapy and Experimental Psychiatry, 16,* 95-100.

Dhammasangani. (n.d.). (E. Muller, Ed.). London: Pali Text Society.

Draguns, J. C. (1981). Cross-cultural counselling and psychotherapy: History, issues, current states. In A. J. Marsella & P. Pedersen (Eds.), *Cross-cultural counseling and psychotherapy.* New York: Pergamon.

Goleman, D. (1976). Meditation and consciousness: An Asian approach to mental health. *American Journal of Psychotherapy, 30,* 41-54.

Goleman, D. (1981). Buddhist and Western psychology: Some commonalities and differences. *Journal of Transpersonal Psychology, 13,* 125-136.

Govinda, A. (1969). *The psychological attitude of early Buddhist philosophy.* London: Rider.

Hirai, T. (1974). *Psychophysiology of Zen.* Tokyo: Igaku Shain.

Jayasuriya, W. F. (1963). *The psychology and philosophy of Buddhism.* Colombo, Sri Lanka: YMBA.

Jayatilleke, K. N. (1963). *Early Buddhist theory of knowledge.* London: Allen & Unwin.

Johansson, R. E. A. (1965). Citta, mano, vinnana: A psychosemantic investigation. *University of Ceylon Review, 23,* 165-215.

Johansson, R. E. A. (1969). *The psychology of Nirvana.* London: Allen & Unwin.

Johansson, R. E. A. (1979). *The dynamic psychology of early Buddhism.* London: Curzon.

Johansson, R. E. A. (1983). Defense mechanisms according to psychoanalysis and the Pali Nikayas. In N. Katz (Ed.), *Buddhist and Western psychology.* Boulder, CO: Prajna.

Kabat-Zinn, J. (1982). An outpatient program in behavioral medicine for chronic pain patients based on the practice of mindfulness meditation: Theoretical considerations and preliminary results. *General Hospital Psychiatry, 4,* 33-47.

Kabat-Zinn, J., Lipworth, L., & Burney, R. (1985). The clinical use of mindfulness meditation for the self-regulation of chronic pain. *Journal of Behavioral Medicine, 8,* 163-190.

Kalupahana, D., & Kalupahana, I. (1982). *The way of Siddhartha: A life of the Buddha.* Boulder, CO: Shambhala.

Katz, N. (1982). *Buddhist images of human perfection.* Delhi: Motilal Banarsidas.

Kazdin, A. E. (1976). Self-monitoring and behavior change. In M. J. Mahoney & C. E. Thoresen (Eds.), *Self-control: Power to the person.* Monterey, CA: Brooks/Cole.

Kishimoto, K. (1985). Self-awakening psychotherapy for neurosis: Attaching importance to Oriental thought, especially Buddhist thought. *Psychologia, 28,* 90-100.

Kutz, I., Borysenko, J. Z., & Benson, H. (1985). Meditation and psychotherapy: A rationale for the integration of dynamic psychotherapy, the relaxation response, and mindfulness meditation. *American Journal of Psychiatry, 162,* 1-8.

Majjhima Nikaya (3 vols.). (1888-1902). (V. Treckner & R. Chalmers, Eds.). London: Pali Text Society.

Malalasekera, G. P. (1928). *The Pali literature of Ceylon.* Colombo, Sri Lanka: R.A.S.

Mannè-Lewis. (1986). Buddhist psychology: A paradigm for the psychology of enlightenment. In G. Claxton (Ed.), *Beyond therapy: The impact of Eastern religions on psychological theory and practice.* London: Wisdom.

Marks, I. M. (1981). *Cure and care of neuroses.* New York: John Wiley.

Maupin, E. (1962). Zen Buddhism: A psychological review. *Journal of Consultation and Psychology, 26,* 367-375.

Meichenbaum, D. (1985). *Stress inoculation training.* New York: Pergamon.

Mikulas, W. L. (1978). Four noble truths of Buddhism related to behavior therapy. *Psychological Record, 28,,* 59-67.

Mikulas, W. L. (1981). Buddhism and behavior modification. *Psychological Record, 31,* 331-342.

Nanamoli Bhikkhu. (1972). *The life of the Buddha.* Kandy, Sri Lanka: Buddhist Publication Society.

Narada Thera. (1968). *A manual of Abhidhamma.* Kandy, Sri Lanka: Buddhist Publication Society.

Nyanaponika Thera. (1962). *The heart of Buddhist meditation.* London: Rider.

Rachman, S. (1978). An anatomy of obsessions. *Behavior Analysis and Modification, 2,* 253-278.

Rachman, S., & Hodgson, R. (1980). *Obsessions and compulsions.* Englewood Cliffs, NJ: Prentice-Hall.

Rachman, S., & Wilson, G. T. (1980). *The effects of psychological therapy* (2nd ed.). Oxford: Pergamon.

Rahula, W. (1959). *What the Buddha taught.* New York: Grove.

Reynolds, D. K. (1980). *The quiet therapies.* Honolulu: University of Hawaii Press.

Rimm, D., & Masters, J. C. (1979). *Behavior therapy: Techniques and empirical findings* (2nd ed.). New York: Academic Press.

Saddhatissa, H. (1971). *The Buddha's way.* London: Allen & Unwin.

Saddhatissa, H. (1976). *The life of the Buddha.* London: Unwin Paperbacks.

Samyutta Nikaya (4 vols.). (1884-1898). (L. Feer, Ed.). London: Pali Text Society.

Sarathchandra, E. R. (1958). *Buddhist psychology of perception.* Colombo, Sri Lanka: University of Ceylon Press.

Sekida, K. (1975). *Zen training.* New York: Weatherhill.

Shapiro, D. H. (1978). *Precision Nirvana.* Englewood Cliffs, NJ: Prentice-Hall.

Shapiro, D. H. (1982). Overview: Clinical and physiological comparison of meditation with other self-control strategies. *American Journal of Psychiatry, 139,* 267-274.

Shapiro, D. H., & Walsh, R. M. (Eds.). (1984). *Meditation: Classic and contemporary perspectives.* New York: Aldine.

Singh, R., & Oberhummer, I. (1980). Behavior therapy within a setting of karma yoga. *Journal of Behavior Therapy and Experimental Psychiatry, 11,* 135-141.

Solè-Leris, A. (1986). *Tranquility and insight.* London: Rider.

Sturgis, E., & Meyer, V. (1981). Obsessive-compulsive disorders. In S. M. Turner, K. S. Calhoun, & H. E. Adams (Eds.), *Handbook of clinical behavior therapy.* New York: John Wiley.

Suzuki, D. T. (1970). *Zen mind, beginner's mind.* New York: Weatherhill.

Tachibana, S. (1926). *The ethics of Buddhism.* London: Curzon.

Thoresen, C. G., & Mahoney, M. J. (1974). *Behavioral self-control.* New York: Holt, Rinehart & Winston.

Vinaya Pitaka (4 vols.). (1879-1883). (H. Oldenberg, Ed.). London: Pali Text Society.

Walley, M. R. (1986). Applications of Buddhism in mental health care. In G. Claxton (Ed.), *Beyond therapy: The impact of Eastern religions on psychological theory and practice.* London: Wisdom.

Ward, C. (1983). The role and status of psychology in developing nations: A Malaysian case study. *Bulletin of the British Psychological Society, 36,* 73-76.

Watts, A. (1963). *Psychotherapy, East and West.* New York: New American Library.

Webb, R. (1975). *An analysis of the Pali canon.* Kandy, Sri Lanka: Buddhist Publication Society.

Woolfolk, R. L. (1975). Psychophysiological correlates of meditation. *Archives of General Psychiatry, 32,* 1326-1333.

Woolfolk, R. L., & Franks, C. H. (1984). Meditation and behavior therapy. In D. H. Shapiro & R. N. Walsh (Eds.), *Meditation: Classic and contemporary perspectives.* New York: Aldine.

Wolpe, J. R. (1958). *Psychotherapy by reciprocal inhibition.* Stanford, CA: Stanford University Press.

Wolpe, J. R. (1973). *The practice of behavior therapy* (2nd ed.). New York: Pergamon.

15

RELATIONAL ORIENTATION
IN ASIAN SOCIAL PSYCHOLOGY

DAVID YAU-FAI HO

The aim of this chapter is to propose a conceptual framework for Asian social psychology and, more ambitiously, to explore its range of cross-cultural applicability and potential contribution to mainstream social psychology. Following Enriquez (1977), the development of such a psychology represents endogenous indigenization, wherein culture is treated as a source for theoretical constructions, rather than exogenous indigenization, wherein culture is treated as a target of investigation.

Considerable confusion arises from the ambiguity of the term *Asian psychology*. An appropriate beginning for the present chapter, therefore, is delineation of the various meanings of this term:

1. *Psychology of Asian people(s):* A body of psychological knowledge, theoretical or empirical, about patterns of thinking and behaving among Asian people(s); these patterns are viewed as psychological phenomena to be investigated.

2. *Psychology in Asia:* The history and current status of psychology, as an academic discipline or a professional specialty, within various Asian countries.

3. *A psychology created by Asian psychologists:* A new theoretical system or school of thought in psychology created by a group of Asian psychologists (or psychologists in Asia) who may be identified by their common adherence to a definite philosophical base (e.g., dialectical materialism). No such psychology has yet developed beyond the embryonic stage.

4. *Asian psychological thought:* Psychological conceptions of Asian thinkers, both historical and contemporary, about human nature, cognition, and behavior. In themselves, these conceptions may be regarded as cultural products or

AUTHOR'S NOTE: I would like to express my gratitude to the Centre of Asian Studies of the University of Hong Kong for its financial support with respect to the preparation of this chapter.

as psychological phenomena subject to further investigation, but they do not constitute a psychology.

5. *Psychology with an Asian identity:* A theoretical system or school of thought in psychology rooted in, or derived from, Asian cultures. Culture is viewed as a source from which methods, concepts, and principles used for theory construction may be derived. Such a source may consist of literary religious-philosophical traditions of the high culture or vernacular folk traditions in the mass culture.

There is no necessary connection between the first meaning and any of the following four—just as, more generally, there is no necessary connection between the behavior of a target group and the psychology employed to study it. There may be nothing particularly Asian about a psychology of Asian people(s), and it is inappropriate to use the term *Asian psychology* to refer to it. Conversely, Asian psychology (as defined in points 2, 3, 4, and 5) is not necessarily confined to the study of Asian people(s) alone. The crucial question is, What contributions does or can Asian psychology make to the study of human behavior in general and hence to the development of psychological science as a whole?

Of particular interest is the idea of an Asian psychology of Asian people(s)—that is, the study of Asian patterns of thought and action from an Asian perspective. As I have noted elsewhere, "An Asian psychology with an Asian identity must reflect the Asian intellectual tradition, which is distinct from the western in its conceptions of human nature, the goal and meaning of life, relationships between the human person and other humans, the family, society, nature, the cosmos, and the divine" (Ho, 1988, p. 55). This may be developed from psychological conceptions of Asian thinkers (a union of the first and fourth definitions above) or from a conscious attempt to create a psychology with an Asian identity (union of the first and fifth). Contention arises, however, when one insists on having an Asian psychology of Asian people(s). Is it necessary to have a psychology developed especially, presumably based on an Asian approach, for studying Asian people(s)? Can its methods, concepts, and principles be differentiated from and represent a viable alternative to or an improvement over those employed in Western psychology? The rationale for an Asian psychology of Asian people(s) rests on an affirmative answer to this question. What is clear, in any case, is that no such psychology is anywhere near maturity.

In the following exposition, I restrict the term *Asian social psychology* to mean social psychology with an Asian identity (as in the fifth definition above). I will take stock of what has been developed by various Asian authors, delineate common themes that appear in their writings, and propose my own conceptual framework. Of course, the domain of Asian social psychology is rather broad and has to be delimited. First, I shall limit myself to conceptions derived from vernacular traditions in the mass culture, rather than literary traditions of the elitist intelligentsia. Second, geographically I shall be concerned primarily with East Asia, specifically with three cultures, Chinese, Japanese, and Filipino; it seems that, in the social science literature, more concepts have been derived and employed as intellectual tools from these three than from other Asian cultures (see Ho, 1982).

CONCEPTUAL FRAMEWORKS
ROOTED IN THREE CULTURES

China

Situation centeredness. In *Clan, Caste, and Club,* Hsu (1963) proposes a hypothesis about the basic nature of three ways of life or worlds: The Chinese world is situation centered, the American world is individual centered, and the Hindu world is supernatural centered.

> The situation-centered world is characterized by ties which permanently unite closely related human beings in the family and clan. Within this basic human constellation the individual is conditioned to seek mutual dependence. . . . The individual-centered world is characterized by temporary ties among closely related human beings. Having no permanent base in family and clan, the individual's basic orientation toward life and the environment is self-reliance. . . . The supernatural-centered orientation enjoins the Hindu society to seek intimacy with the Ultimate Reality and/or Its manifestations and is commensurate with the idea, in interpersonal relations, of unilateral dependence. (pp. 1-4)

Differences in the family system lie at the root of these three worlds: dominance of the father-son relationship in the Chinese system, of the husband-wife relationship in the American system, and of the mother-son relationship in the Hindu system. Dominance of the father-son relationship would lead to greater reciprocity and greater restriction of dependence to well-defined channels and limits, and thus sets the stage for the situation-centered orientation; dominance of the husband-wife relationship leads to greater self-reliance and thus to individual centeredness; and dominance of the mother-son relationship leads to greater unilateral and all-embracing dependence and thus to supernatural centeredness.

Hsu's hypothesis may be criticized on several grounds. The first concerns the choice of the term *situation centeredness,* by which Hsu means that the primary guide for behavior is one's place or the place of one's primary group in the social network, rather than some abstract, universalist moral notion, such as justice. Multiple and differing standards of conduct prevail according to differing social groupings in which particular events occur. Moral conceptions are hence relative to social situations. Hsu calls this *situational determinism*. Similar terms, such as *situation ethics* and *situationalism,* have been used by Japanese as well as Western observers to characterize social interaction in Japan (Lebra, 1976, p. 111). However, the word *situation* has strong temporal and spatial connotations. Situations change, depending on time and location. In contrast, the word *relationship* connotes permanence. Clearly Hsu has in mind something more permanent or enduring than situational factors when he states that "the situation-centered world is characterized by ties which *permanently* unite closely related human beings in the family and clan" (p. 1; emphasis added). It would seem more appropriate to put the emphasis on the relational, rather than the situational, context in which social interaction takes place.

The second criticism concerns the assumption that there is a close link between the kinship pattern of a culture and the psychological disposition of individuals within that culture. In the Chinese case, father-son dominance would presumably predispose people psychologically toward situation centeredness. The notion of dominance of the father-son relationship may have sociological validity, to the extent that the father-son relationship is structurally the most important of role relationships in a patrilineal social system, but its psychological validity is doubtful. In real life, Chinese fathers are not as closely involved as are Chinese mothers in the emotional lives of their children. Furthermore, there is strong evidence that father-child relations tend to be marked by affectional distance, perhaps even tension and antagonism, in contrast to warm and close mother-child (especially mother-son) relations (see Ho, 1987). Thus the empirical basis for linking situation centeredness to father-son dominance is rather shaky.

Psychosocial homeostasis. Hsu (1985) declares, in *Culture and Self,* that "the meaning of being human is found in interpersonal relationships" (p. 27). He argues for a Galilean, as opposed to Ptolemian, view of humankind. In a Galilean view, the individual is seen "in terms of a larger whole," in contrast to a Ptolemian view, which sees the individual "as the center of his world" (p. 33). The central focus of the Chinese concept of *ren* (*jen* according to the Wade-Giles romanization; literally, "person") is "the place of the individual in a web of interpersonal relationships"; it is thus a Galilean concept. In contrast, personality is an individualistic concept, with its central focus on the individual's "deep core of complexes and anxieties"; it is thus a Ptolemian concept. *Ren* is not a "fixed entity," but is in a "state of dynamic equilibrium." It is "a matrix or a framework within which every human individual seeks to maintain a satisfactory level of psychic and interpersonal equilibrium" (p. 33)—a process that Hsu calls *psychosocial homeostasis*.

Hsu's assertions are basically a restatement of ideas he published earlier (Hsu, 1971). But how are the concepts of *ren* and self related? This is a question of crucial importance, inasmuch as his explication purports to be one on the self in cross-cultural perspective. Hsu does not address this question; in fact, he says very little about the self. What he does do is advocate the replacement of one etic (a pancultural concept employed by social scientists to analyze emic phenomena) with another that he claims will work better. His advice is to "forget about the term 'personality' " (p. 27) and to employ the concept of psychosocial homeostasis instead. To regard Hsu's explication as a description or analysis of the self would, in the words of Hsu and his coeditors, confuse "objective 'etic' and experiential 'emic' approaches to social behavior or even to ignore self-consciousness as a nonsignificant determinant of social behavior undeserving serious scientific study in its own right" (Marsella, DeVos, & Hsu, 1985, p. 3). Their thesis is that

> the experience of selfhood—consciousness— . . . is *not* totally derivative of or reflective of personality structure, nor is it reducible to an analysis of the social structure in which an individual participates. . . . [The] analysis of the self in social interaction is a necessary intervening level of analysis between that concerned with social role interaction on the one hand, and personality structure on the other. (pp. 3-7)

To incorporate Hsu's ideas into a study of the self, one would need to investigate how the "elements of man's existence" appear in the phenomenal world of individuals. If his advice were taken, then emphasis would be put on the interpersonal self (corresponding partly to his "intimate society and culture" and "operative society and culture"); the social self ("wider society and culture") and particularly the inner self ("expressible conscious" and "inexpressible conscious") would be secondary in importance. (The "preconscious" and the "unconscious" are, by definition, not represented in the phenomenal world; the "outer world" would be mostly outside its range.) This represents a departure from the intense interest self theorists have traditionally shown in the inner self.

Collectivist orientation. In earlier work, I addressed the subject of the collectivist orientation (Ho, 1979). In contrast to individualism, collectivism affirms that preservation and enhancement of the well-being of the group is the supreme guiding principle for social action. Accordingly, members of the group are expected to subjugate their own inclinations to group requirements, perhaps even to make personal sacrifices. The organization rests fundamentally on the principle of reciprocity, with each member being related to other members in a network of interlocking responsibilities and obligations. Individuality is negated to the extent that pressure toward conformity is exerted on the members. In return, they are assured of collective economic and psychological security inaccessible to the individualist, because built-in group mechanisms ensure that their basic needs are met. Collectivism is exemplified by the traditional Chinese ethos. Empirical research relying on this construct has been generated; an example is the study of the impact of cultural collectivism on reward allocation by Leung and Bond (1984).

Two observations may be made about my work on the collectivist orientation. First, as I have stated, collectivism has appeared in many varied forms throughout the ages and in diverse parts of the world. Both ideology and organization may vary, depending on the type of collectivity involved, but what is invariant is the principle that the interests of the individual or the smaller unit are subservient to those of the larger unit, and ultimately of the collectivity as a whole. Thus in analyzing behavior in a collectivist setting, one should specify the social units involved. Second, the possibility that individualism and collectivism can coexist should be entertained. A creative synthesis of these two ideologies for the realization of human potential takes a dialectic form: the collective actualization of individuals-in-society and, simultaneously, the reflection of this actualization within the individual self. An implication for social psychology is that conceptually individualism and collectivism may be better represented on two (or multiple) unipolar dimensions than on a single bipolar dimension.

Social orientation. Yang (1981) defines social orientation as follows:

> a predisposition toward such behavior patterns as social conformity, nonoffensive strategy, submission to social expectations, and worry about external opinions in an attempt to achieve one or more of the purposes of reward attainment, harmony maintenance, impression management, face protection, social acceptance, and avoidance of punishment, embarrassment, conflict, rejection, ridicule, and retaliation in a social situation. (p. 159)

Social orientation consists of two main components, namely, group orientation and other orientation (Yang & Ho, 1988). The former refers to the emphasis put on maintaining solidarity and harmony in social interaction, particularly within the primary group, the family and clan. The latter refers to sensitivity to opinions others have about oneself and hence to a concern about impression management. Empirical studies of personality change in Taiwan suggest that a set of decreasing characteristics may be identified; these include such interrelated traditional Chinese proclivities as collectivist orientation, other orientation, relationship orientation, authoritarian orientation, submissive disposition, inhibited disposition, and effeminate disposition (Yang, 1986). Yang considers that these proclivities may be subsumed under his concept of social orientation and, therefore, that the Chinese in Taiwan are becoming less socially oriented.

A major difficulty in Yang's formulation concerns his choice of the word *social*. Social orientation is universal—human society cannot be otherwise. A related difficulty is that the concept, as defined by Yang, is overinclusive. What Yang has asserted consists of two main propositions: (a) Chinese place the group above the individual, and (b) Chinese tend to be other directed. Both propositions are commonly accepted by students of Chinese society. Also, Yang assumes that social orientation lies at the opposite end of the *same* continuum as individual orientation. This assumption is questionable, however; conceptually, at least, the two may be better represented by different continua.

Japan

Attribute and frame. Nakane (1970) employed two concepts, attribute and frame, for analyzing Japanese society in comparison with other societies. An *attribute* is a quality that may be acquired not only by birth (e.g., membership in a descent group or caste) but also by achievement (e.g., appointment to high office). The term *frame* is the English translation of the Japanese *ba. Ba* means location, but its normal usage connotes a special base on which something is placed according to a special purpose; it is also used in physics where the word *field* would be used in English. A frame may be a locality, an institution, or a particular relationship that binds a set of individuals into one group; in all cases it indicates a criterion that sets a boundary and gives a common basis to a set of individuals who are located or involved in it.

According to Nakane, groups may be identified by two criteria: one based on the individual's own attributes, and the other on his or her situational position in a given frame. The tendency of the Japanese is to classify individuals on the basis of frame rather than attributes. In identifying themselves, for instance, Japanese are more likely to reveal their geographic or institutional affiliations (e.g., "I come from Village X," "I graduated from University X," or "I belong to Company X") rather than their own attributes (e.g., "I am an office worker")—precisely because the audience is presumed to be more interested in the former than in the latter. Given the primacy of the institution as a social unit, overriding importance would be attached to one's institutional affiliations, which are likely to develop into a strong sense of group consciousness, identification, and loyalty. Such is the heart of social organization in Japan.

The novel concept of frame is potentially a useful analytic tool for investigating not only Japanese but also other societies. Unfortunately, the distinction between attribute and frame is beset by logical difficulties and conceptual confusion. To begin with, logically speaking, group affiliations or memberships are attributes, but the converse of this statement cannot be made. That is, group affiliations or memberships constitute a subset of the universe of individual attributes. A frame is said to refer to an individual's affiliation with, or membership in, a particular group based on geographic or institutional ties. As such, it is logically also an attribute—albeit of a kind different from what refers to affiliation or membership based on blood or marriage ties. For example, belonging to a particular company is an attribute of the employees of that company, just as being a member of a particular family is an attribute of the members of that family. Moreover, an attribute may function as a frame under some circumstances. For example, being a member of a prominent family would be, according to Nakane, an attribute; but it functions as a frame, just as having graduated from a renowned university is a frame. Both function to locate the individual's status within the social system. These examples serve to illustrate that a redefinition of frame is necessary to preserve its utility as an analytic tool.

Social relativism. Lebra (1976) singles out social relativism as the chief characteristic of the Japanese ethos. Social relativism has two integral components: social preoccupation and interactional relativism. *Social preoccupation* refers to the proposition that "Japanese are extremely sensitive to and concerned about social interaction and relationships" (p. 2). *Interactional relativism* refers to the pattern wherein behavior results from interaction and mutual influence between an actor and his or her object. In unilateral determinism, by contrast, behavior results from "an external prime mover such as an environmental force," or from "an internal prime mover such as an irresistible passion or desire" (p. 8). Traditional Western culture comes closer to unilateral determinism than interactional relativism. Social preoccupation and interactional relativism imply each other, and *social relativism* is the term for this combination.

The Philippines

Social acceptance and reciprocity. Lynch (1973) considers social acceptance to be the most important of the

basic aims that motivate and control an immense amount of Filipino behavior. . . . [It is] enjoyed when one is taken by one's fellows for what he is, or
believes he is, and is treated in accordance with his status. . . . Put negatively
. . . social acceptance is had when one is not rejected or improperly criticized
by others. (p. 8)

Values instrumental to the attainment of social acceptance are smoothness of
interpersonal relations, *hiya* (shame), and *amor propio* (sensitivity to personal affront). Smoothness of interpersonal relations may be defined as follows:

a facility at getting along with others in such a way as to avoid outward signs
of conflict: glum or sour looks, harsh words, open disagreement, or physical
violence. . . . It means being agreeable, even under difficult circumstances. . . .
It means a sensitivity to what people feel at any given moment, and a willingness and ability to change tack (if not direction) to catch the slightest favoring
breeze. (p. 10)

Hiya is the general and universal social sanction of shame. *Amor propio* is
more restricted in scope and functions to protect the individual against loss
of social acceptance or to rouse him or her to regain it once it has been lost
or diminished. In short:

Social acceptance is gained and enhanced by smooth interpersonal relations;
its loss is guarded against by two sanctions discouraging behavior disruptive
of these relations. The first and general sanction is hiya, or shame; the second
and specific safeguard is amor propio, or self-esteem, which is a sensitivity to
personal insult or affront. (p. 16)

Two key concepts that are integral to smooth interpersonal relations have
been studied by social scientists. Both are pregnant with meaning about social intercourse in Filipino culture. The first is *pakikiramdam,* which may be
translated as "being sensitive to and feeling one's way toward another person" (Mataragnon, 1988, p. 252). Highly valued by Filipinos, it is subtlety
and sensitivity par excellence and is instrumental to the maintenance of
smooth interpersonal relations.

The second concept is *utang na loob,* which literally means a "debt inside
oneself" and is usually translated as "debt of gratitude." Kaut (1961) singles
it out as a key concept for the analysis of how culturally defined indebtedness regulates and conditions interpersonal behavior among Tagalogs. Refusal to comply with *utang na loob* obligation is rare on an overt level, because
to refuse is to insult, and insults are serious matters. Again, it is imperative
to avoid overt interpersonal conflicts. In a similar vein, Hollnsteiner (1973)
asserts: "To restate the norm of reciprocity as an operational principle in

Philippine life: every service received, solicited or not, demands a return" (p. 82). Between coordinate parties, repayment with interest is expected, but ambiguity exists as to what amount of repayment is sufficient to fulfill completely the debtors' obligation. Between superordinate and subordinate parties, only partial, incomplete repayment is expected. In either case, the sense of indebtedness is never completely erased, and the *utang na loob* relationship is rarely terminated. Failure to honor *utang na loob* would bring shame (*hiya*) on the debtor. Affective sentiment is thus maximally involved in *utang na loob* reciprocity, especially when the debt of gratitude is so great that a lifetime is insufficient for its repayment.

Shared identity. Enriquez (1978) argues that smoothness of interpersonal relations is secondary to, and should be understood in the light of, a more basic value, namely, *pakikipagkapwa* (sense of fellow being). He identifies *kapwa* (fellow being) as a core concept in Filipino social psychology—the only concept that embraces both the categories of "outsider" (*ibang-tao*) and "one of us" (*hindi ibang-tao*). He explains that the Filipino language has two pronouns for the English *we: tayo* (an inclusive we) and *kami* (an exclusive we). *Tayo* includes the listener; *kami* excludes him or her. Unlike the English word *other, kapwa* is not used in opposition to the self and does not imply the recognition of the self as a separate identity. Rather, *kapwa* is the unity of self and others, and hence implies a recognition of shared identity. From this arises the sense of fellow being that underlies Filipino social interaction.

Enriquez points out further that the notion of shared identity has great theoretical import. It appears to contradict the claim that all cultures distinguish between the in-group and the out-group, the member and the nonmember, or the insider and the outsider—an example of a universal or etic. Enriquez (1978) states:

> There seems to be at least one culture that does not fit this mold perfectly: the middle class Filipino from the Philippine province of Bulacan. For the Bulakeno the *ibang-tao* ('outsider') is *kapwa* in the same manner that the *hindi ibang-tao* ('one of us') is also *kapwa* ('the unity of the one-of-us and the other'). (p. 104)

COMMON THEMES

The reader may have discerned that certain themes recur in the conceptual frameworks recounted above. These common themes may be conveniently summarized in the propositions presented below.

The principles for guiding social action are as follows: (a) Collective or group interests take precedence over those of the individual, (b) the fulfillment of external social obligations takes precedence over the fulfillment of internal individual needs, and (c) securing a place in the social order takes precedence over self-expression. The potent determinants of social behavior are thus externally located; that is, they are outside of the individual. It may be added that, whereas Asians tend to be preoccupied with the fulfillment of obligations, Westerners tend to regard self-expression and meeting individual needs as a matter of rights to be defended against encroachments or violations by others or by collective authority. We may term the Asian orientation *obligation preoccupied* and the Western orientation *rights preoccupied.*

The norm of reciprocity binds interacting parties to an interlocking network of obligations and indebtedness. The Filipino concept of *utang na loob* corresponds closely to the Japanese concept of *on.* As explained by Lebra (1976), *on* derives its moral strength from a cultural generalization of reciprocity:

> When applied in the Japanese cultural setting, reciprocity immediately suggests the concept of *on.* . . .
>
> *On* is a relational concept combining a benefit or benevolence given with a debt or obligation thus incurred. . . . it is not a discrete object but is embedded in the social relationship between the donor and the receiver of a benefit. From the donor's point of view, *on* refers to asocial credit, while from the receiver's point of view, it means a social debt. An *on* relationship, once generated by giving and receiving a benefit, compels the receiver-debtor to repay *on* in order to restore balance. (p. 91)

Lebra suggests that *on* is a culture-bound notion of reciprocity for the Japanese. However, one is struck by the commonality between Hollnsteiner's and Lebra's analyses of reciprocity. Further, the ideas contained in *utang na loob* and *on* are by no means unfamiliar to the Chinese. The Chinese notion of indebtedness to a personal favor is expressed by the term *renqing* (favor, present) or, more explicitly, *renqingzhai* (indebtedness to a favor). The affective component involved is reflected in the word *renqing,* which generally means human feelings. An extended time perspective is emphasized in the need to repay one's debt of gratitude. If unable to pay in one's lifetime, the debt may be passed on to the next generation or generations. It may also be assumed in the debtor's next life (see Yang & Ho, 1988). Many legendary tales are centered on the theme of repaying indebtedness owed in a previous life. In short, indebtedness must be remembered and repaid when possible; this obligation has no time limitation. It is thus understandable why an individual does not accept favors from others too readily. In conclusion, it may be said that, whereas the norm of reciprocity is universal, its expressions in Asian cultures take on an imperative quality in regulating social exchanges that is far more pronounced than in Western cultures.

Social behavior is characterized by a high degree of other directedness. The theme of other directedness is expressed in Yang's other orientation, Lebra's social preoccupation, and Lynch's social acceptance. The term *other directedness* (contrasted with inner directedness and tradition directedness) is used by Riesman (1950) to describe a phenomenon in American society. Other-directed people are said to have a paramount need for approval and direction from, and hence the tendency to act in conformity with, contemporary others, especially their peers.

In the Asian context, other directedness differs from Riesman's characterization in at least three important respects. First, it is by far more pervasive. Other directedness pervades a much wider domain of social interaction, in terms of the diversity of situations, of social actions, and of the individuals or groups of individuals with whom one interacts. Second, the primary social sanctions involved are shaming and ostracism; in contrast, Riesman's other-directed people respond to group sanctions with diffuse anxiety rather than shame. Third, the accent is on the avoidance of social disapproval; in contrast, Riesman's other-directed people actively seek approval and popularity. This highlights an important theoretical distinction: The social dynamics involved in avoiding disapproval are quite different from those involved in seeking approval (see Ho, 1976, on losing face versus gaining face). To begin with, the term *social approval* connotes the positive element of liking more so than does *social acceptance.* One may be socially accepted, but not necessarily liked. If the main concern is to be socially accepted, the imperative is to avoid being disapproved, rejected, or ostracized. That means that one must be sensitive to social norms and exercise caution in one's conduct so as not to violate them. Avoiding disapproval is a more fundamental requirement than seeking approval. Not everyone is eager or needs to seek approval, but everyone who cares for maintaining effective social functioning must see to it that disapproval directed at him or her is contained within limits, and that remedial measures are taken to regain acceptance when these limits are exceeded. However, regaining acceptance does not constitute gaining approval; it is merely a restoration of the acceptance lost. Clearly, avoiding disapproval and seeking approval are not simple opposites.

The normative pattern of social interaction is the maintenance of harmony or smoothness and the avoidance of open *conflict.* Smoothness of interpersonal relations, according to Lynch (1973), serves to enhance social acceptance. He gives a descriptive account, not a theory, of social interaction in Filipino society, and almost totally absent from this account is a consideration of the other side of smoothness—that is, tension—in interpersonal relations. However, it is worthy of note that Lynch includes social status as a factor to be considered in his conception of social acceptance. This invites further analysis of the social dynamics involved. Tension would arise, and social acceptance would be disrupted, if the status a person claims for him- or herself is discrepant with (most likely more extravagant than) what others are prepared to recognize and accord that individual. A more provocative question concerns whether social acceptance is predicated on "keeping people in their place." Given the highly stratified and hierarchical nature of Asian societies, one must ask if smoothness of interpersonal relations functions to suppress underlying tensions and maintain the status quo. Indeed, after reviewing the evidence, Lynch reports: "*Interpersonal relations are often stressful* [in the Philippines]. Despite the high value placed on SIR [smoothness of interpersonal relations], or perhaps because of it, interpersonal dealings often fall short of the norm" (p. 50).

In China and Japan, the idea of smooth interpersonal relations receives full ideological backing from Confucianism. The ideal social order is one where harmony is maintained and conflicts are avoided. But Confucianism does not offer a dynamic conception of society. It does not give full recognition to the role of conflicts in social processes and offers no analysis of how conflicts arise and how these may be resolved.

The individual's orientation toward the group is characterized by conformity, not self-assertion. Collectivism, other directedness, and smoothness of interpersonal relations combine forces to generate pressures on the individual to conform to cultural norms and to yield to group demands. Social behavior is regulated by what is considered proper or acceptable; individual sentiments and volition are secondary to group requirements. Thus conformism is highly predictable in Asian societies.

RELATIONAL ORIENTATION

Several assorted conceptual frameworks have been reviewed, and a number of common themes have been delineated. Hsu (1971, 1985) makes an explicit claim that his formulation of psychosocial homeostasis has universal validity and applicability. Other authors have limited themselves mostly to culture-specific theorizing, without universalist aspirations. However, collectivism (Ho, 1979) clearly applies to societies other than China, and social relativism (Lebra, 1976) appears to hold great promise for analyzing social behavior in societies other than Japan.

But what is the defining characteristic that, more than any other, gives a conceptual framework its Asian identity and marks it apart from Western conceptualizations? The answer to this question begins with recognition of the primary importance of the relational contexts within which social behavior takes place. It may be observed that the concepts employed (e.g., *ren, on,* and *utang na loob*) in the frameworks recounted above are characteristically relational in character, in contrast to the individual character of Western concepts, such as actor, ego, and self; indeed, the primacy of relational contexts has been recognized by previous authors. The use of relational concepts has pivotal significance in theory building (Ho, 1982). Relational concepts are powerful tools that promise to free behavioral science from its present intellectual encapsulation, with overreliance on Western concepts.

At this point, the reader may object. The importance of relational contexts has long been recognized in social psychology; it is, therefore, not unique to Asian conceptions. A fundamental belief is that human character itself develops only in the social context—clearly a recognition of the crucial role of interpersonal relations in human development. But Asian conceptions of social existence go beyond this belief. Interpersonal relations are of crucial importance not only historically, in the formation of human character, but also contemporaneously, in defining what it means to be human throughout the individual's lifetime. The life of the individual is incomplete. It derives its meaning only from the coexistence of other individuals; without others, the very notion of individual identity loses meaning. In this sense, Asian conceptions of social existence are relation centered, in contrast to Western conceptions, which tend to be individual centered.

I propose to use the term *relational orientation* to capture the essence of Asian social psychology, in contrast to the individual orientation of Western social psychology. *Relational orientation* is not identical to *relation centeredness,* which connotes a more extreme focus on the relation and a corresponding deemphasis of the related individuals. Similarly, *individual centeredness* connotes a more extreme focus on the individual than does *individual orientation.* Relational orientation differs from situational determinism. Relationships may be culturally defined—called *role relationships*; a notable example is the father-son relationship governed by the Confucian ethic of filial piety in Chinese culture. They may also be socially defined, as in the case of status or authority relationships. Role and status relationships have enduring structural properties that are invariant across social situations.

However, other relationships are temporary in nature and are subject to situational influences. Acquaintanceships formed through chance encounters belong here. Relational orientation also differs from collective orientation. The emphasis is on relationships, rather than on collective interests. Loyalties based on personal relationships within a collective often contradict, even sabotage, the larger interests of the collective. It is thus important to specify the kind and quality of relationship between the individual and the group or between individuals in the group in order to assess the impact of relationships on social behavior.

Relational orientation is more fundamental than other directedness. It implies reciprocity, interdependence, and interrelatedness between individuals. Social actions follow not so much from the individual's own inclinations, sentiments, or needs as they do from the individual's perception of his or her relationships with other people—largely conditioned by cultural definitions. The social "presence" of others always enters into social calculations. Moreover, this process is bidirectional. One assumes that one's own presence is taken into consideration by others; in the same way, one also assumes that others assume their presence is considered by oneself. An appreciation of this relational orientation explains why attempts to predict social behavior by personality variables alone are, in principle, doomed to failure—not only in the Asian context, I might add, but in any social context, a prospect psychologists have become more aware of. The reason is that, again, the potent determinants of social behavior are more likely to be located externally, in the relational context, not internally, within the organism.

Relational orientation is, according to Hsu's (1985) terminology, a Galilean concept. It takes full recognition of the individual's embeddedness in the social network. A methodological consequence is that the psychology of social actions, even when pertaining to a single individual, must extend its domain to include (a) actions by the individual, either self-initiated or in response to those of others; (b) actions by other people closely associated with the individual; (c) actions directed at the individual by people with whom the individual is interacting; (d) actions directed at the individual by people closely associated with those with whom the individual is interacting; and, finally, (e) actions directed at people closely associated with the individual by those with whom the individual is interacting directly or indirectly. An example of this of kind of analysis is my own earlier study of face behavior (Ho, 1976). Clearly, the domain of social actions to be included for analysis is more encompassing and more complicated than has traditionally been envisioned. The social arena is alive with many actors interacting directly or indirectly with one another in a multiplicity of relationships. It is a dynamic field of forces and counterforces in which the stature and significance of the individual actor appear to have diminished. No longer at the center, the individual is not the measure of all things. This new perspective cannot be characterized by anything short of psychological decentering.

I shall now consider the implications of relational orientation for two of the most important topics in social psychology: informal social identification and identity and selfhood.

Informal Social Identification

By *informal social identification* I mean locating a person's position in the social network and thereby activating a set of expectations and behavioral rules implicitly associated with that position. This informs and prepares others for how to proceed with their interactions with the person concerned. The process consists of securing a knowledge of some attributes about the person that are considered important, or even necessary, for locating his or her social position.

The universe of attributes may be divided into two main classes: individual and relational. Individual attributes consist of (a) physical and psychological attributes that are intrinsic to the individual (e.g., personal appearance, maturity, and gender identity) and (b) biographical attributes that are extrinsic to the individual (e.g., age, sex, ethnic background, educational attainment, and occupation). Relational attributes are based on social connections—also extrinsic to the individual. In turn, social connections may be based on (a) geographic origin or institutional affiliation—what Nakane (1970) calls frames—and (b) blood or marriage ties (i.e., family or clan), caste, or achievement (e.g., admission into a prestigious university or learned society)—what Nakane calls attributes. They may be informal affiliations (e.g., acquaintanceships) or formal membership in organizations or groups. Relational attributes should not be confused with social status, although they may serve as one of its indicators. A person who has connections with people of high status may be of humble status him- or herself, and vice versa; however, connections based on achievement (e.g., membership in a prestigious organization) are in themselves status indicators.

Now, consider a social encounter between two previously unacquainted persons. Each party would reveal some information about him- or herself to, and would withhold other information from, the other party; at the same time, each would want to know something about the other. In a given culture, ordinarily there would be a considerable overlap between what one is willing to reveal and what the other is presumably interested in. This overlapping information consists of attributes about a person that provide an initial means for informal social identification. In different cultures, varying degrees of importance would be attached to different attributes. For instance, in relative terms individual attributes tend to be given more importance in American culture; in contrast, relational attributes tend to more important in Asian cultures. An American may become annoyed if the other party shows too much interest in his or her relational attributes, with the feeling that the other party is "more interested in my social background than in me as a person." On the other hand, Asians may feel uncomfortable if the other party's interests are focused on their individual attributes; they may also feel that the other party is not paying enough attention to their social "place."

Social embeddedness means that relational attributes are particularly important in identifying a person or locating his or her place in a given social network. Relational attributes function as a social map, without which one would be at a loss to know how to deal with the person concerned. One needs to know first, in other words, with whom one is dealing; in order to do that, one must gain knowledge of the person's social connections.

Identity and Selfhood

The significance of social connections goes beyond informal social identification to the very definition of identity, I use the term *relational identity* to refer to identity defined by a person's significant social connections. To illustrate, the Chinese term for identity, *shenfen,* has a strong connotation of a person's social "place." Relational orientation thus implies relational identity.

Closely related to the notion of relational identity is collective identity, wherein an individual's identity is defined by membership in the reference group to which he or she belongs. In the extreme, the individual is not regarded as a separate being, but as a member of the larger whole. For Westerners, an individual's identity may be defined quite independent of the group. For Asians, however, individual identity tends to be interwoven with collective identity (Ho, 1985). Each member partakes of the attributes of the group. Each shares the pride that the group claims and bears the burden of its collective humiliation. As Lebra (1976) puts it, "Both the pride and the shame of an individual are shared by his group, and in turn the group's pride and shame are shared individually by its members" (p. 36). Lebra refers to the Japanese, but her description applies no less to other Asian groups.

Self psychology provides a language that is remarkably suited to capturing the meaning of relational or collectivist identity. Phenomenologically, the definition of identity is reflected in the conception of selfhood. In Asian cultures, the self is not an individualistic self, one that is intensely aware of itself, its uniqueness, its sense of direction, purpose, and volition. The boundary between self and nonself is not sharply demarcated; the self is not distinct and separate from others, encapsulated unto itself. Rather, the self is what I would call *relational self,* one that is intensely aware of the social presence of other beings. The appearance of others in the phenomenal world is integral to the emergence of selfhood; that is, self and others are conjointly differentiated from the phenomenal world to form the self-in-relation-with-others. This, in short, is the phenomenological representation of selfhood.

The relational nature of selfhood in Asian cultures has been recognized by previous authors. According to Tu (1985), "The Confucian perception [is] that selfhood entails the participation of the other" (p. 245). Lebra (1976, p. 67) explains that, in Japan, the term for the self is a *bun* compound noun, *jibun*; the concept of *bun* (which means portion, share, part, or fraction) implies an image of society as a organic whole, individuals being parts of that organism. Enriquez's (1978) notion of shared identity goes one step further in negating the individualistic self. Significantly, these relational conceptions appear to strike a common chord with expanded conceptualizations of the self among contemporary Western theorists. Johnson (1985) states, *"The self is no longer regarded as a unitary phenomenon*—that is, as an encapsulated, individual variable. Instead, the self is accepted as an *interpersonal,* i.e. as an *intersubjective,* unit" (p. 129).

Still, the self in Asian cultures tends to be a subjugated self. It is conditioned to respond to perceptions, not of its own needs and aspirations, but of social requirements and obligations. Incongruence between the inner private self and the outer public self is likely to be present. About the self in Japanese culture, DeVos (1985) concludes: "The Japanese sense of self is directed toward immediate social purposes, not toward a process of separating out and keeping the self somehow distinct, somehow truly individual, as remains the western ideal" (p. 179). My contention is that this conclusion applies no less to traditional Chinese and Filipino cultures.

CONCLUSION

Conceptions of social existence derived from Asian cultures recognize the crucial role of relational contexts within which social behavior takes place. Accordingly, Asian social psychology is characterized, above all else, by what I have termed *relational orientation* (or *relation centeredness,* if even more emphasis on the relation is intended)—in contrast to individual orientation (or individual centeredness).

Thus far, I have developed relational orientation as a conceptual framework, not as a theory. Two questions present themselves. The first concerns its range of cross-cultural applicability within Asia, where vast cultural differences exist. For instance, the Hindu conception of life appears to be radically different from Chinese and Japanese conceptions, which have much in common (see Hsu, 1963); this is not to mention important cultural variations within the Indian subcontinent itself. Nevertheless, I maintain that relational orientation is a useful conceptual framework. It makes a demand on the theorist to consider variations in how social relationships are defined, and consequently in how they govern social behavior, in different cultures.

The second question is more vital. It concerns conceptual and methodological contributions by the conceptual framework here developed to mainstream social psychology. Relational orientation offers a perspective for viewing human behavior, as an alternative to the Western perspective preoccupied with the individual. The potency of this perspective derives from a fundamental principle, namely, *Social interaction takes place invariably in relational contexts, regardless of cultural variations.* The unit of analysis is not the individual, but the individual-in-relations. Relational orientation, therefore, redresses the current imbalance in social psychology resulting from its bias rooted in individualism. A systematic investigation of the individual-in-relations now demands its rightful place in mainstream social psychology.

REFERENCES

DeVos, G. (1985). Dimensions of the self in Japanese culture. In A. J. Marsella, G. DeVos, & F. L. K. Hsu (Eds.), *Culture and self: Asian and Western perspectives* (pp. 141-184). New York: Tavistock.

Enriquez, V. G. (1977). Filipino psychology in the Third World. *Philippine Journal of Psychology, 10,* 3-18.

Enriquez, V. G. (1978). Kapwa: A core concept in Filipino social psychology. *Philippine Social Sciences and Humanities Review, 42,* 100-108.

Ho, D. Y. F. (1976). On the concept of face. *American Journal of Sociology, 81,* 867-884.

Ho, D. Y. F. (1979). Psychological implications of collectivism: With special reference to the Chinese case and Maoist dialectics. In L. H. Eckensberger, W. J. Lonner, & Y. H. Poortinga (Eds.), *Cross-cultural contributions to psychology* (pp. 143-150). Lisse, Netherlands: Swets & Zeitlinger.

Ho, D. Y. F. (1982). Asian concepts in behavioral science. *Psychologia, 25,* 228-235.

Ho, D. Y. F. (1985). Prejudice, colonialism, and interethnic relations: An East-West dialogue. *Journal of Asian and African Studies, 20,* 218-231.

Ho, D. Y. F. (1987). Fatherhood in Chinese culture. In M. E. Lamb (Ed.), *The father's role: Cross-cultural perspectives* (pp. 227-245). Hillsdale, NJ: Lawrence Erlbaum.

Ho, D. Y. F. (1988). Asian psychology: A dialogue on indigenization and beyond. In A. C. Paranjpe, D. Y. F. Ho, & R. W. Rieber (Eds.), *Asian contributions to psychology* (pp. 53-77). New York: Praeger.

Hollnsteiner, M. R. (1973). Reciprocity in the lowland Philippines. In F. Lynch & A. de Guzman II (Eds.), *Four readings on Philippine values* (4th ed., pp. 69-91). Quezon City: Ateneo de Manila University Press.

Hsu, F. L. K. (1963). *Clan, caste and club.* New York: Van Nostrand.

Hsu, F. L. K. (1971). Psychosocial homeostasis and jen: Conceptual tools for advancing psychological anthropology. *American Anthropologist, 73,* 23-44.

Hsu, F. L. K. (1985). The self in cross-cultural perspective. In A. J. Marsella, G. DeVos, & F. L. K. Hsu (Eds.), *Culture and self: Asian and Western perspectives* (pp. 24-55). New York: Tavistock.

Johnson, F. (1985). The Western concept of self. In A. J. Marsella, G. DeVos, & F. L. K. Hsu (Eds.), *Culture and self: Asian and Western perspectives* (pp. 91-138). New York: Tavistock.

Kaut, C. R. (1961). Utang-na-loob: A system of contractual obligation among Tagalogs. *Southwestern Journal of Anthropology, 17,* 256-272.

Lebra, T. S. (1976). *Japanese patterns of behavior.* Honolulu: University of Hawaii Press.

Leung, K., & Bond, M. H. (1984). The impact of cultural collectivism on reward allocation. *Journal of Personality and Social Psychology, 47,* 793-804.

Lynch, F. (1973). Social acceptance reconsidered. In F. Lynch & A. de Guzman II (Eds.), *Four readings on Philippine values* (4th ed., pp. 1-68). Quezon City: Ateneo de Manila University Press.

Marsella, A. J., DeVos, G., & Hsu, F. L. K. (Eds.). (1985). *Culture and self: Asian and Western perspectives.* New York: Tavistock.

Mataragnon, R. (1988). *Pakikiramdam* in Filipino social interaction: A study of subtlety and sensitivity. In A. C. Paranjpe, D. Y. F. Ho, & R. W. Rieber (Eds.), *Asian contributions to psychology* (pp. 251-262). New York: Praeger.

Nakane, C. (1970). *Japanese society.* Berkeley: University of California Press.

Riesman, D. (1950). *The lonely crowd.* New Haven, CT: Yale University Press.

Tu, W. M. (1985). Selfhood and otherness in Confucian thought. In A. J. Marsella, G. DeVos, & F. L. K. Hsu (Eds.), *Culture and self: Asian and Western perspectives* (pp. 231-251). New York: Tavistock.

Yang, K. S. (1981). Social orientation and individual modernity among Chinese students in Taiwan. *Journal of Social Psychology, 113,* 159-170.

Yang, K. S. (1986). Chinese personality and its change. In M. H. Bond (Ed.), *The psychology of the Chinese people* (pp. 106-170). Hong Kong: Oxford University Press.

Yang, K. S., & Ho, D. Y. F. (1988). The role of yuan in Chinese social life: A conceptual and empirical analysis, In A. C. Paranjpe, D. Y. F. Ho, & R. W. Rieber (Eds.), *Asian contributions to psychology* (pp. 263-281). New York: Praeger.

16

PSYCHOLOGY IN AND OF CANADA

One Small Step Toward a Universal Psychology

JOHN W. BERRY

Most current attempts to develop an indigenous psychology are being made in Third World countries, where scholars are attempting to decolonize their science and to understand their own populations in their own terms. Largely forgotten is that a major impetus toward indigenous psychology was a set of early analyses and arguments made in Canada by MacLeod in 1955, and in France by Moscovici in 1972, that focused on some essential and distinctive characteristics of populations *within* the broad set of Western industrialized societies.

In addition to arguments for the importance of people in a society understanding themselves in their own terms, it has also been argued that such activity should be viewed as only one step in a broader comparative effort to produce a panhuman psychology (Berry, 1978, 1983). Out of numerous *indigenous* psychologies arises the possibility of generating a *universal* psychology; the *national* precedes the *international,* both logically and empirically. To use other terms (Berry, 1969), and to link the argument to the title of this chapter, psychology done *in* a country is often merely an *imposed etic,* whereas psychology done *of* a country qualifies as an *emic*; the eventual integration will constitute a *derived etic,* and perhaps, eventually, a *universal* psychology (for an elaboration of these concepts, see also Berry, 1989).

This chapter first presents an initial framework to guide our exploration of the issues, then turns to an illustrative example of indigenous psychology from Canada. The issue of integrating across indigenous psychologies with the goal of producing a universal psychology is considered in the concluding chapter of this volume.

PRELIMINARY FRAMEWORK

Three points need to be made in the development of a preliminary frame-work. The first is that contemporary psychology is a discipline that is very much associated with a particular society. When one considers the number of psychologists, their research funding and productivity, and their general impact on the field, it is difficult to escape the conclusion that psychology, as we know it, is something that is largely an American phenomenon. Al-though statistics might be useful here (for example, is 90% or 95% the cor-rect proportion of the world's psychologists living in the United States?), analytic evidence is just as important. Moscovici (1972) has argued persua-sively that social psychology especially was largely developed in the United States, taking "for its theme of research and for the contents of its theories the issues of *its own* society" (p. 19). More recently, Berry (1974, 1978), Faucheux (1976), Jahoda (1979), Kalin and Gardner (1981), Pepitone (1976), and Triandis (1977) have made similar observations and interpretations.

The second point is that there is an important distinction to be made be-tween the *what* and the *how* of the discipline, that is, between the content and the theories and methods employed. Although there is an obvious interplay between the content and the theory and method of a discipline, for analytic purposes it is useful to consider them separately. This distinction was implied by Moscovici, as the quotation above shows; I developed it further in my own work (Berry, 1976). The theoretical and methodological perspectives of many researchers in psychology emerge from the content areas or problems with which they work; at the same time, research questions that receive pri-ority are often those that are congruent with the local societal ideology. For example, Sherif and Sherif (1969, p. 222) note that the emphasis in American political culture is clearly on the individual; this is held to account for the individualist emphasis in American social psychology, in contrast to a col-lectivist one (Sampson, 1977). Another commentator has found that "Ameri-can theories fit American value patterns" in his large study of workers' values in 40 nations (Hofstede, 1980, p. 32).

A third preliminary point is that there are three legitimate goals, or levels of research, in cross-cultural work that need our attention (Berry, 1969). At one level, we attempt the transportation of current psychological knowledge in order to test its applicability in other cultural systems (*imposed etic*); at the second level, we seek out new psychological knowledge from a point within other cultural systems (*emic*); at the third level we compare the psy-chological knowledge acquired from these first two activities, and then inte-grate them into a more general (*derived etic* and eventually a *universal*)

WHAT?

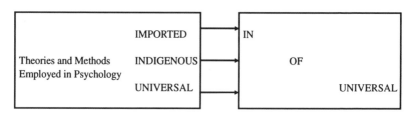

HOW?

Figure 16.1. Preliminary Framework for Distinguishing Imported, Indigenous, and Universal Psychologies

psychology that is applicable to more than one cultural system (see also Berry, 1989).

These three points may be brought together into the preliminary framework in Figure 16.1. The distinction between the what (content) and the how (theory and method) of psychology provides the basic horizontal and vertical structure of the framework. The three goals or levels of cross-cultural research are indicated within each dimension.

Given that the ultimate goal of science is the production of general statements about all relevant phenomena, using appropriate theoretical and methodological tools, it is likely that the psychology we all wish to develop is universal both in its content and in its theory and methods; this ultimate psychology is indicated in the lower right sector of the framework, where all psychological phenomena are included within a comprehensive theoretical system, but one that also takes varieties of indigenous phenomena into account.

In sharp contrast to this universal psychology is the kind indicated in the lower left sector. Here, psychology is imported from one society (often the United States) to another society and is used to study topics that are central to the established literature using extant theories and methods; we can refer to this approach as doing social psychology *in* another society, often with little regard to what is actually happening there or to how it may best be studied.

As this volume illustrates, an emerging antidote to doing psychology *in* another society is to develop the discipline from within, to create a psychology that reflects the local reality (Berry, 1974; Berry & Wilde, 1972; Enriquez, 1979; Kumar, 1979; Moscovici, 1972). The numerous indigenous psychologies *of* various societies are indicated in the central sector of the framework. Of course, what American psychology does now in the United States is included here, and is entirely appropriate. But clearly the two problems with this situation are its importation and use *in* other societies and its masquerading as a universal psychology; this double error is what we face at the present time.

The other sectors in the framework will be described in the following sections, where I will attempt to put some flesh on this skeleton. These are all problematic and involve mismatches between content and theory when employing imported theory or methods to study local phenomena.

IMPORTED PSYCHOLOGY

In Canada, as in many other societies, the materials available for teaching and research in psychology are largely "made in the U.S.A." In physics or even in experimental psychology, this may not pose much of a problem, although even this benign view has been debated by Symons (1975), who argues that *what* is considered important to know about is often a product of values in one's society. Even in experimental psychology, Crutchfield and Krech (1962) argue that "the scientist—like every other person—is a member and product of his society. Certainly no psychologist can escape this influence, no matter what his experimental problem, and no matter how thick and soundproof are the walls of his laboratory cubicle" (p. 12). The uncritical use of the imported product directs us to commit a number of errors.

For one, we incorrectly identify our own social phenomena by either ignoring important local societal issues or assimilating them to the version that exists in the imported literature. These errors of omission and commission abound in social psychology in Canada. With respect to errors of omission, psychological phenomena associated with Canadian ethnic pluralism (for example, intergroup relations and linguistic and multicultural phenomena), with regionalism, and with political, economic, and cultural dependency have with few exceptions been ignored (Berry, 1974; MacLeod, 1955).

With respect to errors of commission, when they occur, they frequently are identified with apparently similar phenomena in the United States (such as equating French Canadians or Canadians from the West Indies with American blacks); numerous examples are documented by Alcock (1978) and Sadava (1978). Such attempts to insert "appropriate Canadian examples" (Wrightsman, 1977, p. viii) into a ready-made (in the United States) psychology is not an appropriate approach to scientific research and or to the making of generalizations.

Another error occurs when we employ imported theory (and methods) to study and explain local phenomena. For example, attempting to understand multiple intergroup relations in the Canadian ethnic mosaic by the mainstream-minority concept (developed in U.S. black-white studies) would have been fruitless (Berry & Kalin, 1979; Berry, Kalin, & Taylor, 1977); in Canada we simply do not have a single mainstream to which minorities relate one by one in neat dyadic interactions.

In summary, it is not difficult to find examples of mismatch between phenomena and theory when psychology is done *in* another society. This situation has been likened to the use of a blueprint to help understand a piece of machinery. Errors exist when one misidentifies either the machine or the blueprint, but also when one uses an inappropriate blueprint for the machine being examined. To continue the analogy:

> The blueprint which we use to help us understand the machine must bear some resemblance to it. Our social science concepts and assumptions are often mere copies of those developed and employed in other societies: to import them uncritically for our special purposes may lead us to serious errors. If our blueprint were printed elsewhere, how can we hope to make sense of the complex machinery we see here? One way to resolve the inconsistency between the machine and the blueprint is to make the machine match the blueprint; this we are in danger of doing. The other is to discard the present blueprint, and make a new one based upon the machine as it is; this is what I hope we will be able to do. (Berry, 1974, pp. 137-138)

INDIGENOUS PSYCHOLOGIES

Making new blueprints to match the local phenomena requires the construction of indigenous psychologies *of* a particular society. As we have seen, this is precisely what has happened in the United States, and it is what is required in other societies who wish to understand themselves. That social psychology from the United States does reflect society in the United States has been pointed out by a number of observers (e.g., Moscovici, 1972; Sampson, 1977).

More generally, as we have seen, Crutchfield and Krech (1962, p. 12) believe that this situation is basic to all science; it is not limited to dominant scientific communities. Again turning to Hofstede (1980), we see that his analyses demonstrate a link between one particular value dimension (uncertainty avoidance) in a society and the type of theory preferred in that society: "In high uncertainty avoidance countries, scholars look for certainties, for Theory with a capital T, for Truth. In low uncertainty avoidance countries, they take a more relativistic and pragmatic stand and look for useable knowledge" (p. 182).

Thus we should accept as normal the existence of a match between societal characteristics and psychological content, theory, and method; this match clearly exists in the one well-developed example that we have available. The situation that is abnormal is the resistance, in many quarters, to the drive to establish other indigenous psychologies. It is claimed that they are unnecessary, that they are nationalistic, and that they are too limited. But they are also potentially threatening to those who are well trained in *the* psychology and who may require a degree of relearning and retooling in order to reduce their ethnocentrism and maintain their credibility. In addition, of course, these indigenous psychologies *of* a people and their society are more likely to be accurate and useful, and so deserve a life of their own for reasons quite apart from the innuendo in the above caricature of a debate.

SPECIAL FEATURES OF CANADIAN SOCIETY

In 1974, I proposed that there were some aspects of life in Canada that required special attention from psychologists, all of which emphasize the *diversity* of the country and the population. In brief, Canada covers a massive area of land and water, entirely within the Arctic and North Temperate climatic zones. It is occupied by a relatively small number of persons of extremely varied ethnic backgrounds, who have arrived over a long time span and have tended to settle in regionally distinct groups.

In more detail, these special features of the Canadian behavioral setting may be divided (somewhat arbitrarily) into three clusters:

- *The North, and other regions:* Low temperatures and low population density, isolation, difficulties of transportation and communication, and sociopolitical fragmentation are all special features of life in Canada that derive from these simple geographic and demographic facts.
- *Cultural, social, and linguistic dualism:* The bulk of the population (about 65%) is composed of two major sociocultural and linguistic groups; those of

British origin account for almost 40% and those of French origin for about 25%. Government policies are in effect (Government of Canada, 1969) that are designed to promote the acceptance of this dualism (mainly through bilingualism), and Quebec is generally recognized as a "distinct society" (in cultural, linguistic and political terms) within the Confederation.

- *Cultural pluralism: Native Peoples, immigrants, and ethnic groups:* The balance of the Canadian population (about 35%) comprises numerous ethnocultural groups that, more so than in most other countries, have managed a large degree of cultural retention. Indeed, a government policy (Government of Canada, 1971) is in effect that is designed to ensure that such cultural diversity persists; this has been institutionalized in the Multiculturalism Act (1988) and in a Department of Multiculturalism and Citizenship.

The multiculturalism policy contains four elements. First, the policy wishes to avoid assimilation by encouraging ethnocultural groups to maintain and develop themselves as distinctive groups within Canadian society (through programs to promote own-group maintenance and development). Second, a fundamental purpose of the policy is to increase intergroup harmony and the mutual acceptance of all groups that maintain and develop themselves (i.e., other-group acceptance and tolerance). Third, the policy argues that group development by itself is not sufficient to lead to group acceptance; intergroup contact and sharing are also required. Fourth, full participation by groups cannot be achieved if some common language is not learned; thus the learning of one or both official languages (French or English) is also encouraged by the policy.

RELEVANT AREAS
OF PSYCHOLOGICAL INQUIRY

Although divisions within a discipline are often arbitrary, it is still possible to discern subareas of inquiry that are characterized by a special focus and a special methodology. For the field of ethnic psychology, I have articulated some of these special features in earlier work (Berry, 1985b). Within psychology more generally, at least four socially relevant fields have attained some independent recognition: social, clinical, educational, and work psychology.

When these four subareas of psychology are crossed with the three special features of Canadian life, twelve kinds of research ventures emerge (see Table 16.1); each is described briefly below, to illustrate the scope and magnitude of the issues.

Table 16.1 Twelve Problem Areas for a Canadian Indigenous Psychology

	Special Features of Canadian Society		
Areas of Psychology	North	Dualism	Pluralism
Social	1	2	3
Clinical	4	5	6
Educational	7	8	9
Work	10	11	12

Social

1. How do individuals in various regions, but particularly in the North, deal with each other, and how do they deal with isolation, alienation, and the like? Most of what we do in social psychology is limited to the study of people in urban and central areas.

2. What is the character of French-English relations (prejudices, attitudes, stereotypes) and communication (bilingualism, linguistic vitality)? Are they such that the country can continue to hold itself together, or will a perpetual cleavage inevitably result?

3. What is the character of relationships among the various ethnic groups (including Native Peoples) that make up the Canadian "mosaic," and how are these groups related to the French and English sectors of the population? Are language issues central to their identity? How do immigrants and refugees adapt to life in Canada, and what is their impact on the overall character of Canadian society?

Clinical

4. Are there particular stresses associated with regional life (poverty, isolation) that serve as risk factors to mental health? How can individuals be served best by social and health institutions to reduce such risks?

5. Is there a possibility that bicultural/bilingual persons will become marginal to both groups, thereby facing greater risk of psychological problems? Is there a chance of identity loss or identity confusion among such individuals?

6. Are there particular risks in being culturally different, remaining over generations as part of distinct ethnocultural groups? What are the extra risks associated with being an immigrant or a refugee?

Educational

7. Schooling in dispersed populations presents a special challenge, particularly when cultural and language factors are also involved (as in the case of northern Indian and Inuit communities). Native Peoples have long had the right to control their own schools (Government of Canada, 1972), but how can this political control best be implemented?

8. Bilingual education has been a prominent feature of life in Canada, and results based on these experiments have been widely disseminated to other countries. What are the long-term consequences for individuals and communities of this massive bilingual experience?

9. Multicultural education, to meet the needs of immigrant and ethnocultural groups as well as the larger society, is an urgent requirement in Canada. Education for understanding cultural diversity and for tolerance is not easy, but can be much assisted by psychological research.

Work

10. Selection and training for work in remote areas of the country (miners, teachers, nurses, and so on) have been serious problems for decades. High turnover, and the resulting loss of continuity in service, has created apprehension, even distrust, among local populations. How can these difficulties be overcome?

11. How can selection criteria for employment be made equivalent and equitable when there are two cultures and two languages that dominate the world of work? How can effective management take place when there is often an interethnic component to all work relationships?

12. Similarly, how can selection criteria be made equivalent and equitable when skills, work attitudes, and credentials from all over the world are represented in the work force? What is the relative effectiveness of ethnically homogeneous work groups compared with the random allocation of individuals without regard to ethnicity and language?

WHAT HAS BEEN ACCOMPLISHED?

The simplest and briefest answer to this question is, Not very much! However, in the area of social and ethnic psychology some progress has been made, particularly in the dualism and pluralism domains. Since the publication of the first "reader" in Canadian social psychology (Berry & Wilde,

1972), three others have appeared (Earn & Towson, 1985, 1990; Gardner & Kalin, 1981; Koulak & Perlman, 1973). Of greatest significance has been the publication of two social psychology textbooks, one in French (Bégin & Joshi, 1979) and one in English (Alcock, Carment, & Sadava, 1988, 1991). Other general volumes have also appeared in overlapping areas such as ethnic studies (Driedger, 1987; Goldstein & Bienvenue, 1980) and the social psychology of education in a multicultural society (Ouellet, 1988; Samuda, Berry, & Laferrière, 1984). Finally, a volume on ethnic psychology, dealing mainly with Canadian ethnocultural group phenomena, has recently appeared (Berry & Annis, 1988).

The following subsections look more closely at accomplishments in the specific areas, following the sequence in Table 16.1.

Social

1. Virtually nothing has been accomplished in the various regions or in the specific area of the Canadian North; the psychological dimension of living in remote areas and in the largest and most challenging region remains virtually ignored.

2. The study of French-English relations has advanced substantially. The McGill research group (led by Wally Lambert) and former students (Gardner, Taylor, Aboud, Simard, Clément, Bourhis, and others) continue to establish important findings in the areas of bilingualism and intergroup relations (see, for example, Clément & Kruidenier, 1985; Edwards, 1985; Gardner, 1985; Lambert, 1981). Most of these studies have been conducted in Montreal, but one national survey (Berry et al., 1977) and follow-up analyses (e.g., Kalin & Berry, 1982) have revealed important positive mutual regard between the French and English communities, one that is enhanced by contact and mutual knowledge.

3. The above-mentioned volumes dealing with ethnicity (especially Driedger, 1987; Gardner & Kalin, 1981) have advanced the accumulation of social psychological knowledge surrounding relationships among the ethnically diverse sectors of the Canadian population and how acculturating groups seek to relate to the larger society (Berry, Kim, Power, Young, & Bujaki, 1989). The national survey by Berry et al. (1977) was specifically devoted to understanding relationships among ethnocultural groups in Canada; it was also concerned with attitudes toward the ideology of multiculturalism and toward immigration. Results indicated a generally positive regard for the idea of a multicultural society and the presence of a highly variable (from positive to negative) set of attitudes toward ethnocultural groups and immi-

grants. Another national survey identified the language-related attitudes of the 10 most populous ethnocultural groups in the country: Although heritage language maintenance is generally highly valued, there tends to be variable maintenance after the first generation (O'Bryan, Reitz, & Kuplowska, 1976). Little has been done with respect to relationships with Native Peoples, except that this is generally recognized to be a problem in urgent need of attention (Berry, 1981; Indian & Inuit Affairs, 1980; Kalin & Berry, 1982; Ponting & Gibbins, 1980). (For a general overview of many of these issues, see Berry, 1984.)

Clinical

4. Once again, little has been accomplished in the area of stresses associated with regional life. Recent conference proceedings in the area of circumpolar health (e.g., Berry & Hart Hansen, 1985) reveal only limited concern with these issues.

5. In the area of bicultural/bilingual persons' risk of psychological problems, there has been little research, and only in the area of anxiety associated with learning the other official language (e.g., Gardner, 1985; Lalonde & Gardner, 1984).

6. The acculturative stress experienced by immigrants, refugees, and Native Peoples has had a moderate degree of attention. A national task force has recently reported on immigrant and refugee mental health (Beiser et al., 1988) and an overview of acculturative stress among immigrant and ethnic groups was prepared by Berry, Kim, Minde, and Mok (1987) after earlier overviews of the situation among Native Peoples generally (Berry, 1985a) and among the James Bay Cree (Berry, Wintrob, Sindell, & Mawhinney, 1982). There is high variability in psychological difficulties, and these problems appear to be related to a number of factors that are amenable to policy management; hence there are some prospects for preventing and reducing mental health problems.

Educational

7. Education in the North has changed a great deal, but mainly because of political factors rather than the impact of psychological research findings. Recent reviews of education and cognitive dimensions of northern Native life show substantial research activity (Berry & Bennett, 1991, 1992; Chrisjohn, Towson, & Peters, 1988; McShane & Berry, 1988), but it appears that little regard is paid to it by those responsible for educational change in the North.

8. Among the most important changes in the education of Canadians in recent years has been the advent of "bilingual education" (meaning most often in Canada the early immersion of English-language students in either totally French-language or both-language programs). This has come about because of a continuing demonstration by Lambert and others in both research and public policy domains (e.g., Lambert & Tucker, 1972) that there are clear cognitive and social advantages to using both official languages, and very few disadvantages. The opposite (English-language education for French mother-tongue students) has not been attended by the same interest.

9. An equally important educational change has been brought about by the dramatic increase in immigrant children in Canadian schools, particularly in major urban areas (of Toronto, Montreal, and Vancouver). Recent books have appeared for use in teacher training and in counseling that attempt to encourage the profession to keep up with these demographic and cultural changes (Samuda et al., 1984; Samuda & Wolfgang, 1985).

Work

10. Few psychological studies appear to have been done with regard to regional and northern work. However, some "experiments" have been tried with respect to work rotation to the North (e.g., fly in for five weeks' work, fly out for three weeks at home), but there has been no formal or psychological evaluation of these alternatives.

11. Some efforts have been made to examine variation in management values between the French and English communities (e.g., Kanungo, 1980). There have also been moves to establish a working knowledge of both official languages as a criterion for employment in the Federal Civil Service and Crown Corporations; this has led to considerable concern about employment selection and equity, and the perception of threat by unilingual (mainly English) groups. However, little systematic research has been accomplished.

12. Access to employment by persons of varying cultural, linguistic, and racial backgrounds has been a topic of considerable recent public concern. The influence of ethnicity (signaled by accent) has been studied experimentally by Kalin (e.g., Kalin, 1982; Kalin, Rayko, & Love, 1980) and others: judgments of suitability for employment have been found to vary with ethnicity in most studies. One government task force (in Ontario) has completed an inquiry into the problem (Cumming, Lee, & Oreopoulos, 1989) and the issue has been part of general national inquiries (Government of Canada, 1984, 1985), but no formal national research has been conducted.

CONCLUSIONS

Unlike many of the examples of indigenous psychologies in this and other publications, the Canadian case represents a situation where some psychologists have been trying to achieve an indigenous perspective in a Western industrialized country. To some observers this attempt is a strange enterprise, especially because it is taking place in a country that is being massively influenced by American society generally, and not just in the psychology that is taught and researched.

It is possible to see this activity as a response to general acculturative pressures being experienced. Historically, France, then Great Britain, and now the United States have been the colonial powers dominating public and private life in Canada. Much of the current activity is in keeping with one of the four acculturation strategies outlined by Berry et al. (1989). Many Canadian psychologists are content to be *assimilated* to the American traditions and institutions: They publish in the United States, they belong to the American Psychological Association, they establish their collegial networks and go to regional and national conferences there; some Canadian psychology departments seek accreditation from the American Psychological Association, and occasionally seek (contrary to Canadian immigration laws) to hire American faculty. The Canadian Psychological Association even encourages the American Psychological Association to hold its annual conventions in Canada—that is, to meet outside its national territory, invading the "scientific space" usually occupied by international congresses. Needless to say, with such a dominant reference group, especially one so close, it is very difficult to gain acceptance for many of the ideas expressed in this chapter. In terms of the acculturation framework (Berry et al., 1989), this has led to a sense of *marginalization* on the part of many Canadian psychologists who have been attempting to promote an indigenous perspective in Canadian psychology.

In contrast to these two acculturation strategies, the intention has been to establish this indigenous perspective initially through a form of *separation,* through a kind of deliberate neglect of dominant American paradigms, and to see ourselves (or "to know ourselves," as the 1975 Symons report is titled). This, of course, has been the strategy of ethnography for more than a century; to understand people in their own terms. As we will argue in the concluding chapter to this volume, the long-term goal is similar to the acculturation strategy of *integration,* where psychology draws upon the ideas, theories, methods, and findings of both (eventually all) societies to yield the generalized *universal* psychology.

Although psychology in Canada remains overwhelmingly in the assimilation mode, efforts to contribute to this long-term universal goal (through the development of an indigenous perspective) are also alive. Whether the generally accepted value of diversity to a society will be recognized specifically with respect to diversity in psychological points of view remains uncertain. This chapter has been one attempt to explain and sustain one indigenous perspective. There is hope, because dominant societies (in the literature on acculturation) do not remain dominant forever, just as dominant scientific paradigms occupy center stage for a time, but are replaced by others.

REFERENCES

Alcock, J. (1978). *Social psychology and the importation of values.* Paper presented to the Canadian Psychological Association, Ottawa.

Alcock, J., Carment, D., & Sadava, S. (1988). *A textbook of social psychology.* Toronto: Prentice-Hall.

Alcock, J., Carment, D., & Sadava, S. (1991). *A textbook of social psychology* (2nd ed.). Toronto: Prentice-Hall.

Bégin, G., & Joshi, P. (Eds.). (1979). *Psychologie sociale.* Québec: Les Presses de l'Université Laval.

Beiser, M., et al. (1966). *After the door has been opened: Report of the task force on mental health issues affecting immigrants and refugees.* Ottawa: Health and Welfare Canada/Multiculturalism and Citizenship Canada.

Berry, J. W. (1969). On cross-cultural comparability. *International Journal of Psychology, 4,* 119-128.

Berry, J. W. (1974). Canadian psychology: Some social and applied emphases. *Canadian Psychologist, 15,* 132-139.

Berry, J. W. (1976). Critique of Triandis "Social psychology and cultural analysis." In L. Strickland, F. Aboud, & K. Gergen (Eds.), *Social psychology in transition.* New York: Plenum.

Berry, J. W. (1978). Social psychology: Comparative, societal and universal. *Canadian Psychological Review, 19,* 93-104.

Berry, J. W. (1981). Native peoples and the larger society. In R. Gardner & R. Kalin (Eds.), *A Canadian social psychology of ethnic relations* (pp. 214-230). Toronto: Methuen.

Berry, J. W. (1983). The sociogenesis of social sciences: An analysis of the cultural relativity of social psychology. In B. Bain (Ed.), *The sociogenesis of language and human conduct.* New York: Plenum.

Berry, J. W. (1984). Multicultural policy in Canada: A social psychological analysis. *Canadian Journal of Behavioural Science, 16,* 353-370.

Berry, J. W. (1985a). Acculturation and mental health among circumpolar peoples. In R. Fortuine (Ed.), *Circumpolar health* (pp. 305-311). Seattle: University of Washington Press.

Berry, J. W. (1985b). Cultural psychology and ethnic psychology: A comparative analysis. In I. Reyes Lagunes & Y. Poortinga (Eds.), *From a different perspective: Studies of behavior across cultures* (pp. 3-15). Lisse, Netherlands: Swets & Zeitlinger.

Berry, J. W. (1989). Imposed etics, emics and derived etics: The operationalization of a compelling idea. *International Journal of Psychology, 24,* 721-735.

Berry, J. W., & Annis, R. C. (Eds.). (1988). *Ethnic psychology: Research and practice with immigrants, refugees, native peoples, ethnic groups and sojourners.* Lisse, Netherlands: Swets & Zeitlinger.

Berry, J. W., & Bennett, J. A. (1991). *Cree syllabic literacy: Cultural context and cognitive consequences* (Cross-Cultural Psychology Monographs, 1). Tilburg, Netherlands: Tilburg University Press.

Berry, J. W., & Bennett, J. A. (1992). Cree conceptions of cognitive competence. *International Journal of Psychology, 27*, 73-88.

Berry, J. W., & Hart Hansen, J. P. (1985). Problems of family health in circumpolar regions. *Arctic Medical Research, 40*, 21-27.

Berry, J. W., & Kalin, R. (1979). Reciprocity of inter-ethnic attitudes in a multicultural society. *International Journal of Intercultural Relations, 3*, 99-112.

Berry, J. W., Kalin, R., & Taylor, D. (1977). *Multiculturalism and ethnic attitudes in Canada.* Ottawa: Minister of Supply and Services.

Berry, J. W., Kim, U., Minde, T., & Mok, D. (1987). Comparative studies of acculturative stress. *International Migration Review, 21*, 491-511.

Berry, J. W., Kim, U., Power, S., Young, M., & Bujaki, M. (1989). Acculturation attitudes in plural societies. *Applied Psychology, 38*, 185-206.

Berry, J. W., & Wilde, G. J. S. (Eds.). (1972). *Social psychology: The Canadian context.* Toronto: McClelland & Stewart.

Berry, J. W., Wintrob, R. M., Sindell, P. S., & Mawhinney, T. A. (1982). Psychological adaptation to culture change among the James Bay Cree. *Naturaliste Canadien, 109*, 965-975.

Chrisjohn, R., Towson, S., & Peters, M. (1988). Indian achievement in school: Adaptation to hostile environments. In J. W. Berry, S. H. Irvine, & E. B. Hunt (Eds.), *Indigenous cognition: Functioning in cultural context.* Dordrecht, Netherlands: Martinus Nijhoff.

Clément, R., & Kruidenier, B. G. (1985). Aptitude, attitude and motivation in second language proficiency: A test of Clément's model. *Journal of Language and Social Psychology, 4*, 21-39.

Crutchfield, R. S., & Krech, D. (1962). Some guides to the understanding of the history of psychology. In L. Postman (Ed.), *Psychology in the making.* New York: Knopf.

Cumming, P., Lee, E., & Oreopoulos, D. (1989). *Access to profession and trades in Ontario.* Toronto: Queen's Printer.

Driedger, L. (Ed.). (1987). *Ethnic Canada: Identities and inequalities.* Toronto: Copp Clark Pitman.

Earn, B., & Towson, S. (Eds.). (1985). *Readings in social psychology: Classic and Canadian contributions.* Peterborough: Broadview.

Earn, B., & Towson, S. (Eds.). (1990). *Readings in social psychology: Classic and Canadian contributions* (2nd ed.). Peterborough: Broadview.

Edwards, J. (1985). *Language, society and identity.* Oxford: Basil Blackwell.

Enriquez, V. G. (1979). Toward cross-cultural knowledge through cross-indigenous methods and perspectives. *Philippine Journal of Psychology, 12*, 9-16.

Faucheux, C. (1976). Cross-cultural research in experimental social psychology. *European Journal of Social Psychology, 6*, 269-322.

Gardner, R. C. (1985). *Social psychology and second language learning: The role of attitudes and motivation.* London: Edward Arnold.

Gardner, R. C., & Kalin, R. (Eds.). (1981). *A Canadian social psychology of ethnic relations.* Toronto: Methuen.

Goldstein, J., & Bienvenue, R. (Eds.). (1980). *Ethnicity and ethnic relations in Canada.* Toronto: Butterworths.

Government of Canada. (1969). *Official languages act.* Ottawa: Queen's Printer.

Government of Canada. (1971). *Multiculturalism policy.* Ottawa: Queen's Printer.

Government of Canada. (1972). *Native control of Native education.* Ottawa: Queen's Printer.

Government of Canada. (1984). *Equality now: Report of Parliamentary Committee on the Participation of Visible Minorities in Canadian Society.* Ottawa: Queen's Printer.

Government of Canada. (1985). *Equality for all: Report of Parliamentary Committee on Equal Rights.* Ottawa: Queen's Printer.

Hofstede, G. (1980). *Culture's consequences: International differences in work-related values.* Beverly Hills, CA: Sage.

Indian and Inuit Affairs. (1980). *An overview of some recent research on attitudes in Canada towards Indian people.* Ottawa: Queen's Printer.

Jahoda, G. (1979). A cross-cultural perspective on experimental social psychology. *Personality and Social Psychology Bulletin, 5,* 142-148.

Kalin, R. (1982). The social significance of speech in medical, legal, and occupational settings. In E. B. Ryan & H. Giles (Eds.), *Attitudes toward language variations.* London: Edward Arnold.

Kalin, R., & Berry, J. W. (1982). Social ecology of ethnic attitudes in Canada. *Canadian Journal of Behavioural Science, 14,* 97-109.

Kalin, R., & Gardner, R. (1981). The cultural context of social psychology. In R. Gardner & R. Kalin (Eds.), *A Canadian social psychology of ethnic relations.* Toronto: Methuen.

Kalin, R., Rayko, D., & Love, N. (1980). The perception and evaluation of job candidates with four different ethnic accents. In H. Giles, W. P. Robinson, & P. Smith (Eds.), *Language: Social psychological perspectives.* Oxford: Pergamon.

Kanungo, R. (1980). *Biculturalism and management.* Toronto: Butterworths.

Koulak, D., & Perlman, D. (Eds.). (1973). *Readings in social psychology: Focus on Canada.* Toronto: John Wiley.

Kumar, K. (1979). Some reflections on transnational social science transactions. *International Journal of Comparative Sociology, 19,* 219-234.

Lalonde, R. N., & Gardner, R. C. (1984). Investigating a causal model of second language acquisition: Where does personality fit? *Canadian Journal of Behavioural Science, 15,* 224-237.

Lambert, W. E. (1981). Bilingualism and language acquisition. *Annals of New York Academy of Sciences, 379,* 9-22.

Lambert, W. E., & Tucker, G. R. (1972). *Bilingual education of children: The St. Lambert experiment.* Rawley: Newbury House.

MacLeod, R. B. (1955). *Psychology in Canadian universities and colleges.* Ottawa: Social Science Research Council.

McShane, D., & Berry, J. W. (1988). The abilities of Native North Americans. In S. H. Irvine & J. W. Berry (Eds.), *Human abilities in cultural context* (pp. 179-202). New York: Cambridge University Press.

Moscovici, S. (1972). Society and theory in social psychology. In J. Israel & H. Tajfel (Eds.), *The context of social psychology.* London: Academic Press.

O'Bryan, K., Reitz, J., & Kuplowska, O. (1976). *Non-official languages.* Ottawa: Supply & Services.

Ouellet, F. (Ed.). (1988). *Pluralisme et école.* Montreal: Institut Québécois de Recherche sur Culture.

Pepitone, A. (1976). Toward a normative and comparative bicultural social psychology. *Journal of Personality and Social Psychology, 34,* 641-653.

Ponting, R., & Gibbins, R. (1980). *Out of irrelevance: A socio-political introduction to Indian Affairs in Canada.* Toronto: Butterworths.

Sadava, S. (1978). Teaching social psychology: A Canadian dilemma. *Canadian Psychological Review, 19,* 145-151.

Sampson, E. E. (1977). Psychology and the American ideal. *Journal of Personality and Social Psychology, 35,* 767-782.

Samuda, R., Berry, J. W., & Laferrière, M. (Eds.). (1984). *Multiculturalism in Canada: Social and educational perspectives.* Toronto: Allyn & Bacon.

Samuda, R., & Wolfgang, A. (Eds.). (1985). *Intercultural counselling.* Toronto: Hogrefe.

Sherif, M., & Sherif, C. (1969). *Social psychology.* New York: Harper & Row.

Symons, T. H. B. (1975). *To know ourselves* (Vols. 1-2). Ottawa: Association of Universities and Colleges of Canada.

Triandis, H. C. (1977). Cross-cultural social and personality psychology. *Personality and Social Psychology Bulletin, 3,* 143-158.

Wrightsman, L. (1977). *Social psychology in the 70's.* Monterey, CA: Brooks/Cole.

17

THE WAY AHEAD

From Indigenous Psychologies to a Universal Psychology

JOHN W. BERRY
UICHOL KIM

Over the course of the various observations and arguments in this volume, there has been a strong emphasis on examining a particular sociocultural context and then drawing insights from it for a psychology that is rooted in that context. Many agree with cross-cultural psychology's main criticisms of general psychology: It is both *culture blind* and *culture bound.*

It is culture blind because general psychology usually does not pay explicit attention to the cultural context in which it is rooted or to some of the most obvious factors (cultural ones) that influence the development and display of human behavior. It is culture bound because many of its theories and findings are not generalizable in other cultures. The development of indigenous psychologies is thus an essential remedy for the culture-blind and culture-bound nature of general psychology.

However, in themselves, indigenous psychologies do not reduce the culture-bound nature of general psychology. It is only when a number of indigenous psychologies are considered simultaneously, as a comprehensive body of knowledge, that psychology can become a more generalized discipline, one that can understand and explain human behavior at large. Thus to remedy the culture-bound problem, a further, comparative, enterprise is called for, one that permits the elaboration of general principles of human behavior. The cross-indigenous approach's potential for complementing and supplementing the cross-cultural approach has been outlined in this volume both by Enriquez in Chapter 9 and by us in our introductory chapter.

The eventual outcome can be termed a *universal* psychology and involves a shift in perspective from indigenous psychologies to a cross-indigenous psychology and an integration with cross-cultural psychology. As described in the introduction, both the cross-cultural and cross-indigenous approaches adopt a stepwise process guided by the notions of *emic* and *etic* (Berry, 1989; Pike, 1967).

In Berry's (1969, 1989) analyses, the terms *emic* and *etic*—which were coined by Pike (1967)—are elaborated into three terms that parallel these three activities: *imposed etic, emic,* and *derived etic.* In the first, the addition of *imposed* signifies the outside origin, and probable mismatch, of the concepts initially employed with those that are relevant to the local culture. They are etic because they are usually assumed (often incorrectly) to be valid in all cultures. General psychology can best be understood as an imposed etic when it is employed in cultures other than the one (Euro-American) that gave rise to it. The concept of emic was used by Pike to signify an approach from within a cultural system, one that provides insight into indigenous phenomena, and in which meaning derives from understanding phenomena *in their own terms.* Derived etics result from attempts, using the comparative method, to pull together the knowledge gained from both the imposed etic and emic approaches. They are etic because they are valid in more than one culture; they are derived because they have resulted from using the two approaches, rather than assumed in advance. Within this framework, the development of indigenous psychologies results from emic strategies of research. Of course, although they need not follow on the initial imposed etic approach, emic research has often been stimulated by, and as a reaction to, misunderstandings and misinterpretations that resulted from *imposed etic* research. The development of an indigenous psychologies approach is both a valuable enterprise in its own right and a necessary step toward the creation of a more universal psychology.

The way ahead, toward a universal psychology that is fully complemented by indigenous psychologies, has been proposed (Berry, 1978, 1983) using the framework in Figure 17.1. The framework shows a cultural dimension across the top, on which cultures can be compared. This should be based upon some *dimensional identity* (Berry, 1989; Frijda & Jahoda, 1966) to enable valid comparison to take place. For example, a cultural dimension (across the top of Figure 17.1) might be the relative emphasis on individualism and collectivism in a society, or the relative degree of social stratification (tightness versus looseness) in a society. We then consider which kinds of behaviors might be studied in relation to these dimensions; for example (down the left side of Figure 17.1), aspects of social, clinical, educational, or work psychology are all conceivably dependent on variations in these cultural contexts.

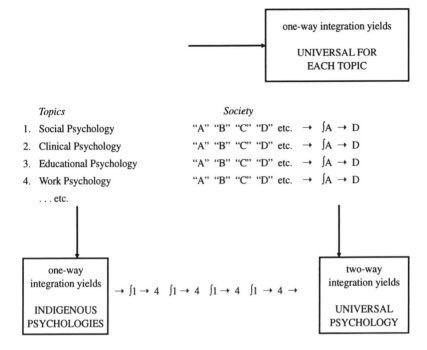

Figure 17.1. Framework for Pursuing a Universal Psychology

Studies may then be carried out on each topic within one or more societies representing each major position on the cultural dimension. The integration of psychological knowledge across topics within a society (down the diagram) yields an indigenous psychology; the comparative integration of psychological knowledge across societies within a topic (across the diagram) yields a universal for that topic; and the comparative integration across all topics and societies produces our overall objective—a veritable universal psychology. Within this framework, such a final product is demonstrably different from either an indigenous psychology or a universal that is produced by the cross-cultural study of a single topic.

Finally, within this framework, it should be clear that the pursuit of indigenous psychologies serves a number of purposes. First, they provide an antidote to premature generalization and ethnocentric psychology. Second, they provide a more accurate picture of the psychology of a particular cultural group. Third, and perhaps most important, they provide the necessary wealth of information for what most cross-cultural psychologists wish eventually to attain—a *universal* psychology.

REFERENCES

Berry, J. W. (1969). On cross-cultural comparability. *International Journal of Psychology, 4,* 119-128.

Berry, J. W. (1978). Social psychology: Comparative, societal and universal. *Canadian Psychological Review, 19,* 93-104.

Berry, J. W. (1983). The sociogenesis of social sciences: An analysis of the cultural relativity of social psychology. In B. Bain (Ed.), *The sociogenesis of language and human conduct.* New York: Plenum.

Berry, J. W. (1989). Imposed etics, emics and derived etics: The operationalization of a compelling idea. *International Journal of Psychology, 24,* 721-735.

Frijda, N. H., & Jahoda, G. (1966). On the scope and methods of cross-cultural research. *International Journal of Psychology, 1,* 110-127.

Pike, K. L. (1967). *Language in relation to a unified theory of the structure of human behaviour.* The Hague: Mouton.

AUTHOR INDEX

SUBJECT INDEX

Ability:
    cognitive, 7
    information processing, 7
Absenteeism, 33
Acculturation, 270
Africa, 84
Age, 148, 215, 255
Altruism, 87
Analysis, 75, 80, 89, 99, 121
    cultural, 15
    ethnographic, 16
    historical, 13, 15, 16
Animal, 18
Anthropology, 2, 68, 109, 136, 149, 180
Art, 14, 114
Asia, 84, 240-258
Attitude, 219
Attributes, 219, 246-247, 255-256
Attribution, 246-247
Autonomy, 63, 75, 84, 90, 204, 207

Behavior, 155, 162, 232, 237
    human, 46, 48, 56, 57, 87, 153, 240,
        278
    modification, 232
    social, 34, 50
Beliefs, 14
Bilingualism, 266, 267, 268, 269, 270,
    271
Biological science. *See* Sciences
Boundaries, 35, 41

Canada, 200, 201-204, 207
Caste, 31, 33, 255
Categorization, 20, 21, 58, 75, 143

Children, 60, 70, 73, 74, 162, 175
Classification, 21, 66, 85
Cognition, 57, 85, 98, 143, 145, 178
Cognitive development, 89
Cognitive representation, 95, 194-206
Collective individualism, 20, 75, 134, 135,
    145
Colonization, 134
Common sense, 185
Communalism, 31
Communication, 59, 70, 71, 95, 194, 265
Community, 68, 74, 176
Conscience, 98, 109, 115
Context:
    acculturative, 25
    spiritual, 25
    historical, 3
    relational, 253
Cross-cultural approach, 4, 23, 26
Cross-indigenous approach. *See* Indigenous
        psychologies
Cultural collectivism, 26
Cultural relativism, 20, 26
Culture, 3, 5, 14, 15, 66, 110, 119, 121, 134,
        159, 162, 176, 184, 214, 267
    change, 183
    non-Western, 6
    pattern, 14
    psychology/sciences, 1
Customs, 102, 139

Developing society, 119
Development:
    cultural, 107
    moral, 49
    national, 33

ABOUT THE AUTHORS

Ruben Ardila (Ph.D., University of Nebraska) was born in Colombia and has been a visiting professor in the United States, Germany, Argentina, and Puerto Rico. Currently, he is Professor of Psychology at the National University of Colombia in Bogotá. He has written 25 psychology books and more than 150 scientific articles for journals in different countries. His main areas of research include the experimental analysis of behavior, social issues, and history of psychology. His latest book is *The Experimental Synthesis of Behavior.*

John W. Berry is Professor of Psychology at Queen's University Canada. He received his Ph.D. from the University of Edinburgh in 1966. He has been a lecturer at the University of Sydney, a Fellow of Netherlands Institute for Advanced Study, a Visiting Professor at the Université de Nice and the Université de Genève, and is a past president of the International Association for Cross-Cultural Psychology. He is the author or editor of 20 books in the areas of cross-cultural, social, and cognitive psychology.

Pawel Boski is Professor of Psychology at the Polish Academy of Sciences in Warsaw. After completing his Ph.D. at the University of Warsaw, he went abroad and spent thirteen years of his career in Nigeria and in North America. At the University of Jos he studied ethnic factors in person perception and attribution. During his years in Canada and the United States he was mainly interested in acculturation and identity processes in immigrants. Most of his published works cover these two topics. Active in IACCP, he is currently organizing the Department of Cross-Cultural Psychology in Warsaw.

E. A. Budilova is affiliated with the Institute of Psychology of the Academy of Sciences in the former USSR.

Sang-Chin Choi is Professor of Psychology at Chung-Ang University. He received his Ph.D. from the University of Hawaii. His recent research has focused on cultural psychology of Koreans. He has published a number of papers on folk concepts and themes associated with Korean psychology.

Soo-Hyang Choi is a Researcher at the Korean Educational Development Institute. She received her graduate training in cross-cultural psychology at the University of Alberta, and she has pursued and written about communication, socialization, and selfhood in Korea and the West. Some of her writings on intercultural communication have been integrated into intercultural training and educational programs in Korea. Currently, she is involved with a cross-cultural study of Korean and English discourse patterns.

Padmal de Silva is Senior Lecturer in Psychology at the Institute of Psychiatry, University of London, where he is also Clinical Tutor to the Clinical Psychology Training Programme. He has been engaged for several years in the study of Buddhist psychology, on which he has published several papers. His other interests include obsessive-compulsive disorder, sexual problems, eating disorders, and post-traumatic stress disorder. He is coauthor, with S. Rachman, of *Obsessive-Compulsive Disorder: The Facts* (1992).

Rogelio Diaz-Guerrero is Emeritus Research Professor at the National University of Mexico (UNAM). He received his M.D. from UNAM in 1943 and his Ph.D. from the State University of Iowa in 1947. His main areas of interest have been culture and personality and cross-cultural psychology. He has authored, coauthored, or edited numerous books and many articles on those subjects. In 1992 he was elected honorary Fellow of the International Association for Cross-Cultural Psychology. His prolific applied research includes the formative and summative studies for *Plaza Sesamo,* the Spanish-language version of *Sesame Street.*

Michael O. A. Durojaiye is Professor of Education at The University of West Indies, St. Augustine, Trinidad, and Tobago. He has written extensively on psychology of Africans.

Virgilio G. Enriquez holds a Ph.D. in psychology from Northwestern University and a master's degree in Filipino from the University of the Philippines. In recognition of his outstanding contributions to the growth and development of Philippine social science, he has received several awards, including the Outstanding Young Scientist Award given by the Republic of the Philippines' National Academy of Science and Technology in 1981. A prolific author, he has to his credit numerous published works in indigenous psychology, Filipino personality, psychology of language and politics, philosophy and values, cross-cultural psychology, and *Pilipinolohiya* (Philippine studies). His latest publication is *From Colonial to Liberation Psychology: The Philippine Experience* (1992).

James Georgas is Professor of Social Psychology at the University of Athens. He received his Ph.D. from Loyola University of Chicago. His publications include the textbook *Social Psychology* and *Acculturation of Ethnic Greeks from the Soviet Union and Albania to Greece,* both in Greek. He has published articles on cross-cultural aspects of intelligence testing and personality testing, family values, and other topics. His current research interests are in the areas of cross-cultural theory, family structure and function, and bonds with people in the immediate community.

David Yau-Fai Ho received his doctoral training in psychology and logic in the United States. In 1968, he returned to his birthplace, Hong Kong, and devoted his time to the introduction and development of clinical psychology in that society. Currently, he is Professor of Counseling at California State University at Fullerton. His research interests have focused on personality development, psychopathology, and social behavior in Chinese culture, and he is the author of numerous contributions in psychology, psychiatry, sociology, linguistics, and education. He is committed to the enrichment of mainstream psychology derived from conceptions indigenous to Asian cultures. He has had multicultural experiences in North America, Hawaii, and the Far East, and has served as President of the International Council of Psychologists (1988-1989).

Denise Jodelet is the Director of L'école des Hautes Etudes en Sciences Sociales in Paris, France. She has published extensively in scholarly journals and books on social representation of mind and body. Her most recent publication is entitled *Madness and Social Representation* (1991).

Uichol Kim is Assistant Professor in the Department of Psychology, University of Hawaii at Manoa. He was born in Korea and emigrated to Canada in 1968. He received his B.Sc. from the University of Toronto, where he majored in psychology and Korean studies, and his Ph.D. from Queen's University. His cross-cultural research has focused on cultures of East Asia, particularly Korean people living in Korea and abroad. His areas of research interest include individualism and collectivism, socialization, group dynamics, acculturation, and ethnic relations.

V. A. Koltsova is affiliated with the Institute of Psychology of the Academy of Sciences in the former USSR.

B. F. Lomov is affiliated with the Institute of Psychology of the Academy of Sciences in the former USSR.

Beatrice Medicine received her Ph.D. from the University of Wisconsin, Madison, in 1982, and is a cultural anthropologist. From time to time she resides at her home in Wakpala, South Dakota, which is located on the Standing Rock Indian Reservation. Retired from California State University at

Northridge, Dr. Medicine is currently a Research Coordinator with Canada's Royal Commission on Aboriginal Peoples in Ottawa. She has written extensively on gender issues among native populations, especially among American Indians. Over the years she has presented numerous invited addresses in many countries focusing on issues concerning native populations. Over the years, Dr. Medicine has received a multitude of awards for her tireless efforts in promoting the concerns of aboriginal groups.

A. M. Medvedev is affiliated with the Institute of Psychology of the Academy of Sciences in the former USSR.

Fathali M. Moghaddam was born in Iran, educated in England, and now teaches at Georgetown University. He previously taught at McGill University and Tehran University and has also worked for the United Nations Development Program. He is the author of *Social Psychology in Cross-Cultural Perspective* (with D. M. Taylor and S. C. Wright) and *Theories of Intergroup Relations* (with D. M. Taylor) and various papers in scientific journals.

Durganand Sinha was educated at Patna University (India) and Cambridge University. He taught at Patna University and the Indian Institute of Technology (Kharaghur) before joining Allahabad University in 1961 as Professor of Psychology and Head of that department. From 1982 to 1987 he was Director, ANS Institute of Social Studies, Patna. He has been UGC National Lecturer and National Fellow, ICSSR National Fellow, and visiting professor in many institutions, including ETS, Princeton, Jawaharlal Nehru University, M.S. University of Baroda, and University of Hong Kong. He is a Past President and Fellow of the International Association for Cross-Cultural Psychology. His current research interests include psychosocial dimensions of acculturation, deprivation, and poverty, and psychology and national development. He is the author of *Psychology in a Third World Country: The Indian Experience* and coeditor of *Social Values and Development: Asian Perspective* and is currently engaged in editing a book with Professor Henry S. R. Kao on Asian perspectives in psychology.

Joseph E. Trimble received his Ph.D. from the University of Oklahoma in 1969. He is a Professor of Psychology at Western Washington University, where he has been a faculty member since 1978. Throughout his academic career, he has focused his efforts on promoting psychological research with indigenous, ethnic populations, especially American Indians. In the past decade or so he has been working on drug abuse prevention and intervention research models with native youth. He has presented more than 20 papers and invited lectures at professional meetings and has generated more than 100 publications dealing with topics concerning psychology and culture.